THE SPANISH JESUIT MISSION
IN VIRGINIA

1570-1572

THE
Spanish Jesuit Mission
IN VIRGINIA

1570 - 1572

by

Clifford M. Lewis, S. J.

AND

Albert J. Loomie, S. J.

PUBLISHED FOR

The Virginia Historical Society

by

THE UNIVERSITY OF NORTH CAROLINA PRESS

CHAPEL HILL 1953

FOREWORD

By E. G. Swem

THIS contribution, *The Spanish Jesuit Mission in Virginia, 1570-1572*, including necessarily a discussion of the Spanish knowledge of Chesapeake Bay in the sixteenth century, is the result of an examination of the printed and manuscript sources now available on this subject, and is submitted with the belief that a more tenable view as to the location of the Mission has been reached than heretofore. Some of the sixteenth- and seventeenth-century English voyagers and geographers were aware of the early reconnaissance by the Spanish of the middle Atlantic Coast, that part of Northern Florida now known as Virginia; but they seem to have been uninformed as to the effort of Governor Menéndez de Avilés of Florida, in 1566, and again in 1570, to settle a colony in the Chesapeake Bay region. In "Notes ascribed to Richard Hakluyt, 1598," in E. G. R. Taylor's *Original Writings and Correspondence of the Two Richard Hakluyts*, we find: "All those large and spatious countries on the east part of America, from 32 to 72 degrees of northerly latitude have not, nor never had any one Spanish colony." Perhaps the writer meant that there had never been a settlement on such a scale as at Saint Augustine in the Florida peninsula; and in this respect, he was correct. Two serious attempts, however, had been made by the Spanish. Lack of knowledge of the first attempt in 1566, may be easily explained, because it was a complete failure, not one ship having landed in the Chesapeake region. Ignorance of the second attempt, the Jesuit Mission of 1570, may be justified by crediting the Spanish officials with the shrewdness of not giving publicity to the seating of a colony that was obliterated in a few months. If any mention of Spanish colonization in the Chesapeake region seeped into English works, it made little impression. Captain John Smith in the First Book of his *General History of Virginia*, with the caption, "How ancient authors report, the New World, now called America, was discovered," after speaking casually of Columbus in six lines, omits any further reference to Spanish discoveries. He mentions the Cabots, Frobisher, and Gilbert, and recounts the voyage of Amadas and Barlow at some length. There was occasionally a glimpse of the truth; for instance, the Virginian, William Stith, in his *History of Virginia*, published in 1747, said: "A gentleman of credit, once assured me, that in a very old Spanish map, which he had seen, our bay was laid down under the name of Madre des Acquas [Madre de Aguas] or some expression to the like purpose." The first American writer to redeem the Mission from oblivion was Dr. John Gilmary Shea, who wrote briefly about it in the *United States Catholic Magazine*, Volume 5, 1846. Dr. Shea continued his investigation and published his best account of the Mission in 1875 in the *Catholic World*. In 1848 Robert Greenhow addressed a "Memoir on the First Discovery of Chesapeake Bay" to the Virginia Historical Society. This was the last chapter in Conway Robinson's *An Account of the Discoveries in the West until 1519, and of Voyages to and along the Atlantic Coast of North America from 1520 to 1573*, published by the Virginia Historical Society in 1848. In the preparation of a volume on the history of the Southern United States, Greenhow, a corresponding member of the Virginia Historical Society, read the old Spanish chroniclers of the New World. He became aware of the early discovery of the Chesapeake by the Spanish, and of the unsuccessful attempt by Menéndez in 1566; but he seems to have known nothing about the second attempt by Father Segura with the permission of Menéndez, the Jesuit Mission of 1570. He wrote the Memoir for the purpose of directing the attention of American historians to the general subject of Spanish activity along the Middle Atlantic Coast. In the period of two years 1846-1848, Shea had written particularly, in a brief account, of the Jesuit Mission of 1570, although he uses an incorrect date 1578; Greenhow had called attention to the exploring efforts of the Spanish; and Robinson had published his work on the general subject of early voyages to America. From that time to the present, numerous studies have appeared about the Jesuit Mission of 1570, but we believe that no one of them has covered the field so exhaustively as the present monograph, for the reason that in very recent years new archival information, both printed and manuscript, has been opened to scholars. Our authors have fortified their contribution throughout by copious and discerning notes. The original documents and narratives upon which the whole discussion is based, with accompanying translations, are printed in full. In their anxiety to offer the reader every facility for solving questions that might arise, the authors have prepared for Part Three: "Navigable Waters and Indian Settlements of Ajacán in 1570"; "The Meaning of Ajacán; its Orthography"; "Cartography of the Chesapeake." Then follows a Bibliography of works that have been consulted. The reproduction of seventeen maps and of two early engravings completes a sincere effort to clear up this controverted event and to give to the public as definitive a conclusion as the evidence at this time will permit.

As a member of the Committee on Publications of the Executive Board of the Virginia Historical Society, it has been my agreeable duty to cooperate with the authors of the monograph; the performance of this assignment with its participation in such an important inquiry has been a refreshing excursion in the midst of a busy retirement. This may be a demonstration of that eternal truth that one in the nebulous period called "age," should betake himself regularly to a fresh intellectual stimulus, such as the study of a new subject, or the revision of an old one. A matter of historical inquiry is never old; at least it never should be. There is always additional information, and an opportunity for a new interpretation. I must acknowledge the deep satisfaction I have experienced in uniting my modest offering with the achievement of my associates, who have joined a liberality of view, with the enthusiasm, the patience, and the devotion so characteristic of true scholars. Their aim has been to discover and present the truth. My own part in the accomplishment of such an admirable addition to our knowledge of early Virginia should be expressed by the term "occasional advisor."

As a resident of the peninsula which enters so much into this discussion, and as a student of its roads, creeks, rivers, and historic sites, may I offer my view of the location of the Jesuit Mission, with my reasons for such view. That the Spanish very early entered the Chesapeake, and gave it a name, Bahía de Santa María, which with variations persisted throughout the sixteenth century, is incontestable. The documents herein printed prove that two attempts were made to colonize in the Chesapeake region. The ships of the Segura Mission of 1570 entered a convenient and comfortable harbor, now known as Hampton Roads, with several ports not far from each other. Practical and sensible navigation would lead them into that river, the James, near these ports, and not into the rough waters of the Bay toward the York, Rappahannock, and Potomac. They went up this river twelve to twenty leagues, to the mouth of a fresh-water stream, which could only be the mouth of College Creek (Archers Hope Creek) or Powhatan Creek. Warwick River and Skiffes Creek, being too near Menéndez' port, must be ruled out. If the Missionaries landed at the mouth of College Creek, they did not remain there, because there was no Indian village in that neighborhood. The early maps show no village on the north bank of the James, below Jamestown. Seeking the village, the Fathers carried their equipment two to three leagues by boat up College Creek, and then landed. From there they crossed the land, at a point near the present site of Williamsburg, reaching Queens Creek or Kings Creek. Going down one of these creeks, they came to a point near the Indian village of Kiskiack, a site well known and always marked on the early maps. This site was on the York River. Near this village the Fathers built their chapel and hut, and it was here five of them were murdered, the other three having been killed at a point farther west. In 1588, the same pilot, Vicente Gonzales, who had brought the Fathers up the James in 1570, was in Hampton Roads, and on returning sailed into the Chesapeake on an exploring expedition. He went into the York as far as present Yorktown, and described it as entirely new territory, and for this reason we must eliminate the York for the 1570 voyage. He then sailed up beyond the mouth of the York, and in his journal always described new waters, until he reached the Susquehanna. In deciding that the 1570 voyage was up the James, the elements of time and distance as indicated by the documents, and the relatively convenient navigation of the James compared with that of the Bay, are of great weight. My view therefore agrees with that of the authors.

In view of former interest shown by the Virginia Historical Society in early Spanish exploration along the middle Atlantic Coast, it is most fitting that the Society should sponsor this comprehensive study of the Jesuit Mission of 1570, a remarkable event associated with that exploration.

Williamsburg, Virginia

PREFACE

OUR debt is heavy to the many persons and institutions who have assisted us in completing this study. It has been most gratifying to discover their interest in the Segura Mission among the Indians, one of the noblest events in all of early American history.

This work would have been impossible without the Jesuit documents on the Florida Mission, carefully edited by Father Felix Zubillaga, S.J., and published as the sixty-ninth volume in the *Monumenta Historica Societatis Iesu*. We are indebted to Father C. de Dalmases, S.J., Director of the Instituto Storico Della Compagnia Di Gesu in Rome, for permission to publish the original texts. Father Maynard Geiger, O.F.M., Archivist of the Old Santa Barbara Mission, California, has graciously consented to the reprinting of certain portions of his excellent translation of Luis Gerónimo de Oré's Relation on the history of Florida. Father Jerome V. Jacobsen, S.J., Director of the Institute of Jesuit History at Loyola University, Chicago, has given us guidance on bibliography. Father William Repetti, S.J., Archivist of Georgetown University, has generously supplied us with transcriptions from the Shea Papers.

In our investigations we have visited many libraries and we are grateful for the patient and courteous service of the various staffs in the Manuscript and Maps Divisions of the Library of Congress, in the Library of the Mariners' Museum at Newport News, in the Library of the United States Naval Academy, Annapolis, and in the Peabody Institute Library, Baltimore. Mr. Lloyd Brown at the last institution gave us many valuable hints on cartographical sources. Mr. Herbert Ganter,

Archivist of The College of William and Mary, sent copies of the Shea-Campbell correspondence. Mr. Lawrence Wroth, Director of The John Carter Brown Library, has supplied information on the Dutch cartography of the Chesapeake. Dr. Hans Neuberger of The Pennsylvania State College has assisted us in meteorological points.

The United States Coast and Geodetic Survey has generously aided us in many ways. Admiral Robert F. Studds, Director, and Admiral Robert W. Knox, Acting Director, Mr. A. A. Stanley, Chief of the Geographical Branch, and Messrs Bruder, Heck, and Marmer advised us on nautical problems and physical changes in the rivers and coast lines, and placed at our disposal the excellent collection of maps and topographical memoranda in the Survey Archives. Also helpful was Mr. Herman R. Friis, Acting Chief Archivist, Cartographic Records Branch, National Archives and Records Service.

Dr. T. D. Stewart, Curator of the Division of Physical Anthropology at the United States National Museum, Dr. John Swanton, Dr. William N. Fenton, Dr. Clifford Evans, and Dr. C. B. Abbot of the Smithsonian Institution have given courteously of their time and knowledge on ethnology and meteorology. Dr. Regina Flannery Herzfeld of the Department of Anthropology of The Catholic University of America has read sections of the manuscript and discussed with us the sources on the ethnology of Virginia. Miss Helene Philibert and Dr. Patricia Mooney of Washington have helped the progress of this book by many kindnesses.

The Reverend Clayton Torrence, late Secretary of the Virginia Historical Society, encouraged us from the start, and we recall with pleasure his countless courtesies to us. Dr. E. G. Swem, Librarian Emeritus of The College of William and Mary, read the manuscript throughout and gave generously of his rich knowledge of Virginia history. It has been a privilege to be associated with one of the country's greatest bibliographers. No less kind have been the members of the Publications Committee of the Society. Mrs. Philip W. Hiden, Mr. Samuel M. Bemiss, and Dr. Malcolm Harris have given us expert guidance in our visits to various sites on the York and James rivers. Dr. Ben C. McCary, an authority on Virginia archeology, with Dr. Swem graciously conducted investigations for the writers along College Creek. At Yorktown we were able to receive the advice of Mr. E. A. Hummel and Mr. C. E. Hatch, Historians of the Colonial National Park, on surveys in that area. Father Thomas J. Walsh, Pastor of St. Bede's Church at Williamsburg, did everything possible to make our trips to Virginia a pleasant experience. Through the kindness of the Honorable John S. Battle, Governor of Virginia, we were able to use the State launch *Chesapeake* in exploring the lower Bay and the mouth of the James River as a means of interpreting the accounts of the Spanish navigators.

It would be difficult to express adequately our indebtedness to our fellow Jesuits at Woodstock College. Fathers Kurt Becker, Edward Bodnar, Francis Canavan, Arturo Gaete, John Laboon, Edward Ryan, and Gustave Weigel have all assisted us at various times in checking translations, preparing photostats and illustrations, and advising us on various historical and navigation problems. We are likewise grateful for the encouragement given us by our Religious superiors and by the Most Reverend Peter L. Ireton, D.D., Bishop of Richmond, who has always been helpful to those investigating the history of the Spanish Mission.

In this study we have intended to present a documentary history of the Spanish attempts to settle the Chesapeake area and we have had no wish to anticipate any possible future pronouncements of the Church concerning the sanctity of the missionaries. Any use of the word "martyr," therefore, is to be understood in the popular, non-technical sense.

In preparing this study, Father Loomie concentrated on historical research and Father Lewis on anthropology and other scientific fields, but there is no portion of this work that has not been revised after discussion by both the authors. While many persons have tried to comb out errors and misinterpretations in the text, some mistakes will inevitably appear. For these we are entirely responsible.

All too inadequately we have tried in these pages to follow the dictum of St. Paul which every Christian historian tries to fulfill: "And now, Brethren, all that rings true, all that commands reverence, and all that makes for right; all that is pure, all that is lovely, all that is gracious in the telling; virtue and merit, wherever virtue and merit are found—let this be the argument of your thoughts."

C. M. L.

A. J. L.

Woodstock, Maryland
February 4, 1953

CONTENTS

CONTENTS

PART II

The Documents with Their Translations

PART III

Ajacán and the Chesapeake

ILLUSTRATIONS

Names That Occur Frequently

Francis Borgia. General of the Society of Jesus from 1565 to 1572.

THE MEMBERS OF THE EXPEDITION

Juan Baptista de Segura. Jesuit priest, Vice-Provincial of his order in Florida, leader of the expedition to Ajacán.

Luis de Quirós. Jesuit priest.

Don Luis de Velasco. Christian Indian who guided the Jesuits.

Alonso de Olmos. A youth who accompanied the expedition.

Gabriel Gómez,
Sancho Zaballos } Jesuit Brothers
Pedro Mingot de Linares,

Cristóbal Redondo
Gabriel de Solís } Lay catechists
Juan Baptista Méndez,

THOSE WHO WROTE LATER OF THE EVENTS

Juan Rogel. Jesuit priest who came to the Chesapeake in 1572.

Juan de la Carrera. Jesuit Brother who outfitted the expedition at Santa Elena, an island off the coast of South Carolina near Port Royal, and came to the Chesapeake in 1572.

Bartolomé Martínez. A Spanish colonist and official who lived at Santa Elena during the events at Ajacán.

SPANISH OFFICIALS

Pedro Menéndez de Avilés. Adelantado of Florida, Governor of Cuba and Admiral of the Spanish fleets, who ruled the Province from 1566 to 1574.

Pedro Menéndez Marqués. Nephew of Pedro Menéndez de Avilés and later Governor of Florida.

Juan Menéndez Marqués. First cousin of Pedro. "Sergeant-Major" of San Agustín, who led the expedition of 1588 to the Chesapeake.

Vicente Gonzales. Pilot of the vessels that carried the Jesuits to the Chesapeake in 1570, 1571, and 1572.

Andrés Gonzales. Pilot of the Spanish vessel that scouted the English in the Chesapeake in 1609.

Francisco de Ecija. Leader of the Spanish expedition that reached the Chesapeake in 1609.

Abbreviations Frequently Used

AA—American Anthropologist

ACHS—Records and Studies of the American Catholic Historical Society

AGI—Archivo General de Indias

AHR—American Historical Review

BAE,B—Bureau of American Ethnology, Bulletin

BAE,R—Bureau of American Ethnology, Report

GHQ—Georgia Historical Quarterly

HAHR—Hispanic American Historical Review

HRS—Historical Records and Studies of the United States Catholic Historical Society

MHM—Maryland Historical Magazine

MHSI—Monumenta Historica Societatis Iesu

   MAF—Monumenta Antiquae Floridae, vol. 69 of the *MHSI*. Paragraph numbers, where given, refer to those inserted in the text by the *MAF* editor.

PMHS—Proceedings of the Massachusetts Historical Society

SMC—Smithsonian Miscellaneous Collections

TRHS—Transactions, Royal Historical Society

VMHB—Virginia Magazine of History and Biography

WMQ—William and Mary College Quarterly Historical Magazine

A modified legal form for footnotes has been used in the text. For example, *The Georgia Historical Quarterly*, vol. 8, p. 228, becomes 8 *GHQ* 228. The full title of a work frequently referred to is in the Bibliography, which is also a guide to works of general reference.

PART ONE

AN HISTORICAL SYNTHESIS

A Narrative Summary of the Documents

SINCE May, 1848, when Robert Greenhow addressed his "Memoir on the First Discovery of Chesapeake Bay" to the Virginia Historical Society, little has appeared in the publications of this state relative to the Spanish attempts of 1566 and 1570 to establish a mission in Virginia territory. Greenhow's contribution was to direct attention to Spanish sources, particularly Barcia's *Ensayo Cronológico*, from which he concluded that the Spanish were familiar with the Chesapeake during the period of 1566-1573.[1]

Generally speaking, the neglect of the subject of the Spanish mission has been in no small measure due to the scattered documentary sources, preserved for the most part in private archives. Therefore, for the benefit of scholars who may wish to pursue the question further, we have thought it wise to present in this study the best available texts and translations of the Spanish and Latin documents. It is anticipated that some popular misconceptions may be revised in the light of the evidence here presented.

---

1. Robert Greenhow's *Memoir* was printed in Conway Robinson, *An Account of Discoveries in the West until 1519, and of Voyages to and along the Atlantic Coast of North America from 1520 to 1573* (Richmond, Virginia Historical Society, 1848), 481-491. Robert Greenhow (1800-1854), a physician of wide cultural and scientific attainments, was born in Richmond, the grandson of John Greenhow, a prominent Williamsburg merchant. Some years after finishing his course at Wil- liam and Mary College he entered the employ of the Department of State as linguist and translator. As an outgrowth of this activity he became interested in Spanish documents and prepared a history of the Spanish colonies which was privately printed two years after his death. Greenhow's *Memoir* has the distinction of being the first historical study in English to publicize widely the Spanish knowledge of the Chesapeake in the sixteenth century.

It will be apparent that the mission in Virginia was born of something more than a sudden storm that blew a ship into the Chesapeake. Rather, it began with a Mexican viceroy's dreams of a vast colonial empire— dreams inherited by the Governor of Florida and slowly brought to maturity against a checkered and fantastic background that embraced a search for a strait leading to China, the political and economic rivalry of France, England, and Spain, the taking of an Indian from Virginia on an earlier voyage, and the missionary failures in Florida. Of greater local interest will be the answer which these documents contain to a question which since Greenhow's day has been the subject of wide disagreement: the location of the Spanish Jesuit settlement of 1570 generally known as Ajacán. Guesses have ranged from the North East River, reaching towards Philadelphia, to some river emptying into Albemarle or Pamlico Sound, North Carolina.[2] Woodbury Lowery, the most authoritative and most widely quoted writer on Spanish Florida, thought it impossible to exclude any of the western or northern tributaries of the Chesapeake as the possible site.[3] The late Father Michael Kenny, S. J., treated the question at length in his *Romance of the Floridas*, but he did not utilize the important Relation of Luis Gerónimo de Oré.

We have tried to contribute toward a solution of this problem by a study of early Spanish cartography, sufficient only to establish that the Spanish long knew of the Chesapeake and that the Jesuits entered it. This we have followed with a detailed analysis of the documents, relating them to what we have been able to deduce concerning the ports and streams and the Indian tribes of the Chesapeake of 1570. We have included a survey of many old English maps, documents, and navigational charts. An immediate conclusion is that we must shift the events of 1570-1572 from the Potomac-Rappahannock region to the James-York. Finally we

2. Louis Dow Scisco, who has contributed occasional articles to the *Maryland Historical Magazine* on the early history of the Chesapeake, thinks the Spaniards did not discover the bay until 1573. "Pedro Menéndez Marqués," he says, "real discoverer of the Chesapeake, has been much cheated of fame by the unfortunate error that has credited the Axacan missioners with prior occupation of the Bay region" ("Discovery of the Chesapeake Bay, 1525-1573," 40 *MHM* 275-286). This view is supported by a 1765 map of Fernando Martínez, which lists the "cabo y Bahía de Santa María" as "discovered by Pedro Menéndez Marqués" in 1573. Martínez, however, goes on

to injure his own authority by crediting Raleigh with settling it in 1574.

The priority of Menéndez Marqués' discovery seems to have been conceded also by Arredondo in listing Spanish claims to Georgia: "He . . . sailed as far as the bay of Santa María, in 36° 30', keeping an itinerary and diary of his voyage" (Herbert E. Bolton, ed., *Arredondo's Historical Proof of Spain's Title to Georgia* [Berkeley, 1925] 139). Part of the burden of the early part of our study will be to disprove Menéndez Marqués' priority.

3. See his Appendix EE, "Site of the Segura Mission," in *The Spanish Settlements* 2:461-464.

have advanced a more detailed but less firmly held hypothesis as to the exact site. Following the story of the Ajacán mission is a summary of our findings, page 62, below.

EARLY KNOWLEDGE OF THE CHESAPEAKE

THE STORY OF THE Ajacán mission is the interweaving of two threads representing the temporal and the spiritual, each dependent on the other but not always compatible, a common theme in both French and Spanish exploration and settlement. The temporal lords were interested in the east coast of North America at various times for four reasons: (1) the search for a strait that would provide a quick sea route to the cloves, nutmeg, sandalwood, and pearls of the Spice Islands;[4] (2) Indians for the slave trade; (3) furs for the nobility of Europe; (4) ports for the storm-tossed galleons returning from the silver mines of Mexico and for the pirate ships that preyed upon the galleons.[5]

The possible short cut to the Moluccas that had lured Columbus was destined to be the preoccupation of navigators for two centuries after his death. It is barely possible that Amerigo Vespucci found the Chesapeake on such a search as early as 1497.[6] England claimed discoveries as far south as the Chesapeake for John Cabot in the next year.[7] It has been

4. The dire need for a shorter route safe from Moslem pirates is well demonstrated in Henry H. Hart, *Sea Road to the Indies* (New York, 1950) and Felix Plattner, *Jesuits Go East* (Dublin, 1951).

5. An excellent introduction to our own study is available in "Spain's Route to the New World," the first chapter of Frank Wesley Craven, *The Southern Colonies in the Seventeenth Century* (Baton Rouge, 1949) and C. H. Haring, *Trade and Navigation Between Spain and the Indies in the Time of the Hapsburgs* (Cambridge, Mass., 1918).

6. For a good summary of the historical controversy over Vespucci's voyage to North America, see the review article by Charles E. Nowell, "América la bien llamada," 30 *HAHR* 501-511. The review deals with a recent work by Roberto Levillier, *América la bien llamada*, Vol. I, *La conquista de occidente*, Vol. II, *Bajo la cruz del sur* (Buenos Aires, 1948). Accord-

ing to Levillier, Vespucci sailed as far north as the Chesapeake on his first voyage. His argument is based chiefly on maps of La Cosa, Canerio, Cantino, and Waldseemüller, all made shortly after 1497, which show a solid land mass west of Cuba that demands the Vespucci exploration as their sufficient reason. The reviewer, while favoring Levillier's general disposition to regard Vespucci's accounts as authentic, does not think he got north of Cuba in his first voyage and that the land masses reflect the cartographers' attempts to draw in the coast of Asia.

7. Whether or no one agrees that Cabot explored as far south as Florida, there seems to be little textual or cartographic proof that he found the Chesapeake Bay. Henry Harrisse, who believes the second Cabot voyage (1498-99) explored from Newfoundland to Florida, admits it strange that no mention is made of the Hudson, Delaware, or Potomac (*John*

vigorously disputed whether Giovanni da Verrazano's landfall and exploration in 1524 were north or south of the Chesapeake, but recent studies have practically established his exploration from Florida to Cape Breton.[8] Estevan Gómez, a Portuguese sailing for Spain in 1524-25, is credited by J. B. Brebner, George Dexter, J. G. Shea, and Woodbury Lowery with probably having followed the whole Atlantic Coast to at least 40° N. Lat. in 1525, and like Cabot and Verrazano, he too was looking for a strait leading to China.[9] Gómez may have found the Chesapeake, and the same may be said with more certitude for Francisco Gordillo and Pedro de

Cabot, The Discoverer of North America, and Sebastian His Son [London, 1896] 141). The map of 1544 attributed to Sebastian Cabot, many years after he had been in Spain's employ, shows the Chesapeake as the Baya de Espírito Santo. But the shape of the bay differs significantly from Ribero's, being deeper and narrower and containing three small islands. It divides into two branches like a rabbit's ears, one corresponding to the James, the other to the upper part of the Chesapeake. It is much nearer the truth than Ribero's bay and may indicate personal knowledge of its shape. The 1498 voyage of Cabot is hazy; according to John Bartlett Brebner, we cannot be sure that Sebastian was on this trip. Brebner, however, credits Sebastian with exploration of the Atlantic Coast from Newfoundland to Hatteras in 1509 (The Explorers of North America, 1492-1806 [New York, 1933] 113). But since Sebastian Cabot entered Spanish employ in 1512, we must assume that he kept details of his trip secret, since the maps do not reflect them before 1529, if then. Perhaps the Spanish policy, too, was opposed to the publication of the results of his voyage, for this would admit the prior claims of England. James A. Williamson, in The Voyages of the Cabots and the English Discovery of North America under Henry VII and Henry VIII (London, 1929) undertakes a closely reasoned cartographical proof of Cabot's voyage of 1508 or 1509 (see especially 228 ff.).

8. James C. Brevoort, in Verrazano, the Navigator (New York, 1874) 51, basing his conclusion on Verrazano's omission of the Chesapeake and Delaware bays, contends that "His most southerly point must have been, therefore, in 39° .05', a few miles north of Cape May." Others assume that he missed these bays while sailing at night, a practice

which he seems to have followed up to a certain period in his voyage. J. R. Swanton, in The Indians of the Southeastern United States (137 BAE,B 57), says that Verrazano "recorded a few interesting particulars regarding the inhabitants of the region [North Carolina] agreeing very well with what later writers tell us." The map attributed to Verrazano's brother gives in 1529 a quite faithful outline of the coast of North America in general character (Justin Winsor, Narrative and Critical History of America [Boston, 1884-89] 4: 26).

From 1521 to 1523, under the alias of Juan Florín, Verrazano had operated in the Atlantic as a French corsair preying on Spanish commerce.

William Herbert Hobbs, writing in 41 Isis (December, 1950) 268-277, gives a very convincing demonstration that Verrazano's landfall was in Florida, and that he deliberately falsified his latitudes so that the map would not be useful to rival mariners. He explains the origin of Verrazano's Mare Occidentale, which leaves but a six-mile strip of land in the vicinity of Pamlico and Chesapeake, as due to the impression that he would obtain from looking over the low sandpits across the sounds of Carolina and the bay of Chesapeake. Hobbs thinks the mouth of the Chesapeake was missed in the fog or during night sailing. He believes that Quexos' discovery of the Chesapeake in 1525 may have led Verrazano to omit French claims to that region when he published his account of exploration in 1527.

9. 3 Winsor 28 ff. Kohl and Harrisse do not think Gómez' journey can be stretched as far south as the Chesapeake. See Henry Harrisse, Discovery of North America (London and Paris, 1892) 251; J. G. Kohl, Die Beiden ältesten General-Karten ... (Weimar, 1860) 67 ff. For Brebner's opinion, see op. cit. 32.

Quexos, who were hunting Indian slaves along the coast in 1521.[10] Quexos, moreover, in 1525 was sent by Lucas Vásquez de Ayllón to explore the coast for a distance of 250 leagues, preparatory to settlement by Ayllón's colony. The first serious attempt to colonize the east coast resulted in Ayllón's failure of 1526. Writers again divide on the location. Shea, Guilday, Kenny, Harrisse, Navarrete, Herrera, and Kohl, to name but a few, think Ayllón went north from his first landfall and thus settled on the James River or somewhere in North Carolina. Arredondo, Lowery, and Zubillaga, along with the anthropologists J. R. Swanton and Douglas L. Rights, think he went south, perhaps as far as the Savannah River. The trend of modern historians is toward the latter viewpoint. We shall not now entangle ourselves in this question.[11] Several writers are willing to concede that John Rut of England sailed the Atlantic seacoast to the West Indies in 1527.[12]

We might pause here, however, to determine if a cursory examination of early maps discloses any reflection of these expeditions in so far as they may have touched Chesapeake Bay. The first conclusion, which is generally accepted, is that one or more of these explorers—most likely Quexos in 1525—must have supplied the characteristics and nomenclature for the official Spanish *Padrón General* maps which, shortly after this period, begin to portray a Bahía de Santa María along with rivers called del Espíritu Santo and Salado emptying into it. Map discussions logically begin with the opinions set forth by the great German geographer, J. G. Kohl, in his work *Die Beiden ältesten General-Karten von Amerika ausgefuhrt in den Jahren 1527 und 1529.* This work contains two large reproductions in color of the so-called Hernando Colón map of 1527 and the Ribero-Weimar map of 1529, prototype of many maps of the Atlantic

10. 1 Lowery 154-164. However, there seems to be no support for Mooney's statement that "throughout the remainder of the 16th century the Virginia coast was frequently raided by Spanish slave hunters from the West Indies..." ("The Powhatan Confederacy, Past and Present," 9 *AA* [1907] 129).

11. The arguments concerning the Ayllón location are summarized in 1 Lowery, Appendix H, "Ayllón's Last Voyage," 447-452; by J. G. Shea in 2 Winsor 238-241, 285 f; by J. R. Swanton in *Early History of the Creek Indians* 73 *BAE,B* 31-48. Shea's case for the James rests on the well-grounded supposition that Ayllón knew of the James, plus the fact that in the Ecija report of 1609 the Indians of the Carolinas called the English settlement at Jamestown "Guandape," which was also the name of Ayllón's settlement. Others believe De Soto found signs of the Ayllón settlement on a southern river, possibly the Savannah.

12. For John Rut's mysterious voyage from England, see Arthur P. Newton, *The European Nations in the West Indies, 1493-1688* (London, 1933) 49, and Bolton, *The Spanish Borderlands* (New Haven, 1921) 1. This voyage provides the *terminus a quo* for Irene Wright's first volume of documents, covering 1527-1568, which reflect the Spanish attitude to foreign trade in the Caribbean.

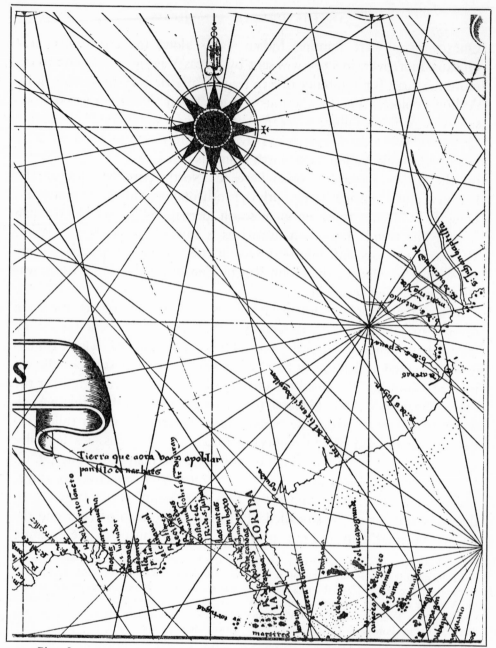

"PADRÓN GENERAL" MAP OF 1527 SHOWING AYLLÓN TERRITORY

Most writers regard the bay below "tierra del licençia doayllon" as too far south for the Chesapeake. There is the added difficulty that it is shown south of the Ayllón Territory. For a definitive answer, it would be necessary to identify "C de arenas," variously supposed to be Cape Henlopen, Sandy Hook, or even Cape Cod.

Coast during the remainder of the sixteenth century.[13] The Colón map shows the "tierra del licençia de ayllon" above a long, narrow bay between 33° and 34° N. Lat. According to E. B. Mathews in *The Maps and Map-Makers of Maryland*, "This sketch is supposed to furnish the first representation of Chesapeake Bay based upon authentic information." [14] In the Ribero-Weimar map the "b.de s.mᵃ" is shown between 34° and 35° as a wide shallow bay confronted by islands with the Río del Espíritu Santo running into it from the west and another unnamed river in the general position of the Potomac. Meantime the long, narrow bay of the Colón map is either dropped entirely or identified with the new broad bay or one of the rivers in the south. Kohl insists that the bay shown on the Ribero map is the Chesapeake, despite the error in latitude. His arguments are taken from the development of later cartography, which keeps the same bay but tends to elevate it to 37°, properly narrowing its mouth and bending the northern branch straight up in the direction of the northern Chesapeake and Susquehanna and naming it the Río Salado, or "Salt River," appropriate enough to the salt water of the bay itself.[15] He supplements this argument with the historical testimony of Oviedo and Barcia and of later Spanish explorers such as Menéndez Marqués in 1573, who make it clear they mean to identify St. Mary's Bay with the Chesapeake. He therefore prefers to think Ribero made an error in latitude rather

13. For a discussion of the Ribero-Weimar map which at the same time presents the background for its construction, see Jean Delanglez, S.J., *El río del Espíritu Santo* (New York, 1945). Reproductions of those sections of the 1527 and 1529 maps pertaining to the Chesapeake may be found in E. B. Mathews, *The Maps and Map-Makers of Maryland* (Baltimore, 1898) 344. In 341-346 he discusses the significance of these maps and quotes extensively from the Kohl work cited in note 9, above.

14. *Ibid.* 341. Against this opinion is the fact that the Ayllón and Ribero maps both have "c. de Arenas" at 40°, yet there is a difference of nearly 1½° between Ayllón's long narrow bay and Ribero's broad bay. Agnese portolan charts of 1536-1580 distinguish a "c. de. s. maría" from "aillon" farther down the coast.

15. A few examples will illustrate: The *Harleian Mappemonde* (*post* 1542) gives the "B. de Se Marie" at 36½°; the *Descliers Mappemonde* (1546) shows the "B de St. Marie" at 35°. The Villard map of North America (*c.* 1547) names the "R. de S. Esprit," the "Rio Salado," and "B. Ste. Marie," placing the bay at 37°. The shape of the bay in all three is a reflection of the Spanish *padrón* after 1536. These maps are shown in H. P. Biggar, *The Voyages of Jacques Cartier* (Ottawa, 1924) 128, 192, and 160, respectively. Pamlico as a distinct entity disappears, but it is hardly conceivable that the Spanish could have been ignorant of it or could have forgotten its existence. Its coast, like a ship's prow, is preserved but deprived of its bay.

We shall not now follow the vagaries of a "cabo de Santa María" which shows up first in the Maiollo map of 1527 (3 Winsor 39) but is not always identified with one of the Chesapeake capes. Harrisse (*Discovery of North America* 228) concludes, from the Maiollo and other maps, that Verrazano discovered from 27° to 43°. It is true that the faithfulness in large outline of the east coast in the maps of Verrazano, Maiollo, and Colón requires its having been observed by some explorer.

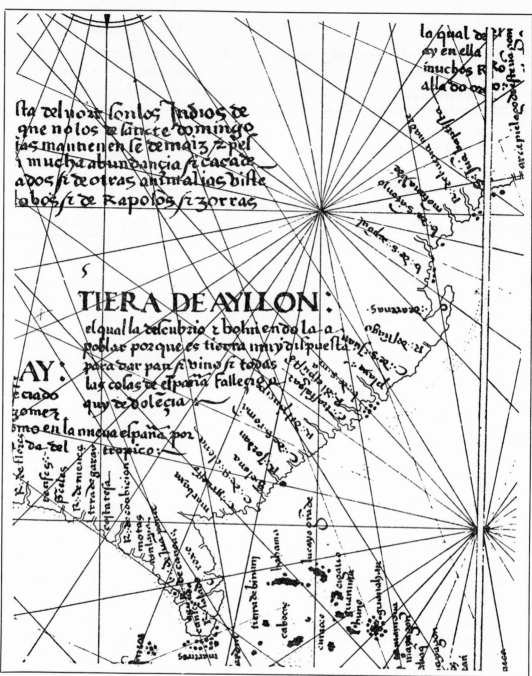

RIBERO-WEIMAR MAP OF 1529 SHOWING THE BAHÍA DE SANTA MARÍA

The bay is shown as "b: de S.M.ª" just below "playa" and above "R: del espu sto."
The bay is located below the 35th parallel, which gives rise to the question as to
whether Ribero was actually showing Pamlico rather than the Chesapeake. The
existence to the north of a "R: de St. Iago," later applied to a Currituck Sound
inlet, strengthens the impression, but we are inclined to favor Kohl's identification
of Ribero's Santa María with the Chesapeake.

than admit that the Spanish might have used the same name for both Pamlico and Chesapeake. But there remains the possibility that the Spanish may have regarded the two bays as one, imagining they were connected.[16] In this event the Salado would be the Chesapeake. However, Ribero's map, more correctly than those of his successors, shows an indentation near C. Traffalgar [sic] corresponding to Pamlico Sound, though he curiously omits the long sand bar separating it from the Atlantic. It is likely that if confusion of Pamlico and the Chesapeake was a fact, it arose at a later date when the memory of the early explorations was dim. If, as we may suppose, the English in 1585 had seen any of the Spanish maps, they evidently (from their ignorance of the Chesapeake) imagined that the Bahía de Santa María was Pamlico. In confirmation of this is the legend on an early map of the North Carolina coast drawn by John Smith.[17] Below "Wococon" (Island) off Pamlico Sound he writes: "The Port of Saynt Maris, where we arrived first." By "we" he probably means the English as represented by Raleigh's colony, and it is feasible that he thought he was giving the Spanish name for Pamlico. William Strachey, however, in a side note to his *Historie*, written about 1616, says the Spanish name for the Chesapeake was Santa María.[18]

The representation of islands rather than a solid peninsula in front of the Chesapeake has led some writers to insist that Ribero meant to show Pamlico Sound. However, to explorers following the Atlantic Coast, the shore line would have looked very much like two rows of islands, for Assateague on the Maryland shore was then broken up into islands. Even admitting that their ship sailed up the bay, unless they carefully examined the shore they might have carried away the impression of a coast composed of "shallow broken Isles," as Smith's party later described it. This supposition, however, is weak, for if Quexos had sailed all the way up the bay it is not probable that he would have described the upper part of it

16. Scisco, in "The Voyage of Vicente Gonzales, 1588" (50 *MHM* 99) thinks the Spanish pilot believed the Chesapeake to be joined to the Carolina Sounds.

17. Reproduction in Alexander Brown, *Genesis of the United States* 2: 596. This crudely drawn map Brown supposes to have been made in 1608 and sent to Lord Bacon in 1618. See Appendix A below.

18. In William Strachey, *The Historie of Travaile into Virginia Britannia* 4, there is a side note which reads as follows: "Within the Chesopoke Bay six leagues, which Bay the Spaniards in their cartes call Sante Maria." In developing England's claim to Virginia, Strachey, writing in 1616, emphasizes the failure of Spain effectively to occupy the territory. "Noe Prince may laye claime to any more amongst these newe discoveries (and soe it was heretofore, a just distinction being therefore kept between the Kinge of Castile and Portugall) then what his people have discovered, tooke actuall possession of, and passed over to his right..." (*ibid.*).

as it is in the 1529 map, terminating at the westward-trending river which resembles the Potomac.

For more than a generation the attention of Europe was diverted from the central Atlantic Coast to the furs and fisheries of the north and the gold and silver of the south, but in 1564 the enterprising and imaginative Pedro Menéndez de Avilés fell into proprietorship of the vast licentiate of Ayllón, and we may be sure that he dusted off the old maps that showed his holdings, for he soon began talking of the Bahía de Santa María and the Río Salado and including them in his plans for the future. We shall now deal with the events which led up to this new interest in the Chesapeake.

Rediscovery of St. Mary's Bay

DURING THE 1550's the Spanish government became increasingly nervous at reports of French activity along the Atlantic Coast coming closer and closer to the route that its stream of silver must follow from Mexico. The trade winds, and to an extent the Gulf Stream, operate in a vast clockwise movement in the Atlantic, making it advantageous to follow a southern route, as did Columbus, when sailing west, and a northeastern route when sailing back to Europe with the treasure-laden vessels. The warm Gulf Stream flows north at a speed of about 60 miles a day until it reaches Cape Hatteras, where within 60 miles of the Chesapeake it veers off to the east across the Atlantic. The treasure fleets followed it NE to 32°, then E¼ NE to 38° or 39° and the Azores.[19] Close to the coast a narrow cold stream creeps southward. If a hostile power were to seize this coast it would provide bases for pirate operation against the fleet, and Spain, following the economic philosophy of her day, was spawning English and French corsairs by her monopoly.[20] The journey up the coast was dangerous enough without that. Even on good days there were perilous winds off Hatteras, and in winter, winds howling down the shore line made sailing next to impossible. We can enumerate wrecks that piled up on this

19. Antonio Vásquez de Espinosa plots the course of the treasure fleets to and from Spain in his *Compendium and Description of the West Indies* (ed. C. U. Clark, Washington, 1942) 1 f.

20. A recent book by George Woodbury, *The Great Days of Piracy in the West Indies* (New York, 1951), should supply a vivid picture of Spain's problem in defending its monopoly.

coast in 1528, 1545, 1551, 1553, 1554, 1559, 1561, and 1564, and there were doubtless many, many more. Hence harbors would have the added advantage to the Spanish of refuge for their ships in time of storm. Therefore Philip II in 1558 demanded settlement of that coast. The energetic empire-builder, Don Luis de Velasco of New Spain, was charged with the undertaking.

The expedition that he sent out in 1559 under Tristán de Luna y Arellano was a nightmare of ineffectual activity, and it came to grief on the west coast of Florida. From the correspondence that followed between Velasco and Luna we have the first clear-cut reference to a discovery of the Chesapeake Bay. A group of sailors had landed at Campeche, chief town on the Yucatán Peninsula. It came to Don Velasco's ears that one of their number, an Englishman, had been on the Atlantic Coast years before and might prove to be a capable guide to the discovery of ports in that region. The following is his deposition, signed by the Viceroy:

"He is called John, an Englishman born in Bristol. In the year '46, being a boy of ten years, he left Artamua [Ardmore?] which is in England in a ship of the fleet as a cabin boy. As it was coming to await the ships which went from the Indies, a storm struck them which forced them to make the land of La Florida in 37°. They found a very good bay where they anchored. Soon there came alongside over thirty canoes in each of which were fifteen to twenty persons with bows and arrows. They would not permit more than two to come on board, and they gave them as many as a thousand marten skins in exchange for knives, fishhooks and shirts. After two days they went away from there toward the south down to 33° where according to his opinion is the Punta de Santa Elena...." [21]

From this statement it is not clear what kind of ship called at 37°, but from what Velasco wrote to Luna on August 20, 1560, it might be inferred that this Englishman, who was married in France, was sailing on a French ship. "There are suspicions and some indications," the Viceroy writes, "that the French who have settled at Los Bacallaos, which is

---

21. Both Hariot of the 1585 North Carolina colony and John Smith of Virginia report trapping of "martens." It is possible that the animal referred to in all these accounts is the muskrat rather than the weasel-like animal. An Irishman of Virginia in 1610 told the Spanish that the Indian king had his treasure-house full of sable-martens. The text of this document is in Priestley, *The Luna Papers* 2: 177 ff. (hereafter cited Priestley). A facsimile is given, with transcription and translation. The Punta de Santa Elena is on the coast of modern South Carolina. There are other references to this Englishman's account in the August 20 letter, vol. 1, and in the September 13 letter of Velasco to Luna, vol. 2. Artamua may mean Dartmouth (Lowery). Los Bacallaos is the modern Newfoundland.

not far from the Punta de Santa Elena, are trying to come and take the port or ports which may be there, and settle them so as to impede the passage of the Bahama Channel." [22] Still trying to sell Luna on the importance of struggling through with his mission, Velasco assures him that "since . . . the French come quite near to Santa Elena nearly every year to buy from the Indians gold, pearls, marten-skins, and other things, it must not be said that it is not a suitable country to colonize. . . ."

At this time Pedro Menéndez de Avilés, who had been a captain of the treasure fleets since 1554, was in Mexico between trips. Velasco enlisted his help in the coastal enterprise. He was expected to leave for Spain not later than February, 1561, taking the Englishman to Luna for use in exploring the east coast. Velasco wrote Luna: "I think I wrote by Luis Daza that General Pedro Menéndez was still here but was to set out to return to Spain about the middle or the last of February and would take with him two light ships so that he might go from La Havana to discover what ports there are at the Punta de Santa Elena and the coast for eighty or one hundred leagues from there on towards Bacallaos. One of these ships, it seemed best, ought to give information to his majesty of what occurred there, and the other was to come to report to you and to me on what it might find. This measure was not to be taken if Don Martín and Biedma have gone to discover the port and have made a settlement in it. . . ." [23]

So far as we know, the only fleet that actually left Mexico that spring was commanded by Ibarra in April. It is thought that Menéndez went with this fleet. It is probable also that two of the sloops, as planned, explored the coast north of Santa Elena, for Biedma failed to reach it, and a royal order of September 23, 1561, indicates that Menéndez had examined the coast and had made his report thereon to the king.[24] This accords with Velasco's statement that "everything that has happened will be reported to him [His Majesty] in detail by General Pedro Menéndez, with information as to what ought to be done, so that he may promptly order it. . . ." [25] It is probably of such a report that Menéndez makes mention in his letter of January 30, 1566, to the King: ". . . the way in which we must proceed to learn this secret [the passage to China] is that which

22. 1 Priestley 195. Actually, the years 1541-1545 were a period of intense commercial activity by the French in the Atlantic (4 Winsor 61).

23. Velasco to Luna, September 13, 1560, 2 Priestley 139.

24. Brown, 2 *Genesis* 947.

25. Velasco to Luna, September 3, 1560, 1 Priestley 196.

I communicated to Your Majesty in a memorial some years ago...."[26]
We cannot infer that Menéndez himself was in the sloops ordered to explore the coast; in fact his correspondence indicates that he had not seen
it with his own eyes.

A month or more after Ibarra sailed for Spain, Angel Villafañe, who
had assumed Luna's command, began exploration of the east coast with
four vessels. On June 14 in the vicinity of Hatteras his caravel nearly
foundered, and two smaller vessels perished.[27] What happened next is
vague, but we know that the two remaining vessels met at sea a week
later on their way to Havana. We do not know whether or not either
ship entered the Chesapeake.

The Taking of the Indian Don Luis

IT MAY HAVE BEEN one of Villafañe's vessels or one of the Menéndez
sloops which picked up an Indian chief of Virginia who is to play a very
important role in our narrative from here on. He it is who seems to have
supplied the Spanish name for the northern province—Ajacán. Without
his advice and persuasion it is doubtful if the missionaries and Menéndez
would have attempted the settlement of the Chesapeake, and he it was
who brought death to eight of the Jesuits. He was called Don Luis de
Velasco, after his sponsor, the Viceroy. Mystery surrounds his appearance
on the scene. One explanation stems from Francisco Sacchini:

"Ajacán is a large province in Florida, 37° north of the Equator and
170 leagues distant from Santa Elena. Some eleven years earlier [therefore
in 1559 or 1560], the brother of a principal chief of that region gave himself up to some Spaniards sailing near Ajacán. None of his family knew
of this. After he was brought to Spain and treated honorably and kindly,
he was baptized by Luis de Velasco, Viceroy of Mexico, whose name
he received. When King Philip thought it fitting, he later ordered the man
to be returned to his province in company with some Religious of the
Dominican order. After spending some years fruitlessly on various islands,

26. From a translation by Henry Ware in
8 *PMHS* (2) 466. Ware has translated seven
letters of Menéndez to Philip which throw
much light on their plans for the Chesapeake.

The Spanish is given in Ruidíaz, *La Florida*,
vol. 2.

27. 2 Winsor 260.

he was living at this time in Havana. A man of fifty years, he afforded Father Segura very convincing proofs that he was a good man. . . ." [28]

Luis Gerónimo de Oré, who is confused in his dates, says Don Luis was picked up in 1570 by a ship from Santa Elena which lost its course towards the north, in 37½ °, and put into a large bay which the sailors called the Bahía de Madre de Dios. "From among some Indians who came aboard they retained a young *cacique*, whom they took along with them to Spain. . . ." Here he was baptized, clothed by the King, educated by the Jesuits at Seville, and inspired some of these Religious to take him back to his own country in a missionary enterprise. [29] Pedro de Ribadeneyra narrates that Menéndez had taken him to Spain, where he was baptized, and that he accompanied Father Segura to Florida in 1568. Bartolomé Martínez maintains that Menéndez himself, after the Ribault massacre, discovered the port of Jacán 300 leagues north of Santa Elena, and there, with the permission of the Indians, took the young son of a chief to Spain, where he was six or seven years with the Jesuits of Castile until, after the age of twenty, he desired to return to his country. [30]

Solís de Meras and Barrientos, contemporaries of Menéndez, say that in 1566 Luis had been "six years with the Adelantado." [31] Brother Juan de la Carrera and Father Juan Rogel, however, had seen the Indian; it is significant that they agree so well in saying that Don Luis, a native of Florida, was taken to Mexico by Dominicans, baptized there with Velasco as godfather, later taken to Spain and presented to Philip II, who clothed and (according to Carrera) educated him. Father Rogel says that Menéndez brought him back to Havana, where he was taken to Father Juan Baptista de Segura. Carrera says the Dominicans brought him to Havana and left him there and that he then sought out the Admiral. [32]

We submit the following summary of the evidence. First, as to age, Oré and Martínez speak of Don Luis as young. Rogel speaks of a son of a petty chief. Carrera describes him only as a self-styled "big chief" and a "big talker." Sacchini gives him an age of fifty at the time he was discussing plans in 1570. From the time of Columbus until the middle of the seventeenth century, explorers of all nations made a practice of abducting

28. Francisco Sacchini, *Historiae Societatis Iesu, Borgia*, Book VI, No. 267. The relevant passages are translated in Part II below.

29. "The Martyrs of Florida," by Luis Gerónimo de Oré (hereafter cited Oré).

30. See the Martínez Relation, paragraphs 23-25, translated in Part II below.

31. Jeannette Connor, *Colonial Records of Spanish Florida* 1: 208. Barrientos' almost identical recital is found in Genaro García, *Dos antiguas relaciones de la Florida* (Mexico, 1902) 126.

32. *MAF* 552 for Carrera, 611 for Rogel.

young Indians who could easily acquire a European tongue, yet old enough to retain their own; thus they could act as interpreters. Although cases of taking older Indians are not uncommon, it is less likely that the Spaniards would have wanted to bring with them an Indian forty years old. From the Segura and Rogel letters we know that Don Luis had a three-year-old "brother" and an "uncle," not too easily associated with a man aged fifty, but the terms are also applicable to more distant relatives.

Where was Don Luis found? Oré and Martínez say in a bay which the former locates at 37½° N. Lat. Solís de Meras and Barrientos give 37° as the latitude for St. Mary's Bay, the land of Don Luis. The others do not mention the location. Shea thinks Villafañe may have picked up the Indian somewhat south of Virginia, and in view of what Sacchini says concerning the ignorance of his tribe about his disappearance this might be true.[33]

When and by whom was Don Luis found? First it is important to note that the correspondence of Velasco with Luna does not mention Don Luis in 1560, and yet we note how often he quotes the Englishman who had been on the coast fifteen years previously. It is almost certain that no Spanish ships sailing from east to west ever took a route far enough north to touch the Chesapeake. It is even more certain that no Spanish ships, unless blown from their course, sailed north so far along the coast in 1559 and 1560, for that is the very thing Velasco was desperately trying to accomplish. The Indians of North Carolina had retained a tradition in 1584 of a wreck on Wococon Island twenty-six years previously (1558 or 1559), but the survivors, in an improvised craft, again came to grief farther down the coast.[34] Villafañe was accompanied by Dominicans; one of his ships may have found Don Luis.[35] Fathers Contreras and Beteta are said to have been seeking a mission site and so would have been interested in the education of an Indian of that region. It seems equally probable that the Menéndez ship which was to return to Mexico and report may have exceeded the hundred leagues assigned it and may have entered the Chesapeake. One thing nevertheless somewhat militates against any Spanish ship's actually having gotten into the Chesapeake at this time: that is the fact that Menéndez later seems to be drawing

33. 2 Winsor 260, note 1.
34. From the account by Amadas and Barlowe, in *Hakluyt's Voyages* (*Everyman's Library*). Hereafter cited Hakluyt (EL) 6: 239f.

35. Activities of the Dominicans are treated by Father V. F. O'Daniel, O.P., in *Dominicans in Early Florida* (New York, 1930). The Dominicans with Villafañe are discussed *passim* in this work.

all his information of that bay from the Indian and sailors of other nations rather than from any Spanish pilot, and he speaks of the desirability of sending a pilot there in 1566 "in order that with his own eyes he may see this arm of the sea. . . ." [36]

In two letters of 1565 he has been relying on the same sources of information. He locates Don Luis' home and St. Mary's Bay at 37° and states that 80 leagues north and inland from that bay is to be found another arm of salt water, going west-northwest. [37]

In his letters of 1565 Menéndez identifies Luis as "The Indian who is in New Spain," thereby implying that he had not yet been introduced to King Philip. [38] It seems most probable that Don Luis was only once in Spain—for a period of two years or more immediately after the abortive attempt of 1566 to establish a mission on the Chesapeake. We cannot be sure when or with whom he returned to Havana.

MENÉNDEZ DE AVILÉS PLANS A SETTLEMENT AT AJACÁN

IT WILL be of interest now to try to reconstruct as nearly as we can the geography of the Chesapeake and the interior as Menéndez conceived it. Thus we can appreciate the importance he attached to a settlement in the north. [39] First he had information from a rescued sailor and possibly others

36. Menéndez to the King, January 30, 1566, 8 *PMHS* (2) 467.

37. *Ibid.*, 433. The translation here might give the impression that Don Luis lived 80 leagues south of St. Mary's Bay, but the idea Menéndez wants to convey is that St. Mary's Bay is the land of Don Luis.

38. *Ibid.* 433, 456.

39. This reconstruction is based on Menéndez' memorial already cited; his letters to the King of October 15, 1565, December 25, 1565, and January 30, 1566; a letter to a Jesuit friend of October 15, 1566 in 2 Ruidíaz; Hernando de los Ríos, "Memorial on Navigation and Conquest," in E. H. Blair and J. A. Robertson, eds., *The Philippine Islands 1493-1898*, 55 vols. (Cleveland 1905-1909) 9: 299-314; and H. H. Bancroft, *History of the Northwest Coast*, 2 vols. (San Francisco, 1884) 1: *passim*, especially notes on Menéndez and Urdaneta. We have also built on Navarrete, *Viajes Apócrifos*,

34-39, which is Bancroft's main source. A retired colonel and mathematician, Ríos carefully collected the traditions concerning two passages to the Orient: one sailed by the Portuguese through the Arctic and the "Strait of Anian," the other through New Spain at about 45°, the latter being the passageway in which Menéndez was particularly interested. The information about this route came to Ríos from Fray Andrés de Aguirre, an Augustinian cosmographer and former companion of Urdaneta, and from Father Sedeño, Jesuit superior in the Philippines and former associate of Menéndez in Florida, who, as we shall see, opposed the establishment of a mission in Ajacán. "Father Antonio Sedeño, rector of the Society of Jesus of this city [Manila], who died about two years ago [1595], said that it was told him many times by Pero Meléndez in Florida" (Blair and Robertson 9: 311). Fray Andrés had gotten

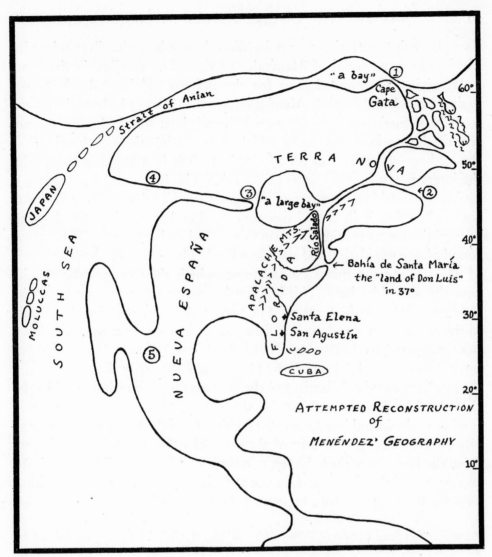

Plate III

THE GEOGRAPHY OF PEDRO MENÉNDEZ DE AVILÉS

Stories of the strait to the South Sea, popular at the time of the Adelantado, are compiled in this drawing. It was generally believed that two straits existed: the first (1) was discovered by Bretons in 1545 and navigated by Portuguese as far as China. The reality corresponding to Anian was Bering Strait. Whales seen south of Terra Nova were believed to have come through this strait. In 1554 Menéndez met a Biscayan who claimed to have sailed with a French pirate through an opening (2) about 45° north latitude, which ended in a large bay. At a quarter of a league from this bay (3) in latitude 42° they found another arm of the sea. Here they built four brigs and sailed to 48° (4) where they found a large colony of people who built houses for them. From there they could have gone by boat to a point near the mines of Zacatecas (5). The Río Salado, a tributary of the Bahía de Santa María, Menéndez believed to run north 80 leagues to the strait.

about French penetration to a point directly north of the silver mines in
Mexico. In a memorial of Menéndez to the King, possibly in the year
1561, giving recommendations for the defense of the Atlantic Coast
against French and English, Menéndez says that in 1554 he brought a man
from New Spain who had been on a French boat that had gone up "an
arm of the sea in Terra Nova which goes cutting through Florida." [40]
Proceeding west they had been brought to halt in a bay 400 leagues in
the interior. (In later accounts he puts down both 500 and 600 leagues.)
Going overland but a quarter of a league they found another arm of the
sea, and having built four brigs they explored it another 300 leagues
toward the west, entering this arm at 42° and ending at 48°. There they
found a large population and abundant food. They were 500 leagues north
of Mexico and the mines of Zacatecas, which they conceivably could
have threatened by boat. This imaginative account has its counterpart in
the cartography of the century. The French maps exaggerated the length
of the St. Lawrence and made it flow from a bay whose nature may have
been suggested by Indian reports of the Great Lakes.[41] Many of these
maps showed a strait by which the Hudson and Richelieu rivers afforded a
passage between the Atlantic and the St. Lawrence. Menéndez evidently
thought the Chesapeake might be the starting point for another strait
leading to the inland bay 80 leagues northwest of the Chesapeake or actually connecting with the arm of the sea which lay a quarter of a league
from the bay. From there he felt certain it would be possible to navigate
to the "Sea of the West" and thence to China and the Moluccas. Writing
to a Jesuit friend in Cádiz, he named the Río Salado as the river "which

the story direct from a Biscayan, sailing with
a French pirate, who entered a strait around
45°. In Andrés' version there was only one
brigantine. The people inland built wooden
houses for them where they stayed until, one
of them having had a difficulty with a woman,
they were driven away. Their ship was
wrecked and the Biscayan rescued by a Portuguese vessel. He later was in Mexico with
Francisco Ibarra's army. Here he circulated
his fanciful story, perhaps based on some penetration of the St. Lawrence and Great Lakes,
and caught the ear of Menéndez, Urdaneta,
and Aguirre, among others.

40. Memorial of Menéndez, 2 Ruidíaz 323.
This arm of the sea, if it really existed, was
evidently the St. Lawrence, explored by
Cartier. The French boat in question perished

at sea. Menéndez' informer was rescued by
a Portuguese ship.

41. For such a bay, see the prototype Molineaux map of 1600, 3 Winsor 216. The
tempting concept of a Hudson River strait
and of a northern sea passage leading to
Japan and the Moluccas is pictured in a map
attributed to Jean Cossin, 1570, under the title,
*Carte geographique, ou universelle description
du monde,* in the Karpinski collection. Mat-
thias Quadus' map of 1600 shows two straits.
In the cartography of Menéndez' time the
east-west longitudinal distances were col-
lapsed. Reasons for the tardiness in accurate
measurement of longitude are well brought
out by Lloyd A. Brown, *The Story of Maps*
(Boston, 1949).

goes to China." [42] We believe he was thinking of the Chesapeake and its tributaries, not so much in terms of the later maps of Martínez and Dircks or a Paris map of 1580, in which the Río Salado seems to represent the Potomac, but in terms of Homem, in which it would correspond to the upper bay and the Susquehanna. [43]

The Governor's speculations were advanced by the help of Don Luis when the King, by an order of March 22, 1565, to the President and *audiencia* of New Spain, remanded the Virginia chieftain to the custody of Menéndez. [44] According to Kenny, the Archbishop of Mexico had been trying to prevent the return of Don Luis to his homeland, fearing his corruption. [45] Don Luis, with typical Indian boastfulness, was most willing to impart all knowledge of his native country and wanted to lead the missionaries there, as he said, for the conversion of his brethren. We know that crude map-drawing was an accomplishment of Indians in general and of Virginia Indians in particular, so that it is reasonable to picture Don Luis sketching the outlines of the Chesapeake for the interested Menéndez. [46] We may be sure that Luis shared the common belief of his

42. 2 Ruidíaz 159. Menéndez in discussing the strait seems to be appealing to Jesuit interest in the missions of China and Japan started by Xavier. In March, 1565, he wrote Francis Borgia, Father-General of the Jesuits: "This land of Florida should be connected with Tartary and China, or there should be an arm of the sea . . . by which one may go to China and Maluco and return to the land of Florida" (*MAF* 1 f.). That Borgia was interested in the Florida mission as a stepping stone to the East is suggested in his letter to Nadal, October 9, 1567, where he speaks of the advantage of having missionaries in Honduras, on the way to China and Japan (8 *MHSI* "Nadal" 533). Early maps and reports indicate the possibility of encountering Tartars, Chinese, and Japanese by sailing through straits entering the interior or leading to the west coast of the North American continent. This fact should not be minimized when we question why Francis Borgia (*post factum*) should have approved the missionary enterprise in Virginia among a sparse population of natives. Actually he was in no position to set limits to the possibilities that might open up with Ajacán as a wedge.

43. Lowery gives a somewhat similar analysis in 2: 212. Shea and others have pictured the Potomac as the river supposed to

lead to China, but as the Spanish knew of only one northern branch of the bay, and inasmuch as the 1588 explorers passed by the Potomac in preference to an attempt ultimately blocked by the rocks of the Susquehanna, we may conclude that Menéndez and his successors were looking for a wide channel of salt water. Juan Menéndez Marqués, while still exploring the Chesapeake in 1588, evidently entered each of the tidewater rivers far enough to discover that it was freshening, then continued on his way up the bay. Pedro Menéndez de Avilés related the story of a trade in buffalo hides through the lower continental strait, the Indians carrying them by canoe to Terra Nova.

44. F. Zubillaga, *La Florida* 394, note 9, quotes the mandate which provides for the delivery of Juan [*sic*] Velasco, "with his Indian servant." This would seem to mean Don Luis' servant, for if Menéndez had one, he would hardly have needed permission for his services.

45. Michael Kenny, *Romance of the Floridas* (Milwaukee, 1943) 148.

46. Swanton, *The Indians of the Southeastern United States* 735 f. Archer writes of meeting an Indian in Virginia who was going to draw a map in the sand with his foot, but was successfully persuaded to use pen and

brethren on the Atlantic Coast concerning the nearness of their river sources to a western sea. When Ralph Lane was in Raleigh's North Carolina settlement in 1585 he was told that the River Moratoc (Roanoke) gushed from a huge rock fronting on the western sea.[47] Later, men of the Virginia colony had a similar account of the neighboring James.[48] The Algonkin tribes, hemmed in by Siouan neighbors in the Piedmont, either through trade or tradition may have preserved vague knowledge of the Great Lakes, the Gulf of Mexico, or even the Pacific which circumstances did not permit them to verify.[49]

In the winter of 1565 Menéndez ostensibly was confirmed in his speculations on the strait leading to China by conversations with Fray Andrés Urdaneta, who was passing through to Spain to give an official report on López de Legaspi's administration of the Philippine Islands. Father Urdaneta, an ex-soldier, pilot, and cosmographer, "had a full account for many years" of the strait going in the direction of China.[50] In his various

paper (E. A. Arber, ed. with A. G. Bradley, *Travels and Works of Captain John Smith* [hereafter cited Arber], 1: xli). Powhatan also demonstrated this ability to Smith on another occasion. A list of about thirty such instances has been compiled by Delf Norona in "Maps Drawn by Indians in the Virginias," *The West Virginia Archaeologist* (March 1950) 12-19.

47. 6 *Hakluyt* (EL) 145.

48. Brown in his *Genesis* has several documents containing these narratives, which were retailed in England and dutifully picked up there by the Spanish ambassadors Zúñiga and Velasco and relayed to King Philip III. When John Smith returned to Jamestown after a tour of the Chesapeake in 1608, his men reported that "the good newes of our Discovery, and the good hope we had by the Salvages relation, that our Bay had stretched into the South Sea, or somewhat neare it, appeased their fury..." (2 Arber 420). Smith is said to have motivated Hudson's search for the strait to China (Brown, 1 *Genesis* 184). Powhatan once told Smith that his people were lying about the western salt sea, but he may have said this to deter the English from going into the enemy Monacan territory and forming alliances there. In Smith's earlier accounts Powhatan himself seems to believe the report (1 Arber 19 f.). From his first conversation with that chief, Smith seems to have learned about the Iroquois as situated on the great

sea to the north, while the Roanoke (Maratoc) arose near the southern part of that great body of salt water. Without knowing it, he was equating the Great Lakes with the Pacific Ocean. Such tales were not the exclusive property of the Algonkin. Oñate in 1604 heard almost identical recitals about the proximity of a western ocean from the Mojave, who may have had the Great Salt Lake in mind.

49. That the enmity of the Sioux and Algonkin known to exist in Smith's day was true in 1570 is indicated by the account given by Alonso, sole survivor of Ajacán, to Martínez: "The Indians of the long wide valleys are the enemies of those in the mountains and in summer a savage war is waged." (See the Martínez Relation, Part II below, para. 45 and note 23.)

50. 8 *PMHS* (2) 466-467. For sketches of Urdaneta, who went to the Philippines with Loaysa's 1525 expedition, helped Legaspi discover the best route to Manila, and in 1552 joined the Augustinian order in Mexico, see Blair and Robertson 2: 33, note 5, and *passim*. When he met Menéndez in 1565 he had just piloted a fleet on a new and better route from the Philippines across the Pacific. He had been informed that some French had navigated a northern strait to China beginning about 70° and had returned through another to Florida below 50°. He never put full credence in

letters to the King, Menéndez presented St. Mary's Bay as the key to all the fortifications in Florida, controlling a rich trade with the Indians of the interior, and giving access to the distant lands of the East. Lowery cites a document to show that the King made a generous contribution to the financing of Menéndez's plans.[51] In all this matter one can be certain that the Governor was really interested in the Chesapeake as a base for the protection of his fleet and for profitable operations against pirates, but he manifests less immediate interest in his own recitals concerning a route to China. He or his pilots were four times in the bay during his lifetime without exploring it. Nevertheless, his theory on the strait became the dominant motive behind the later Spanish explorations of the coast, including the important 1588 expedition which we shall treat in detail.

When Menéndez had returned to Spain in 1563 he was for the second time taken to prison to answer charges filed by the jealous Casa de Contratación, which had been established to govern trade with the Indies. After the French occupation of Port Royal, South Carolina, the King released Menéndez from his difficulty and made him successor to the tragic Ayllón as proprietor of the Atlantic Coast. His destruction of the French colony and building of Fort San Agustín are well-known history that need not delay us here. We have already seen how he immediately turned his attention northward to Santa Elena and Santa María. In the summer of 1566, during a two-day stop at San Mateo, just north of San Agustín, he found two Dominican monks, possibly those whom he had ordered Solís de Meras to bring from New Spain the year before as missionaries in his new territory. He felt that the time was ready for colonizing the Chesapeake.

"He sent a captain with 30 soldiers and 2 Dominican friars to the Bay of Santa María, in 37°, with an Indian who was the brother of the *cacique* of that country, and who had been 6 years with the *Adelantado:* he was very crafty, a good Christian with very good understanding, called Don Luis de Velasco; so that with his assistance they might settle in that land and try to make the Indians Christian.

these rumors, but subsequent writers even credited Urdaneta himself with personal discovery of the strait (Bancroft 51 f.).

51. A letter of Fourquevaux to Catherine de' Medici, May 8, 1568, cited in 2 Lowery 367, note 2, informs us that Philip had been so impressed by Menéndez' importunity that he had advanced 230,000 crowns for the undertaking. Menéndez' deposition of March 28, 1568, cited in note 3, pp. 367-368, partially explains the King's interest, for in it the *Adelantado* claimed that the Portuguese had been fortifying themselves for two years in the interior, probably near the "bay" he so often describes. If the King's providence is a fact, one can scarcely exonerate Menéndez from extreme niggardliness in his economy with the Jesuit missionaries, later.

"The friars were from Peru and New Spain, a very fertile country [*sic*]: they had suffered hunger, hardships and danger in Florida. As it appeared to them that they could no longer endure such a difficult life, they secretly drew some of the soldiers into a conspiracy, for there was no need of much effort to accomplish this, and won over the pilot; and being in accord, and taking testimony to the effect that on account of a storm they had been unable to go to the Bay of Santa María, they went to Seville, defaming the country and speaking ill of the King and the *Adelantado*, because they wanted to conquer and settle it." [52]

The recently discovered report of the pilot, Pedro de Coronas, puts no blame on the friars, Pablo de San Pedro, of Jérez, and Juan de Acuña, of Granada. He says that he had directed the ship to 37°, then back to 36°, then up again to 37½°, but that Don Luis was not able to recognize the territory as his own. When a heavy wind drove them out to sea they decided to return home. There are two difficulties with his narrative. It is strange, first of all, that Don Luis seemed to have no trouble in finding his tribe in 1570, and secondly, if the wind arose at 37½° it hardly would have blown them out of the bay. There remains the possibility of the usual exaggeration of latitude, in which case Coronas may not have reached Cape Henry. If, however, the Dominicans depreciated Florida and Menéndez, they were not without material for complaint, as we shall see later. Whether or not Solís de Meras' report was true, it is probable that Menéndez agreed with him, for he put through a regulation providing for the most severe penalty, perhaps even death, for any captain who would make an unauthorized voyage from Florida carrying a missionary. [53] He later rescinded this order under pressure from Francis Borgia, Father-General of the Society of Jesus.

Menéndez began to woo the Jesuits in earnest in 1565, and until his death in 1574 he never ceased begging Francis Borgia for more priests, Brothers, and catechists for the missions in Florida, the chapels in the forts, and the school for sons of Indian chiefs in Havana. [54] In 1566 came Fathers Pedro Martínez and Juan Rogel and Brother Francisco Villareal. Pedro Martínez was killed by Indians near St. Johns River in Florida.

---

52. 1 Connor 207. See also Barcia 128, 132.

53. Kenny 149 cites AGI 2-5-4/12 as the source of Coronas' report. Menéndez may have been angered not only by the return of the Dominicans but by the participation of a Seville cleric named Rueda in the mutiny at San Agustín (1 Ruidíaz 190).

54. The personnel and background of the Jesuit mission in Florida are treated in detail by Kenny and Zubillaga, to some extent by Lowery, and by Ugarte, "First Jesuit Mission in Florida," 25 *HRS* 59-68.

Father Portillo, who was sent over to Peru as provincial, included the Florida mission in his jurisdiction. He was sceptical from the first about the new enterprise of Menéndez. On April 10, 1568, there sailed from Spain Fathers Baptista de Segura, vice-provincial, Gonzalo del Álamo, and Antonio Sedeño; Brothers Juan de la Carrera, Pedro Linares, and Domingo Agustín Báez; five catechists; and six Florida Indians, one of whom, Don Jaime of Tegesta, proved a valuable missionary ally. Father del Álamo was later chief chaplain of the Armada. Father Sedeño was a pioneer Jesuit in Mexico and the Philippine Islands. Brother Báez is famous for having composed an Indian grammar before his death after only one year as a missionary. Of the five catechists, all of whom entered the Society, Méndez, Solís, and Redondo were killed at Ajacán. Salcedo was in charge of the 1571 relief expedition to the Chesapeake.

After one year Segura had made two or three trips throughout the Florida missions and had become convinced of the futility of trying to convert the natives in the circumstances that existed. In a report to Borgia, the vice-provincial calls attention to the failing health of his men, the slight benefit to the natives, the diversion of valuable missionary personnel to the forts, where they had to act as chaplains, and finally to the earlier Dominican decision to abandon the mission because of the little hope it contained. That he was already thinking in terms of the Chesapeake is evident from the following passage:

"Your Paternity will judge whether it will not be more for the greater hope for the conversion of King Philip's Indians, for instance, should the opportunity offer to go to China from here, for the Indians have found a route, or should some other such enterprise be presented, or finally should they be sent to some other land discovered by our countrymen, where more abundant fruit may be expected in Our Lord. In what I have said I do not refer to myself, for I am fully aware of my unworthiness and that the least trial seems heavy to me. May God in His bounty grant that I may profit if only from the least crosses to be borne." [55]

From the letters of Father Rogel, who worked at Santa Elena and surrounding territory as well as at Havana and San Carlos in western Florida, we gather additional reasons for the failure of the Jesuit mission.[56] The Indians, because of the poverty of the land, lived scattered throughout the forest nine months of the year. Menéndez' lieutenants were care-

55. Segura to Borgia, Havana, December 18, 1569, 25 HRS 109; MAF 406.
56. Letter of December 9, 1570, MAF 471-

479. Swanton discusses its anthropological import in Early History of the Creek Indians 57-58.

less, cruel, and unjust in their treatment of the Indians and thus created an almost continual state of enmity. Finally, Father Rogel himself, in company with most of the missionaries of his day, felt that it was morally reprehensible to temporize with "devil-worship," and his outspoken criticisms offended the Indians. Father Sedeño, in his turn, emphasized the multiplicity of tongues and a widely scattered population living in unhealthy and inaccessible swamps.

From the documents that we have it is difficult to follow the movements of Menéndez during these years, but apparently he was in Spain trying to enlist the help of the King while his garrisons were rebelling and disintegrating. Las Alas, one of his lieutenants, finally took about half the men back to Spain. It was Menéndez himself who brought the last party of Jesuits to Florida, sailing February 7, 1570. They were Father Luis Quirós and Brothers Sancho Zaballos and Gabriel Gómez.[57]

THE MISSION TO AJACÁN

ROGEL SAYS the Governor brought Don Luis to Havana and Carrera relates that there Menéndez, Don Luis, and Father Segura discussed the proposed mission in Ajacán, territory of the Indian.[58] Father Segura, whom we might term an enthusiast, felt that he had in this Indian a helper as valuable as was Timothy to St. Paul.

A study of the correspondence makes it clear that Segura must have been given broad powers of decision by Borgia, as indeed the remoteness of Florida would demand, for there is no indication in Borgia's letters that he gave specific permission for the Ajacán enterprise. Sedeño, writing to Borgia on May 14, 1570, is the first to mention the mission and indicates

57. Kenny 245, following Martínez (Part II below), para. 25, says Menéndez took Don Luis back to Florida. For the correct information see note 6 of the Martínez Relation in Part II.

58. In relation to this meeting Kenny cites a remark of Brother Carrera without noting the source. It may be a letter of Brother Carrera written March 10, 1572, which he quotes on other occasions, but such a letter is not known by Zubillaga even under *epistolae deperditae*. According to the source quoted by Kenny (247), Segura had written for advice to the other Florida Jesuits, who were opposed to the Chesapeake plan, but their replies, on a ship delayed by storm, arrived at Havana after Segura had left. *MAF* 478, note 30, criticizes a similar statement by Sacchini. Menéndez is represented as originally opposing the plan, then consenting and cooperating. It is known that he did not think highly of Father Segura's administrative capabilities and tried to have him replaced, as did Father Sedeño, who felt that he was lacking in eloquence and mastery of the languages, highly regarded in those days for the missions and still emphasized with good reason in the Jesuit constitutions.

that Father Segura will give more particulars, which he evidently did in lost letters of May 26 and 31.[59] Father Borgia, writing to Segura September 7, 1570, had received only his December and March letters, but a general policy for new enterprises is certainly couched in his efforts to provide liberty of movement for his Jesuits. He says, "But although Your Reverences do well in rejoicing in your trials and in asking always to be in them, I am here fulfilling my duty so that His Majesty may know of the situation there and give orders for an efficacious remedy which as I hope will soon be forthcoming, by commanding that the Religious enjoy the freedom that God and his Holy Church have given them, so that if they don't realize the fruit that is to be hoped for in that place, they may go to another where hearts are better disposed. . . ."[60]

Borgia's letter of November 14, 1570, to Segura belatedly wishes him success in the voyage with Don Luis "for the greater glory of His Divine Majesty and the salvation of many souls."[61] In this letter he acknowledges receipt of Segura's letters of April 14, 15, 17, May 27 and 31, and July 18, all now lost. Their discovery might materially advance our knowledge of the missionaries' plans.

Brother Carrera, who had responsible charges in connection with temporal necessities, retained a vivid memory of the preparations made by the vice-provincial: ". . . he prepared himself for the trip and had a boat made and equipped with everything necessary for both the sea voyage and that land, which was to be stocked with different sorts of animals and birds and many other things. With all this equipment he sailed from Havana. . . . He arrived in good weather at the point of Santa Elena in Florida where I was staying at the time, and there we all had a meeting."[62]

At Santa Elena there ensued a conference among Fathers Sedeño, Rogel, Quirós, Segura, Brother Carrera, and several of the Brothers and catechists. Brother Carrera distrusted Don Luis and thought an experienced Father should go ahead and spy out the land. Fathers Rogel and Sedeño offered their services, but Father Segura "had decided beforehand to take with him Father Quirós and Brother Gabriel Gómez, both recently arrived from Spain, and Brother Sancho de Zaballos who was still

59. Sedeño to Borgia, May 14, 1570, *MAF* 430.

60. Borgia to Segura, September 7, 1570, *MAF* 437.

61. Borgia to Segura, November 14, 1570, *MAF* 458.

62. Carrera Relation (Part II below), para.

35. The "animals" are explained by the clause in Menéndez' contract, typical of Spanish policy, providing for the production of livestock in the New World. When the *Adelantado* went to Florida he took with him, horses, sheep, swine, lambs, goats, and perhaps other stock (2 Lowery 143).

a novice, and Brothers Juan Baptista [Méndez], Pedro de Linares, Cristóbal Redondo, Gabriel de Solís [a relative of Menéndez], and other young men who sought to enter the company." [63] Also in the party was a young lad named Alonso de Olmos, son of a Santa Elena settler.

Father Segura was determined to establish himself at Ajacán without the encumbrance of any garrison of soldiers who might give bad example and stir up trouble among the natives as they had in Florida. One can hardly imagine Menéndez' consenting to such an arrangement under favorable circumstances, but his garrisons were decimated, and conditions were so bad that Fathers Rogel and Sedeño were ordered to go back to Havana.

Father Quirós called at Brother Carrera's storehouse and took the greater part of his ecclesiastical furnishings and his best articles in the way of chalices, monstrances, and vestments for the new mission. The novices, in tears, took their leave of Brother Carrera and the others and bravely boarded ship. Their craft stood out to sea on August 5 for the new adventure, as Father Segura relates. Storms and the necessity for feeling their way up the unfamiliar coast delayed them, so that it was early in September when they came in sight of the Chesapeake.

First Landfall in the Chesapeake

FATHER SEGURA does not describe the harbor, but Brother Carrera from his 1572 voyage gives us a good picture of it: "Our Fathers and Brothers disembarked [1570] in a great and beautiful port, and men who have sailed a great deal and have seen it say it is the best and largest port in the world. So, if I remember rightly, the pilot remarked to me. It is called the Bay of the Mother of God, and in it there are many deep-water ports, each better than the next. I saw this port myself when I went with the Governor, as I will narrate later. It seemed to me (for as it looked to me and I was given to understand), it was about 3 leagues at the mouth,

63. Rogel Relation (Part II below), para. 8. Carrera in his Relation (Part II below), para. 36, describes the men somewhat differently. Linares is a brother, Méndez, de Solís, and Redondo are novices. The admission into the Society of these last three men by Father Segura is discussed together with biographical details in the introduction to Part II. It is prac-

tically certain that Father Segura would have rewarded the young men by admission to the novitiate of the Society to which they were aspiring, in view of the hardships they had suffered. This information could easily have been passed along to Rogel by the boy Alonso de Olmos.

and in length and breadth it was close to 30. They say that at the end of it the other sea begins. Also there is the very important navigation route, mentioned before, which the Governor wanted to explore. I understand he would have done this, had he lived long enough. There is a large population on the shores of this port and inland." [64]

A port of one mouth 3 leagues wide cannot apply to Pamlico or Albemarle Sound. "The other end of the bay" recalls Menéndez' hope that the Río Salado at the northern end of the bay might be the way to China. There may be some confusion about the 30 leagues' length and breadth. Kenny takes the remark to mean that Carrera was viewing the bay at its maximum extension, which is the Potomac, whose mouth could easily be confused with the bay.[65] But he would have had almost the same impression of width at the mouth of the James. At any rate, it does not follow that Carrera himself saw that extension, for he clearly indicates he is supplementing his own knowledge with that of others. It is also true of the Chesapeake that there are many deep-water ports. A recent yachting guide lists 232 with a depth of more than 6 feet.[66] The North Carolina bays, to the contrary, have very narrow and shallow entrances and satisfactory deep water only toward the mainland. This was true even in the time of Walter Raleigh.[67]

The large population that Brother Carrera mentions on the shores of the port were doubtless the Kecoughtan, who, according to Strachey, numbered a thousand persons and were situated near Hampton.[68]

Fortunately, from the later relation of Luis Gerónimo de Oré we have a fairly accurate notion of the direction taken by the ship once it reached

64. Carrera Relation (Part II, below), para. 39. Those familiar with Percy's description of the bay and its people when the English first arrived will have a good idea of the scene viewed by the Spanish (Brown, 1 *Genesis* 152-156; 1 Arber lxi-lxiii).

65. Kenny 287. Carrera's statement is, in itself, sufficient proof that neither he nor Father Rogel was near the northern end of the bay.

66. Fessenden S. Blanchard, *A Cruising Guide to the Chesapeake* (New York, 1950) 17.

67. "In this sea [Pamlico] are 100. Iles of diuers bignesses, but to get into it, you have but 3 passages and they very dangerous" (2 Arber 309 quoting Amadas and Barlowe, 1584).

68. For our tribal sizes, names, and locations we are relying on various documents published by Arber, by Brown in his *Genesis*, the maps and writings of John Smith, the map of Tindall, and the *Historie* of Strachey. These have been summarized by James Mooney in F. W. Hodge, *Handbook of American Indians North of Mexico*, by Frank Speck some years ago in various articles in the *AA*, and in the Heye Foundation, *Indian Notes and Monographs*; and more recently by Maurice A. Mook in several articles in *WMQ* including: "The Aboriginal Population of Tidewater Virginia," "The Anthropological Position of the Indian Tribes of Tidewater Virginia," "Virginia Ethnology from an Early Relation," and "The Ethnological Significance of Tindall's Map of Virginia, 1608."

the bay. Oré was exercised to see that the Spanish King do something about the "encroachment" of the English in the Chesapeake. "From these ports of Jacán and Bermuda, boats of the enemy set out every year and run along the islands of Cuba, Puerto Rico, Jamaica, and Santo Domingo. They rob what they can without our being able to punish them." [69] He therefore gives most detailed information, collected from mariners' accounts, of the ports within the bay and the exact measures that must be taken to dislodge the English:

"Because the description of the Bahía de Madre de Dios and of the ports with their latitudes, and of the directions of their explorations is so trust-worthy and so necessary for the time when Your Majesty may be pleased to command that the bay be cleared of the robbers who have occupied it and fortified it for thirty years, it seemed well that I should dwell on it at some length." [70]

We will resume the Franciscan's account as the 1588 expedition, in the month of June, nears the Chesapeake: "The mouth of the bay is about 3 leagues wide, without shoals or reefs, and is more than 8 fathoms deep. It runs northwest-southeast and forms a large round gulf. Between the entrance and the place where one reaches the mainland, it extends toward the west and the northwest for about 3 leagues. In the east-west direction, with the mouth, on the mainland, there is a good port which at its entrance has a depth of 3 fathoms. A little less than 2 leagues from there, there is another port toward the northwest, where Captain Gonzales said he landed when he brought the religious of the Society [of Jesus], whom Don Luis and his accomplices put to death, as has already been told.

69. Oré 53. A contemporary of Oré, the Carmelite Antonio Vásquez de Espinosa, makes almost the same statement: "The English of *Xacal* [Virginia] keep raiding, in conjunction with the other pirates' nest which they maintain in Bermuda...." See his *Compendium and Description of the West Indies* 110. John Smith himself was detained by both English and French pirates on his return to Plymouth from New England in 1615 (1 Arber 217-227). In this narrative he puts his finger on the ultimate reason for piracy: the Spanish refusal to permit trade in the West Indies. Percy in 1607 wisely states that "If this River [James] which we haue found had beene discouered in the time of warre with Spaine, it would haue beene a com-moditie to our Realme, and a great annoyance

to our enemies" (1 Arber lxxi). Spanish writers almost universally thought of the English Atlantic coastal settlements in terms of piracy, not distinguishing the peaceful aims of the colonists from those of some of their leaders, whose raids struck terror in the hearts of Spanish settlers in South America (Vásquez de Espinosa 55, 60) and Argall, who was not too gentle in breaking up the foothold of the French on the New England coast. Spanish attitudes are described by David B. Quinn, "Some Spanish Reactions to Eliza-bethan Colonial Enterprise," 1 *TRHS* (1951) 1-26.

70. Oré 48 f. "Thirty years" embraces both the Carolina enterprise beginning in 1584 and Jamestown. This dates Oré's report at about 1615.

"He [Captain Gonzales] said that on a plain which is beyond a bluff and where there was a group of pine trees, an altar had been erected and Mass had been said and that from there he returned toward the east, where on the mainland of that area, but within the bay and near some small islands and an inlet, the *Adelantado* had been. It was there that the *Adelantado* finished the gunwales of two frigates in which he sailed for Castille from that place [1572].

"Thereupon they departed from the said port, and coasting along the shore of the mainland toward the north, they discovered another port which appeared to be a good one and of great depth. On the shore there was an abundance of large stone, while the cape of land to the north formed a high headland. These three ports can be seen at one glance from the mouth of the bay; the last, however, only faintly." [71]

Before discussing this excerpt we add one from the Menéndez Marqués Relation: "From the Bay of Santa Elena to the Bay of the Mother of God of Ajacán, which is at 37° latitude, if necessary I offer to point out ports of suitable entrance where even vessels of 50 tons can be anchored and repaired, especially in the said harbor and bay of the Mother of God, whose entrance lies northwest-southeast without any kind of sand bar or reef inside or outside the entire mouth. Here in the sea's direction, at one observation, there was a depth of 7 or 8 fathoms or more, and the width of the mouth was more than 2 leagues in my opinion. After entering inside, there is such a gulf that the land almost disappears from one side to the other, and when one has entered about 3 leagues in a northwest direction, the shore of the mainland is reached and there is another large harbor with a depth of 3 fathoms or more at its mouth." [72]

We shall now proceed to an interpretation of the valuable hints contained in these reports, leaving to Part III a more detailed analysis and proof for those interested in a more technical discussion of the question. Our procedure was to strive for a re-creation of 1570 navigation conditions by a study of the movements and statements of the early Virginia colonists, and by an examination of the earliest maps and pilot's charts. In general it may be said that the chief significant changes that have taken place in four hundred years are in the erosion of the north shore of the James and the York, the bank in some places having been cut back a hundred yards or more with consequent blocking of the entrances

71. *Ibid.* 44 f.
72. This Relation is described fully in Part II of this work, where the necessary excerpts are given. It is also discussed by Scisco in 22 *MHM* 502.

to small streams, and in the dredging of channels and construction of docks in the Hampton Roads and Norfolk area. Fort Wool, in Hampton Roads, is an artificial island. The James was probably somewhat deeper in early days, though it has not been much subject to siltage. The small fresh-water streams entering it were in former days much more navigable than now, a condition found everywhere in this country before deforestation. Small low islands along the entrances to Back River and Poquoson River have largely disappeared.

In evaluating directions found in the documents we make allowance for the deviation of the magnetic pole from true north.[73]

Oré's description of the mouth of the bay is quite correct, except that he underestimates the distance to both Cape Charles and the mainland. The entrance to the James is west-northwest from the mouth, though the shore line goes west before going northwest. Lynnhaven Inlet and Little Creek were not accessible, though in our times a way has been dredged into the latter. Gonzales would have proceeded northwest through the Thimble Shoal channel in sight of the south shore, probably only occasionally taking soundings. He would have found enough water in Willoughby Bay, but the low sand spit that surrounds it would have given no protection. From Sewall's Point to Norfolk he would have found about 12 feet of water in several sheltered areas fairly close to the shore, enough for almost any of the Spanish vessels. In general, the desirability of a port was enhanced to the degree one could draw close to the shore and avoid the building of docks. Here we have a spot directly west of Cape Henry, on the mainland, which well might have been our first port. A little less than 2 leagues from there in a northwest direction is Newport News, where the channel of the river comes close to the shore. This spot meets all the requirements of all the narratives. There is a *barranca,* or bluff, about 25 feet high, a stand of Loblolly Pines towering over a hundred feet once graced the area,[74] there are level places beyond

73. W. H. Hobbs treats of the relation of the magnetic compass variation to an historical problem in "The Track of the Columbus Caravels in 1492," 20 *HAHR* (1950) 63-73. The pole moves in a complete circle every 129 years. In 1588 the variation from true north at the mouth of the James would have been at its minimum, but the extreme range of variation in that area is so small as to make it possible to utilize the deviation found on modern charts, which is between 6° and 7° inclination toward the west.

74. A communication from George W. Dean, Virginia State Forester, Charlottesville, informs the writers that "Near Newport News there was a stand of virtually virgin timber, predominately Loblolly Pine, which was cut off within the last five years. On the property of the Mariners' Museum, also at Newport News, there still exist scattered pine trees 200 to 300 years of age. Some of these trees reach as high as 120 feet." P. A. Bruce, in his *Economic History of Virginia* 1: 89, states that these giant pines in Virginia were numer-

the bank where Mass could have been said,[75] and there is an ancient village site at the yacht basin which could have been inhabited by Indians who talked to the Jesuits on their stopover here before ascending the river.[76]

From here it would have been necessary for Gonzales in 1588 to return "toward the east" in order to continue his examination of the bay. He would not have gone as far as the eastern shore of Virginia at this time, only to swing back to the west, which would have meant an extra 40 miles of navigation. Therefore the 1572 port of the Admiral "inside the bay" must refer to the mainland near Point Comfort. The inlet might refer to Hampton Creek, with a minimum of 9 feet at its mouth, or more probably to Mill Creek, today a little bay formed by the Point, but then a stream. Early maps indicate that the Phoebus shore once extended nearly a mile farther toward the channel. It is on this shore, northwest of Mill Creek, that we believe Menéndez landed. Off the shore between the creeks Menéndez would have found about 6 feet of water, more than today, sufficient for his frigates. The west side of the point itself would have had from 8 to 12 feet, described by John Clark, English pilot of 1611, as a protected and excellent port. The small islands could have been the islets once found at the entrance and still along the southern shore of Mill Creek, or Oré may have meant Point Comfort itself, described to the Spanish by a Virginia Irishman as an island.[77] Later in his Relation discussing Ecija, Oré speaks of "the islands" in the mouth of what we know to have been the James; so regardless of their existence we still have a key to the location of Menéndez' port.[78] Why Point Comfort would have ap-

ous only on the coast and along the shores of the bay and the mouths of the large rivers, hence their aptitude as a landmark. In the earliest land patents "old pines" on a broad creek in Elizabeth City constitute a landmark, as do lone pines at the mouth of the Nansemond River and Pagan River.

75. It is quite possible that ceremonies of taking possession were held here in connection with the Mass, a prominent spot such as this being a likely choice.

76. We understand that a number of Indian pipes were recovered from this site by Mr. Jerome Knowles, of Newport News.

77. "This Cape Comfort is an island which lies at the mouth of a great river on which the English live" (statement by an Irishman who had been eight months in Virginia, in a "Report to Spanish Council of State" July 1, 1610,

Brown, 1 *Genesis* 394). Oré, who reports Molina's adventures at Point Comfort in 1611, believed there were islands at the mouth of the James, as also did Ecija. See the documents in Part II below.

78. Still another check on Menéndez' port is the mention of the "*encenada* where the *Adelantado* had been" on the 1588 return trip of Gonzales down the eastern shore. It seems that the ship came to shore above Kiptopeke at a spot where the explorers could look across the bay directly into the mouth of the James River. Here Oré was probably speaking of *encenada* in the sense of the mouth of the James. From that angle of observation they could have noted the break in the tree line between Point Comfort and Willoughby Point. Scarcely any other feature of the western shore would have been distinguishable.

Plate IV   Drawing by D. T. Netter, S.J.

MOUTH OF THE JAMES RIVER AS FORMERLY SEEN
FROM AN APPROACHING SHIP

Early instructions to English pilots state that Point Comfort at a distance looked like two small islands detached from the mainland. They were evidently the *cayos*, or "keys," that Écija was asked to investigate in 1609 and the *isletas*, or "islets," mentioned by Oré, where the English sentinel ship stood in 1609 and near which Menéndez repaired his frigates in 1572. The cape of Newport News in the background, being higher ground, would have appeared a more attractive place to make the first landfall in the 1570 expedition, and there is evidence that this is the first port touched by Gonzales. The arm leading to the left beyond the point goes to Norfolk and was mentioned as a port by the leaders of the 1588 expedition.

peared to Ecija as two islands is clear from the following description found in Walter Hoxton's *Mapp of the Bay of Chesepeack*, published in London in 1735 or later: "Point Comfort is chiefly covereed with woods, but there are two places on it where no trees grow, which makes it appear like two Islands."

Menéndez Marqués' account can be harmonized with Oré's if we remember that it is more general. His harbor northwest would be the mouth of the James in general. From the Ecija report, which we reproduce in Part II, it is clear that Gonzales and Menéndez Marqués knew of the existence of the James River and therefore could not have omitted its ports from a careful report to the King.

When the 1588 sailors left "said harbor" (the James), they coasted along the shore of the mainland toward the north. Then they discovered the port at Yorktown, one of the world's best inland ports, as we know. It may be positively identified from Oré's Relation by the huge rocks on the southern shore, found nowhere else in that part of the Chesapeake, and by the cape forming a high bluff to the north, which is Gloucester Point. The water off the south shore is 70 feet deep. It is important to note here that the discovery of the York—at least this port—in 1588 was literally true: Oré uses the word *descubrir*, which in this context probably means to come upon an unknown site. Therefore it is highly probable that Gonzales did not ascend the York River in 1570-72.

The hardest part of the narrative to adjust to facts is the statement that all "three ports" can be seen from one point of observation from the mouth of the bay. Supposing tree tops at an elevation of 150 feet above sea level and a 40-foot lookout, the maximum range of observation is 25 statute miles, putting Gloucester Point too far from the mouth to be seen. By climbing a tree on Cape Henry, even a trained lookout under ideal conditions could never have seen the entrance to the York.[79]

Another difficulty arises from the latitude assigned by Oré for the first port: "Captain Vicente Gonzales and the pilot Ginés Pinzón took the latitude which they found to be a good 40° at the head of the bay. They had taken it also at the first port after they entered the bay and here they found it to be 37° and some minutes." [80] The Spanish is *treinta y siete grados y tantos minutos*, which Father Geiger had originally rendered 37° 37'. It is uncertain if Oré meant *tantos* to signify "as many" rather than "some" minutes, even though he earlier gave 37½° as the latitude of St. Mary's Bay. However, the estimate at the mouth of the Susquehanna is 27' too high, and it is not unlikely that a similar error in observation affected the estimate for the first port. If we are correct in selecting Sewall Point as the first port, then in terms of 37° 37' we must posit an error of 40' in Gonzales' estimate. Errors of even a degree were still occasional in the navigation of that day.

A passage in Father Quirós' letter, written while the crew was unloading the ship, suggests a stop such as Gonzales mentions on the river. He says, "From some Indians whom we met farther down this river we have some information about the region farther inland. Three or four days' journey from there lie the mountains. For two of these days one travels on a river. After crossing the mountains by another day's journey or two, one can view another sea. If any new information can be had with more certainty and clarity, we will get it." [81]

Earlier he had remarked that they did not have as good information as they should have had "from the Indians" about the stream they should have entered. In treating of such detailed matters they must have gone ashore, and it may be noted that he says "down the river" rather than "at

79. Oré did not call Menéndez' *encenada* a port (*puerto*), perhaps because it was too exposed. Therefore it is best to assume that his "three" ports are Norfolk, Newport News, and Yorktown.

80. Oré 47.

81. Quirós-Segura Letter to Juan de Hinistrosa (Part II below), para. 5.

the mouth of the river," entirely compatible with a stop at Newport News. Why then *un río* rather than *este río* ("this river") for the journey to the mountains, especially since they were already on the James and that is the stream most frequently mentioned as leading to the western ocean? [82] First, note that Father Quirós' information was vague; secondly, that the James divides into several branches with various names, and the Fathers would not have been sure if the same river was meant; and lastly, the writer wanted to emphasize that two days of river travel were involved, for which a boat was required. Any one of these reasons would have warranted omission of the definite *este*. The last-named is probably the reason, for the initial part of the journey "from there" was to be by a river, and therefore logically the river on which the Indians were situated, the James, and therefore known to the writer.

Some time must have elapsed from entry of the river to the writing of the letter, to give time for trading difficulties and for a changed attitude on the part of the savages to arise, as we shall see later.

PROBABLE PORT OF DEBARKATION

THE MISSIONARIES arrived at their destination "in the land of Don Luis" on September 10 and began to unload. The date is sometimes given as December 10, because Father Quirós says "only with great difficulty can they find roots by which they usually sustain themselves, and the great snows found in this land do not allow them to hunt for them." [83] The solution is simply that Father Quirós was not speaking of the conditions as he found them but of the anticipated winter snows, and such snows, though not of long duration, were not infrequent even in the Virginia colony.

Where was this port of debarkation? [84] Oré says "Having arrived at the

82. Opechancanough, brother to Powhatan, during Smith's imprisonment by him on the Pamunkey, spoke of a "great turning of salt water" within four or five days of the falls of the James. This gives the impression that it was specifically the James they most frequently thought of as heading near the western sea (1 Arber 16 ff.).

83. Quirós-Segura Letter (Part II below),

para. 3. Proof of the September date for arrival is logical when the August departure from Santa Elena is clearly in the sources. Moreover, the "parched soil" is incompatible with December snows and Father Quirós hoped to receive aid in the winter, if at all possible.

84. It is well to note that from now on the discussion of locations will be on progressively insecure ground. We shall present an hypo-

Bahía de Madre de Dios at Jacán, they ascended the river for a distance of twelve leagues. On the banks of this river, the *cacique* Don Luis had his towns. Two brother *caciques* of Don Luis together with other Indians received them and gave them lodgings amid demonstrations of great joy." [85]

Another directive on the location of the point where they left ship is given by Father Rogel in his letter of 1572: "Anchoring the fleet in a port of this bay, the Governor sent an armed *fragatilla* with 30 soldiers to a fresh-water stream where Ours disembarked when they came here. This place is 20 leagues from this port." [86]

Unfortunately, we do not know whether Rogel and Oré were presenting their own estimates or those of others, in the distances for either Virginia or Florida. In the one comparison we can make of their Florida estimates, the 50-mile distance between Gaule and Santa Elena, Rogel gives 22 leagues, Oré, 14. If we apply their respective league values of 2.27 and 3.57 miles to Virginia, Father Rogel would have the Jesuits going up the river 45.4 miles, Oré, 42.8 miles. Every account of the mission stresses or even overstresses its inland location.[87]

Father Rogel informs us that the small frigate, a boat with a shallow draft, proceeded up a narrow stream 3 leagues by oar. This stream was wide at the mouth. The mention of a fresh-water stream led Kenny to choose Aquia Creek, a branch of the Potomac, as the stream. We know from Oré's relation that Aquia Creek is completely out of the picture. Furthermore, the Spanish term *agua dulce* is a very relative phrase which was applied to any potable water. It is not necessary to go out of the tidewater area to verify these conditions, and indeed with the distances given us we cannot get near the fall line, no matter what hypothesis we adopt within the scope of Oré's report.[88]

thesis which has, we believe, a better than even chance of being correct, while realizing that the discovery of lost letters such as that written to Philip II by Segura might present contrary evidence.

85. Oré 21.

86. Rogel August, 1572, Letter (Part II below), para. 2.

87. Carrera says that they went "inland," "many leagues from the sea," Ribadeneyra, "far from the sea." For a discussion of the value of a league, see Appendix D.

88. Juan Menéndez Marqués and Vicente Gonzales described the head of the Chesapeake as composed of *agua dulce* brought down from the streams that flow into it there. A communication from D. W. Pritchard, Director of the Chesapeake Bay Institute, enables us to interpret the Spanish remarks on fresh water. Their estimate would stem from potability. Dr. Pritchard believes that "fresh water" would contain less than 1.0 parts per thousand salt content, since more than that is scarcely potable. The Institute found that the water ten miles south of the Susquehanna's mouth is potable, the salt ranging from 0.05 to 0.06 parts per thousand. At Deep Water Shoals on the James, just below College Creek, the

From the documents we have seen so far we may set up the following requirements for the port of debarkation: (1) On a narrow fresh-water stream wide at the mouth; (2) some forty miles from Point Comfort (Menéndez' port); (3) on a stream whose navigable portions came within 2 leagues (4 to 6 miles by land) of another stream in which they could launch an Indian canoe; (4) the entrance of this last stream evidently being far from the port of debarkation, else the pilot would have pulled up anchor and taken them directly to it.

It is relatively easy to eliminate most of the tributaries of the James from consideration as the small stream entered. The Elizabeth River is not navigable 40 miles from Menéndez' port. The Nansemond in its navigable portions is not near any other stream. Deep Creek and Warwick Creek are not far enough from Point Comfort, though a case might be made out for Warwick, wide at the mouth, its head being within 2 leagues of the York, but probably not navigable that far up. Though near the path that led to Chiskiac, Skiffe's Creek, as today, probably had a shallow entrance and is a bit too near Point Comfort. Powhatan Creek, then flowing into the Thorofare, in its navigable portions did not come within 2 leagues of another navigable stream. The Chickahominy is too far away, too wide, and too heavily populated. College Creek is nearly 40 miles by river from Point Comfort, and Jamestown itself, only 5 miles farther on, was described in two early independent Spanish reports as 20 leagues from Point Comfort. It is wide at the mouth, has fresh water, and in colonial times, when it was known as Archer's Hope Creek, was navigable for 5 miles, to a port only 1 mile from Williamsburg. From that port to Queens Creek it is only about 4 miles, and to Kings Creek, another York tributary, only slightly farther. To enter either Kings Creek or Queens Creek after leaving the port on the James would have required a water voyage of a hundred miles. Thus every one of the requirements that we have set up is met by College Creek.

Since we are dealing with Indian tribes and villages, not only geographical but ethnological harmony must be satisfied by the locations selected. The possibility of such a harmony is based on the stability of Algonkin settlements in Virginia, some of which have persisted to this day near their original sites. The archaeology of Virginia, still in its infant stages,

water has a mean salinity of 5 parts per thousand but varies down to 1 part. This confirms an observation made by Beverley in 1705. Therefore for the water in the tributaries to be fresh they would necessarily have to be fed by surface runoff and by springs, and there are several such tributaries entering the James.

has already demonstrated that the larger linguistic and cultural groups maintained rigid boundary lines over a period of many years, and knowing as we do from Smith and Strachey the Indian sense of property lines for hunting, fishing, and agriculture, we have no right to suppose major changes in alignment of tribes in the thirty-five years that elapsed from their punishment by Menéndez to the coming of the Virginia settlers. The tribal locations of 1607 are well known to us from the famous map [89] of John Smith and the extensive literature that has come down to us from colonial times, most of which is to be found in Arber-Bradley's two-volume collection of early colonial writings, in Strachey's history, and in *Force's Tracts*. The ethnological harmony of the sites we suggest will become apparent as the narrative advances.[90]

The Site of the Mission

WE SHALL resume the narrative in the words of Father Quirós at the point where their ship came to the end of its journey. "We find the land of Don Luis," he says, "in quite another condition than expected, not because he was at fault in his description of it, but because Our Lord has chastised it with six years of famine and death, which has brought it about that there is much less population than usual.[91] Since many have died and many also

89. For reproductions of Smith's map, first published in 1612, see J. T. Scharf, *History of Maryland* (1879), vol. 1; Arber, vol. 2; and Mathews, *Maps and Map-Makers of Maryland*. Of the map Mathews says: "If all knowledge of the region were lost it is doubtful if many, even of the most highly trained topographers with Smith's instruments and methods, could spend less than a month in exploring Chesapeake Bay and produce a sketch of the country as free from distortion and exaggeration as the map drawn by Smith in 1608" (360). Speck has given it equal praise. Bushnell found it reliable in locating Indian tribal sites on the upper James and Rappahannock, but it has proved less useful in some other sections of Virginia. See also Appendix A.

90. The Algonquian stability upon which many of our suppositions is based was confirmed in conversations with Dr. T. D. Stewart and Dr. Clifford Evans of the United States National Museum. Dr. Stewart has ex-

cavated ossuaries on the York River and Potomac Creek, and Dr. Evans is accumulating data on the ceramics of the various Indian tribes of Virginia.

91. Quirós-Segura Letter (Part II below), para. 2. Famines were not unknown among the Indians of the Jamestown colony, and of course the effects on the whites are too well known to bear repetition. Pedro Menéndez Marqués in a letter to the King of Spain in 1588 says there was so severe a drought in Florida that year that no corn at all had been planted (*Hist. Mag.* 1859, 175 f.). In the Maryland Jesuit mission in 1640 famine due to drought was so bad among the Indians that the whites had to relieve them from their stores (letter of a missonary in Father White's *Relatio Itineris in Marylandiam* 75). The severity of the 1570 drought, or the degree of exaggeration, may be judged by Smith's remark that in September "men could not want victuall." By August in good times the

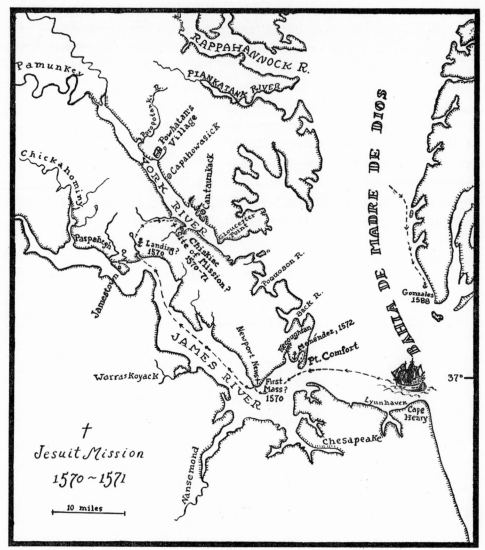

Plate V

JESUIT MISSION, 1570-1571

We have placed the cross indicating the mission on the north bank of Kings Creek, though it could have been at any place in the Chiskiac area or in the settlements across the river below Powhatan's village of Werowocomoco. Menéndez' anchorage could have been on Point Comfort itself. On the eastern shore we have indicated approximately the point where Gonzales crossed from the west on his return from the head of the bay in 1588. At the point where he anchored and picked up an Indian youth, he was within sight of Menéndez' anchorage, which is to say, in sight of the mouth of the James, which would appear as a break in the shore line from that distance.

have moved to other regions to ease their hunger, there remain but few of the tribe, whose leaders say that they wish to die where their fathers [92] have died, although they have no grain, and have not found wild fruit, which they are accustomed to eat."

It is difficult to turn one's back on an enterprise for which one has carefully prepared, and Father Segura elected to stay. Because of the delay in reaching Ajacán, the Jesuits were forced to give much of their supplies to the crew. Father Segura was very anxious to send the ship away as quickly as possible, so that its food supply might hold out long enough for the return voyage.

All that we know definitely about the final encampment is contained in the following passage: "As to information about the land that touches the route along which the pilot must be directed, he himself will give it. It is not convenient to enter by the river we did, but we did not have as good information from the Indians as was necessary about the place we should have entered. And so, today, the pilot has gone overland 2 good leagues away to see a river, which he will enter when with good fortune he comes again to help us. Through this region he can go by water up to the place where we plan to make our encampment. To reach this spot, it is 2 good leagues by land and 2 others or more by water, so that the goods, which we have unloaded in this uninhabited place reached by this river where we are now, must be carried by the Indians on their shoulders for these 2 leagues and then embarked in canoes." [93]

Fathers Segura and Quirós wrote two letters, one, already quoted, to Hinistrosa in Cuba asking for immediate supplies of food and grain seeds which the Indians could plant, and another to the King, also requesting provisions. It is evident that the Jesuits were planning to increase the agricultural activities of the Indians, as they had done in Florida, both to reduce their suffering and to make them more sedentary. There is another indication that their location on the river examined by the pilot was not far from the second landing place, for as Father Quirós states: "...it is imperative that some provisions arrive some time during March

---

Indians had returned to their village sites. Somewhat parallel to the 1570 drought was the seven-year period in Virginia from 1925 to 1931, six of these years having below-average precipitation with 1930 almost half normal. Bruce, however, in 1: 176 f. maintains that riverside corn plantings were not greatly affected by drought.

92. The mention of "ancestors" suggests that this was already a well-established tribal site and leads one to suppose that this same attachment to place persisted up to the time Smith made his map.

93. Quirós-Segura Letter (Part II below), para. 4.

or at the beginning of April so that we can give seeds to the tribe for planting. At this time the planting is done here and thus many of the tribes will come here after being scattered over the region in search of food and there will be a good opportunity for the Holy Gospel. The chief has sought this very thing especially." [94]

From the excerpts quoted above it is evident that the Jesuits must either have seen the spot in which they were going to settle or had met and talked with Indians from that spot, which could not have been a great distance away. There is evidence of a general exodus from the peninsula to the headwaters of the rivers. The region where the ship anchored is described as *desierto*, which carries more the meaning of uninhabited than deserted. The English colonists do not speak of encountering any tribes here. Father Quirós seems to be giving this as one of the reasons for their removal to another stream. The 2 good land leagues walked by the pilot would take him 6 or 7 miles across to the York, up which on a relief trip he could sail to the Indian settlement of Chiskiac, probably then composed of scattered settlements reaching from the "Indian Fields" below Felgate's Creek to Queens Creek. To reach one of these hamlets, the Jesuits would have had to carry their goods 2 leagues to Queens Creek, and then would have paddled 2 leagues or more to their destination near the York. Nothing in the narrative would exclude their having crossed the York and having settled in one of the hamlets ruled in 1607 by Powhatan, but it is not at all probable that they did so.

In a footnote to his letter, Father Quirós penned some instructions on how the relief expedition should find their dwelling: ". . . from the time it is understood that the frigate is to come with the help requested, one or two Indians will be sent with a letter to the mouth of the arm of the sea, along which any ship coming must sail. Thus, when they see the ship, they will make a large smoke signal by day and a fire at night. Furthermore the people there will have a sealed letter of yours and they will not return it until they receive another like it, which is to be a sign that those who come are friendly and are the ones who bring the message

---

94. Hariot gives the middle of March to June for planting by the North Carolina tribes. Smith says, "In Aprill they begin to plant, but their chiefe plantation is in May, and so they continue till the midst of June" (1 Arber 62). Among the things they planted, according to Smith, were corn, pumpkins, beans, peas, wheat, squash, and a wild fruit called "maracocks," like a lemon. The peas referred to are probably a smaller variety of beans (Hariot). Some of the corn raised during the time of the English colony grew higher than a man's head and was the chief reliance in time of famine.

... our letter will carry information about the way which must be followed in entering and serve as a guide." [95]

The system of signal fires was doubtless suggested by Don Luis, since it was an Algonquian practice along that coast. From the words "must sail," we may assume that the Indians were to take up their station at Cape Henry, or perhaps Point Comfort. The use of the Indians suggests that the settlement was far enough from the cape to make it difficult or dangerous for Jesuits to meet the ship. We may also infer that the relief ship was not to enter the James in order to reach the Jesuits' final settlement.

A hint of the strict control Father Segura wished to exercise over the mission environment is contained in the paragraph he adds to the Quirós letter, calling attention to the fact that one of the crew had been engaged in trade with the natives without his permission. Clearly, he wanted to teach the Indians their duty of supporting the missionaries and also keep the natives from contamination from white traders and their wares.

With Father Rogel's Relation we resume the story: "Thus was brought about what came to be the cause of their death; for if they had remained a few days with the ship, they would have acquired an early experience of the bad dispositions there and the promise of little fruit, and might have returned to Santa Elena to wait for a better opportunity. Seeing themselves abandoned and without other resources, they built a small cottage where they might have shelter and say Mass. . . ." [96]

Martínez says the Jesuits took along boards, nails, and a carpenter to build their house. Unless the carpenter was one of their company, he would have had no opportunity to erect a house for them. We need not suppose the structure differed a great deal from the Florida model described by Segura in a letter from Havana. [97] The walls of that model were of rough wood, the roof thatched, capable of erection in fifteen days. Brother Carrera imagined that there was a kitchen, that the floor of the hut was the cold earth, and the roof of palm leaves, but he was wrong about the latter, unless they had brought palm leaves with them for the purpose or used marsh grass. Oré writes that they lodged "in a house . . . made of palms. This had a small apartment to one side where the Fathers were to say Mass until they could build a more commodious church." [98]

95. Quirós-Segura Letter (Part II below), para. 7.

96. Rogel Relation (Part II below), para. 8.

97. Segura to Borgia, November 18, 1568, MAF 358-370; 25 HRS 99.

98. Oré 21. See also the Carrera Relation (Part II below), note 12.

From the first, Don Luis provides an interesting study in psychology. He helped energetically in getting the Fathers adjusted and persuaded Father Segura to send one of the company from the ship 6 or 8 leagues into the interior to baptize his three-year-old brother, who was dying. If Sacchini is correct, the head chief, Don Luis' brother, had died, and a younger brother was ruling in his stead. The latter offered the headship to Don Luis upon his return, but Don Luis assured him that he had come back on spiritual business and not for temporal gain.[99] Don Luis seems to have been a member of a large ruling family. From the more trustworthy accounts we may conclude that he had a brother and an uncle near the site of debarkation, and therefore in the Paspahegh territory that reached from there to a point beyond the Chickahominy. This uncle was a big *cacique* and the chief target for the avenging Menéndez. Another "brother" lived in the village where the Fathers and Brothers erected their hut, and he it was who prevented the death of Alonso. One can hardly escape noticing the similarity with Powhatan and his three brothers, whose orbit of operations embraced the upper York River, the Pamunkey and Mattaponi, and extended across the upper part of the Chickahominy to the James.[100] One of the prerogatives of the "werowances," or chiefs, was polygamy, and the reports are unanimous in ascribing marital aberrations as the cause of Don Luis' downfall, "for he took unto himself many wives after the manner of the Gentiles." He lived with the Fathers but two nights and not over five nights in the village. Then with various excuses, such as gathering students for the mission and chestnuts for food, he went to live in the territory of his uncle a day and a half journey away. From subsequent events, it is clear that Don Luis returned to the general vicinity of the port of debarkation, but perhaps as far north as the Chickahominy.[101]

The nine missionaries soon must have consumed their remaining two

99. Sacchini, Book VI, No. 270, translation in Part II below. If, as other accounts state, Don Luis had an uncle who was an important chief, the uncle and not the brother would have been the more important.

100. Shea in "Log Chapel on the Rappahannock," *Catholic World* (March, 1875) 856, speculates on the possibility of Powhatan's having participated in the martyrdom of the Jesuits. Speck thinks the foundation of Powhatan's empire was laid as early as 1570. It would be interesting to know if Don Luis played a part in the beginning of this empire.

101. Archaeological investigations reveal heavy Indian settlements between Jamestown and the Chickahominy, but not on the James above the mouth of the Chickahominy, contrary to Smith's map. However, Paspahegh activities in Smith's accounts take place below rather than above the Chickahominy. The Indians themselves referred to Jamestown as Paspahegh. The Paspahegh probably controlled the whole peninsula along the path that led to Werowocomoco.

barrels of flour, and then were driven to seek for roots and berries in the forest. Twice Father Segura sent a message to Don Luis by a novice brother. We are told by the various writers that he censured Don Luis for his way of life and explained their helplessness in converting the natives without him as interpreter. But like Wanchese of the Raleigh colony and Chicora, Ayllón's Indian, whose promise paralleled Don Luis' in many respects, he had abandoned Christian associations for the ways of his tribe.

Until February of 1571 the Jesuits continued this haphazard existence, united to God in their prayers. Antonio Astraín, who does not give the source of his information, says, ". . . there remained only the slender hope of the ship, which was due to come back with provisions at the end of four months. This period terminated January 11, 1571. . . ." [102] From the accounts of Carrera and Rogel we learn that they bartered as well as they knew how, exchanging copper, brass, tin, and possibly some axes for corn in the neighboring villages. Finally Father Segura, confined by illness, sent Father Quirós and Brothers Solís and Méndez on a last mission to Don Luis. They were asked to take along mats (a common article, constructed of reeds, with many uses among the Algonkin) as a protection against the cold and to barter for corn among the villages that lay on the path by which they would return. Don Luis seems to have greeted them cordially on this occasion, promising that he would set out after them and return to the missionaries. He did follow them, and on the Sunday after the Purification, February 4, with several other Indians, he killed Father Quirós and Brother Solís with a shower of arrows.[103] Brother Carrera adds that "Brother Baptista Méndez fled to the woods with blood running from his deep wounds. There he hid himself that night and in the morning [of February 5] he was discovered and killed. After that the murderers burned the bodies and stole their clothing and bundles." [104]

102. 19 *ACHS, art. cit.,* 7; Antonio Astraín, *Historia* 296 f.

103. Carrera (Part II below), para. 45, apparently means that all the murders took place on Candlemas Day, February 2. Oré (23) puts all the deaths on the eve of Purification, February 1, the feast of St. Ignatius of Antioch. Rogel's August Letter (Part II below), para. 6, the best source, states that the Quirós murder took place on "the Sunday after the Purification," and that the others were killed five or six days later. The 2nd of February was on a Friday, so that the first deaths occurred on February 4, as Tanner has it in *Societas Iesu . . . Militans* 449. The Segura group therefore were killed on February 9 or 10. John Tate Lanning, in his fine book, *The Spanish Missions of Georgia* (Chapel Hill, 1935) 54, following an error of Barcia, states that Quirós was killed on February 14.

104. Carrera (Part II below), para. 44. Both the Raleigh colony and the Virginia colony were plagued by Algonkin thieves, but Smith says they waged their wars not so much for spoil as revenge (1 Arber 71).

The party of Indians led by Don Luis next approached the cabin of the Jesuits. Rogel, Carrera, and Oré and all the others are overly descriptive here, agreeing only in the essentials. The Indians arrived early in the morning of February 9, asked for all the axes in order to cut wood for the Jesuits (Carrera says for firewood, Oré, to build a chapel).[105] Brother Zaballos went with them. Then the Indians set upon the helpless Jesuits, killing them with the axes and their native weapons.

An important difficulty arises in connection with the part now played by Alonso. In his letter, Father Rogel states, "This boy says that when he saw them killing the Fathers and Brothers, he sought to go among the Indians as they inflicted the wounds so that they might kill him too. For it seemed better to him to die with Christians than live alone with Indians. A brother of Don Luis took him by the arm and did not let him go."[106] In his Relation Rogel says, "A brother of Don Luis stopped him by hiding him in a house and locking him up. He was doing a kindness, when others were murdering the Fathers."[107] According to Carrera, Alonso accompanied Zavallos to the woods. The Indians split the head of the old brother, but "They did not touch the boy who had gone with him, saying that they did not want to kill him, but only the Fathers. When he saw them dead and so badly wounded, he asked them in deep sorrow of soul to kill him too. He preferred to die with them rather than live without them among infidels and barbarians."[108] Oré, who thinks the murder was perpetrated during Mass, reports that "Alonso de Lara [*sic*] was in the house of a *cacique*, a brother of Don Luis, who was also a conspirator with his brother for the death of the religious. He had pity on Alonso for he did not kill him after the others, but took him to his house and gave him some breakfast." When Alonso heard the noise from the massacre, he ran to the scene, but the *cacique* caught him by the arm and detained him.[109] Various reasons are advanced for their having spared Alonso—the fact that he was not a Religious, his youth, etc. Inasmuch as the social instincts of the Indians often led them to adopt the children of their enemies, it is quite probable that he was saved by his youth.

Because of the importance of Alonso as a witness, we cannot afford to overlook a point reiterated by the sometimes unreliable Martínez, who

105. In the provisions supplied from the royal treasury for the company sailing from Spain with Father Segura had been "six woodchopper iron axes at four reals each; four iron adzes at seven and one-half reals each." Kenny 218, quoting from AGI 2-3-31/32.

106. Rogel, August, 1572, Letter (Part II below), para. 6.

107. Rogel Relation (Part II below), para. 8.

108. Carrera Relation (Part II below), para. 45.

109. Oré 23.

had many opportunities to talk to Alonso in later years. Alonso, "according to his own story did not witness the actual martyrdom," is the testimony of Martínez. In his version, Alonso, because he was a friend of Don Luis, was sent to bring him back. He lost his way and came to the village of the friendly chief who protected him. He learned all the details of the massacre from the Indians. It is probable that Martínez is confusing two events. It may be that Alonso was sent on one of the earlier missions to Don Luis, for as a resident of Santa Elena and most probably a catechist like his younger brother, he would have been the most experienced woodsman of them all, even though the youngest. At any rate, it seems certain that Alonso was at least in the vicinity when the massacre took place.

When a crime has been committed, it is logical to look for motives. There is hardly any room for doubt as to Don Luis' being the chief perpetrator. How, we may ask ourselves, could a man who had received gentle and generous treatment from these Spanish priests and Brothers resolve to take their lives in such bloody fashion? Brother Carrera seemed to think at least a contributing cause was to be found in the precious vessels they possessed, for Father Quirós' request for supplies at Santa Elena had caused him to remonstrate: "When I saw the list I was a little upset, and I said to him, 'Father, I would gladly give you everything you ask of me, even though I know that it is all going to be lost, were it not for the fact that I know for certain that all this will contribute greatly to the death of everyone going there.'" This motive may have induced Luis' companions to follow him, and it would have been a strong motive in a tribe where wealth meant greater power and possession of more women. But it hardly explains Luis' own actions, which seem to have been immediately occasioned by the third visit and the importunity of the Jesuits, calling upon him to abandon his sins and to return to the practice of his religion. In the light of A. I. Hallowell's studies of historic Indian psychology (if they can be applied to the Virginia Algonkin), we may expect Don Luis to manifest extreme sensitivity to overtones of anger or public criticism, in his case a sensitivity perhaps heightened by a disturbed conscience if his conversion had been genuine. The parallel between this massacre in Virginia and that of the Franciscans in Guale in 1597, is remarkable enough to note here.[110] "One of the Fathers would not permit an Indian youth, who was a Christian and heir to the caciquedom,

110. For a description of the Guale massacre and background for the motives, see Oré 73 f., 77, 91 f., 101.

to have more than one wife to whom he was married." With other chiefs who rankled under similar prohibitions he planned the massacre of the Fathers. The instrument of the killing was the macana. Like Don Luis and his companions, they afterwards dressed themselves in the habits of the Religious. Also like Don Luis, some of the criminals experienced great remorse, though this element may well be legendary. In a trial held at San Agustín some of the Indians testified that the friars had enjoined monogamy upon them, and this was the cause universally ascribed by the Religious. The Indians themselves maintained the cause was interference with their elections, but as Swanton, who favors the Indian account, admits, the Christian Indian who was backed by the friars was one of the chief conspirators.[111]

Like the Christian Indians in Guale, the weeping Don Luis saw to the burial of the last five slain. Whether he or Alonso took the initiative cannot be determined from contradictory reports. Rogel, Martínez, and Oré agree that the bodies were buried—Carrera says in a long trench, and Rogel says beneath the chapel. Martínez again casts his shadow of doubt, for Alonso told him that "God willed they should be buried by His Holy Angels." But Father Rogel's letter, by far the most reliable document of all, reflects his certainty of their burial by the Indians.

The Indians immediately plundered the Jesuits' goods, attiring themselves in the cassocks, chasubles, even the linen altar cloths, and hanging the patens about their necks. In connection with this looting, Alonso related a story to the Spaniards which the reader, according to his inclination, may attribute to divine intervention, coincidence, or a fertile imagination. When three of the Indians attempted to break open a locked chest in which was a crucifix and some other sacred objects, they fell down dead. Oré says that Don Luis and Alonso then lifted the chest for reverent safe-keeping into a *garita*, or Indian granary.[112] In his Relation, Rogel states that an old soldier who had been in Ajacán said that the Indians still venerated the chest forty years later.[113] Whatever the basis in fact for the story, it has found its way into all the accounts and early histories of the massacre.

To resume with Father Rogel: "The boy stayed in the same hut for 15 days. Because of the famine in the land, Don Luis told him that

111. Swanton, *Early History of the Creek Indians* 84-88.

112. Oré 24. The occasional embellishments introduced into the narratives by pious imaginations do not interfere with the validity of other soberly related parts of the accounts.

113. See the Relation, para. 10, translated in Part II below.

they should go and seek grain. Alonso came in this way with him to the chief where he remained. This chief told the boy to stay and he would treat him well and hold him as a son. This he did. Finally Don Luis distributed the clothes of the Fathers among himself and his two brothers who shared in the murders. The boy took nothing but the relics and beads of Father Baptista [Segura], which he kept until now and handed over to us. After this Don Luis went away very anxious to get hold of the boy to kill him, so that there would be no one to give details of what happened to Ours, but because of his fear of the chief with whom the boy was staying, he gave up the idea." [114]

THE FIRST RELIEF EXPEDITION

IRONICALLY enough, only a week or two after the death of the missionaries, on receipt of Segura's petition, King Philip signed an order addressed to the Governor of the island of Cuba directing him to provide for the necessities of the Jesuits and their companions. "As I have before me the spiritual advancement of the said Indians and that so good and holy a work should go ahead, it is my will that the said Religious and persons with them be provided with food. . . ." [115] Thus were the wheels of the cumbersome system of colonial administration slowly grinding along, while the Jesuits were being starved.

The last letters of Quirós and Segura had reached Havana in the winter of 1570, and the Fathers there became anxious to send help at once. From the report of a soldier who had been serving Segura they perceived the grave danger and quickly provisioned a ship, probably late in the spring of 1571, and sent it to Ajacán under the direction of Vicente Gonzales and Brother Juan Salcedo, who had come over with Father Segura as a catechist and was now admitted to the Society. Rogel, Carrera, and

114. Rogel, August, 1572, Letter (Part II below), para. 7; Oré (28 ff.) has an amusing and probably apocryphal sidelight: "The *cacique* had disguised him during the night to make him look like Don Luis' niece for he knew Alonso's 'uncle' would not kill him." There is a strong hint here that we are dealing with another "brother" of Don Luis in the person of the chief of the tribe near the port. Relationship between Kecoughtan and the tribes inland can by no means be excluded. When Gates settled at Kecoughtan, Pochins, one of Powhatan's sons, was werowance. The chief who protected Alonso may well have been the powerful werowance who died shortly after 1600, whose death was the signal for Powhatan's subjection of these people, according to Strachey (61).

115. Philip II to Menéndez de Avilés, February 19, 1571, *MAF* 642.

Oré agree that Gonzales did not find the signs he was looking for on his arrival and was immediately suspicious. The Indians, clothed in the Jesuits' cassocks, walked up and down the shore and made signs to Gonzales to land. This seems to have been a ruse on the part of Don Luis to get the crew to land so that they might be overpowered. As the pilot began to draw nearer to shore, several boats of Indians attacked. Carrera says that the artillery was of less effect against the Indians than "a great pile of rocks which they were carrying for ballast," which made the Indians retire with damage and the loss of two chief Indians, who were captured.[116] When the Spaniards were returning through the strait of Bahama one of the Indians leaped overboard and was not seen thereafter; the other was taken to Havana in chains and kept in the Jesuit house.[117] He gave very little information, except to indicate that the boy Alonso alone was still alive, with the implication that Don Luis' uncle and some other *caciques* were somehow responsible for the deaths of the Jesuits.

When they heard Gonzales' pessimistic account, Father Rogel, still trying to fulfill Segura's request made when he left Santa Elena, took upon himself the responsibility of allowing Brother Carrera to equip another relief ship, which sailed from Havana in company with two other boats and reached Santa Elena in September of 1571, shortly after the arrival there of Governor Menéndez with two Jesuits, Padre Sedeño and Brother Villareal. The Governor forbade the supply ship to go any farther because of the difficult sailing conditions, giving as an additional excuse the necessity of finding the missing captives. Since the garrison at Santa Elena was always short of food, he requisitioned the supplies for the starving Spaniards. Father Sedeño sent Rogel's ship back to Havana with a letter saying that the relief trip could not be made until the spring of 1572.

The Basque spirit of Rogel could not endure this wait. In Havana he made a deposition against Menéndez before a public notary and before the Governor of Havana, Menéndez' nephew, and then proceeded to

116. Carrera Relation (Part II below), para. 50. The Brother says the Indians had never seen large rocks. Of course they had, but the remark does suggest the type of shore line which the Brother observed, recalling Verrazano's statement that in 200 leagues along the Atlantic shore he did not see any large rocks.

117. From a letter of Father Sedeño to Borgia, from Santa Elena, February 8, 1572, *MAF* 507, it is clear that more than two Indians were brought back from Ajacán or else both the Indian who leaped overboard and the one taken to Havana had somehow gotten onto the Florida mainland. One of the reasons advanced by Menéndez for delaying a second relief expedition was "because two Indians were missing whom the pilot had brought from there. These had fled to other Indians who dwell near San Agustín. The Governor proposed to recapture them and take them with him on the journey." At least one of the Indians accompanied Father Rogel on the second relief expedition.

pester the officials into sending the ship northward with another load
of supplies. When this second load of precious provisions sailed into
Santa Elena in the winter of 1571, it was Padre Sedeño's turn to be provoked. In a long letter to the Jesuit Father General in Rome, the good
Padre gave a bitter description of the well-meaning efforts of Juan Rogel:

"He caused the officials much annoyance," wrote Sedeño, "by his requests that the ship be provisioned, not considering, if he considered anything at all, that they could not approach the coast in December. . . . He
did not realize that all he did was futile and without rhyme nor reason,
that he did but exasperate the Governor and the officials and alienate them
when we needed favor." [118]

Needless to say, while the Governor was angry over Rogel's independence, he was very glad to receive another load of supplies for the
undernourished Spanish garrison.[119]

PUNITIVE EXPEDITION OF 1572

IN THE spring of 1572, Padre Rogel again began his efforts to send supplies to Ajacán and learn the fate of Segura and his companions. In a letter
of March 10, 1572, Rogel wrote to Borgia that as yet there were no definite plans.[120] However, on June 27, he wrote jubilantly that Menéndez
had arrived in Havana and had agreed to search for the missing Fathers.[121]
The next letter, written from the Chesapeake in August, gives complete
details on the death of the Jesuits and on the punishments inflicted on
the natives there. To this on-the-spot report we shall add bits judiciously
from Brother Carrera and Fray Gerónimo de Oré to fill out the picture.

It was no great inconvenience for Menéndez to stop at the Chesapeake
in the summer of 1572. All expenses for the relief of the Jesuits and the
support of thirty soldiers and sailors had been paid from the royal treasury. The King had ordered him home to prepare an armada at Santander,

118. *MAF* 509.

119. On his return to Havana with the Governor and Father Sedeño, Brother Carrera
experienced the discomforts of a shipwreck in
freezing weather off Cape Cañaveral. See his
Relation (Part II below), paras. 52-56, and the
letter of Father Sedeño to Polanco, from Santa

Elena, February 8, 1572 (*MAF* 493-506; 25
HRS 116-126), which tell of an escape more
stirring than fiction.

120. *MAF* 512-515, and Rogel, June, 1572,
Letter, Part II below, note 5.

121. Rogel to Borgia, from Havana, June 27,
1572. Translated in Part II below.

and the Chesapeake was very little out of the way. When he reached San Agustín, where he was having two new frigates built, he decided to accompany the Jesuits, Father Rogel, Brother Carrera, and Brother Villareal. They left San Agustín on July 30, where the Jesuits collected the last of their belongings, stopped at Santa Elena for five days, then proceeded north to the Bahía de Madre de Dios. We do not know exactly how long the voyage from Santa Elena required, but from the events at the port we can conclude it was made in from fifteen to twenty days, not unusual in favorable winds and taking advantage of the Gulf Stream current. Father Rogel admirably summarizes the events that took place in the Chesapeake:

"Reaching this bay, the Governor immediately ordered that we were to search for Alonso. . . . Anchoring the fleet in a port of this bay, the Governor sent an armed *fragatilla* with thirty soldiers to a fresh-water stream where Ours disembarked when they came here. This place is 20 leagues from this port. It seemed best to me to take the bound native in my company to be our interpreter. The order of the Governor was to take the uncle of Don Luis, a principal chief of that region, as well as some leading Indians. On taking them, we were to ask them to give us the boy and we would let them go. Everything happened in excellent fashion, for within an hour after our arrival he took the chief with five of his leaders and eight other Indians.

"This was the method of capture. After we had anchored in the middle of the narrow stream, Indians soon appeared on the bank and some entered the boat. To these the Spaniards gave gifts and made some exchanges. When they left the boat very contentedly, others arrived. With a third group came the chief and his leaders; one of them wore as a decoration or trinket a silver paten, that Ours had brought. At once the Spaniards seized them and forced them down into the boat and dressing the ship, passed to the mouth of the stream 3 leagues away by oar. On the way, the soldiers killed some Indians who were trying to shoot arrows at us and had wounded a soldier.

"At the mouth of the river, which was very wide, we anchored again an arquebus shot away from the shore. Canoes of Indians came in peace, and they said that the boy was in the hands of a leading chief who lived two days' journey from there, near this port [Menéndez' port, from which Father Rogel was writing]. They asked that we give them time to send for him and bring him. This we did, and we gave them trinkets to give to the chief who held the boy and we stayed there waiting for him. It seems that as soon as the chief learned of the capture of the others and about the fleet and the imminent death of the Indians, he sought to curry favor with the Governor. For he did not want to let the boy be brought to our ship but he sent him to this port with two Indians. It is a marvelous thing in how short a time the Governor learned what was happening there from the mouth of the boy.

"When the Indians did not bring the boy, we fought off an ambush of many canoes loaded with archers ready to attack the vessel. First there came two large canoes filled with Indians who were so concealed that no one was seen except the two who steered and they pretended they brought us oysters. Before they got aboard, the watchman discovered them. We made ready and the others retreated. At my request, the steersmen were not fired upon, for we were still not certain whether it was an ambush or whether they came in peace. When the time was up and the boy did not come, we waited for a night and further into midday and finally set sail with our captives. By way of farewell, the pilot steered the ship towards land with the excuse that he wanted to speak to them and then he ordered a blast from the arquebuses into the group of Indians who were standing crowded together on the shore. I believe many of them were killed, and this was done without any knowledge of mine until it happened. Then we returned to this port." [122]

Oré adds some interesting details, among them that the Spanish soldiers hid in the hold of the ship until the Indians on board were dining on honey and biscuits, delicacies that, as Solís de Meras reports, Avilés more than once offered in his negotiations with Florida Indians; then they seized thirteen and killed twenty. On the rescue of Alonso, Oré has information that completes rather than contradicts Rogel, and he may have had it from the mouth of Alonso's brother, "Juan," who met some Indians at Menéndez's port and inquired for his brother.[123] They told him he was with a *cacique* a day's journey distant.[124] "The *Adelantado* told them to say that Alonso was his son and that they should tell their *cacique* to send him to him. At the same time he sent some gifts." This admirably explains why the chief sent Alonso to Menéndez rather than to Gonzales. Martínez, nearly always at variance, says Alonso escaped at

122. Rogel, August, 1572, Letter (Part II below), paras. 2 to 6.

123. Oré calls the brother "Juan de Lara." Martínez Relation (Part II below), para. 43, says Alonso's mother was Marina de Lara and his two brothers were Francisco and Pedro. Juan may have been one of these brothers. See note 19 to the Martínez Relation.

124. Strachey estimated the Indians' "day's journey" at 14 to 16 miles.

night and swam out to the flagship, naked as an Indian, then knelt at the feet of his father.[125] He had nearly forgotten his Spanish. With him was an Indian boy, a close friend of Alonso, whom Menéndez took back to Europe.

Father Rogel's remark that the blast of the arquebuses was without his permission is in keeping with the character he displayed in Florida while protecting the Indians against unjust demands and injuries of the soldiers, on occasions offering his life in their defense. Now, after a trial that reveals Menéndez as a judge holding court in what he considered his own territory, Rogel with the help of Alonso gave religious instruction and baptism to the eight or nine Indians who were adjudged guilty of complicity in the murder of the Jesuits. Carrera reports that when the chief saw the black-robed Jesuits on the ship he thought the slain men had risen from the dead. The Admiral told the captured *cacique* that unless Don Luis and his two brothers were brought to justice, he would punish those he had captured. A volunteer Indian, perhaps the *cacique*, was given five days to round up the renegade Luis. When the time expired and he failed to return, the condemned Indians were hanged from the ship's rigging. It should be noted here that there was opportunity during the trial and later religious instruction to get confirmation from the Indians of Alonso's story, so that it is hardly true to say that all we know of the deaths of the Jesuits hangs from one thread. That this information must have been quite detailed is evident from the apparent release of at least five Indians as not involved in the murders.

We may give the following interpretation of the preceding events. All three voyages ended at the same stream—College Creek, because Gonzales had not learned how to enter the York, even though the trip to Kings Creek would have been shorter than to College Creek from Point Comfort. Further evidence of this is the fact that the stream entered in 1572 was in the territory of Don Luis' uncle, where the murder of the first three Jesuits took place, and that, we know, was at some distance from the final settlement. The stream entered in 1572 was two days' journey from Alonso's village. If that were in the vicinity of Newport News, it would be about 30 miles by the wandering path from College Creek, or two days' journey. Alonso logically would have chosen to stay near the entrance of the river in the hope of a rescue, and his location here in turn would have caused Don Luis to worry for fear he might be

125. See his Relation (Part II below), para. 45.

taken by the Spanish and tell them the whole story of the mission. New-port, 10 miles away, again would have fitted Oré's datum on the village's being one day's journey from Point Comfort.

At the end of his letter, Father Rogel observes that the population in the Chesapeake was greater than in any other region through which he had traveled, that the people there were more sedentary than the Florida tribes, that the Governor's sternness had impressed them in a salutary way, and that he would be willing to labor there if his superiors saw fit.[126]

The missionaries, in a stormy voyage in which they nearly lost their lives, in September returned to Cuba, where they awaited orders to move on to New Spain. The Governor returned directly to Spain, where he died two years later. The Ajacán experiment was at an end.

SPANISH SEQUELS TO THE MISSION

WHILE Menéndez was in port at Ajacán and finishing the gunwales on his two frigates, he sent his son-in-law, Don Diego de Velasco, with some soldiers to reconnoiter the interior.[127] Because he was in a hurry, he did not look for the bodies of the Jesuits, but Menéndez promised to return for them. Death prevented his carrying out the promise, and there is no indication that any of the future Spanish expeditions to the Chesapeake looked for the spot. In 1573 the Governor's nephew, Pedro Menéndez Marqués, was sent to make a careful exploration of the coast of Florida. He gives a detailed description of the "harbor and bay of Santa María, which is three leagues wide, wherein one enters to the north north-west," placing the bay at 37° 30', thereby conforming to the error which is now so familiar to us.[128] He made a voyage in 1587 to investigate the

---

126. See Appendix B for population esti-mates. Rogel's mission philosophy displays a realism born of experience. The Franciscans succeeded in Florida where the Jesuits had failed, and one of the factors doubtless was better protection from the Spanish garrisons. George Thorpe, the Virginia idealist, was killed by one of his Indian "converts" as a reward for his kindness (2 Arber 574 f.). In the words of Smith, "...those are still but Saluages as they were, onely growne more bold by our owne simplicities, and still will be worse and worse till they be tormented with a continuall pursuit..." (*ibid.* 594). Menéndez, who began with the utmost diplo-macy, became progressively stern and ended by asking permission of the King to enslave the Indians.

127. Oré 29.

128. 2 Connor, Appendix C, "A fragment of a description of the voyage of Pedro Menéndez Marqués along the east coast of Florida, in 1573," 323.

Raleigh settlement and look for a strait to the South Sea but was driven off by stormy weather around Hatteras.

In the following year, Gonzales and Pedro Menéndez Marqués' cousin Juan Menéndez Marqués, treasurer and sergeant-major, renewed the investigation. They were told by Indians along the coast that the English had established themselves in a location which Gonzales identified as on a stream that "passes to the South Sea." [129] When they investigated Roanoke Sound on their return they found evidences of ship repair but no English. While in the Chesapeake they seized two Indian youths, one on the west bank not far from the Potomac, the other on the eastern shore. Both died later, the latter from grief, the other, who became a Christian, from small-pox in Viana, Santo Domingo. He was buried in the convent there. [130] The cousins Menéndez Marqués reported to the King in 1589 and were ordered to erect a fort of three hundred men in the Chesapeake and look for precious metals, but the course of events prevented these plans from fructifying.

Of course the English settlement at Jamestown provoked a great deal of interest in Spanish circles; the Spanish ambassadors Zúñiga and Velasco kept King Philip III as well informed as the English rulers of developments there. [131] In 1609 a scouting expedition under Captain Francisco Fernández de Ecija entered the Bay of Ajacán, July 24. The following day he withdrew because of a ship "in the region of the islands," according to Oré. Others, who had previously sailed with Captain Vicente Gonzales, pointed out there a river that carries much water (río caudaloso), [132] a proof that Gonzales knew the James. We believe that he and Menéndez Marqués certainly would have wished to include its ports in their accounts to the King. Ecija said he believed the "English plan to go up rivers that connect to other rivers that will admit them to the riches of Mexico . . . and overrun the whole coast of New Spain, Tierra Firme, Peru, and China. . . ." [133] That was his view on the strategic importance of the Chesapeake, a prolongation of the preoccupation of

129. Scisco, "Voyage of Vicente Gonzales in 1588," 42 MHM 97 f.

130. Oré 51; 2 Ruidíaz 503.

131. Brown in his Genesis translates about fifty thousand words of the information sent out by the ambassadors. A fine broad view of Spanish-English relations with authoritative bibliographical notes is provided in Irene A. Wright, "Spanish Policy toward Virginia, 1606-1612," 25 AHR 448-479. Her forthcoming book to be published by the Hakluyt Society, Further English Voyages to the Spanish Main, promises to throw further light on Anglo-Spanish relations.

132. See the text of the Ecija Report translated in Part II, below.

133. Wright, art. cit., quoting from the Consulta of the Council for War in the Indies, March 5, 1611.

Menéndez. The English for years were apprehensive that Spain might some day assert her claims, but the Spanish Empire was too widespread and vulnerable to merit the military expenditure needed to dislodge the English, who by that time were firmly planted and meant to stay.

One of the last documents to mention Ajacán is a *declaración* by Alonso Botello y Serrano and Pedro Porter y Casanate dated September 17, 1636. It summarizes the available knowledge of a strait between California and Florida and indicates the diversity of opinions held by explorers:

"Another indicates Xacal, with its strait and the new northern sea assuring the navigation to Spain. Others doubt this, saying that these straits lead up to so high a latitude that the passage is impossible, by reason of cold. Some say this *ensenada* [the Chesapeake?] runs N.W., others N., others N.E., and some say that it ends in three rivers flowing down from lofty sierras [from Juan Menéndez Marqués?]. The finding of the passage will facilitate military and commercial communication with Spain; and in the opinion of different persons it will afford a means of succoring New Mexico, reveal the dwelling-place of white and clothed men, lead to the discovery of *La Gran Quivira*, the towns of the crowned king, island of the giantess, lake of gold, rivers Tizon and Coral. By it the foe may be harassed on both seas and forced to abandon Xacal, and prevented from attacking California and drawing aid from Florida. . . . . the Conde del Valle says a Dutch vessel entered the strait of Anian, and the enemy is advancing from Xacal day by day." [134]

In 1611 a Spanish caravel on the pretext of looking for a lost vessel came to Point Comfort to spy on the fortifications. Three leaders went ashore and were imprisoned. The Spanish retaliated by seizing John Clark, "pilot of Xacán" and later mate of the *Mayflower*, who also may have been the son of Captain John Clarke of the Raleigh Colony. Molina, one of those left behind, in a letter of 1613 gave his location as $37\frac{1}{3}°$ "in which is also the bay which they call Santa Maria . . . and at 4 leagues distance from its mouth is this river [the James] from the south, nine fathoms in depth." [135] Like Clark, he gave his distance from Jamestown as 20 leagues. He estimated Henrico as 40 leagues from Point Comfort, where he was confined. It is impossible to say how much Molina knew of the Spanish mission that he could have relayed to the English, but Strachey may have learned from him the Spanish name for the Chesapeake.

134. 1 Bancroft 107, note 12. "Xacal" is equivalent to "Jacán."

135. *Narratives of Early Virginia* 222 f.

VIRGINIA TRADITIONS OF THE SPANISH OCCUPATION

QUITE NATURALLY it may be asked why the early Virginia colonists heard nothing from the Indians about the Spanish mission and its grim consequences: the death of so many Europeans and Indians. There is a partial explanation in a more famous question: How is it that two of Raleigh's groups in North Carolina, the second involving more than a hundred people, simply disappeared, leaving no more than vague rumors of their massacre and the subsequent survival of a small remnant? More-over, the Virginia colonists made an energetic attempt to find out the true story of the Raleigh colony from the natives, but they hardly suspected that the Spanish had preceded them in Virginia, and so were not alert to clues.

But actually the silence is not complete. We believe there are enough indications available to link Don Luis with the ruling Powhatan clique in circumstances which of their nature involve the presence of the Spanish.

The first and most important clue is the statement of an early settler, Raphe (Ralph) Hamor. The "Chickahominies, a lustie and daring people, who have long lived free from *Powhatans* subjection," asked for a treaty in 1614. Captain Argall, Hamor, and Governor Dale with fifty men in a barge "went up an arm of our river some seven miles from James Town...." [136] Before admitting the Chickahominy Indians as English subjects they demanded, among other conditions: "Thirdly, they should at all times be ready and willing to furnish us with three or four hundred bowmen to aide us *against the Spaniards*, whose name is odious among them, for Powhatan's father was driven by them from the *west-Indies* into these parts, or against any other *Indians* which should, contrary to the established peace offer us any injurie." (The term "West Indies" was applied not only to the Caribbean islands, but to any Spanish-held terri-tory on the mainland.) An even stronger intimation of Spanish influence on the ruling family of Virginia is to be found in the following paragraphs of Beverley's history of Virginia:

"This *Oppechancanough* was a Man of large Stature, noble Presence, and extraordinary Parts. Tho' he had no Advantage of Literature, (that being no where to be found among the *Indians,*) yet he was perfectly

---

136. Raphe Hamor, *A True Discourse of the present estate of Virginia, and the success of* the affaires there till the 18 of June 1614 (Lon-don, 1615; reprinted Albany, 1860) 11-13.

skill'd in the Art of Governing his rude Country-men. He caused all the *Indians* far and near to dread his Name, and had them all entirely in Subjection.

"This King in *Smith's* History is call'd Brother to *Powhatan*, but by the *Indians* he was not so esteem'd. For they say he was a Prince of a Foreign Nation, and came to them a great Way from the South-West: And by their Accounts, we suppose him to have come from the *Spanish Indians*, some-where near *Mexico*, or the Mines of St. *Barbe:* But, be that Matter how it will, from that Time till his Captivity, there never was the least Truce between them and the *English*." [137]

Rounding out the picture of this chief, Beverley earlier tells us: "Powhatan died in April the same Year [1618], leaving his Second Brother *Itopatin* in Possession of his Empire, a Prince far short of the Parts of *Oppechancanough*, who by some was said to be his Elder Brother, and then King of *Chickahomony;* but he having debauch'd them from the Allegiance of *Powhatan*, was disinherited by him. This *Oppechancanough* was a cunning and a brave Prince, who soon grasp'd all the Empire to himself: But at first they jointly renew'd the Peace with the *English*, upon the Accession of *Itopatin* to the Crown." [138]

An additional account of Opechancanough's southern origin, this time bearing the marks of interpretation and elaboration, is quoted by Thomas J. Wertenbaker to the effect that Opechancanough, accompanied it would seem by a whole tribe, "conquered all along from Mexico" to Virginia.[139]

In evaluating these data it is important to know something of the age of Powhatan and his brother. Captain John Smith estimated Powhatan's age as about sixty in 1608, and Strachey gives him nearly eighty years about 1616. Opechancanough was generally believed to be about a hundred when he died in 1644 after having perpetrated the massacres of 1622 and 1644. Beverley thus described him: "now grown so decrepit, that he was not able to walk alone . . . his Eye-lids became so heavy, that he could not see, but as they were lifted up by his Servants." [140]

What Beverley says about Opechancanough's relation to the Chickahominy tribe is generally accurate. When the Chickahominy failed to live

137. Robert Beverley, *The History and Present State of Virginia* 61.

138. *Ibid.* 45.

139. *Virginia under the Stuarts* 80. See p. 89, where Wertenbaker gives as his reference Public Record Office, CO5-1371-6 to 16. A review in 22 *VMHB* 221, takes issue with the credence placed by Wertenbaker in this source, citing the fact that Thomas Rolfe, son of Pocahontas, sought the Governor's permission to visit "his kinsman Opecancanough."

140. Beverley 62.

up to their promise to supply corn, the English engaged Opechancanough, whose headquarters were near by at Pamunkey (West Point), to subject the Chickahominy to English domination. Shortly afterwards a party of English met Opechancanough near Lanexa, and the old Indian made a great show of having conquered the Chickahominy and of having received the title "King of Ozinies," the village at that point. There are many indications that Powhatan and perhaps his ancestors made repeated attempts to bring the Chickahominy under subjection, but they never seem to have succeeded beyond the point of exacting certain tribute. Powhatan was doubtless angered by Opechancanough's cooperation with the English plan, but even before that he had indicated Itopatin as his immediate successor, with Opechancanough next in line. All this came after Hamor's visit of 1614, so that the Chickahominy would not have complained against this chief before that date.

The common-sense conclusion to the above accounts seems to reduce itself to this: The persistence of such a belief about Powhatan's father or brother demands some cause; sufficient cause is to be had in the fact that the Spanish actually did bring the Indian Don Luis from Mexico to Virginia. It is hardly possible that Ayllón's Chicora fled that far north to start all the trouble for the Chickahominy, although Swanton believes the Shakori of southern Virginia may have been his displaced tribe. Powhatan himself was too naive to have been Don Luis. The latter would never have sent a representative to England to count population by cutting notches in a stick. Opechancanough is a more logical candidate for the role of Don Luis. When Smith was at West Point the Indians under his control were fascinated by Smith's compass and showed that they believed the world to be flat. However, Smith does not attribute these reactions and beliefs to their leader, who showed himself interested in the nations of the world and the manner of sailing the seas and the Englishman's God. George Thorpe later found him well informed in religion. Even so, he gives the impression of learning for the first time about things Don Luis would easily know.

Despite the cultural affiliation which Swanton and others have found between the Powhatan and the lower Mississippi Indians, one would hesitate to postulate any mass movement from there under Opechancanough.[141] There is absolutely no linguistic or archaeological proof of such a transplantation, which would be indeed unique over such a distance.

141. See Swanton, "Aboriginal Culture of the Southwest," 42 BAE,R 718.

We are therefore left with the following guesses: If Don Luis was a young man when picked up for the first time in Ajacán, then he was possibly an elder brother of Powhatan. If, as is also possible, he was about forty years of age in 1560, as Sacchini has it, he was in all probability the father of Powhatan, a probability that draws strength from the superiority of Hamor's testimony over Beverley's. If the reader wishes to satisfy the details of both accounts, there is one more angle on which he might work—the Indian servant of Don Luis.[142] We know of no reason why Don Luis would not have taken him to Ajacán, if he was still alive, nor is there reason why we should insist on documentary evidence for the presence of such a minor character. He is an Indian from Mexico, the servant of Don Luis and thus the foster-brother of Powhatan—Opechancanough. A possibility, admittedly, but one that will appeal more to the novelist than to the historian.

One wonders why Hamor of all people identified the rumored white men at Ocanahowan as Spanish, where all the other English accounts assume that these men were survivors of the Raleigh colony. His statement: ". . . and even this Summer Cole and Kitchins plot with three more, bending their course to Ocanahowan, five daies journey from us, where they report are Spaniards inhabiting."[143] Perhaps he thought it was from this region that Powhatan's father had been driven.

It may be concluded from remarks of Smith in his *True Relation* that some party of whites preceded the English on the Rappahannock. Smith was taken to various Rappahannock tribes to see if they could identify him as the tall captain who had sailed up their river, killing their king and taking their people captive. Brown raises the question of the 1572 punishment, but according to Smith the marauders had been there from one to four years previously, which would coincide with the 1603 tragic exploration by Bartholomew Gilbert.[144] Powhatan, however, may

142. See note 44 above and citation there.

143. "Out of Master Hamors Booke," *The Generall Historie of Virginia*, 1: 214. See also Appendix C, "Rumors of the Lost Colony," p. 274, below.

144. See Brown (*Genesis*, 180) on Smith, and (*ibid*. 1: 26 f.) for the massacre of Captain Gilbert and several companions in Chesapeake Bay territory. In connection with the Spanish on the Rappahannock mention must be made of a cache of rare Spanish trade beads found in 1925 near Leedstown on the site of the Rappahannock Indian village of Pissasec. As Bushnell demonstrates, they were unlike any English product. They could have been bartered by Juan Menéndez Marqués in 1588. However, what with the rivalry of England and Spain on the sea, their presence can be explained in terms of booty taken after an English sea victory (Bushnell, "Indian Sites Below the Falls of the Rappahannock, Virginia" [96 *SMC* (1937) 27-35]).

Smith in an address to Princess Anne in behalf of Pocahontas said that he was the first

have been including a recollection of the Spanish revenge of 1572 when he told Smith he did not wish war, for he had "seene the death of all my people thrice and not one living of those three generations but my selfe," [145] an exaggeration, of course, but doubtless containing some truth.

The English in Virginia, we conclude, discovered vague traditions of the Spanish on their soil, which we, from our vantage point in history, can explain more clearly than they.

The English did not follow the Spaniards in applying the word Ajacán to Virginia.[146] Some writers on this Jesuit mission have attempted to locate it by discovery of some modern equivalent of this Indian word. In the third Part of this study, in a separate essay, we present a summary of the meaning and use of the name "Ajacán."

SUMMARY

IN REVIEWING this mission and its background we have tried to utilize all the sources upon which one can draw in determining locations and establishing the route of the Jesuits to the point of final settlement. We have let the maps and the documents speak for themselves as much as they can; when they have ceased, remembering that Powhatan was already an adult in 1570, we have reached across a span of only thirty-five years, recreating in general the position of the Algonkin tribes of 1607, trying to adjust the narrative to fit the demands of anthropology. From these combined methods it seems possible to offer the following conclusions: (1) The 1570 missioners stopped to say Mass at Newport News, then proceeded up the James to College Creek before disembarking; (2) They next carried their

Christian Powhatan and his attendants ever saw, though a "great captain" had been up the York as well as the Rappahannock from one to four years before Smith's captivity (2 Arber 531). Tindall, writing to Prince Henry, June 22, 1607, enclosing a map since lost, calls the James "our River...where never christian before hathe beene...." If the Spanish could forget they had been on the James, we can understand how the English may have failed to find out about it, but even if they knew, their knowledge would scarcely have found expression in English publications, most of which were intended as promotional pieces coupled with a defense of the English right to the territory.

145. 1 Arber 135.

146. A letter of Governor de Canzo of Florida to the Spanish King states, "if your Majesty wishes to inquire about the town of *el Jacan* through England, you must ask about Virginia, which is the name the English have given it, because about *el Jacan* they will know nothing" (Katherine Reding, "Letter of Gonzalo M. de Canzo, June 28, 1600," 8 *GHQ* 228). A transcript is available in the Lowery Papers, "Florida," vol. 6, Library of Congress.

supplies over to Queens Creek or Kings Creek and paddled them down to the York River to a Chiskiac village; (3) The martyrdom of Quirós and his two companions occurred in Paspahegh territory not far from Jamestown; (4) The remaining Jesuits were killed at the village on the York; (5) Menéndez anchored his ships in 1572 at or near Point Comfort, and the subsequent events described by Father Rogel took place at the mouth of College Creek; (6) It is certain that all the events connected with the mission took place in Virginia.[147]

A study of the early sixteenth-century maps reveals that the Bahía de Santa María was known in a confused manner as a good harbor near the 37th parallel. Menéndez, hopeful of discovering the chimerical passage to China, had long desired to explore it. But the defense of his sprawling, poorly financed, and rebellious province of Florida, coupled with his responsibility for getting the treasure fleets safely across the pirate-infested Atlantic, kept this ambitious official wholly engaged. The decision of Juan de Segura to establish a mission at Ajacán should have brought hearty support, despite the fact that the Jesuits were to work alone. The missionaries were justifiably afraid that a garrison of soldiers would sabotage their work with the Indians.

Although the Jesuits had in the main volunteered for the Orient, when they were sent to the less promising lands of Florida they went willingly, even eagerly. They had not been absent long enough from the civilization of Spain to have learned the art of survival in the wilderness. Their hopes that the Christian Indian Don Luis would be an invaluable interpreter and example for his people were cruelly frustrated. The massacre of the missionaries was but the last act of a tragedy.

Various writers have attempted to assess the importance of the mission on the course of American history. We know that Spain did cling to Florida for more than two centuries and for most of that time was a cause of real concern to the Virginia colony and other southern colonies. If the Jesuits had succeeded, Avilés might have erected some fortifications in the Chesapeake. In this event the course of English colonization might at first have been diverted to other areas. On the other hand, Menéndez de Avilés and Philip II were much stronger leaders than their successors. English enterprise was growing while Spain was entering her economic decadence, her interests still hopefully trending in the direction early

---

147. Of all those who have written concerning the Ajacán mission, Mooney (seconded by Swanton) comes the nearest to our conclusion, in 1 *Handbook* 877: "...the exact location is uncertain, but it seems to have been on or near the lower James or Pamunkey r."

pointed out to her by Peter Martyr—"To the South! To the South! For the great and exceeding riches of the Aequinoctiall, they that seek riches must not go unto the cold and frozen North."

Unless, like the English, they had discovered the market for tobacco, the Spanish certainly would have found Ajacán as unprofitable as the rest of Florida. Had they found the region economically rewarding, their very success would have been an invitation to their conquest by the British sea-dogs. Thus they would have saved the English the tragic and costly mistake of Roanoke Island and would have pointed out to them much earlier the advantages of the great bay of the Chesapeake.

PART TWO

THE DOCUMENTS
WITH THEIR TRANSLATIONS

Introduction

A SYNTHESIS of the events of the Segura mission needs to be complemented by the documents. The historical picture that then becomes discernible is vivid with the authentic colors of many incidents that were perforce omitted. In this task we are fortunate in having at hand several letters, relations, and reports that have received scant attention up till now. Some were written on the scene of events; others are the later recollections of eyewitnesses. These sources of information have already been used to reconstruct events as we believe they happened. Now, after an introduction dealing with the biography of the writers and the character of their narratives, the texts and translations are offered.

The problem of testimony may be placed this way: Who witnessed the events at Ajacán in the fall of 1570, in the spring of 1571, and in August of 1572? In any enumeration of the close witnesses we have Fathers Quirós and Segura, the boy Alonso, and the Indians who gave information to Alonso and to the Spaniards when captured. Father Juan Rogel saw the Fathers leave Santa Elena in August, 1570, he received a report from Brother Salcedo and the pilot who explored the rivers in the spring of 1571 looking for the missionaries, and he was at hand for the final scene in 1572. Pedro de Lara, the brother of Alonso de Olmos, also witnessed the events of 1572, according to Oré. The pilot Vicente Gonzales, another witness in 1572, supplied Oré either in person or in writing with information on ports and locations and perhaps some of the events that occurred. Oré's sources were good, for he tells almost the same story as the Jesuits and without having read any of their reports, as we know because of his failure to learn the names of more than Father Segura. Brother Juan de la Carrera was responsible for equipping the expedition at Santa Elena and he was also a member of Pedro Menéndez de Avilés' party in 1572. Every other source can be traced back in some fashion to Alonso, Rogel, Carrera, Pedro de Lara, or Gonzales, so that an order of importance for these documents can be established. In our opinion this order should be as follows: The Quirós-Segura Letter, the Letters and Relation of Juan Rogel, the Relation of Carrera, the later recollections of Bartolomé Martínez—who knew Alonso de Olmos and his family at Santa Elena— set down in a Relation, and the Relation of Luis de Oré, far more accurate than that of Martínez. There is also an excellent general account by Francisco Sacchini, who seems to have had available many original documents when he wrote in Rome in 1622. Later Jesuit historians followed Sacchini very closely. Among these, Mathias Tanner [1] has written the best account, although he provides no new details.

The geography of Ajacán is discussed at length in Parts I and III. There is room here, however, for a brief alignment of sources. For the site of the mission, the best clue is furnished by the pattern of journeys to creeks and various villages sketched in the Quirós-Segura Letter. The Rogel Letter of August adds details to the initial picture. For an over-all description of the Chesapeake, the Oré Relation is the best source by far. Here the indefinite phrases of the Rogel Relation and letters find clarification in a full account of the 1588 voyage to the Chesapeake. The importance of this event sixteen years afterwards lies in the information supplied by the captain, Vicente Gonzales, for whom this was the fourth voyage to Ajacán. He recalls the place where the Jesuits said Mass in 1570 and the port used by Menéndez. His own Relation, which is reproduced here, is, except for a clear description of the Chesapeake, strangely jumbled in its geography and its data. However, it offers the local color of the contemporary exaggerations about the wealth of Florida.

The continued Spanish interest in the Chesapeake as a possible strait leading to China is shown in a brief letter written in 1587 by Pedro Menéndez Marqués describing his explorations north of Santa Elena to the mouth of the Bay of Jacán, where they ended abruptly in a storm that drove his fleet down to the Bahamas. A letter and a relation by the sergeant-major of San Agustín, who went on the 1588 expedition, Juan Menéndez Marqués, are here presented and their confirmatory details

1. Mathias Tanner, S. I., *Societas Iesu usque ad sanguinis et vitae profusionem militans in* *Europa, Africa, Asia et America, ...* (Pragae, MDCLXXV) 447-451.

should illustrate the care and accuracy with which Oré drew up his fuller description. It is probable that both of these documents are addressed to a friar, possibly the commissary-general of Florida, in the hope that he would use his influence at the Spanish court to strengthen and fortify the Florida coast against the incursions of the French and English. The reports of Juan Menéndez Marqués and Vicente Gonzales are dated many years after the time of actual exploration. This will not occasion surprise when one recalls the unbelievable carelessness with which geographical information was gathered and retained in those times. Apparently the court had to be reinformed again and again on the location of ports and rivers and the character of the coast line. Pedro Menéndez de Avilés, Pedro Menéndez Marqués, Juan Menéndez Marqués, Francisco Ecija, and Andrés Gonzales covered almost identical ground, and still the court seemed to remain essentially uninformed.

In 1609 the Ecija expedition scouted the English in Virginia. From this came two useful reports, one by the leader, and the other by the ship's pilot, Andrés Gonzales. Some of the members of this expedition, in turn, recalled the experiences of the 1588 voyage, certifying that it must have entered the mouth of the James during its exploration and so adding clarity to the description given by Oré. Thus, far from straying from the topic, these documents offer many details that shed considerable light on the Jesuit mission. We trust there is a concomitant importance in the presentation of the texts of documents very useful for the general history of the Chesapeake region. They have been too long neglected.

Carrera and Rogel

Since there are several persons, such as Carrera, Rogel, Segura, and his first companions who landed first at Ajacán, who are present constantly throughout these documents, it will be useful to give their biographies in so far as the meager sources afford details.

Juan de la Carrera was born in Benbibre del Biezo, near León in the winter of 1536. He was a merchant in business with his uncle before he entered the Society of Jesus as a coadjutor-Brother at Burgos on December 6, 1552. He was then appointed to various domestic offices in the colleges at Burgos and Villímar until 1566. He tells us that he finally expressed his desires to go to the missions on the urging of Father Segura,[2]

---

2. Carrera Relation, para. 4, *MAF* 539.

and he accompanied the vice-provincial in his voyage to Florida in 1568. He is known to have assisted Father Rogel at the small college for the sons of native chiefs at Havana, and we can see his great piety in a request to Father Francis Borgia, the General of the Society of Jesus, for permission to receive Holy Communion frequently.[3] In 1574 he was ordered to go to Mexico City, where he stayed for six years at the Colegio de San Pedro y San Pablo performing domestic duties. Then he was stationed at Puebla de Los Ángeles until 1585 and afterwards at Pátzcuaro in Michoacán until 1592. He was a member of the Guadian mission for three years, after which he returned to the college at Puebla, where he had a holy death on January 4, 1601.[4]

Brother Carrera colored his account unwittingly with reasonings after the fact. He is shown to be warm-hearted, but worrisome. Nothing is more typical of him than the phrase in his Relation, "my forebodings were fulfilled." Yet his account is substantially correct and in harmony with that of Juan Rogel. Being of less education than the other Jesuit writers on these events, he would incautiously attribute the ordinary to the supernatural. He does not err in excess as much as Bartolomé Martínez, who has the handicap of recollecting the reports of the young man Alonso, some thirty-five years after the events.

Francisco Sacchini was an historian whose five folio volumes record the early period of the history of the Society of Jesus with a remarkable sweep and color, yet with considerable detail. His ornate Latin style is excellent, but at times his history is closer to Cicero's definition in the *De Legibus* of an *"opus . . . oratorium maxime."*

Another general chronicle of the Jesuit mission at Ajacán is contained in the *Chronological History of the Continent of Florida* by Andrés Barcia which is a classic history of the Atlantic Coast from 1512 to 1722. His Decades consist principally in an accumulation of various relations arranged in chronological order. His history of the Jesuit mission appears to rely heavily upon Ribadeneyra and Sacchini, although he mentions only the former in connection with his narration of the events of 1571. There are some significant deviations in the Barcia account of the Jesuit mission. He mistakenly lists six Fathers and four catechists, naming the pilot "Brother" Vicente Gonzales, and dates the massacres on February 14 and February 18. He also asserts that Pedro Menéndez de Avilés returned from the Chesapeake to Santa Elena. He exaggerates the cunning

3. Rogel to Borgia, Havana, Feb. 5, 1569, *MAF* 383.   4. Editor's note to the Carrera Relation, *MAF* 535.

of Don Luis and attributes the story of the sudden deaths of three of the Indians who murdered the Fathers (see the Rogel Relation below, paragraph 10) to a Father Andrés de Rivas and adds that Father Rogel rescued a crucifix from the belongings of the Jesuits. In his version neither of the two captured Indians of the second expedition gave information, and the failure of Governor Pedro Menéndez to recover the bodies is explained by his fear of meeting a superior force of Indians.

Juan Rogel emerges as the most competent, reliable narrator of all in his letters and Relation. This might be expected considering his education. Born in Pamplona in 1519, he enrolled in 1547, in the University of Alcalá, where he studied the classics and philosophy and received his licentiate. He then studied medicine at Valencia for two years after this. At the age of twenty-five he entered the Society of Jesus and was ordained a priest in January, 1556. For eleven years he labored in the parishes in Toledo and Cuenca and elsewhere, while he constantly urged his superiors to send him to the Indies.[5] Typical of his efforts is a letter written in August, 1560, to Father Laínez, second General of the Society of Jesus. He states his desire simply but fervently and then adds that he has good bodily health, and that he should be of less use in Europe since he stutters and knows more medicine than theology.[6] Juan Rogel is the veteran of the Florida Mission of the Jesuits: he was in the first group to arrive in 1566, and he labored with great zeal but small fruit in Tacobago, Guale, and Orista. After the tragedy in Ajacán, he went to New Spain, and from 1579 to 1619 he labored in the unhealthy, turbulent port of Vera Cruz. There his career was distinguished by his toil as doctor, pastor, and preacher. Many years later the Mexican Jesuit historian Francisco Alegre was to write in fond tribute: "he was among the most notable men whom the Company has ever had."[7]

The Companions of Segura

IN A LETTER TO Governor Menéndez dated December 9, 1570, Juan Rogel states that nine had departed from Santa Elena, "five members of the Company and four catechists."[8] One of the catechists was the boy Alonso de Olmos, who went along to serve the Fathers' Masses according

5. See the excellent summary of a doctoral dissertation on Juan Rogel in Rosemary Griffin's "Rogel, Padre of the Ports," 30 *Mid-America* (1948) 3-43.

6. *MHSI* "Epistolae Lainii" 5: 192-199.

7. Francisco Jávier Alegre, *Historia de la Compañía de Jesús en Nueva España* 2: 115.

8. Rogel to Menéndez, Havana, Dec. 9, 1570, *MAF* 478.

to the Rogel Relation.[9] He survived during his Indian existence of a year and a half. We know little about him except that he was the son of a colonist at Santa Elena, and his death some years later as a soldier at Orista is described by Oré and Martínez.[10] The other three catechists are known by their names only, Cristóbal Redondo, Gabriel de Solís, and Juan Baptista Méndez.[11] The last two accompanied Father Quirós on the journey that ended in their tragic death. It may be safely inferred, we believe, that these three catechists were received into the Society of Jesus in Ajacán, some time before their massacre. This would explain Rogel's noticeable change in the titles he gives them. In the letter of December, 1570, quoted above, they are called *mancebos de doctrina;* in the letter of August, 1572, he calls them *hermanos,* reserved to novices and brothers in this series of documents.[12] Ribadeneyra and Sacchini, earliest Jesuit historians of these events, always called them "Religious." Moreover, if they were not Jesuits, perhaps they would have been spared as Alonso was.[13]

Three coadjutor-Brothers were members of the expedition also. Gabriel Gómez was born in Granada and entered the Society there in 1568. In a letter of his provincial he is mentioned as a teacher "in the third class" at the college in Seville,[14] and in another letter he is called "a very estimable grammarian." [15] Sancho Zaballos also taught at Seville before entering; he was appointed to the Florida Mission very soon after his entrance into the Society, which caused Father Francis Borgia to send a sharp letter of rebuke to his provincial.[16] Pedro Mingot Linares was born in Valencia, but entered the Society in Rome, on May 31, 1564.[17]

9. Rogel Relation, translated below, para. 8.

10. Martínez Relation, translated below, para. 43.

11. In the membership of the Jesuit band at Ajacán, F. Zubillaga mistakenly places an "Alonso Méndez" (*La Florida* 395, note 13, and *MAF* 478, note 28; *MAF* 525, note 6; *MAF* 526, note 12). The only Alonso present was Alonso de Olmos, who was not a Jesuit. There is no mention in any of the documents of this Alonso Méndez.

12. See the Letter of Rogel, August, 1572, translated below, para. 6.

13. Rogel says, in his Relation, translated below, para. 8, that Alonso was spared "because of his youth, or God's design." Carrera, in his Relation, translated below, para. 45, says "they did not want to kill him, but only the Fathers."

14. Avellaneda to Borgia, Seville, Feb. 10, 1570, *MAF* 413.

15. "gramático muy aprovechado," Avellaneda to Borgia, Seville, Sept. 23, 1568 (Archives of the Society of Jesus, Rome, *Hisp.* 1109, f. 58). See Zubillaga, *La Florida* 393, note 7.

16. Borgia to Segura, or in his absence, Sedeño, Rome, Nov. 14, 1570, *MAF* 459; Borgia to Juan de Cañas, Provincial of Andalucía, *MAF* 466.

17. The researches of F. Zubillaga can discover this slight datum in an old catalogue: "Pietro Mingota, of Valencia, came here on the last day of May, 1564, and he was examined for a coadjutor. Since he had no impediments, he showed himself ready to do whatever was proposed to him in the examination. He brought with him an old black cape, a used *parzetta,* an old pair of stockings, a

Father Polanco, Secretary of the Society, records a meeting in Sienna with Fr. Antonio Sedeño and Brother Linares in his diary for August 16, 1567.[18] The two were en route to Spain to embark for Florida. Brother Linares sailed with the second group of Jesuit missionaries, which arrived at San Agustín in June, 1568. Soon after, when he became sick, he was sent to rest in Havana with Brother Carrera.[19] After teaching catechism for several months at Santa Elena,[20] he was chosen by Father Segura for the Ajacán expedition.

Father Luis Francisco de Quirós was born in Jérez de la Frontera in Andalucía, but the dates of his birth and entrance into the Society are unknown. There is extant a letter he wrote to his superiors in Rome on December 29, 1562, from the Society's college in Trigueros (Huelva). The college had been but recently opened and he speaks of the great numbers of confessions and the many works of the ministry he and two other Fathers were able to perform there.[21] He was also stationed at the college in Seville in 1567, and took part during the same year in the provincial congregation of his order in Granada.[22] He was then made superior of a mission among the Moriscos at Albaicín near Granada. The mission was closed after two years,[23] and he was appointed to the Florida Mission which he reached in June, 1570. The journey to Ajacán was his first assignment in the New World.

JUAN DE SEGURA

JUAN BAPTISTA DE SEGURA was born in Toledo in 1529. At an early age he enrolled in the University of Alcalá where he obtained the degree of Master of Arts, after studying Latin, Greek, and Hebrew. He then began his studies in theology and Holy Scripture at the same university for four more years. All this time he must have been preparing himself for the religious life, because he took his vows two days after entering

pair of ordinary black cloth trousers" (Archives of the Society of Jesus, Rome, *Rom.* 170, f. 143). See *La Florida* 327, note 75.

18. *MHSI* "Polanci Complimenta" 2: 654.

19. Zubillaga, *La Florida* 332.

20. John Tate Lanning, in his *Spanish Missions of Georgia* 246, states that five Jesuits reached Ajacán: Fathers Segura and Quirós, and the catechists Méndez, Solís, and Gómez: "There is no evidence beyond sheer authority to indicate that Redondo, Linares, and Cevallos [Zaballos] ever went to Virginia,..." The Rogel Relation, para. 8, and the Carrera Relation, para. 36, give all the names of the party of nine. The Rogel Letter of Dec., 1570 (cited above), states that "nine departed for Ajacán."

21. Zubillaga, *La Florida* 392, note 2.

22. Antonio Astraín, *Historia de la Compañía de Jesús en la Asistencia de España* 2: 279.

23. Zubillaga, *La Florida* 393; *MHSI* "Borgia" 5: 31-45.

the Society at Alcalá on April 19, 1556.[24] After teaching a few months at Medina del Campo, he went to Valladolid, where he reviewed his theology at the Dominican priory of San Gregorio. He was ordained in 1557. For the next eight years he labored—preaching, teaching catechism near Burgos, at the college of Villímar, where he was rector from 1560 to 1563. Then he was made rector at Monterrey for the next two years, and finally he went to Valladolid to be the rector from early in 1566 until June, 1567.

Father Segura had desired to go to the Indies from the time of his entrance into the Society. On March 19, 1565, he penned these lines to Francis Borgia: "The Lord has always made me confident that through this mission of the Indies, His overflowing goodness will give me spiritual strength to begin to serve Him in earnest." [25] For over a year after this, his assignment in the missions fluctuated among several possibilities, Honduras, Peru, Florida—or should he sail and be assigned later? He was finally appointed to Florida, over which he was constituted vice-provincial on September 26, 1567.[26] He arrived at San Agustín on June 21, 1568, and sent back a report telling of his great hopes in the new field, and asking for some information on difficulties in canonical jurisdiction.[27]

There are eight letters extant that Juan de Segura wrote during his two years as superior of Florida before going to Ajacán. Several of them were addressed to Father Francis Borgia.[28] These writings reveal Segura's plans

24. This account will but summarize the many details of his life pieced together from provincial catalogues and letters by F. Zubillaga, *La Florida* 317-323. See also the Carrera Relation, paras. 3-6, *MAF* 538 f.

25. From a letter, Segura to Borgia, March 19, 1565 (Archives of the Society of Jesus, *Hisp.* 102, ff. 143), *MAF* 25.

26. See especially *MHSI* "Borgia" 4: 420, 442; also Borgia to Araoz, Rome, March 16, 1567, *MAF* 162, and Bustamente to Borgia, Alcalá, May 31, 1567, *MAF* 168. Segura's letter of appointment from Jerónimo de Portillo, provincial, is in *MAF* 205 f.

27. Segura to Borgia, San Agustín, July 9, 1568, *MAF* 315 ff.

28. Francisco de Borja y Aragón (1510-1572) was born of a powerful and wealthy Spanish family, the hereditary Dukes of Gandía in Valencia. From the age of eighteen, Francis Borgia lived at the court of the Emperor Charles V, who conferred on him the title of Marquess of Lombay. In 1539 he was made Viceroy of Catalonia and in 1543 he inherited the title of Duke of Gandía. At this time he was made Master of the Household of Prince Philip, which promised great political influence when the Prince should ascend the throne. However, on the death of his wife in 1546, Francis Borgia decided to renounce his titles and in 1550 he took the habit as a member of the newly founded (1540) Society of Jesus. He was a man of considerable administrative experience who had a deep enthusiasm and zeal for the religious revival which pervaded southern Europe during this half century. In 1558 he preached one of the funeral eulogies at the obsequies of Charles V. After a succession of responsible posts, he was elected General of the Society of Jesus in 1565, and his term of office coincided with the pontificate of Saint Pius V. In 1670 he was canonized by Pope Clement X; his liturgical feast is celebrated on October 10.

and are a primary source for the early Jesuit endeavors in Florida, Georgia, and South Carolina. He established Havana as the center of the mission. There the Fathers were to rest from their journeys and seek the advice of the others, and visit the sons of the native chiefs studying there.[29] He traveled to all the mission posts at Tegesta, Calus and Guale, teaching the natives and the Spanish garrisons, and despite the disappointments that his relations with Menéndez produced, his letters retain a spirit of bold determination.[30] He insisted on the freedom of movement of the Jesuits, and refused to let them be relegated to the status of garrison chaplains as Menéndez preferred. By the close of 1569, Segura was debating whether or not to recommend the withdrawal from the mission. The results of the previous four years were very meager; the blood of martyred Fathers and catechists and the sweat of the living were of slight effect. He wrote to Francis Borgia that though the Fathers were willing to suffer, it would be better to fulfill their missionary purpose also. "I have decided to declare to your Paternity," Segura said, "that with all their constant toil, their health and bodily vigor seem to weaken, and there is little benefit to the souls of these natives, and slight hope of any, if we judge by what has been seen up till now."[31] The Father-General in Rome agreed with Segura in a letter dated September 7, 1570. The letter was never received by Segura as he had already decided to make a last effort at Ajacán. Before sailing at the end of August, he had sent all the other Jesuits to Havana to await orders.

What sort of man was Segura? He was well educated and admired by his brethren for his virtues.[32] He was believed to have considerable administrative ability, for he was made a superior at the age of thirty-one and held various offices in succession until his death ten years later. But the most urgent question will always be why he attempted the Ajacán jour-

29. Segura to Borgia, Havana, Nov. 18, 1568, *MAF* 358-370. The first half of this letter deals with the plans for this college, its finances and curriculum. The college never prospered though the Consejo de Indias encouraged it, for it was difficult to get natives to send their sons. Carrera (*MAF* 548 f.) relates a touching story of the baptism after long instruction of three Indian boys who died shortly after the ceremony, "a thousand thanks to the Lord," for Pedro Menéndez de Avilés would have sent them back to their people who were a danger to their new faith.

30. For examples see the following letters to Francis Borgia available in an English translation in 25 *HRS*: from Havana, Nov. 18, 1568, 96-102; from Havana, June 19, 1569, 107-108; from Santa Elena, Dec. 18, 1569, 108-112.

31. Segura to Borgia, Santa Elena, Dec. 18, 1569, *MAF* 406 ff.

32. This tribute by Juan de la Carrera echoes the praise in Martínez and Sacchini: "He gave a fine example and edification with his deep humility, patience and obedience, prayer and mortification, in which he was very distinguished. He was beloved by everyone..." (Carrera Relation, para. 3, *MAF* 538).

ney at the risk of so many lives. Segura was an intellectual, and beyond that an idealist. The failures of his missionaries after so much hard work must have made him anxious to work alone according to the advice of the great missionary Bartolomé de las Casas. There is no finer commentary on Segura's intentions than this passage in the treatise called *The Only Way to Draw All Nations to the True Religion* by Bartolomé de las Casas: "If the truth is proposed quickly with angry shouting or perhaps amid the clatter of arms and the terror of threats and beatings and domineering cruelty, it is clear that the human mind is prostrate with fear . . . so that the will cannot be moved but is forced to hate." [33]

Segura was studying at Alcalá when the celebrated debates between Juan Ginés de Sepúlveda and Bartolomé de las Casas on the theology of the *Conquista* and the enslavement of the Indians were held at Valladolid in 1550 and 1551,[34] in which city he was rector of the Jesuit college fifteen years later. Since he had entertained a desire to go to the missions from his youth, by his own admission, surely the inspiring doctrine of "good example and gentle persuasion" expounded forcibly by Las Casas may have become part of the young Jesuit's missionary credo.[35] The expedition to Ajacán has the same nobility in purpose and courage of conviction.

33. *Del Único Modo de Atraer a todas las gentes a la religión verdadera*, [Lewis Hanke, ed.] (Mexico, 1941) Book V, Chap. 4, p. 40.

34. See the account in *Las Casas, Disputa con Ginés de Sepúlveda* [M. de Olivart, ed.], (Madrid, 1908), and Lewis Hanke, *The Spanish Struggle for Justice in the Conquest of America* (Philadelphia, 1950) 111-133.

35. Mention must be made of another earlier effort to apply these principles on the Atlantic Coast. Fr. Luis Cáncer, O.P., an experienced missionary and close companion of Las Casas in his peaceful missionary experiments in Guatemala in 1537, was later killed by suspicious and unfriendly savages near Tampa in June, 1549, before he could begin preaching the gospel.

The Jesuit policy in this regard had been laid down in 1567 in a long letter from Francis Borgia to Jerónimo de Portillo. The Father-General believed it best to build permanent residences near the praesidios and then to work elsewhere as need arose. He urges the Fathers to attract the natives by kindness of speech and good example. Father Segura must have had complete confidence in the certainty of Don Luis' protection, for Francis Borgia had warned: "Let them not quickly place themselves in a notable danger of life among a tribe not yet subdued. Though it would be beneficial for them to die in God's service, it does not help the common good, for there is a great need of workers in the vineyard." (See *MHSI*, "Borgia" 4: 421.) There is a good summary of Jesuit missionary procedure in F. Zubillaga, "Métodos Misionales," 12 *Archivum Historicum Societatis Iesu* (1943) 55-88.

Segura was really in complete agreement with an admonition in a letter of Pope St. Pius V to Pedro Menéndez de Avilés: "Nothing, however, is more important in the conversion of the Indian idolaters than to make every effort to prevent their being scandalized by vices and bad habits on the part of those who go to those regions from the West. That is the key to this holy work, within which is enclosed the entire essence of your endeavor" (Pope Saint Pius V to Pedro Menéndez, Rome, August 18, 1569, translated in Barcia's *Chronological History* 150-151).

THE SPANISH COLONIAL SYSTEM

IT MAY BE useful here to indicate the relation of the Province of Florida to the Spanish colonial system. During the period of the Jesuit mission in Florida, 1566-1572, the powers of government were concentrated in the office of *Adelantado*, an ancient Castilian title once reserved to the officials who controlled the civil and military affairs of the hostile regions bordering on the Arab caliphate in Spain. Since Florida was considered to be a land unsubdued by the *Conquista*, Pedro Menéndez de Avilés was *Adelantado* with sweeping powers in political, judicial, and military affairs. He was also Captain-General of Cuba (sometimes entitled "governor"), to which Florida was annexed at this time. Nominally, Cuba and Florida both belonged to the vast territory assigned to the Viceroyalty of New Spain, stretching northward from the Isthmus of Tehuantepec and encircling the entire Gulf of Mexico. Judicial powers within the Viceroyalty were conferred on four *audiencias* or boards of magistrates; these had jurisdiction over different territories. While some documents pertaining to the affairs of Florida are found in the archives of the *Audiencia* of Santo Domingo, the general practice was to bring judicial disputes to the *Audiencia* of Mexico.

Over all the Spanish dominions overseas was the powerful Consejo Supremo de Indias, the Supreme Council of the Indies, in permanent session from August, 1524, to March, 1834. This body held from the Crown executive as well as judicial powers over every department: civil, military, or ecclesiastical. Its laws were to be obeyed equally in Spain and the Indies and it permitted no ecclesiastical independence. Supreme in commercial matters, but subordinate to the Council of the Indies, was the Casa de Contratación, or Board of Trade. In this governmental system, the difficulties of distance and ineffective communication were added to the defects inherent in any large centralized bureaucracy. The wide powers conferred by the Council of the Indies on Pedro Menéndez de Avilés and the remoteness of his province made him practically his own master in his territory.[36]

36. See R. R. Hill, *The Office of Adelantado* (New York, 1930); Lillian E. Fisher, *Viceregal Administration in the Spanish American Colonies* (Berkeley, 1926); J. M. Ots Cápdequi, *El Estado Español en las Indias* (México, 1941).

THE JESUIT PATTERN OF GOVERNMENT

SOME KNOWLEDGE of the Jesuit system of government is essential as background to the understanding of the documents. In the Florida Mission where the Jesuits worked alone or in groups of two or three, there were no established houses of the Society of Jesus, and the Religious were assigned their itineraries by the one superior, Juan Baptista de Segura, called "Father Vice-Provincial." He was directly responsible to the Father-General, Francis Borgia, who by the large powers granted in the Constitutions of the Society of Jesus had direct authority over every member of the Order. The older mendicant orders, which were originally federations of independent monasteries and which later placed their supreme authority in an assembly of abbots and delegates called a Chapter, gave their general superiors less direct authority. The supervision of the missions was not onerous to Francis Borgia at this time because of the relatively small numbers of Jesuit missionaries in the Spanish overseas empire during the sixteenth century. After the closing of the Florida Mission in 1572, the General delegated some of his authority to the two provincials whom he had appointed, Jerome Portillo in the Province of Peru, and Pedro Sánchez in the Province of New Spain. Thus the more customary subdivisions of Jesuits came into the New World: a group of Religious in one house under a rector; a group of houses under a provincial; a group of provinces under an assistant, and the assistants advised the General in the Roman curia on the problems of their large territories.

The personnel of the Florida Mission was drawn from the various Jesuit provinces in Spain, so that the General ordered each of the provincials to release from his jurisdiction one or two men for this new assignment. The Council of the Indies granted permission to the Jesuits to travel to their new posts and ordered Pedro Menéndez de Avilés to use the funds of the royal treasury for their support. Even during the Florida Mission, Francis Borgia appointed a Jesuit to remain in Seville to supervise the supplies and correspondence for the mission and to deal with the all-powerful Council. From this appointment there later developed the Jesuit official called the "Procurator-General of the Indies," who was to handle in the name of the Order all the government demands pertaining to the overseas missions, and secure the proper funds, permits, and orders from the Council of the Indies. This office gave no authority within the Society, unlike the wide jurisdiction the Franciscans gave to their "Commissary-General of the Indies." [37]

THE DOCUMENTS

A WORD ABOUT the character of the documents themselves is now in order. Most of the letters and relations are written with simplicity, candor, and conciseness. Some are private communications from Jesuits to their brethren; thus the story is told without any contrivance, and piety is expressed with unabashed freedom. To those unfamiliar with the fervent religious spirit of this century, one need but recall the flowering of mysticism with the contributions of Saint Teresa of Ávila, Saint John of the Cross, and Saint Ignatius Loyola, to name some of the more prominent only. [38]

In the notes to the documents, we have tried to add specific useful information drawn from contemporary sources and from modern scientific data in such fields as meteorology, cartography, and anthropology. Several of the documents are excerpts only, since they narrated many other incidents not connected in any way with the story of the Jesuits in Virginia. We have added striking parallels between the experiences of the Spanish Jesuits and the English colonists. The volatile conduct of the Indians, the methods of barter, the geographical descriptions recorded by John Smith and others seem to be but a reflection of the accounts of these earlier travelers. Despite the antipathies of Spain and England during this period, their explorers had a common reaction to the New World. We have cited only the more obvious similarities, but those familiar with the English sources for the first decade after the founding of Jamestown will easily supply others. This link between Juan de Segura and John Smith seems to fulfill the adage, "Coming events cast their shadows before."

In the translations we have avoided making descriptions of places more specific than the original text would permit. It is a commonplace for this period of historiography that these documents are written in a certain

37. See F. Zubillaga, *MAF*, Introduction, 17-46; L. de Aspurz, *La Aportación extranjera a las Misiones Españolas* (Madrid, 1945) 168-172; J. Broderick, *The Progress of the Jesuits* (London, 1946) gives a survey of the Society's activities in Europe at this time.

38. A recent historical survey of the religious atmosphere of sixteenth-century Spain may be read in the opening chapters of Leturia-Owens, *Íñigo de Loyola* (Syracuse, 1949). A sketch of the scholastic and religious training of the Jesuits of these days may be had in the introduction to J. V. Jacobsen's *Educational Foundations of the Jesuits in 16th Century New Spain* (Berkeley, 1939).

context that told their original reader more than readers over three and a half centuries later can hope to grasp. Moreover, many documents are lost, so that there will always be lacunae in the corpus of material available today. In reconstructing an event care must be taken that a prejudice or hypothesis does not force more meaning from words than what is objectively clear.

We have preferred to submit the original documents exactly as they were found available. Their sources, given in the notes accompanying each one, will show that a number of them have been previously edited, in varying degree, when published, while others are transliterations of originals in photostats or in typed or handwritten transcriptions in the manuscript collection of the Library of Congress. No attempt has been made to modernize the texts of the latter group.

Various words such as "port," "point," "ship," demand some further elucidation, since they occur regularly in important passages of the documents that follow. As a guide we offer here a short glossary that is based mainly on four sources: (1) words as used in the documents themselves; (2) their use in the excellent contemporary geography, *Compendium and Description of the Indies,* by Antonio Vásquez de Espinosa; (3) the *Index to the Map of Hispanic America,* published by the American Geographical Society in 1943; and (4) the notes in the Dictionary of the Spanish language of the Royal Spanish Academy.[39]

GLOSSARY

BAY—*Bahía* and *baya* mean an opening in the coast line of considerable size. One of the documents refers to the northern end of the Chesapeake as a gulf (*golfo*), but in general "gulf" would be larger than "bay." In Oré the word *ensenada* occurs, which connotes a concave curve in the coast line that makes a bay or cove; the word does not necessarily give an idea of the size or shape of the bay.

MAINLAND—*Tierra Firme* is a relative term meaning not merely the continent, but any large body of land in relation to the headlands and islands about it. Thus *Tierra Firme* is the large James peninsula in Menéndez Marqués. *Costa* means coast, but *banda* is also used for shore or beach.

---

39. *Compendio y descripción de las Indias Occidentales,* edited and translated 108 SMC (Washington, 1948); Spanish text by Charles Upson Clark, in 102 SMC (Washington, 1942). *Diccionario de la Lengua Española,* Real Academia Española [16th ed.] (Madrid, 1939).

POINT—*Punta* can mean a headland, or also a cape. Thus Andrés Gonzales
described Cape Henry as *una punta taxada a la mar*. Oré refers to
the cape of the land to the north that formed a high headland (Gloucester
Point). The word *barranca* can mean either a steep bluff or a ravine. A
more common word for ravine or gorge is *quebrada*, which can also refer
to a stream in a ravine. *Morro* is used by Oré for a headland. The steep
cliff at the entrance to Havana harbor was so named. A *morro* is usually
higher than a *barranca*.

PORT, HARBOR—*Puerto* means a place on a coast protected from the winds
and affording security to ships. It can mean a seaport; e.g., Havana,
San Agustín, and Santa Elena. It can also be a cove in a large river, a
harbor within a wide bay, or the mouth of a river in a bay. At times
puerto appears in a rhetorical couplet where the two words make up one
idea, or where the second specifies the first more clearly. Thus in Vásquez
de Espinosa we find *puerto y río de Uvare, la villa y puerto de Campeche*.
Menéndez Marqués writes of the *puerto y baya de la Madre de Dios*
which appears in the context to be a general reference to the Chesapeake
and its suitable harbor. The fortified seaport of San Agustín is called *la
ciudad y fuerte* by Vásquez de Espinosa and then *puerto y presidio* by
Oré. Espinosa also uses *buenos puertos y surgideros*, i.e., good harbors
and anchoring places. In the northern part of the Chesapeake there are
fine ports and rivers, *puertos y ríos*, according to Menéndez Marqués.
Juan Rogel in his Relation speaks of the port where the Fathers were,
meaning the harbor where they landed. Thus if a distinction can be made,
a "port" would emphasize the actual place of anchorage, and "harbor"
the natural suitability of the place, but the Spanish use one word for both.

RIVER—*Río* was used according to the judgment of the writer, rather than
corriente or *arroyo*, which is a stream. Where the river is called
angosto, "narrow," we have translated it stream. Rivers are also described
as *caudaloso*, which Vásquez de Espinosa uses to show the river has
abundant waters. Thus the Río de Berbís and the Orinoco are so described without any reference to width. *Caudaloso* could refer to mountain streams as in Menéndez Marqués, or the James River as in the Ecija
Report of 1609.

SHIP—In these documents *nao* and *navío* are the most common words, but
the notes of the Spanish Academy are too generic to be of use. The
specific designs of the various types are not known in detail. Vicente

Gonzales speaks of a *lancha* in his relation of 1588. This was a lighter with both sails and oars, and the largest of the boats used for communication within a *flota* or fleet; it was also used for short hauls along the coast. Pedro Menéndez Marqués speaks of this vessel as "fast of sail and oar" and it undoubtedly was designed to outmaneuver most of the larger piratical ships that it might meet on the Atlantic Coast. It was probably similar to the type designed by Pedro Menéndez de Avilés in 1567 for his fast run across the Atlantic to the Azores in 17 days. This ship, weighing only 20 tons but carrying 38 men, is described at length in Barcia's *Chronological History* 142 f. When he appeared off the European coast he struck terror in the hearts of the Portuguese and Spanish sailors, who mistook him for a Moorish pirate. The vessel used in 1572 to capture the Indians involved in the murder of the Fathers is described by Barcia as small, but strong and fast (156 f.).

Quirós in his letter of 1570 requested from Cuba a *chalupa*, the Spanish for sloop, which was a large tender with a deck and two masts. In his June letter, Rogel speaks of a vessel styled *baxel*, a generic word for bark, which was of too deep a draught for the Chesapeake expedition. In the August letter, Rogel calls the ship sent out under the command of Vicente Gonzales, *fragata*, *fragatilla*, and *navío*. Carrera calls it *navío bien armado*. The armament might have been from one to four small carriage guns, four- or six-pounders. This same ship Oré calls *patage* or tender. Martínez says that Alonso de Olmos returned to Havana in a *pataxe*, which obviously is the same vessel. The word "packet-ship" is sometimes used as a translation for this word. In identifying Vicente Gonzales' early career, Martínez writes that he was captain of the *buscarruido*, which vessel the Spanish Academy describes as a small craft that is sent out to explore from a fleet. Thus considering Gonzales' experience, and Oré's and Martínez' identification, one of the vessels in Governor Menéndez de Avilés' fleet must have been a *patache*, which Cesáreo Fernández Duro identifies as a small vessel used to relay orders, sound out the depths of bays, and be an auxiliary to the larger ships of the fleet.[40] Its design is unknown, but it probably had a lateen rig.

In a communication to the writers, Dr. Vernon Tate, Director of Libraries at the Massachusetts Institute of Technology, offered these notes from his readings on the problem of the *fragata*:

"In the 16th Century the term frigate in general referred to a small

---

40. See *Disquiciones náuticas* 6 vols. (Madrid, 1877-1891) 5: 117 ff.

boat usually again, not decked; propelled by oars and sails. I expect that the most accurate English equivalent would be pinnace, and for *fragatilla*, boat or shallop—a term current somewhat later. It is apparent that many of these small vessels originated in the Mediterranean and along the coast where they are now largely used for fishing. Larger war and merchant vessels carried them then as now for communication with the shore, and sometimes for the largest craft a ship's longboat could be a rather respectably-sized vessel.

"I would assume that these vessels would be lateen-rigged. This would mean a relatively short mast, and the lookout post for a vessel of fifteen *codos* [cubits] keel length might be somewhere between 15 and 20 feet. I should guess on the draught of a vessel of that type at being somewhere around 2 to 3 feet, loaded. . . . I have an idea that some of the large rowing sardine boats still in use along the Spanish coast would provide a reasonably accurate model, allowing, of course, for better selection of wood and workmanship."

Rogel calls Oré's *patache* a *fragatilla*, and neither was a professional sailor, so allowance must be made for some vagueness and confusion, although the boats might have been similar in design. It is possible that, like the shallop carried aboard the Spanish caravel of 1611, this *fragatilla* may have been a quite small craft lashed to the deck of one of Menéndez' larger vessels.

The Documents with Their Translations

Carta de Luis de Quirós y Juan Baptista de Segura

Septiembre 12, 1570 *

JHS

Illustre Senor

[1] La gracia del Espiritu Santo sea siempre en el anima de Vuestra Merced, Amen. Por no tener lugar el Padre Vice Provincial de escrevir a Vuestra Merced atento a la priessa q convenia darse en bolver el piloto a essa tierra me ordeno q hiziesse yo esto en su nombre dando cuenta de nuestra jornada y lo demas.

[2] Ha sido la tardanca en llegar hasta aqui mucho mayor de lo que se pensava por las difficultades que Vuestra Merced entendera q suele aver en descubrir tierras nuevas, y las incommodidades del tiempo como mas largamente dara cuenta el piloto a Vuestra Merced, y llegamos aqui adonde se descargo la ropa ayer que fueron dies dias de Setiembre aviendo partido como Vuestra Merced sabe a cinco de Agosto de Sancta Elena. Hallamos la tierra de don Luis muy de otra manera q se penso, no porque aya avido falta en don Luis en el dar relacion della, sino porque la ha Nuestro Senor castigado con seis años de esterilidad y mortandad que ha sido causa de quedar muy despoblada conforme a lo que ella solia ser y porque son muchos los muertes y tambien los q se an ydo por otras tierras a proveer a su hambre, han quedado poca mas jente de los principales que dizen q quieren morir donde sus padres murieron, aunque ya ni tienen mais, ni se hallan frutas de las silvestres que ellos suelen comer, ni raizes ni otra cosa q comer sino muy poco y alcansado con mucho trabajo por estar ya muy agostada la tierra y por esta causa no han tenido los indios que offreser a nosotros ni a los q venian en el navio mas q buena voluntad q cierto esta han mostrado estos indios de don Luis buena de la manera q ellos han podido paresceles q ha don Luis resuscitado y que viene del cielo y como todos los mas que han quedado son sus parientes han se consolado con el muy mucho y cobrado animo

* The source of the document, in each case, is given in the first note following the English translation. The authors have made no attempt to edit the documents.

85

y esperanca q Dios los quiere favorescer y dizen q quieren ser como don Luis y rogado q nos quedamos en esta tierra con ellos y teniendo el cacique hermano de don Luis un hijo de tres años muy enfermo q estava siete u ocho leguas de aqui paresciendole q ya se queria morir a hecho instancia que se le fuessen a baptizar por lo qual parescio al Vice Provincial embiar a noche a uno de los nuestros q le baptizasse por estar ya muy propinco a la muerte. [3] Visto pues la buena voluntad q esta gente mostrava aunque por otra parte como ya dize estan tan hambrientos q todos pensavan perescer de hambre y de frio este invierno como lo han hecho muchos en los inviernos pasados porque de mas de q con difficultad hallan ya los raizes de q se solian sustentar las grandes nieves q ay en esta tierra no les dexan buscarlas mirando tambien la esperanza grande q se tiene de las conversion desta gente y servicio de nuestro Senor y de Su Magestad y entrada para la sierra y la China & le parescio al Padre aventurarnos aquedar aunque con tan poco matalotaje y recaudo porque nos hemos comido por el camino los dos barriles de biscocho de los quatro y el pequeno de harina q se nos dio para el viaje porque tambien ha sido necessario socorrer con algo dello a todo el navio porque venian muy faltos de mantenimiento. [4] bien creo q no nos faltara materia para exercitar la paciencia y a bien succeder se avia de padeser mucho pero a todo esse riesgo ha parescido ponernos y especialmente por parescernos que con la buena diligencia de Vuestra Merced se podra proveer buena cantidad de maiz para q nos podamos sustentar y tenga toda esta gente q siembre y assi por lo que toca al servicio de nuestro Senor y de su Magestad conviene mucho q Vuestra Merced procura si fuesse possible proveernos con mucha presteza y sino fuesse possible hazerse en el invierno es necessario que por todo Marco o a mas tardar al principio de Abril se haga alguna buena provision de manera q se les pueda dar para sembrar a toda esta gente. Y porque en este tiempo se puede sembrar aca y desta manera se llegara mucha gente q esta derramada por toda la tierra a buscar de comer q sera grande disposicion pa el Sancto Evangelio y particular- mente q lo ha pedido esto con mucha instancia el cacique de la informacion desta tierra lo que toca a la derota q se ha de traer el piloto la dara porque no conviene q se entre por el rio que nosotros entramos a causa de no tener tambuena informacion quanto convenia de los indios por donde aviamos de entrar y por esso es ydo oy el piloto por tierra dos buenas leguas de aqui a ver un rio por donde se ha de hazer la entrada quanto con la buena ventura nos vengan a proveer y visitar, pues por aquella parte se puede yr por mar hasta el lugar donde hemos de hazer la habitacion y por aqui ay dos buenas leguas por tierra y otras dos o mas por la mar de manera que la ropa q hemos desembarcado en este desierto adonde se puede llegar por este rio la han de llevar los indios a cuestas estas dos leguas y despues se ha de tornar a embarcar en canoas q es harto trabajo.

[5] La informacion que hasta ahora se ha podido aver de la tierra adentro es que unos indios que encontramos alla abaxo en este rio nos informaron que tres o quatro jornadas del alli estava la sierra y las dos dellas se yva por un rio y despues de la sierra otra jornada o dos se via otro mar. Si otra cosa se pudiere saber con mas certidumbre y claridad se procurara, aunque para esto haze grande falta una buena chalupa porque con la hambre y mortandad aun no tienen canoas esta gente de que se puede hazer caso. El piloto ha hecho muy bien su viaje y trabajado lo possible en el y nos entrego todo el hato que se embarco nuestro en Santa Elena y aun vista la necessidad en que quedamos para llevar por tierra este hato nos ayudo con una botija vazia porque en ellas se avia de llevar el vino, y con un costal porque tambien sera menester llevar en costales la harina y con la mitad de la brea q traya pa remendar alguna de las canoas rotas que tienen estos indios y nos dio un esculpil que traya. Por la mucha necessidad que trayan todos los del navio de mantinimiento ha sido necessario q llegando como llegamos aqui ayer se vayan oy dixandonos aqui en este despoblado con las incommodidades ya dichas y por esto no ha habido lugar de tener mas informacion ni la ay de alargarme mas. Dios nuestro Senor prospere a Vuestra Merced y a todus sus cosas en su Sancto Servicio como Vuestro Merced lo dessea. Deste puerto a 12 de Setiembre de 1570.

Por comission del Padre vice Provincial Capellan de Vuestra Merced
Quiros

[6] Senor mio por no poder mas ordene al Padre Quiros diese larga cuenta a Vuestra Merced de todo yo escrivo a Su Magestad la disposicion que hallo en esta tierra para plantar el Santo Evangelio y la grave necesidad en q quedamos a trueco de cumplir este ministerio, yo entiendo no sera necesario tornar yo a suplicar de nuevo a Vuestra Merced nos embie con toda brevedad una fragata cargada de mais y no otros regalos pues vea Vuestra Merced muy bien quanto importa se haga esto con toda presteca para el remedio y amparo de toda esta gente, servicio de Dios Nuestro Senor y de Su Magestad a quien tambien escrivo como Vuestra Merced embiara a Su Magestad clara noticia y informacion de la derota para venir a Axacam como quien tambien lo sabe etc. En ninguna manera me

parecio convenir embiar alla muchacho alguno de estos indios por lo que dira el piloto y otras cosas. Guarde nuestro Señor a Vuestra Merced muchos años y prospere en su Santo amor y gracia.

J. BAPTISTA DE SEGURA

JHS

[7] Arivase me olvidado de escrivir a Vuestra Merced q desque se entienda ser tiempo en que venga la fragata q se pide con el socorro, se embiara un indio o dos con una carta a la boca del braco de mar por donde se ha de passar para que viendo algun navio haga humada grande de dia y de noche fuego y mas de esso que desque llegue el navio la gente del alli tenga su carta guardada y no la de hasta que le den a el otra como aquella lo qual sera para señal de que los que vienen son amigos y los que traen el recaudo Vuestra Merced tenga cuenta desta seña o de aviso a quien viniere della llevara la carta el aviso del modo que se ha de tener para entrar y servira de guia.
Sea Cristo Nuestro Señor con Vuestra Merced. Amen.
[8] Don Luis lo haze bien como del se esperava y esta muy obediente a lo que en el Padre le ordena con mucho respecto asi al Padre como a los demas q aca estamos y se encomienda mucho a Vuestra Merced y a todos los demas sus amigos y señores.
[9] Por un descuido que ubo de no se quien en el navio de hazer algun rescate de comida sevido luego el inconveniente que se siguio dello que como antes los indios que encontravamos en el camino nos davan de la pobreza q tenian despues como vieron q aquellos avian llevado no se que juguetes por las macorcas etc. de maiz traian las macorcas y otras comidas y pedian que les diessen algo y las darian alegandole q asi lo avian hecho a los otros y como el Padre avia prohibido que aquello no se hiziesse porque no se acostumbrassen y despues nos lo quisiessen a nosotros rescatar se bolvian con ello, [10] parescio le al Padre que diesse cuenta desto a Vuestra Merced para que pues hemos de estar en esta tierra a lo que los indios nos dieren por la mayor parte Vuestra Merced provea que la gente q viniere en ninguna manera rescate si fuere menester si graves penas y si algo traxeren que rescatar dando lo aca a don Luis se dara orden como don Luis haga que les den en correspondencia algo segun que fuere los rescates y que no traten con los indios mas ni de otra manera q como aca se juzgare convenir. Cristo Nuestro Senor con todos. Amen.

QUIROS

LETTER [1] OF LUIS DE QUIRÓS AND JUAN BAPTISTA DE SEGURA TO JUAN DE HINISTROSA *

From Ajacán, September 12, 1570

JHS

ILLUSTRIOUS LORD,[2]

[1] The grace of the Holy Spirit be always in your soul, Amen. Since Father Vice-Provincial [Segura] has no opportunity to write to you, because of his concern over despatching the pilot in haste to your land, he has asked me to forward to you in his name an account of our journey up till now.

[2] After having been delayed in arriving here much more than we had expected by those adversities[3] which you understand are usual in the discovery of new regions, and by the discomforts of the weather, as the pilot will narrate to you more at length, we arrived here and unloaded our cargo yesterday, which was the tenth day of September. We departed as you know on the fifth of August from Santa Elena. We find the land of Don Luis in quite another condition than expected, not because he was at fault in his description of it, but because Our Lord has chastised it with six years of famine[4] and death, which has brought it about that there is much less population than usual. Since many have died and many also have moved to other regions to ease their hunger, there remain but few of the tribe, whose leaders say that they wish to die where their fathers have died, although they have no maize, and have not found wild fruit, which they are accustomed to eat. Neither roots nor anything else can be had, save for a small amount obtained with great labor from the soil, which is very parched. So the Indians have nothing else to offer to us and to those who came on the ship but good will, and certainly these Indians have shown that in a kindly manner. They seemed to think that Don Luis had risen from the dead[5] and come down from heaven, and since all who remained are his relatives, they are greatly consoled in him. They have recovered their courage and hope that God may seek to favor them, saying that they want to be like Don Luis, begging us to remain in this land with them. The chief has kept a brother of Don Luis, a boy of three years, who lies seriously ill, 6 or 8 leagues

* The notes follow the English translation.

from here and now seems certain to die. He has requested that someone
go and baptize him, for which reason it seemed good to Father Vice-
Provincial to send last night one of Ours [6] to baptize the boy so close to
death.

[3] Thus we have felt the good will which this tribe is showing. On the
other hand, as I have said, they are so famished, that all believe they will
perish of hunger and cold this winter. For only with great difficulty can
they find roots by which they usually sustain themselves, and the great
snows found in this land do not allow them to hunt for them. Seeing
then the good will that this tribe has shown, great hope is had of its
conversion and of the service of Our Lord and His Majesty and of an
entrance into the mountains and to China, etc. Therefore, it has seemed
best to Father to risk remaining despite such scanty stores, because on
our trip we have consumed two of the four barrels of biscuit and the
small amount of flour which was given us for the journey. We had to
help the entire ship with some supplies, as we were ill-provisioned for
the journey.

[4] I am convinced that there will be no lack of opportunity to exercise
patience, and to succeed we must suffer much. But it has seemed good
to expose ourselves to that risk and this especially so, since in your
kindness you might be able to send us a generous quantity of corn to
sustain us and to let all this tribe take some for sowing. As it touches the
service of Our Lord and His Majesty, it would be best that you see to
it that we are supplied with all speed possible. If it cannot be done in the
winter, it is imperative that some provisions arrive some time during
March or at the beginning of April so that we can give seeds to the tribe
for planting. At this time the planting is done here, and thus many of
the tribes will come here after being scattered over the region in search
of food and there will be a good opportunity for the Holy Gospel. The
chief has sought this very thing especially. As to information about the
land that touches the route along which the pilot must be directed, he
himself will give it. It is not convenient to enter by the river we did, for
we did not have as good information from the Indians as was necessary
about the place we should have entered. And so, today, the pilot has
gone overland 2 good leagues [7] away to see a river, which he will enter
when with good fortune he comes again to help us and visit us. Through
this region he can go by water [8] up to the place where we plan to make
our encampment. To reach this spot, it is 2 good leagues by land and
2 others or more by water, so that the goods, which we have unloaded

in this uninhabited place reached by the river where we now are, must be carried by the Indians on their shoulders for these 2 leagues and then embarked in canoes, which is sufficiently laborious.

[5] From some Indians whom we met farther down this river we have some information about the region farther inland. Three or four days' journey from there lie the mountains. For two of these days one travels on a river.[9] After crossing the mountains by another day's journey or two, one can see another sea. If any new information can be had with more certainty and clarity, we will get it. Furthermore, in making this trip a good shallop is a necessity, since with the famine and death this tribe does not have the canoes in which the trip could be made. The pilot has managed his voyage very well and has toiled in every possible way and has brought all the provisions that we took at Santa Elena. Moreover seeing our need of getting these provisions overland, he has helped us by giving us a large earthern wine jug,[10] sacks for transporting the flour, and a chisel he brought along. He has also given us half his supply of tar to patch up one of the leaking canoes that the Indians have. With the great need of provisions for the entire crew, it has been thought necessary that they leave today, and we will remain here in this lonely region amid the trials mentioned above. So there has not been opportunity to get more information or to write further. May God Our Lord grant you prosperity in all your undertakings in His holy service as you desire.

From this port on the 12th of September, 1570.
By order of Father Vice-Provincial.   Your chaplain
                                                       QUIRÓS

[6] My Lord, Since I could not do more, I ordered Father Quirós to give a long account to you of everything. I am writing to His Majesty about the conditions which I find in this region for spreading the Holy Gospel, and about the grave necessity in which we remain in the course of accomplishing our mission. I believe there is no need to return, but I must entreat you anew to send us with all speed a shipload of grain, but no other trifles, since you easily see the great importance of this being done at once. It is for the help and protection of the entire tribe, and for the service of God Our Lord and His Majesty. I am also writing to His Majesty that you will send on to His Majesty detailed information of the route to Axacam as far as it is known. In no way does it seem best to me to send you any Indian boy, as the pilot will explain, and for

other reasons too. May Our Lord protect you unto a long life and favor you in His love and grace.

J. Baptista de Segura

JHS

[7] Above I had forgotten to write to you that from the time it is understood that the frigate is to come with the help requested, one or two Indians will be sent with a letter to the mouth of the arm of the sea, along which any ship coming must sail. Thus, when they see the ship, they will make a large smoke signal by day and a fire at night.[11] Furthermore the people there will have a sealed letter of yours and they will not return it until they receive another like it, which is to be a sign that those who come are friendly and are the ones who bring the message. Take heed of this sign or inform whoever comes about it. Our letter will carry information about the way which must be followed in entering and will serve as a guide.

May Our Lord be with you, Amen.

[8] Don Luis has turned out well as was hoped, he is most obedient to the wishes of Father and shows deep respect for him, as also to the rest of us here, and he commends himself to you and to all your friends.

[9] By a bit of blundering (I don't know who on the ship did it) someone made some sort of a poor trade in food. I see now the misfortune which followed, in that while up till now the Indians whom we met on the way [12] would give to us from their poverty, now they are reluctant when they see they receive no trinkets for their ears of corn. They have brought the ears of corn and other foods and asked that they be given something when they handed them over. They say that they have done that with the others. Since Father had forbidden that they be given something, so that they would not be accustomed to receiving it and then afterwards not want to bargain with us, the Indians took the food away with them.[13]

[10] Thus it seemed good to Father that he should tell this to you since we must live in this land mainly with what the Indians give us. Take care that whoever comes here in no wise barters with the Indians, if need be under threat of severe punishments, and if they should bring something to barter, orders will be given that Don Luis force them to give in return something equal to whatever was bartered, and that they may not deal with the Indians except in the way judged fitting here.

Christ Our Lord be with everyone, Amen.

Quirós

NOTES

1. This letter is found in the Buckingham Smith Papers, vol. 2, Florida, 1526-1743, at the library of the New York Historical Society. The transcription has the annotation: "carefully corrected by the original, Seville, July 14, 1889,—B. Smith." Robertson lists this letter as being in the Archivo de Indias (*List of Documents in Spanish Archives Relating to the History of the United States* 82), but recently Father Zubillaga was unable to discover it in Madrid or Seville (*MAF* 480). While sections of the letter are available in Lowery, *Spanish Settlements, 1562-1574* 361-363, this is the first publication of the complete text. We have added the paragraph numbers, but otherwise have attempted no editing. Smith's transcript has been checked against one (source unknown) made by John Gilmary Shea and forwarded to us by Father William Repetti, S.J., Archivist at Georgetown University. The two are virtually identical except for minor differences in spelling.

2. Juan de Hinistrosa was the son of Emanuel Rojas, the Governor of Cuba from 1525 to 1538. Hinistrosa was made Governor of Havana in 1555, and in 1565 he was made Royal Treasurer of Cuba (2 Ruidíaz 116). He was a friend of the Jesuits in Havana, providing them with a house and food and showing them many favors during the Florida Mission (Segura to Borgia, Nov. 18, 1568, *MAF* 361).

3. Among the adversities would be the necessity of proceeding slowly, taking frequent soundings, following the contour of the shore rather than standing boldly out to sea as they could do later, and perhaps coming to anchor occasionally at night because of uncharted waters. Pedro Menéndez Marqués in 1573 kept 2 or 3 leagues from land in sailing from Santa Elena to Ajacán.

4. Within the modern period of accurate weather observation there have been years of severe drought in Virginia, as in 1930, when there was only half the normal rainfall. However, the Indians were probably exaggerating when they spoke of six years of famine, though six years of below-normal rainfall is not improbable. The present development of dendrochronology does not permit a check on this statement concerning the Virginia weather of 1570. See, however, J. C. Hoyt, "Droughts of 1930-34," *Water-Supply Paper* 680, U.S. Geological Survey.

5. Almost the same statement is made about the welcome accorded Don Jaime of Tegesta upon his return to Florida from Spain. See Sacchini, *Historiae*, III, *Borgia*, Book IV, No. 304, p. 201.

6. "Ours," when written by a Jesuit, always refers to other members of the Society of Jesus. This baptism, if performed, would doubtless have been the first in the territory of Virginia. The request probably came from Don Luis rather than from the chief.

7. Father Quirós was probably speaking of land leagues here. A land league roughly was about 2 or 3 miles. Even if we knew the standard used, we would not have more than a general idea of distance covered in terms of leagues, for the methods of estimating distance by land or sea were crude at best. (See Appendix D for a fuller discussion.)

8. From this expression it cannot be concluded that the settlement was to be on the sea or even that it could be reached directly by one of the large salt-water tributaries of the Chesapeake. The expression is used by the Spanish even for travel on fresh-water streams. The portage made in this journey might well have followed the line to Queens Creek later used by the English in erecting the palisades in 1633 to confine all stock in the colony to the eastern end of the peninsula.

9. This river is probably the James (see Part I above, note 49). Strachey said: "Yt [the James] falleth from rocks far west, in a country inhabited by a nation, that they call Monacan . . . from high hills afar off within the lands, from the topps of which hills, the people saie they see another sea, and that the water there is salt; and the journey to this sea, from the Falls, by their accompt, should be about ten daies, allowing, according to a march, some fourteen or sixteen miles a day" (Brown, 1 *Genesis* 186, 397 ff.). Opechancanough told Smith the salt water was four or five "daies iourney of the falles" (1 Arber 17). Powhatan and an Indian who had been Powhatan's prisoner confirmed this account, the estimated distance ranging up to eight days beyond the falls (1 Arber 19). From the Spanish it is impossible to determine whether or not Father Quirós was writing from the river he describes, or from a neighboring river.

10. An earthen wine jug of Spanish origin and a Spanish olive jar were recently recovered by the Smithsonian Institution following excavations at Kecoughtan, near Hampton, but the jug is probably too small to be the one mentioned here. Spanish treasure ships plying the northern course were sometimes seized by the English, and wine is sometimes mentioned as part of the seized cargo. This would easily explain the presence of the wine jug at Hampton.

11. These were the signals commonly employed by the Indians along the coast. They were used in 1609 to advise the English of the approach of Ecija's ship. See the Ecija Report below.

12. There is indication here of a stop or stops farther down the river or bay and also the lapse of some time from the day of entering the bay until they finally dropped anchor.

13. The Jesuits' trading experience is similar to that of the early English. Archer reports the Indians clustered on both sides of the James "proferring vs victualls" (1 Arber xliii). The Virginia Company warned the settlers: "You must take care that your marriners that go for wages, do not marr your trade; for those that mind not to inhabite, for a little gain will debase the estimation of exchange, and hinder the trade for ever after" (1 Arber xxxvii). Studley and Todkill (1 Arber 101) and Wiffin and Phettiplace (1 Arber 128) describe the sad results in 1608 of permitting the mariners to trade with the Indians. The exchange was debased and the Indians acquired weapons which they could use with effect against the whites. Smith in his "Voyages and Discoveries" (1 Arber 74) says: "Their manner of trading is for copper, beads, and such like; for which they giue such commodities as they haue, as skins, fowle, fish, flesh, and their country corne. But their victuall is their chiefest riches."

Cédula real
Febrero 19, 1571

El Rey. Nuestro gobernador de la isla de Cuba o vuestro lugarteniente en el dicho oficio. El Padre Juan Bautista de Segura a escripto quel y algunos religiosos de la Compañía de Jesús y ciertos niños de la doctrina y don Luis de Velasco, indio, que por todos son diez personas, han llegado a las provincias de la Florida, donde avían hecho mucho fruto en la instrución y conbersión de los naturales dellas y al presente lo quedavan continuando con su dotrina; y que por no aver ido proveídos de comida, estavan con mucha necesidad de ser socorridos dello y con qué senbrar alguna cosa para mejor reparo suyo. Y porque teniendo atención al provecho speritual de los dichos indios, y que tan buena y santa obra vaya adelante; es mi voluntad que los dichos religiosos y las personas que con ellos están, sean proveídos de la dicha comida, vos mando que, luego questa veáis, proveáis y deis orden de embiar a los religiosos de la dicha Compañía de Jesús, y a las demás personas questán en su aconpañamiento en las dichas provincias de la Florida, el maíz que os pareciere ser necessario para su comida y sustenación, conforme a la necesidad que tubieren dello. Y ansimismo que puedan sembrar alguna cantidad del dicho maíz, dando orden que se les llebe con mucha brevedad, que la costa que [16v] se hizere en lo susodicho, mandamos a los nuestros oficiales desa isla que, por librança vuestra lo den y paguen de qualesquier maravedís de su cargo; y que a ellos con la dicha librança y testimonio signado de escrivano público de como se enbía (?), mandamos que les sea rescivido y pasado en quenta lo que en ello se montare; y de lo que hiciéredes y proveyéredes, nos daréis aviso.

Fecha en Madrid a diez y nuebe de hebrero de mil e quinientos y setenta y un años.

YO EL REY

Por mandado de su Magestad, Antonio de Herasso, señalada del Consejo.

CEDULA [1] OF PHILIP II

From Madrid, February 19, 1571

THE KING. To our Governor of the island of Cuba or your lieutenant [2] in the said office. Father Juan Baptista de Segura has written [3] that some Religious of the Company of Jesus and certain catechists and Don Luis de Velasco, an Indian, ten persons in all, had reached the provinces of Florida where they had been obtaining great fruit in the instruction and conversion of the natives there, and at present they intend to continue their teaching. Since they had not gone with provisions, they were in great need of help with food and something to plant to improve their situation. As I have before me the spiritual advancement of the said Indians, and in order that such a good and holy work should procede, it is my will that the said Religious and persons with them be provided with food, and I command that, as soon as you see to this, you order that there be sent to the Religious of the said Company of Jesus and also to the persons staying with them in the said provinces of Florida, such maize as you deem necessary for their food and support, according to their needs. In order that they can sow a quantity of this maize as soon as possible, give orders that the supplies be conveyed with all speed. We command that the officials of that island pay the cost of the enterprise from their treasury, through your kind efforts, and we demand, through the aforementioned kind efforts, an account signed by the public notary of how [the maize] was sent and that the sums were received and spent in this business. Inform us of the measures taken in this regard.

Done at Madrid, on the nineteenth of February, fifteen hundred and seventy one.

I THE KING

By command of His Majesty, Antonio de Herasso, with the seal of the Council.

NOTES

1. The autograph signed by the King is in the AGI, Santo Domingo, leg. 2828 f.16. It is reproduced in *MAF* 642 f. This decree came in response to the urgent appeal of Father Segura, written from the Bay of the Mother of God, mentioned in the Quirós-Segura Letter above, para. 6. Whether the five-month period between the sending of the letter and the royal action was due to the letter's cir-

cuitous route to Spain or to the inefficiency of the royal bureaucracy can never be known. The direct appeal to friends and fellow Jesuits in Havana made by Quirós had nearly the same result as Segura's request since the King referred the affair to the officials in Havana. This decree is dated but a few days after the death of the Fathers.

2. Pedro Menéndez Marqués, nephew of Pedro Menéndez de Avilés.

3. Despite the barriers of authority that the Spanish administrative system established, it was the jealousy guarded right of every loyal subject to write directly to the King. Their letters would contain blunt criticism of the royal decrees as well as requests for royal aid for their immediate problems. For an excellent treatment of this little known facet of the Spanish colonial system see Lewis Hanke, "Free Speech in Sixteenth Century Spanish America," 26 *HAHR* (May, 1946) 135-149.

CARTA DE JUAN ROGEL

Junio 27, 1572

† JHS. MUY RDO. PADRE NUESTRO EN CHRISTO.

[1] Pax Christi etc. Porque por essa del Padre Sedeño, que escribió estando de partida para Nueba España por orden del Padre doctor Pero Sánchez, provincial, entenderá V. P. las cosas desta casa y de la Florida, sin tratar yo dello, daré cuenta de lo que después de su partida se a hecho.

[2] Cinco días después que el salió deste puerto, vino el Adelantado y començamos a entender de propósito en esta jornada de Ajacán, para ir a buscar los nuestros y saber la certinidad dellos. Ya, gloria al Señor, está concluído todo, y nos aprestamos con toda prissa para salir deste puerto el díe de S. Pedro y San Pablo. Los oficiales del Rey an dado más de mil ducados de la real hazienda para esta jornada; porque van treinta hombres de mar y guerra, pagados por tres meses, y mas el matalotage para ellos, sin lo que se lleba de mantenimiento, para que, hallando los que están de paz y haziendo fruto, podérselo dexar.

[3] Pero todo esto lo a proveído con una sobrecarga, y es que, en acabando de hazerse la jornada, no emos de tornar acá camino derecho, sino que dize convenir al servicio del Rey (pues a su costa se haze ello), nos vamos a las islas de los Açores. El porqué no lo dize; mas lo que yo e entendido es porque quiere a este piloto para que descubra la costa de España, y sepa si ay cosarios, antes que salga la flota de las Terceras. Yo e resistido quanto e podido a esto, mas tómanos por hambre; porque no ay al presente baxel ninguno que sea a propósito para nuestra jornada sino los que él tiene (porque uno que se compró para este efecto dixo el piloto que no era apto porque pidía mucha agua); y como no ay en el puerto otro alguno que esté aprestado, esnos forçoso tomarlo con las condiciones que él pide. El me a dado su palabra que desde allí me a de embiar acá; pero yo témome que a de rodear los negocios de suerte que me lleben a España; porque a mostrado voluntad de llebar u[no de no]sotros consigo; y assí me temo que dando el Señor buen viaje, que esta carta y yo juntos iremos a España. Lo que yo tengo determinado de hazer es que, no yendo el mesmo Adelantado a buscar los nuestros (lo qual pienso no dexará de ir,

según él me lo dize muchas vezes casi afirmándolo), persuadir a la gente que nos tornemos camino derecho a la Habana.

[4] En llegando de camino a Sancta Helena, plaziendo al Señor, embiaré acá a los Hermanos Juan de la Carrera y Francisco, que están allá; porque assí me lo dexó ordenado el Padre Sedeño, para que aguardemos aquí la resolución del Padre Provincial.

[5] Otra cosa no se me ofrece que escribir a V.P. más de pidir, quan encarecidamente puedo, encomendarme en los sanctos sacrificios y oraciones de V.P. y de toda de la Compañia.

[6] Dios nuestro Señor dé a V.P. su sancto spíritu con augmento de su divina gracia y dones para que en todo acierte a cumplir su divina voluntad, amén.

De la Habana a 27 de Junio de 1572.

De V.P. indigníssimo hijo y siervo en el Señor,

JUAN ROGEL.

LETTER [1] OF JUAN ROGEL TO FRANCIS BORGIA

From Havana, June 27, 1572

JHS

MOST REVEREND FATHER IN CHRIST

[1] The Peace of Christ, etc. Since by the letter [2] of Father Sedeño,[3] written before his departure for New Spain on the order of the Reverend Doctor Pedro Sánchez,[4] Your Paternity is aware of past events in this house and in Florida, I need not discuss them here, but only relate what has happened since he left.

[2] Five days after he left this port for New Spain, the Governor arrived and we began to reach an understanding about the journey to Ajacán to go and search for Ours and learn certainly about them.[5] Now, glory to the Lord, that is all settled and we are preparing to leave here with all speed on the feast of Saints Peter and Paul.[6] The King's officials have granted more than a thousand ducats from the royal treasury for this trip. Thirty soldiers and sailors are going with all their equipment. They have been paid for three months. Furthermore, there is a supply of provisions to leave behind, when we find those who are in peace and have gathered fruit.

[3] All this has been provided under a condition, namely, after finishing the trip, we will not head for here by a direct route, but it is more to the service of the King—since he is financing the voyage—that we go to the Isles of the Azores. The Governor gives no reason, but I have understood that he wants this pilot to sail close to Spain, and learn if there are corsairs lurking there before the fleet leaves the Islas Terceras.[7] I resisted this as much as possible, but "beggars can't be choosers." There are no ships at present suitable for our trip as planned except those in the Governor's command. One purchased for this purpose was declared by the pilot to be unsuitable, because it had too deep a draught. Since there is no other useful ship in the harbor, we are forced to agree to the conditions that the Governor placed. He has given me his word that he will send me back from there, but I fear that he will arrange the trip in such a way that he will take me to Spain. Because of his clear desire to take one of Ours with him, I believe that, with the Lord granting a good voyage, this letter and I will arrive together in Spain.[8] So I have decided to persuade some good man to return directly to Havana, if the Governor does not go in search of Ours. But from his many assurances, I don't think he will give up the search.

[4] After arriving en route at Santa Elena, the Lord willing, I will send here Brothers Juan de la Carrera and Francisco de Villareal who are staying there. When leaving, Father Sedeño ordered this. Thus we will all await together the decision of Father Provincial.

[5] Nothing else presents itself to write to Your Paternity, except to beg as insistently as I can, a remembrance in the holy sacrifices and prayers of Your Paternity and the entire Company.

[6] God Our Lord grant Your Paternity His Holy Spirit and an increase of His divine grace and gifts so that you may certainly fulfill His Divine Will, Amen.

    Your Paternity's unworthy son and servant in Our Lord,

      From Havana on the 27th of June, 1572.

JUAN ROGEL

NOTES

1. The autograph is in the Archives of the Society of Jesus in Rome, codex *Hisp*. 116 f. 387 (prius 645, 499). The text is in *MAF* 521 ff. The letter tells of the preparations for the trip to Ajacán and the uncertainty of Menéndez' assistance at this time.

2. This important letter has been lost.

3. Antonio Sedeño was born in the town of San Clemente near Toledo. While still a boy he was sent to Italy and placed in the service of Count Francisco Landriano, who was a great benefactor of the Jesuits. Sedeño entered the Society at the college at Loreto on July 4, 1559, while still a young man. In the Archives of the Society of Jesus there is his written reply to questions about his interests: "ad studia quidem non tam propensum quam ad externam actionem me sentio" (Zubillaga, *La Florida* 324, note 68). After studying the humanities at the Society's college at Macerata he went to the University of Padua for a year's study of rhetoric in which he believed himself "less than mediocre" (*ibid.*, note 70). In 1664 he went to Rome and while residing at the Colegio Germanico, he heard lectures in philosophy for three years at the Colegio Romano. Without any formal studies in theology he was ordained in 1566, and after repeated requests he was sent to the Florida Mission together with Brother Pedro Linares and Father Segura in 1568. In Florida his abilities as a preacher and catechist found many outlets. He labored in Tegesta, Calus, and Guale for two years, then in the ill-fated college for the sons of native chiefs in Havana. In Father Segura's absence he was appointed vice-provincial of the mission (Nadal to Sedeño, Rome, June 20, 1572, *MAF* 516 ff.). In 1578 he was made vice-rector of the college in Mexico City, then in 1581 he went to the Philippine Islands to be superior of the mission there. After a distinguished career, he died a holy death on Sept. 1, 1595 (see Carrera Relation, para. 7, *MAF* 540). For his Philippine activities there are many citations in Blair and Robertson, *The Philippine Islands, 1493-1803*, especially 13: 197 ff., 223-232.

4. Pedro Sánchez, formerly rector of the college at Salamanca, was made first provincial of the province of New Spain on October 26, 1571. In his instructions from Father-General Borgia, he was ordered to visit Florida and Havana, to inspect the work of the Fathers and take along with him those unnecessary for the restricted purposes of the mission, in preparation for closing it. "Más en caso que aya de quitar la gente de la Florida y Havana, es bien que lo haga poco a poco y quanta se puede, sin offensión del Sr. adelantado D. Pero Meléndez" (from a document in the Roman Archives [Instructiones I, 1546-1547, f. 219] quoted in *MAF* 516, note 6). The early career of Father Sánchez is ably recounted in J. V. Jacobsen, *Educational Foundations of the Jesuits in 16th Century New Spain* (Berkeley, 1938), and G. Decorme, *La Obra de los Jesuitas Mexicanos 1572-1767*, 2 vols. (Mexico, 1941) 1: 3-28.

5. Rogel is referring to the following passage in a previous letter: "Since the Governor has for his own reasons detained at Santa Elena the ship which was going to Ajacán, it seemed best to me in Our Lord, that Brother Carrera be sent to ask the Governor not to delay the trip so long, and to ask Father Sedeño not to give way to the Governor in a matter so important. I know that he reached San Agustín, where he met Father Sedeño and the Governor and all three set sail on the same ship for this port, but they have never arrived nor has any vessel come from Florida at all since then. We are afraid that some disaster has happened either with the Indians or on the sea, what with the storms that have

been blowing. On the other hand we have hope that they have gone back and reached Santa Elena, and so we are only guessing here at present *inter spem et metum.*" Rogel to Borgia, Havana, March 10, 1572, *MAF* 513-515.

6. June 29.

7. The necessity for vigilance in the vicinity of the Azores and the coast of Spain is well illustrated in later incidents recounted about John White's fifth voyage to Virginia in 1590. White's little fleet took several Spanish prizes on the way to Virginia, leading him later to complain that the English pilots were more interested in booty than colonization. On White's return trip they met near the Azores a large fleet under the command of John Hawkins, which planned to spread out along the Spanish and Portugese coasts in what proved to be an unsuccessful attempt to prevent the Spanish treasure fleet's slipping by unchallenged (6 Hakluyt (EL) 213-227). Hawkins had been at work on the Atlantic Coast as early as 1564, but in 1572 it was Francis Drake with three ships who was on the prowl for booty in the Atlantic. At the time Menéndez sailed for Ajacán in August, Drake was busy sacking ports in the Caribbean. Cf. Irene A. Wright, *Documents Concerning English Voyages to the Spanish Main, 1569-1580* (London, 1932) 42 f.

8. Fortunately, this circuitous trip was never made, as will be seen in Rogel's August, 1572, Letter below, para. 1.

Carta de Juan Rogel

Agosto 28, 1572

IHS. MUY. RDO. PADRE NUESTRO IN CHRISTO.

[1] A los postreros de junio próximo pasado escribí a V.P. desde la Habana, dando cuenta cómo, por orden de la santa obediencia, me aprestaba para hazer esta jornada a buscar a los nuestros que vinieron a esas partes; y aunque allí escribí que, en acabando esta jornada, avía de ir a las islas de los Açores, porque al adelantado Pero Menéndez le era forçoso llebar desde aquí el navío en que yo venía camino de España; pero en llegando a S. Agustín mudó parecer, porque determinó de hazer por su persona, con su armada, esta jornada, y en acabando de hazerla darme un navío en que tomasse a la isla de Cuba. Y assí a treinta de julio salimos de San Agustín con esta determinación; y deteniéndonos en Santa Elena cinco días, vinimos a esta baía de la Madre de Dios, y traxe conmigo a los Hermanos Juan de la Carrera y Francisco de Villarreal con el hatillo que teníamos en Santa Elena, para que todos fuéssemos a la Habana a esperar orden del P. Provincial, porque ansí me mandó el P. Sedeño lo hiziesse.

[2] Llegados a esta baía, luego el Adelantado dio orden cómo fuéssemos a buscar a Alonsico, que es el mochacho que vino con el P. Baptista, del qual teníamos noticia que no lo avían muerto, de uno de los indios destas partes, que prendió el piloto, quando vino la 2ª vez, y lo traíamos con prisiones en nuestra compañía; y quedándose él con su armada en un puerto desta baía, embió una fragatilla armada con treinta soldados a un río dulce, donde desembarcaron los nuestros quando acá vinieron, que está veinte leguas deste puerto; y parecióme ir en ella llebando al indio aprisionado en mi compañía, para que nos fuesse lengua. El orden que dio el Adelantado al piloto desta fragata fue que procurasse de prender a un cacique principal de aquella ribera, tío de don Luis, con la gente principal suya que pudiesse; y en prendiéndolos, pidir que nos diessen al mochacho y que luego los soltaríamos: y assí se hizo al pie de la letra; porque en llegando dentro de una hora prendió al cacique con cinco de los más principales que él tenía y otros ocho indios.

[3] El modo de prenderlos fue que aviendo hechado el ánchora en medio del río, que era angosto, luego acudieron indios a la ribera y entraron algunos en el navío, a los quales regalaron y les dieron algunos rescates; y como estos salieron tan contentos del navío, vinieron otros de nuevo; y a la tercera lechigada vino el cacique con sus principales; y el uno dellos traía una patena de plata, de las que llebaron los nuestros, por chaguala o joyel; y luego hecharon mano destos y los pusieron debaxo de cubierta y empavesaron la fragata y salimos hasta la boca del río, tres leguas, al remo, y en este camino mataron los soldados algunos indios que se pusieron a flecharnos y hirieron a un soldado.

[4] A la boca del río, que era muy ancho, tornamos a dar fondo a tiro de arcabuz de tierra, y vinieron canoas de indios de paz, los quales dixeron que al mochacho tenía un cacique principal, que estaba a dos jornadas de allí, y estaba junto deste puerto, y que les diéssemos término para embiar por él que ellos lo traerían. Dióseles el término que pidieron y rescates para que diessen al cacique que tenía al mochacho, y estubimos allí esperándolo; y parece ser que, como supo este cacique la prisión del otro, y que tenía tan vezina la armada y la muerte de los indios, quiso ganar las gracias con el Adelantado, y no lo quiso dar para que nos lo llevassen a nuestro navío, sino embiólo a este puerto con dos indios; y es cosa maravillosa en quán breve tiempo supo el Adelantado lo que allá passaba por medio del mochacho.

[5] Como no llevaron los indios al mochacho, armáronnos una celada de muchas canoas cargadas de flecheros para dar assalto a la fragata: y primero vinieron dos canoas grandes llenas de indios, que venían cubiertos que no se veían sino dos que las governavan y dezían que nos traían hostiones; y antes que llegassen a bordo, los descubrió la centinela, y luego se apercibieron los nuestros, y los otros se retiraron; y a petición mía no mataron a los que venían governando, porque aún no estábamos ciertos si era celada o si venían de paz. Acabado el término, como no vino el mochacho, aguardamos una noche y medio día más, y luego nos hizimos a la vela con la presa; y por despedida acercóse más a tierra el piloto con la fragata, con achaque que quería hablarles, y dio una rociada de arcabuzazos a un montón de indios que estaban en la orilla del río, apiñados, donde creo que murieron hartos: lo qual se hizo sin que yo lo entendiesse hasta que estubo hecho el negocio; y con esto vinimos al puerto.

[6] Daré agora quenta a V.P. de cómo passó la muerte de los nuestros que aquí estaban, según lo refiere este mochacho. Dize que luego en

llegando allá, los desamparó don Luis, porque no durmió en su casa más
que dos noches, ni estubo en aquel pueblo donde los Padres hizieron su
assiento, más de cinco días; y luego se fue a vivir con un hermano suyo,
que vivía jornada y media de donde estaban los nuestros; y aviéndole
embiado por dos vezes a llamar el Padre maestro Baptista con un Hermano
novicio, nunca quiso venir, y quedaron los nuestros en grande afflictión,
porque no tenían con quien poderse entender con los indios y sin mantenimiento, ni quien se lo comprasse; y vandeábanse, como podían, yendo
a otros pueblos a rescatar maíz con cobre y latón: y desta suerte passaron
hasta principio de hebrero, Y dize que el Padre Baptista cada día hazía
hazer oración por don Luis, deziéndoles cómo el demonio lo traía muy
engañado. Y como lo embió dos vezes a llamar y no vino, determinó de
embiar al P. Quirós y al Hermano Gabriel de Solís y al Hermano Juan
Baptista al pueblo deste cacique, que está preso, adonde estaba entonces
don Luis, para que lo llevassen consigo, y de camino rescatassen maíz. Y el
domingo después del día de la Purificación, salió don Luis a los tres que
tornaban para casa con otros indios, y el don Luis dio un flechazo por
el corazón al Padre Quirós: y allí mataron a los tres que fueron a llamarlo.
Y luego se fue al pueblo, donde estaban los Padres, de paz y con dissimu-
lación con otros indios muchos, y mataron a los cinco que quedaban; y el
mesmo don Luis fue el que dio las primeras heridas con un machete
destos que embían para rescates de indios, y acabó de matar con una hacha
al Padre maestro Baptista, y luego los que con él venían acabaron de
matar a los demás. Y dize este mochacho que quando vio que mataban a
los Padres y Hermanos, él quiso ir entre los indios que los estaban
hiriendo, para que a él también lo matassen, porque, dize, que le pareció
que era mejor morir con los cristianos que vivir entre los indios solo; y
que lo tomó del braço un cacique, hermano de don Luis, y no lo dexó ir.
Y esto passó al quinto o sexto día después que mataron a los tres. Y después de muertos, dixo este mochacho al don Luis que pues los avía muerto
los enterrassen; y en esto siquiera usó de misericordia con ellos, que los
enterraron entrambos.

[7] Y el mochacho estubo en la mesma casa hasta quinze días; y como
avía hambre en la tierra, díxole don Luis que fuessen a rescatar maíz; y
assí se vino con él a este cacique, donde se quedó el mochacho por averle
dicho el cacique que se quedasse con él, que él lo regalaría y ternía en
cuenta de hijo: y assí lo a hecho. Y luego entre el don Luis y sus dos
hermanos, que fueron en matarlos, distribuyeron la ropa toda; y no traxo
otra cosa el mochacho más de las reliquias y cuentas benditas del Padre

Baptista, las quales las a guardado hasta agora y nos las a entregado. Y después acá dize que a andado el don Luis muy solícito procurando de aver al mochacho para matarlo, porque no hubiesse quien diesse nuebas de lo que a sido de los nuestros; y que por el temor que tenía a este cacique con quien el mochacho estaba, lo a dexado de hazer.

[8] Lo que el Adelantado a hecho, después de aver sabido la verdad, es que a dicho a este cacique preso que haga que le traigan a don Luis y sus dos hermanos para hazer justicia dellos; si no que la a de hazer de todos los que están presos, pues en su tierra mataron a los tres, y no pueden dexar de tener culpa en la muerte; y assí a prometido que los hará traer dentro de cinco días; y este término estamos esperando, y no sé si, antes que se cumplan, nos embiará el Adelantado la buelta de la isla de Cuba; él dirá en España, plaziendo al Señor, lo que en ello abrá hecho. Queda esta tierra muy amedrentada deste castigo que haze el Adelantado, porque antes dezían que se dexaban matar los Españoles sin hazer resistencia; pero, como an visto lo contrario de lo que en los Padres, tiemblan y a sonado mucho este castigo en toda la tierra; y si haze este castigo será aun más sonado.

[9] Lo que e visto en esta tierra es que ay más gente que en ninguna de las que hasta agora e visto en la costa descubierta; y paréceme que viven aquí más de assiento que en ninguna de las otras partes donde yo e estado; y no estoy [497] desconfiado que, si aquí poblassen Españoles de assiento, de suerte que tubiessen occasión de temer los naturales si quisiessen hazernos daño, pordíamos predicar el sancto evangelio con más comodidad que en ninguna otra parte emos tenido; y es que tenemos este mochacho, buena lengua, que casi se le a olvidado la española, criado en la Compañía conforme a nuestro modo de vivir, y agora después de aver salido del captiverio preguntándole si quería ir con su padre (que también está aquí) o con nosotros, dixo que no quería sino irse con nosotros. Y para hazer que conserve esta lengua y no se le olvide, estoy en duda si llevaré conmigo un mancebito indio, que a venido con él, negando a sus padres y su natural por venirse con él, para que exercite la lengua en el entretanto que V. P. o el Padre Provincial otra cosa ordenaren.

[10] Lo que yo de mi parte puedo dezir a V. P. es que, juzgando V. P. en el Señor que se deva abraçar esta empresa, si me cupiesse a mí la suerte, me ternía por muy dichoso. Bien me temo que la mesma dureza abrá en estos para convertirse, que la ay en los demás donde emos estado; y que si a de aver algún fruto, a de ser por discurso de tiempo cavando en ellos como una gotera en una piedra; pero para hazerse esto ay menos in-

comodidades y contradictiones que en otras partes donde yo e estado: lo 1°
porque la tierra es tan fría que no dará lugar para que hagan los inviernos
largas ausencias de sus casas; lo 2° porque me parece que ay más gente
y es más poblada de naturales esta tierra que las otras donde yo e estado.
[11] Quando fue este mochacho con don Luis, después de aver muerto
a los otros, dize que dexó los ornamentos y libros y lo demás que avía,
cerrado en las arcas; y después que tornó el don Luis hizieron su reparti-
miento; y un hermano de don Luis, dize, que anda vestido con los ornamentos de dezir missa y del altar; y el cáliz de plata me a dicho este
cacique preso que lo dio don Luis a un cacique principal que está la tierra
adentro; y la patena a uno destos indios que están presos; y algunas
imágenes que las hechó por la calle; y entre otras llevaron los Padres un
Crucifixo de vulto grande en una arca; y an dicho unos indios a este
mochacho que no osan llegar a esta arca, porque tres indios que quisieron
mirar lo que avía en ella, murieron allí luego; y assí dizen que la tienen
cerrada y guardada. De los libros dize que le an dicho que, quitándoles las
mañezuelas, los hechó en la calle y los rasgaron todos.
[12] Las otras particularidades que entendiere, si traxeren al don Luis y a
sus hermanos, que los a embiado a prender el Adelantado, desde la
Habana lo escribiré a V. P. quando, plaziendo al Señor, allá llegáremos.
[13] Y pues otra cosa no se me offrece que escribir, cesso encomendán-
dome en los sanctos sacrificios y oraciones de V. P. y de todos los Padres y
Hermanos de la Compañía. Dios nuestro Señor dé a V. P. su sancto spíritu
para que en todo acierte a cumplir su divina voluntad.

Desta baía de la Madre de Dios de la Florida a 28 de agosto de 1572 años.

De V.P. indigníssimo hijo y siervo en el Señor,

† JUAN ROGEL.

LETTER [1] OF JUAN ROGEL TO FRANCIS BORGIA

From the Bay of the Mother of God, August 28, 1572

JHS

OUR MOST REVEREND FATHER IN CHRIST,

[1] At the end of last June, I wrote to Your Paternity from Havana,
telling how, under an order of holy obedience,[2] I made ready to make
this journey in search of Ours who had come to these parts. Although I

had written from there that at the end of the trip I had to go to the Isles of the Azores, because the Governor Pedro Menéndez was obliged to take the ship, in which I had come here, for the trip to Spain; nevertheless, when he reached San Agustín, he changed his plans. He decided to make this trip in person at the head of his fleet, and on completing the trip, to give me a ship in which I might go back to the island of Cuba. Thus, on July 30, we left San Agustín for this purpose, and after staying at Santa Elena for five days, we arrived at the Bay of the Mother of God. With me are Brothers [3] Juan de la Carrera and Francisco de Villareal and the small store of supplies we had on Santa Elena. After this we will all go to Havana to await the order of Father Provincial [4] since Father Sedeño would order me to do that.

[2] Reaching this bay, the Governor immediately ordered us to search for Alonso, the boy who came with Father Baptista. He has not died, according to what we heard from one of the Indians of this region, who was captured by the pilot on his second trip. This Indian has been brought along in chains. Anchoring the fleet in a port of this bay, the Governor sent an armed *fragatilla* with 30 soldiers to a fresh-water stream where Ours disembarked when they came here. This place is 20 leagues from this port. It seemed best to me to take the bound native in my company to be our spokesman. The order of the Governor was to take the uncle of Don Luis, a principal chief of that region, as well as some leading Indians. On taking them, we were to ask them to give us the boy and we would let them go. Everything happened in excellent fashion, for within an hour after our arrival, he took the chief with five of his leaders and eight other Indians.

[3] This was the method of capture. After we had anchored in the middle of the narrow stream, Indians soon appeared on the bank [5] and some entered the boat. To these the Spaniards gave gifts and made some exchanges. When they left the boat very contentedly, others arrived. With a third group came the chief and his leaders; one of them wore as a decoration or trinket a silver paten that Ours had brought. At once the Spaniards seized them and forced them down into the boat, and dressing the ship, passed to the mouth of the stream 3 leagues away by oar. On the way, the soldiers killed some Indians who were trying to shoot arrows at us and had wounded a soldier. [6]

[4] At the mouth of the river, which was very wide, [7] we anchored again an arquebus shot away from the shore. Canoes of Indians came in peace, and they said that the boy was in the hands of a leading chief who lived

two days journey from there,[8] near this port. They asked that we give them time to send for him and bring him. This we did, and we gave them trinkets to give the chief who held the boy and we stayed there waiting for him. It seems that as soon as the chief learned of the capture of the others and about the fleet and the imminent death of the Indians, he sought to curry favor with the Governor. For he did not want to let the boy be brought to our ship, but he sent him to this port with two Indians. It is a marvelous thing in how short a time the Governor learned what was happening there from the mouth of the boy.[9]

[5] When the Indians did not bring the boy, we fought off an ambush of many canoes loaded with archers ready to attack the vessel. First there came two large canoes filled with Indians who were so concealed that no one was seen except the two who steered and they pretended they brought us oysters.[10] Before they got aboard the watchman discovered them. We made ready and the others retreated. At my request, the steersmen were not fired upon, for we were still not certain whether it was an ambush or whether they came in peace. When the time was up and the boy did not come we waited for a night and further into midday and finally we set sail with our captives.[11] By way of farewell, the pilot steered the ship towards land with the excuse that he wanted to speak to them, and then he ordered a blast from the arquebuses [12] into the group of Indians who were standing crowded together on the shore. I believe many of them were killed, and this was done without any knowledge of mine until it happened. Then we returned to this port.

[6] Now I will relate to Your Paternity how Ours who were here suffered death, as this boy tells it. After they arrived there, Don Luis abandoned them, since he did not sleep in their hut more than two nights nor stay in the village where the Fathers made their settlement for more than five days. Finally he was living with his brothers a journey of a day and a half away. Father Master Baptista [13] sent a message by a novice Brother on two occasions to the renegade. Don Luis would never come, and Ours stayed there in great distress, for they had no one by whom they could make themselves understood to the Indians. They were without means of support, and no one could buy grain from them. They got along as best they could, going to other villages to barter for maize with copper and tin, until the beginning of February. The boy says that each day Father Baptista caused prayers to be said for Don Luis, saying that the devil held him in great deception. As he had twice sent for him and he had not come, he decided to send Father Quirós and Brother Gabriel de Solís and

Brother Juan Baptista [14] to the village of the chief near where Don Luis was staying. Thus they could take Don Luis along with them and barter for maize on the way back. On the Sunday after the feast of the Purification, Don Luis came to the three Jesuits who were returning with other Indians. He sent an arrow through the heart of Father Quirós and then murdered the rest who had come to speak with him. Immediately Don Luis went on to the village where the Fathers were, and with great quiet and dissimulation, at the head of a large group of Indians, he killed the five who waited there. Don Luis himself was the first to draw blood with one of those hatchets which were brought along for trading with the Indians; then he finished the killing of Father Master Baptista with his axe, and his companions finished off the others. This boy says that when he saw them killing the Fathers and Brothers, he sought to go among the Indians as they inflicted the wounds so that they might kill him too. For it seemed better to him to die with Christians than live alone with Indians. A brother of Don Luis took him by the arm and did not let him go. This happened five or six days after the death of the others. This boy then told Don Luis to bury them since he had killed them, and at least in their burial, [15] he was kind to them.

[7] The boy stayed in the same hut for 15 days. Because of the famine in the land, Don Luis told him that they should go and seek grain. Alonso came in this way with him to the chief where he remained. [16] The chief told the boy to stay and he would treat him well and hold him as a son. This he did. Finally Don Luis distributed the clothes of the Fathers among himself and his two brothers who shared in the murders. The boy took nothing but the relics and beads of Father Baptista which he kept till now and handed over to us. After this Don Luis went away very anxious to get hold of the boy to kill him, so that there would be no one to give details of what happened to Ours, but because of his fear of the chief with whom the boy was staying, he gave up the idea.

[8] When he had learned the truth, the Governor acted in this fashion. He told the captured chief that he must bring in Don Luis and his two brothers for punishment, and if he did not do this, the Governor would punish all those captured. Since three had been killed in that chief's lands, he could not escape blame for the murders. The chief promised that he would bring them within five days. We are waiting for this time to elapse, and I am not sure whether the Governor will send us on our trip to the island of Cuba before the time is up. He will report to Spain, God willing, whatever action he will have taken. The country remains

very frightened from the chastisement the Governor inflicted, for previously they were free to kill any Spaniard who made no resistance. After seeing the opposite of what the Fathers were, they tremble. This chastisement has become famous throughout the land, and if this further one is done, it will be all the more famous.

[9] I have noticed something about this region. There are more people here than in any of the other lands I have seen so far along the coast explored. It seemed to me that the natives are more settled than in other regions I have been and I am confident that should Spaniards settle here, provided they would frighten the natives that threaten harm, we could preach the Holy Gospel more easily than elsewhere. We are keeping this boy with us. He is very fluent in the language and had almost forgotten his Spanish. After he was freed from his captivity, we asked him if he wished to be with us, or go with his father who is also here.[17] He said that he wanted to be with us only. In order to make sure that he retains the language and does not forget it, I am debating whether to bring along with me an Indian boy,[18] who has come along with Alonso, leaving his parents and home to be with him. Thus he might train in the language, unless, meanwhile, Your Paternity or Father Provincial order otherwise.

[10] For my part, I can say to Your Paternity that if it is judged in Our Lord that this enterprise ought to be begun, and if you desire that the task should fall to me, I would consider myself most fortunate. I fear that there will be the same difficulty among these people in making conversions, as has been found in the places where we have been. If there is to be some fruit here, it will have to be by wearing them away like water on a rock.[19] I believe there are fewer inconveniences and difficulties than in regions where I have already stayed. First, because the country is so cold, there will be no reason for long absences away from their huts in winter. Also it appears to me that there are more tribes and more natives in this region than in others where I have dwelt.

[11] When this boy was with Don Luis, following the death of the others, Don Luis left the vestments and books and everything else locked up in chests. On returning, they took up their share of spoils. He said that a brother of Don Luis is going around clothed in the Mass vestments and altar cloths. The captured chief told me that Don Luis gave the silver chalice to an important chief in the interior. The paten was given to one of those Indians we captured, while the other images were thrown away. Among other things there was a large crucifix in a

chest; some Indians told this boy that they do not dare approach that chest since three Indians who wanted to see what was in it, fell down dead on the spot. So they keep it closed and protected. About the books, Alonso said that after pulling off the clasps, the Indians tore them all up and threw them away.

[12] If I should learn any other details, whether those sent out by the Governor bring in Don Luis and his companions, I will write them from Havana to Your Paternity, when, in Our Lord's pleasure, we arrive there.

[13] As I can not think of anything else to write, I close. I commend myself to the holy sacrifices and prayers of Your Paternity and of the Fathers and Brothers of the Company. God Our Lord grant Your Paternity His Holy Spirit for all success in fulfilling His Divine Will. From the Bay of the Mother of God in Florida, August 28, 1572.

Your Paternity's unworthy son and servant in Our Lord,

JUAN ROGEL

NOTES

1. The autograph is in the Archives of the Province of Toledo of the Society of Jesus, AT 1157 (2) ff. 496-497. The text is in *MAF* 523-530. The same letter except for minor differences in spelling is found in the Appendix of the second volume of Antonio Astrain's *Historia de la Compañía de Jesús en la Asistencia de España*, 2: 640-644. The Astrain text was translated by E. I. Devitt, S.J., in his article "Axacan: The Martyrs of the Rappahannock," 19 *ACHS* (1908) 1-17. Since Francis Borgia died on October 1, 1572, he probably never received this letter.

2. Rogel had not received new orders from Sánchez or Sedeño, so that he evidently felt bound by Segura's request for supplies made known in the letter brought back by the pilot. See the Carrera Relation below, para. 49.

3. The term "Brother" is given to those members of the Society of Jesus who are not ordained priests but serve in some temporal capacity.

4. Father Pedro Sánchez was the provincial of the Jesuits in New Spain and the actual superior of the Florida Mission. In the absence of Father Segura, Antonio Sedeño was acting vice-provincial of Florida. Both were responsible to Father Sánchez.

5. The news of the Spanish ships' arrival would have traveled fast up the peninsula. Therefore it is not certain that the Indians that soon appeared on the banks were from nearby villages. Upon the return of Smith from his exploration of the Chesapeake, Russell and Todkill reported that rumor of their meeting with the Masawomeekes "went faster up the river than our barge" (1 Arber 114). The behavior of the Indians in coming aboard resembles Smith's experience with the Iroquois in the upper Chesapeake: "At last, they sent two of their company unarmed in a Canowe: the rest all followed to second them, if need required. These two

being but each presented with a bell, brought aborde all their fellowes; presenting the captain with venison, beares flesh, fish, bowes, arrows, clubs, targets, and beare-skins" (1 Arber 117).

6. The extreme limits of the width of the stream are suggested by the arrow incident. Smith in his "Voyages and Discoveries" (1 Arber 70) estimates their range at 40 yards for accurate shooting, 120 yards at most for random shooting. Since the boat presumably kept to the middle of the current, the stream could not have exceeded 240 yards in width at that point and was probably considerably less.

7. There were five streams on the north side of the James with wide mouths: Powhatan Creek, College Creek, Skiffe's Creek, Warwick Creek, and Deep Creek. The second is preferred for the reasons given in Part III.

8. Kecoughtan was about two days' journey (30 miles) from College Creek. In the excitement the distance was probably covered in one day.

9. The chief did not give the boy to Rogel's exploring party, but sent him directly to the Governor's ship.

10. The strategy employed is typical of the Virginia Algonkin. Smith's barge was attacked on the Rappahannock by Indians advancing under cover of tree branches, reminiscent of Shakespeare's Birnam Wood. Each boat could have concealed as many as forty men. However, it is possible that the mercurial Indians were in good faith. Archer relates that Indians followed his party along the shore of the upper James for 6 miles with dried oysters which they offered in trade (1 Arber xlii). We cannot determine from the sale of oysters how far inland was the narrow stream entered by the Spanish. Oyster beds are found in both salt and brackish water, but not above College Creek.

11. The setting sail suggests emergence into the estuary of the James, where sails became more practical than oars.

12. It may be significant to note here that the Indians were apparently unafraid of the Spanish ships and arquebuses, probably from lack of experience with them. Perhaps memories of this experience lasted long enough to cause Wingfield to say in "A Discourse of Virginia," "They feare much our shipps" (1 Arber lxxvi).

13. It was customary in the early days of the Society of Jesus to retain the title of Master, Doctor, or Licentiate if one possessed the academic degree. Father Segura was a Master of Theology.

14. Brother Juan Baptista Menéndez (or Méndez).

15. We do not know exactly the method of burial. If Don Luis followed his tribal instincts, he would probably have performed the task as Smith describes it in the case of ordinary burials: "... they digge a deep hole in the earth with sharpe stakes; and the corp[s]es being lapped in skins and mats with their iewels, they lay them vpon sticks in the ground, and so couer them with earth" (1 Arber 75).

16. It is reasonable to suppose that Alonso would have made his way toward the entrance of the bay, hoping against hope for a rescue by a Spanish ship, trying to put distance between himself and Don Luis' associates. Thus in any supposition

concerning the site of the Jesuit settlement, it is feasible that Alonso would have ended up among the peaceful Kecoughtan near Point Comfort. Smith too found corn at Kecoughtan in his necessity. Don Luis may have employed Alonso to carry extra baskets of corn, while Alonso seized the occasion to break away from Don Luis.

17. In the margin Rogel added: "En esto me e engañado, porque se a estragado mucho después que a vivedo solo entre indios, ni quiere estar con nosotros, no conviene." ("I was deceived in this respect, since he has been quite spoiled after living alone with the Indians. He does not want to be one of us, he is not suitable.")

18. In the margin was written: "No lo traxe conmigo, porque lo lleve el Adelantado a España." ("I have not taken him with me because the Governor is taking him to Spain.")

19. Father Rogel's remarks on the need of force and patience recall the statement of Smith: "It is more easy to ciuilize them by conquest then faire meanes; for the one may be had at once, but their ciuilizing will require a long time and much industry." That Rogel's methods would have been not only firm but fair is quite clear from his Florida letters.

Relación de Juan Rogel

1607-1611

[8] Y bolvió a España, donde topó con un indio christiano, natural de la Florida, que, pasando por ella unos frailes dominicos, le llevaron a Mexico y allí recivió el baptismo, siendo su padrino don Luis de Velasco, padre del que aora es virrey. Y así el indio se llamava Don Luis, hijo de un caciquillo de la Florida. Trúxolo de España el Adelantado y era muy ladino; entrególo en la Havana al Padre Baptista porque publicava que era hijo de un grande cacique, y como a tal, nuestro Rey en España le mandava dar ración y lo vistió; y sabía tanto, que confesava y comulgava, y assí pareció a propósito para que el Padre Viceprovincial le llevase por intérprete, y él entendió llevava la ayuda que San Pablo en Timotheo, tomando tan a pechos la empresa que no quiso fiarla de otro; y consultándolo en Santa Elena, donde estava el Padre Rogel y se halló el Padre Sedeño, nunca quiso poner en consulta quién avía de ir con Don Luis; y aunque se ofrecieron entrambos a ello, como personas de experiencia en aquella tierra, no los admitió ni a ninguno por compañero, antes se determinó de llevar consigo al Padre Quirós y al Hermano Gabriel Gómez, recién llegados de España, y al Hermano Sancho de Çavallos, que también era visoño, y a los Hermanos Joan Baptista, Pedro de Linares, Cristóval Redondo, Gabriel de Solís y otros mancebos que pedían la Compañía. Todos los quales fueron con don Luis a la converssión de aquella tierra de la Florida y en entrando en la provincia de Ajacán, don Luis maleó luego y se apartó de los Padres entregándose a mugeres, quedando los Padres y Hermanos solos; porque el mesmo día que llegaron al puerto, mandó el Padre Viceprovincial al piloto, que luego en desembarcando lo que llevavan, saliesen del puerto y se bolviesen a la Havana. Y assí se hizo, que fue la causa de su muerte; porque si se detuvieran algunos días con el barco, con la experiencia que en los primeros sacaron de la mala disposición que hallavan y el poco fructo que se prometían, se bolvieran a Santa Elena a esperar mejor ocassión. Pero viéndose desamparados y sin otro recurso, hizieron una casilla donde alvergarse y decir missa, estando solos, sin ayuda alguna, padeciendo muchíssima hambre e incomodidades. De manera que para sustentarse

ivan algunas leguas a los montes a buscar nísperos y desta manera se sustentaron seis o siete meses. Quando Don Luis se apartó dellos, fuese a un pueblecillo que era de un pariente suyo, que estaría como diez leguas de donde hizieron assiento los Padres. Y el Padre Baptista, como desseava començar a tratar de la conversión, y Don Luis no venía y no tenían otra guía ni medio para hazerlo, embió adonde estava al Padre Quirós a rogarle que viniese; y como el desdichado se avía estragado en todo, respondióle al Padre Quirós que se fuese que luego iría tras él; y a la noche lo cumplió; porque llevando gente consigo, lo mató antes que llegase donde estava el Padre Baptista y desde allí se fue el indio adonde estavan los nuestros, y halló al Viceprovincial en la cama, indispuesto y en oración, que parece los disponía Nuestro Señor para aquel trançe; porque la víspera de la Purificación de Nuestra Señora confesaron todos generalmente y comulgaron con mucha ternura; que esto se supo de un muchacho, hijo de un vezino de Santa Elena que le avía llevado el Padre Viceprovincial consigo para que les ayudase a missa, el qual se llamava Alonso y por su poca edad no le mataron los indios o por ordenarlo Dios assí. Este dio noticia del suceso y dixo que, aviendo llegado Don Luis con su gente armados de macanas y botadores (que son unos palos largos a manera de hastas de lança) saludó al Padre Baptista que estava como avemos referido, y que alçar la macana y saludarle fue todo uno, de manera dándole saludes, le quitó la vida; y a todos los demás dieron la muerte; y saliendo en busca del Hermano Sancho de Çavallos, que en esta sazón avía ido al monte por leña, le mataron en él; y assí escapó solamente Alonsico, del qual se advierte que tuvo grande desseo de morir juntamente con los Padres y estorvóselo un hermano del Don Luis que lo encerró y escondió en una casa, saliendo a buscar favor quando matavan a los Padres. Y después de sosegados, el don Luis llamó a Alonsico y le dixo que enseñase a los indios cómo avían de enterrar los cuerpos de los Padres, como lo acostumbravan los cristianos. Y assí hicieron una sepultura en la capilla donde decían missa y los enterraron en ella.

[9] El modo cómo se supo con certidumbre la muerte del Padre Viceprovincial y sus compañeros fue por aver dexado encargado antes de su partida al Padre Joan Rogel, que quedava en Santa Elena, viniese a la Havana después de algunos días a solicitar con el Governador y officiales que se les embiase algún bastimento. Y el Padre se partió a esto y hizo quanto le fue posible, pero por no aver más de un piloto que supiese aquel puerto de Ajacán donde estavan los Padres [77] y a este le tenían occupado en otras cosas, no se pudo hazer este socorro hasta que pasó año y medio;

y entonces se despachó con este piloto (llamado Vicente Gonçález) al Hermano Salcedo que llevava el más bastimento que pudo juntar el Padre Joan Rogel. Llegados a dar fondo en el puerto, recelosos de algún mal suceso, no quisieron saltar en tierra hasta que viniese alguno de la Compañía o tuviesen noticia dellos. El don Luisillo, según se entendió después, desseava mucho que desembarcasen para cogerlos y matarlos; y viendo cómo reparavan y aguardavan hasta ver algunos de los Padres, usaron los indios deste ardid, que fue tomar las ropas de los muertos y vestírselas y pasearse por la playa; y los demás davan voces que allí estavan los Padres que viniesen; pero confirmándose más en su sospecha nunca quisieron salir a tierra. Estando en esto, vinieron al barco de la nao, a los quales prendieron, y levando las anclas dieron vela y se bolvieron con ellos la buelta de la Havana, aunque entrando por la canal de Bahama, como venían muy cerca de tierra, el uno dellos se arrojó al agua y no se supo más dél; y el otro truxeron en prissión hasta la Havana, y le tuvieron en la Compañía, para bolver después con él a certificarse del suceso (que no lo confesaron quando los prendieron en el navío) ni el que quedó quiso descubrir la verdad.

[10] Visto que no se sabía de cierto el suceso de los Padres, y porque hazía viaxe entonces el Adelantado a España, parecióle pasar por la Florida y llevar en su compañía al Padre Rogel y al Hermano Carrera y al Hermano Francisco de Villarreal. Llegados al puerto, saltó en tierra el Adelantado con acompañamiento de soldados, con grande deseo de enterarse del suceso y castigar los culpados; y aviendo prendido algunos indios de los que avían ayudado a Don Luis y enterádose del caso, trató de hazer justicia de ocho o diez; los quales por medio de Alonsico, que servía de intérprete, fueron catequiçados y bautiçados del Padre Rogel, y los ahorcaron en el barco donde iva el Adelantado, colgándolos de las entenas. Hecha esta justicia, el Padre Rogel rogó al Adelantado le diese algunos soldados de guarda para entrar adonde estava la sepultura de los Padres para traer sus cuerpos y recoger sus vestiduras; pero, por estar ya muy de partida el Adelantado y entrar el invierno, no se pudo detener ni tuvo efecto este desseo; pero prometió que bolvería dentro de un año y que él iría por ellos. Y en esta ocassión se supo de un milagro que sucedió con los ornamentos de los Padres quando los mataron; y fue que un indio, con la cobdicia de los despojos, fue a una caxa en que tenían los Padres los ornamentos de decir missa, y dentro de la caxa estava un Christo de bulto; y queriendo abrirla o quebrarla para sacar lo que estava dentro, el indio cayó allí muerto; y luego otro quiso descerrajarla y le sucedió lo proprio; y otro

que, sin escarmiento de aquellos dos desventurados, quiso intentar lo que
ellos, les acompañó en la muerte: entonces no osaron llegar más a la caxa,
sino se guarda hasta oy día con mucha veneración. Este suceso lo contó
Alonsico y después unos soldados viejos que vinieron de la Florida y avían
estado en Ajacán, dixeron al Padre Rogel que tienen los indios guardada la
caxa sin osar tocar a ella hasta aora. Visto que no se podía hazer otra cosa,
se bolvieron el Padre Joan Rogel y los Hermanos Villarreal y Carrera a la
Havana, donde hallaron al Padre Sedeño.

RELATION OF JUAN ROGEL [1]

Between 1607 and 1611, as edited by Juan Sánchez Vaquero, S.J.

EXCERPTS

[8] Menéndez returned from Spain where he had chanced upon a Christian Indian, a native of Florida. Some Dominican friars traveling through
that country had brought him to Mexico, where he was baptized under
the sponsorship of Don Luis Velasco, the father of the present viceroy.
Thus the Indian son of a petty chief of Florida was called Don Luis. The
Governor brought him back from Spain and he was very crafty, for
when he was brought to Father Baptista in Havana, he gave out that he
was the son of a great chief, and as such our King in Spain had ordered
him an allowance and clothing. He was well instructed so that he con-
fessed and received communion and thus it seemed wise that the vice-
provincial should take him on as an interpreter, and that he should believe that Don Luis afforded the help which Timothy gave to Saint
Paul.[2] Taking the enterprise to heart, Father did not wish to entrust it
to any other. Having called a meeting in Santa Elena where Father
Rogel and Father Sedeño were, he never wished to discuss who was to
go with Don Luis, and although both Fathers offered to do so as persons
experienced in that region, he did not admit them as companions in any
respect. Instead, he had decided beforehand to take with him Father
Quirós and Brother Gabriel Gómez, both recently arrived from Spain,
and Brother Sancho de Zaballos, who was still a novice, and Brother
Juan Baptista, Pedro de Linares, Cristóbal Redondo, Gabriel de Solís
and other young men who sought to enter the Company. All these
went with Don Luis for the conversion of that region of Florida. On

entering the province of Ajacán, Don Luis presently fell into evil ways and leaving the Fathers and Brothers alone, he took up with women. On the day they arrived at the place the vice-provincial told the pilot that after disembarking the cargo, he should sail from the place and return to Havana. Thus was brought about what came to be the cause of their death; for if they had remained a few days with the ship, they would have acquired an early experience of the bad dispositions there and the promise of little fruit, and might have returned to Santa Elena to wait for a better opportunity. But, seeing themselves abandoned and without other resource, they built a small hut where they might have shelter and say Mass, alone, without any help, enduring great hunger and inconvenience. In order to sustain themselves they went some leagues into the woods looking for persimmons and thus they fed themselves for six or seven months. When Don Luis left them he stayed in a small village which belonged to a relative. This lay about 10 leagues from where the Fathers were. As Father Baptista wished to start preaching and Don Luis did not come and they had no other guide or means of speaking, Father Quirós [3] was sent to where the Indian lived to ask him to come back. That unfortunate man was now completely corrupted; he told Father Quirós to go and he would follow after. At night he carried out his plan. For, taking his tribe with him, Don Luis slew Father Quirós before he reached the place where Father Baptista stayed. Then the Indian went on to where Ours were living, and he discovered the vice-provincial in bed, sick and praying. It seemed that Our Lord disposed them for that crisis, because, on the eve of Our Lady's Purification, all made a general confession and communicated with great devotion. This was learned from a boy, the son of a colonist of Santa Elena, whom the vice-provincial took along to serve Mass. His name was Alonso, and because of his youth or by God's design, the Indians did not kill him. This boy described the event. He said that when Don Luis arrived with his tribe armed with clubs and lances, he greeted Father Baptista who was as we described. Raising his club and giving his greeting were really one gesture, and so in wishing him well, he killed him. All the rest were murdered also. Then going out to search for Brother Sancho de Zaballos, who at that time had gone to the forest to get firewood, they slew him there. Alonso alone escaped. It is known about him that he had a deep desire to die with the Fathers, but a brother of Don Luis stopped him by hiding him in a house and keeping him there. He was trying to do a kindness, when they were murdering the Fathers. After the Indians were sated, Don Luis summoned Alonso and told him to show the Indians how to bury the bodies of the Fathers as was the custom of the Christians. And so they dug a grave in the chapel where Mass had been said and there they were buried.

[9] The manner in which the death of the vice-provincial and his companions was known with certainty was this. Previous to their sailing, Father Rogel, who remained at Santa Elena, was ordered to go to Havana in a few days and beg the Governor and the officials to send some aid. Father Rogel went to do this and did the best he could, but because there was only one pilot who knew the port in Ajacán, where the Fathers were, and the officials kept that one engaged in other duties, it was impossible to bring help until a year and a half went by;[4] Brother Salcedo, who brought as much provisions as Father Rogel could gather, was sent back with the pilot, whose name was Vicente Gonzales. When they arrived and dropped anchor in the harbor, they feared some evil event, and did not want to land on the shore until some of the Company appeared or they had news of them. As was later learned, Don Luis was very eager for them to land so as to overwhelm and kill them. The Indians, noticing that they were wary and watching for the appearance of the Fathers, used this stratagem. Taking the robes of the dead Fathers, they put them on and walked along the shore, and the rest of the Indians called out that there were the Fathers and to come ashore. More confirmed in their doubts, those on the ship decided not to land at all. Meanwhile, some Indians came from the shore to the ship. These were seized and then raising anchor and spreading sail, they started to return with them to Havana. However, when passing through the strait of Bahama, they came quite close to the land, and one of the Indians dove into the water and nothing more was known of him. They took the other in chains to Havana. They kept him under bonds at the house of the Society in order to return with him to make certain of the facts (for the Indians did not admit anything when they were in the boat) and the one remaining did not divulge the truth.

[10] As the fate of the Fathers was still not known with certainty, and the Governor was returning to Spain, he decided to travel by way of Florida and bring in his company Father Rogel and Brother Carrera and Brother Villareal. Arriving at the port, the Governor landed with a band of soldiers, and he was most anxious to know the fate of the Fathers and punish the culprits.[5] After seizing some of those Indians who had aided Don Luis and learning the facts, he decided to punish eight or

nine of them. Father Rogel, with the assistance of Alonso, who served as interpreter, catechized and baptized them, after which they were hanged from the rigging of the Governor's ship. After justice was done, Father Rogel asked the Governor to order some soldiers of his guard to go to the burial site of the Fathers and remove the bodies and gather up the vestments, but since the Governor was on the point of leaving and winter approached, he could not remain to fulfill this wish but he promised to return within a year and come for the bodies.[6] On this occasion we learned of a miracle which happened with the sacred vestments of the Fathers when they were killed. There was a certain Indian, eager for spoil, who came upon a box where the Fathers kept the sacred vestments for saying Mass, and in it was a crucifix. When he wanted to break and smash the box so as to drag out its contents, he dropped dead on the spot. Then another Indian tried to force it open and had a similar fate. A third Indian, who had no warning from these two unfortunates, sought to break open the chest also, but he was a companion in their death. As a result the rest dare not approach the box any more. After this the Indians kept it carefully and would not dare touch it. Little Alonso and also some old soldiers[7] who came from Florida and had been in Ajacán told this to Father Rogel. Seeing that they could do nothing else, Father Juan Rogel and Brothers Villareal and Carrera returned to Havana, where they found Father Sedeño.

NOTES

1. The autograph of this relation is lost and the text reproduced here is from a manuscript that paraphrases Rogel's narrative, which is in the Archives of the Society of Jesus in Rome, *Mex.* 19, ff. 76-77. This text is printed in *MAF* 606-616. This version was prepared by Father Juan Sánchez Vaquero for his history entitled: "Fundación de la Compañía de Jesús en Nueva España, 1571-1580," which was never printed. In 1927 a typed version by Father F. Ayuso was prepared but never published. For more details see R. Griffin, "Rogel, Padre of the Ports," 30 *Mid-America* (1948) 15, note 36.

Father Sánchez Vaquero was born in Puertollano, Spain, in 1548 and after taking the degree of Bachelor of Philosophy, he entered the Society in 1568. Sent to New Spain in 1572, he was ordained a year later and then began a distinguished career as rector, preacher, and teacher. He lived with Juan Rogel for some years. In 1598 the Father-General, Claudio Aquaviva, ordered the composition of histories of the missions, and this may be classified as one of the relations written after this ordinance. (For the Latin text of this decree, see *MAF* 603, note 87). There is a serious question whether this version is exact, but it has the merits of good style and contemporaneity with Rogel. An estimate of Sánchez' fidelity must be based on these few lines from his history. "Entre otras cosas que el Padre Francisco de Borja ordenó para el buen govierno de la nueva provincia de México fue una que los sugetos que avían quedado de los nuestros de la missión de la Florida estuviesen sugetos al Provincial de México y se juntasen a esta provincia... *cuya relación escrita por el Padre Juan Rogel es la que se sigue...*" (see *MAF* 605). Yet a century and a half later, Francisco Alegre, in his *Historia de la Compañía de Jesús en Nueva España*, published in three volumes after his death in 1841, recounts the incident of the crucifix in the chest (see this Relation, para. 10) with details different from the Sánchez version. Yet he writes that he follows the original: "con las *palabras mismas* del Padre Juan Rogel, que de su letra y pluma se halla entre los papeles del archivo de esta casa" (1 Alegre 32). Alegre, who was living before the suppression of the Society of Jesus, probably saw the original of Rogel's Relation that was lost in the confiscations of Charles III. There is no way of knowing who has deviated from the original; probably both have been guilty in some respect.

There are some clues as to the date of the composition of this Relation. In para. 8, we read that Don Luis was baptized under the sponsorship of Don Luis de Velasco, "the father of the present Viceroy." Luis de Velasco II was Viceroy on two occasions, 1590-1595 and then again in 1607-1611. There are two reasons for dating the Relation during the second term of Velasco. First, the ordinance of 1598 of Aquaviva probably occasioned its composition. Secondly, in the Alegre version of the Rogel relation, there are the words: "even today after forty years." Since the Ajacán deaths occur in 1571, the date of 1611 for this Relation becomes likely.

2. See Romans, 16:21 and I Corinthians 4:7.

3. From other accounts we know two others were along: Gabriel de Solís and Juan Baptista Méndez. See Rogel's August Letter above, para. 6.

4. It was a half year rather than a year and a half later when Salcedo and Gonzales sailed to Ajacán, for Carrera speaks of the ship's being sent with all dispatch, and Sedeño describes the results in his February, 1572, Letter (25 *HRS* 116-126).

5. Rogel here may be referring to the soldiers under Velasco who went ashore at the harbor, as described by Oré.

6. The time that would be consumed in retrieving the bodies is another confirmation that the burial site must have been a considerable distance inland from the port. The Governor's nephew, Pedro Menéndez Marqués, returned to Ajacán the following year, but we have no indication that he looked for the bodies.

7. Perhaps, as the Alegre version implies, these soldiers were in Ajacán as late as 1611, but we have no way of knowing who they were or whether they were merely spinning yarns.

RELACIÓN DE JUAN DE LA CARRERA
Marzo 1, 1600

[35] Poco antes desto que acavo de referir, llegó a la Habana un indio natural de la Florida, que se dezía don Luis de Velasco, que por ser principal y averse criado en México con los frailes de Sancto Domingo, y bautizados allí por mano del virrey don Luis de Velasco, siendo a lo que creo su padrino, le dio su nombre. Este se avía criado en la corte del rey Felipe 2°, y reescevido dél muchas mercedes: finalmente le inbió el Rey a su tierra, que dezía ser allá gran señor, con unos frailes Dominicos, los quales le bolvieron a traer no sé por qué causa, y viéndose desechado de los frailes, vino a tratar este negocio con el adelantado Pero Meléndez; el qual por lo que el indio le dixo de las grandezas de su tierra, y por la noticia que el Adelantado ya tenía de atrás de aver por su tierra otra mar y otra nabegación de grande importancia para el descubrimiento de grandes reinos como es la Tartaria y otros que con ella confinan, le dio oídos al indio el Adelantado, y lo trató con el Padre Vautista, que estava a la sazón con el Adelantado en la Habana, adonde todo esto se tratava. Concertáronse los dos fácilmente, y sin más consulta, entendiendo el Padre que Dios le avía deparado, como al Padre maestro Francisco Xavier, otro Paulo de Sancta Fe y otro Japón mayor y de más importancia, con los deseos que él tenía de dilatar nuestra sancta fe católica, se preparó para la jornada haziéndose navío a propóssito, y cargándolo de todas las cossas necesarias, no sólo para la nabegación sino tanbién para poblar aquella tierra de jénero de animales y aves y otras muchas cossas; y con todo aparato se hizo a la vela de la Havana por el mes de julio o agosto de 1571, a mi quenta, y llegó con buen tiempo a la puncta de Sancta Elena, en la Florida, adonde todos nosotros nos juntamos, y yo residía a la sazón.

[36] Con el amor grande que nos teníamos, y familiaridad con que nos tratávamos, me dio parte de todos sus dissingnos y traças y pretensiones, que en esta jornada tenía asentados, que todos cierto eran de loar en él, por salir de un pecho cristiano, sancto y sinzero que él tenía: loéle mucho esto: mas púsele dificultad en la esecución, diziendo que aquel indio no

me contentava; y conforme a lo que me avía dicho, entendía no le tratava
verdad, que le suplicava y pedía con encarescimiento lo mirase mejor y
comunicase con todos los Padres que allí estavan, y conforme a eso viese
lo que más conbenía; porque querer irse el superior a partes tan remotas
y apartadas, y desampararlo todo, fiado de un indio, sin arrimo de soldados
ni otra jente más que la suya, no lo tenía por tan conbeniente como ir
otro Padre a la ligera, y ver y descubrir la tierra, y ver lo que avía en
todo, e informarse si el indio mentía o dezía verdad: que esto me parescía.
Junctos todos los Padres llegáronse a este parescer, si no fue el Padre
Quirós que avía de ir con él, y acavaba de llegar d'España sin esperiencia
alguna: con todo eso se resolvió a ir, como lo tenía tratado, y quedarse
allá solo con los suyos, porque no ubiese quien diese mal exemplo a los
indios. Los quales eran él y el Padre Quirós y el Hermano Linares y el
Hermano Zavallos y el Hermano Graviel Gómez y tres novicios, el uno se
llamaba Juan Baptista Méndez y Graviel de Solís y Cristóval Redondo,
y un muchacho que se dezia Alonso. [156] Esto le pareció ser más conforme a la voluntad de nuestro Señor, que él en todo deseava cumplir, y
con esta resolución salió muy firme en su buem propósito.

[37] Vino luego a mí el Padre Quirós su compañero, docto y de muy
buenas prendas, con una memoria larga en que me pedía le diese lo más y
mejor que a mi cargo tenía de todo, especial de las cossas de la iglesia. Yo
quando vi la memoria, me turbé un poco, y le dixe: Mi Padre, yo de muy
buena gana le daría todo lo que me pide, aunque entiendo que todo se a
de perder, si no entendiese por más cierto que todo esto a de ser mucha
parte para la muerte de todas los que allá ban. V. R. me haga caridad de
dezir esto de mi parte al Padre Viceprovincial, y si con todo esto quisiere
que le dé lo que pide, en buena ora, aquí está todo a su mandado. Vino
con la respuesta le diese todo lo que pidiese: yo lo cumplí y tanbién se
cumplió lo que yo le dixe temía. Díle quanto el Padre Quirós me pidió, que
era lo más y mejor y más rico que yo tenía, de cosas de iglesia, como son
cálizes y custodias, hornamentos, y las demás cossas que no eran de iglesia,
y con esto se acavaron de aviar para su jornada.

[38] Viniéronse a despedir de mí los Hermanos novicios que él llevaba,
con mucha ternura y lágrimas; y yo me enternecí con ellos no poco,
porque los amaba tiernamente, como quien los avía criado; y diziéndome
ellos que iban a la muerte, les dixe que fuesen consolados adonde la sancta
obediencia los inbiaba, que Dios sería con ellos, y dél rescivirían el pago y
galardón de sus travajos, que gran bien era morir por Dios y por la
obediencia. Y la mesma ternura y dolor me causó la despedida del Padre

Viceprovincial y los demás compañeros, que no avía de ber más en esta vida, acompañada de muchas lágrimas que todos derramamos.

[39] Llegaron a aquella tierra deste indio, que se dezía don Luis, llamada Jacán, por el mes de agosto, con grandes esperanças que por medio dél se avían de hazer grandes cossas en aquella tierra y en todo lo demás que se esperaba descubrir, por ser el indio principal y muy discreto en sus razones. Desenbarcaron estos nuestros Padres y Hermanos en un hermoso y grande puerto de aquella tierra, que los que an nabegado mucho, y lo an visto, dizen ser el mejor y mayor puerto del mundo: y así, si bien me acuerdo, me lo dixo el piloto. Llámase la baía de la Madre de Dios, y en ella ay muchos puertos muy fondables, uno mejor que otro. Este puerto vi yo, quando fui con el Adelantado, como después diré, y paresció me era gran cossa; porque, según me paresció y entendí, ternía de voca como tres leguas y de ancho y de largo cerca de treinta. Al fin dél se dize comiença la otra mar y nabegación de tanta importancia como queda apunctado, a lo qual el Adelantado estava inclinado a descubrir, y entiendo lo hiziera si la vida le durara. A la orilla deste puerto ay mucho número de jente poblada y tanbién la tierra adenctro.

[40] Desenbarcado en este tan hermoso puerto todo su hacto, y resuelto de quedarse sin soldados ni gente de guardia, más que los nuestros Padres y Hermanos, fiados de Dios y de su anparo y proteción y ayuda de su Madre Santísima y de los sanctos y ángeles del cielo, y puesto en manos deste indio en quien confiaba, que cierto, si él fuera el que devía, mucho fructo se hiziera por su medio; mas fue muy al revés, por ser muy muy diferente de lo que mostró, y el Padre Baptista tenía creído dél. Despidió el Padre el navío y toda la jente con él, y quedóse solo con los suyos, los quales pasaron mucho travajo y fatiga en llevar todo el hacto al pueblo de un hermano de don Luis, ansí por estar lexos del puerto, como por los malos caminos y pantanos que avía en todo él.

[41] [156v] Viéndose este mal indio señor del Padre y de sus hijos y de todo lo que llebaban, sin tener a quien temer, por estar entre sus hermanos y parientes y amigos, y apartados de la mar muchas leguas, para que así como en tierra no tenían quien les favoresciese, así tanbién por la mar les fuese dificultoso el socorro y aunque a los principios, a lo que e entendido, no mostró luego su mal ánimo que tenía, y los Padres hizieron su pobre casita y capilla y lo demás, y començaron a tratar dél el oficio de la predicación del sancto Evangelio a que abían benido, este mal indio y otro Judas, començó a darse a vicios y a pecados públicamente sin temor de Dios y de las jentes, y apartarse de su conbersación y trato. Y tratándose

él más como jentil, que como cristiano en su trato, traje y costumbres, y yéndose a vivir a las tierras de un cacique, tío suyo, que estava vien apartado de los nuestros, adonde se dio más desenfrenadamente y sin rienda a todo linaje de pecados, casándose con muchas mugeres al uso gentílico, sin bastar con él razón alguna ni los muchos y diversos medios que el Padre Baptista tomó para apartarle de su mala vida y atraerlo a sí.

[42] Vivieron estos bendictos religiossos, nuestros Padres y Hermanos, en aquella tierra, a mi quenta, dende fin de agosto hasta la Purificación de Nuestra Señora en un continuo llanto y sobresalto, esperando cada día la muerte, estando en manos deste indio y de los deudos y hermanos suyos el dársela quándo y del modo que quisiesen dársela, sin ressistencia alguna; y así fueron grandes los aparejos y preparaciones que el Padre Viceprovincial hizo para aparejarse y disponerse él y los suyos para la muerte que tenían por cierta. Y así lo primero que hizo fue que todos se diesen a más larga y continua oración, preparándose con continuas pláticas y exortaciones que a menudo les hazia, y con otros buenos exercicios espirituales; hizo que todos se confesasen generalmente de su vida passada. La penitencia era mayor y la austinencia, aunque no quisieran, la avían de tener muy grande, porque les faltó el mantenimiento que avían llevado, y así les era forzoso sustentarse de raízes y yervas del campo, como los indios, que faltándoles de ordinario por equel tiempo el mantenimiento, se sustentan de lo propio.

[43] Afligido el buen Padre más del travajo y fatiga de sus hijos que del suyo propio, como era de suyo conpasibo, piadoso y manso y de mucha caridad, como los vía padescer tanto, enternecíasele el coraçón sobre ellos; y así paresciéndole a él que sería remedio de sus males procurar de reduzir a su amistad aquel indio rebelde y malo, determinó inbiar al Padre Quirós y dos Hermanos con él para que se lo procurasen con buen término traer, y de camino algún mantenimiento y algunas esteras para que les fuese alguna defensa para el mucho frío que padescían, por scr la tierra fría y la casa en que bivían tan pobre y miserable que el mayor abrigo della eran ojas de palma que servían de techo y de paredes, como yo vien sé por esperiencia, pues bibí muchos tiempos en semejantes casas con harta fatiga de fríos, aun en tierras no tan frías.

[44] Hizieron este Padre y Hermanos su enbaxada, con cuidado, a la tierra del tío del don Luis, adonde se avía retirado, como está dicho; y viniendo ya seguros con sus cargas a qüestas de lo dicho, ele aquí a do viene el traidor con armas y compañeros para los matar, saliéndoles de repente al camino con sus arcos y flechas; y como así de improviso se

vieron acometer, bolvióse al don Luis el Padre Quirós y díxole que qué
era aquello que querían hazer y por qué los mataban; y començóles a
predicar el buen Padre; mas las respuestas eran flechaços, y fueron tantos
los golpes y heridas que les dieron, que mataron al Padre Quirós y al
Hermano Graviel de Solís. El Hermano Baptista Méndez mal herido
se huyó al monte corriendo sangre, y allí se defendió aquella noche, mas
a la mañana fue hallado y muerto, y los cuerpos fueron quemados de los
matadores y robados sus bestidos y lo que llebaban.

[45] El buen Padre Baptista, que con deseo esperaba los compañeros y el
buen suceso de su enbaxada, dolíase mucho de su tardança y temíase de
algún mal suceso, y a menudo lo dezía a sus compañeros con gran fatiga de
su coraçón y alma. El día mesmo, a lo que entiendo, de nuestra Señora de
la Candelaria por la mañana, estando en su oración, antes de amanescer,
él y todos sus hijos, como era su costumbre, oye llamar a la puerta y
gran ruido de jente de la qual estava cercada toda la casa con su capitán
y adalid don Luis, que los capitaneaba. Y dízenles que todas las hachas y
machetes [157] con que cortaban leña se las prestasen, porque iban al
monte por leña. El buen Padre, que no pensaba en tal maldad como los
indios le tramaban, innocente de su mal intento, dixo que se lo diesen
todo, y que dos de los de casa fuesen con ellos al monte, y truxesen sus
cargas de leña para calentarse. Viéndose el traidor de don Luis señor de
las armas con que a su parescer se podían defender dellos, usaron de la
traça que se sigue.

Cercaron la casa en derredor de indios flecheros, para que si alguno
saliese, fuese luego muerto de ellos. El don Luis vestido con las ropas
que avía robado al Padre Quirós en el camino, quando lo mató, entró
dentro con los que le paresció con aquellas hachas y machetes, que tenía
en su poder, y repartiólos de tal modo, que unos acudiesen a uno y otros
a otro, de modo que todos a un mesmo tiempo fuesen muertos sin que
se pudiesen ayudar unos a otros; y el malo y perverso de don Luis
acometió primero al Padre Baptista para darle el pago de tanto regalo
como con él el Padre avía usado, que fue mucho; y quando le bio entrar y le reconosció, entendiendo que benía a otra cossa diferente, dizen
que le dixo con mucha alegría de verlo: « Seáis muy bien benido, don
Luis »; por cierto antes que prosiguiese más adelante, le respondió con
la hacha que traía, y le dio muchas heridas en la caveça, en los braços
y en las piernas y en todo su cuerpo, que quedó gravemente herido
y maltratado: y mientras esto hazía el capitán con su Padre, se ocupavan
los demás matadores con los demás por el mesmo tenor, como lobos

con corderos mansos, que a nadie hazían mal sino a todos vien. Llegaron
a la cozina adonde hallaron a un Hermano que se dezía Cristóval
Redondo que en alma y cuerpo y condizión y boz era más todo de
ángel que de honbre, y como se vio acometer de aquellos lobos aquel
manso cordero, y siendo herido dellos, alçó la boz diziendo: Padres míos,
baledme, que me matan; mas ya a esta sazón era por demás ser socorrido
dellos, porque ya todas eran muertos sin quedar ninguno de los que en
casa estavan. Los dos que avían ido fuera, al Hermano Zavallos, Hermano
antiguo y de mucha birtud allá en el monte le abrieron por medio la
caveça y allí quedó muerto. El moço que con él avía ido, no le tocaron,
diziendo que a él no le querían matar, sino a los Padres; y como él los
viese muertos y tan mal heridos, con gran dolor de su alma les rogó que
tanbién le matasen a él, que más quería morir con ellos que vivir sin ellos
entre infieles y bárbaros. Mas ellos con todo eso le dexaron: él les rogó
que ya que los avían muerto, diesen sepultura a sus cuerpos desnudos y
despedaçados a manos de aquellos enemigos de nuestra sancta fe, que
tanto deseaban y procuraban traerlos al conocimiento de su Criador y
Señor: mas el mal indio, autor desta maldad, aunque malo y endurecido
en sus errores y maldades, dize el moço, que se enterneció tanto de verlos
muertos, que lloró mucho, diziendo que eran mártires. Hizieron un grande
hoyo a la larga, y allí los enterraron cada uno por si con sus cruzes en
las manos, al Padre Baptista el primero y los demás por su horden.
[46] Diéronse luego a robar quanto en casa hallaron, sin dexar cossa
alguna de quanto avían llevado, si no fue una caxa en que estaba un
devoto Crucifixo rebuelto con otras cosas de devoción; que, como ellos
abriesen la caxa con desacato, fueron allí de repente muertos tres indios y
con espancto de los demás que no se atrevieron a tocar en aquella caxa.
Profanaron las cossas sagradas y dedicadas al culto divino, y bevían en
los cálizes y colgaban de los cuellos las patenas y bestíanse las vistiduras
sagradas.
[47] Fue nuestro Señor servido que quedase con bida este moço que
se dezia Alonso de Olmos, porque de su boca, como testigo de vista,
supiésemos todas estas cossas; el qual, como después de todo esto le
quisiesen matar a él tanbién, se acojió a las tierras de un cacique, enemigo
destos matadores, el qual lo defendió de sus manos y lo tubo en su poder
hasta que nosotros, quando el Adelantado fue en persona a castigar la
muerte y nosotros con él, lo sacamos de su poder. El modo diré
adelante....

[49] Volviendo a atar el hilo de nuestra istoria, después de la ida del Padre y sus compañeros a Ajacán, quedamos nosotros, como queda apunctado, en el puerto de Sancta Helena, en la Florida, y nos enbarcamos todos para la Habana conforme a su orden, y allí rescevimos cartas del mesmo Padre con el navío que los abía llebado, que nos dio un soldado que los servía; y ansí por su relación como por ellas vimos el mucho peligro en que quedaban todos nuestros Padres y Hermanos, y así se procuró con la mayor presteza que se pudo, despachar un navío de socorro con jente, mantenimiento y todo buen recado. Mas fue nuestro Señor servido que por presto que esto se hizo, ya ellos eran muertos.

[50] Avía dado el Padre por señal cierta al piloto, para quando el navío llegase al puerto, que verían ciertas cossas que el Padre les dio por señal, y que si aquellas señales no hallasen, era señal de que eran muertos: mas como el piloto fue y no halló aquellas señales, tubo mala sospecha, y no quiso saltar en tierra, antes se hizo a la mar; y por muchas señales que los que estaban en tierra hizieron llamándoles, nunca el piloto como cuerdo, quiso llegar a tierra. Quando ellos vieron esto, determinan de enbestir con ellos con sus canoas y mucha jente, para coger el navío. Estas canoas son sus navíos de ellos, y ansí se tubo una rezia pelea de una parte y de otra; y no les fue de tanta importancia la artillería que llebaban, como una gran suma de piedras que en el navío llebaban por lastre; mas como vieron caer sobre ellos tanta multitud, cosa que ellos nunca avían visto, porque en toda aquella tierra no ay piedra ni saven qué es, los hizieron retirar con daño suyo y pérdida de dos indios principales que les cojieron; y con ellos dieron la buelta no llebando nueba cierta de si eran muertos o bivos, ni se pudo sacar de los indios cossa alguna.

[51] En grande perplexidad y congoxa nos pusieron a todos estas nuebas, y con grandes temores y sobresaltos vivimos mucho tiempo sin poder saver cossa cierta dellos; antes con más probabilidad teníamos por más cierto que nos avían muerto a nuestro Superior tan amado, y nuestros Padres y Hermanos; y dándome [158] esto a mí en particular mucha pena y cuidado, esto le dixe al Padre Juan Rogel, que era el superior, porque el Padre Antonio Sedeño estaba en la Florida con el adelantado Pero Meléndez, y le dixe mi sentimiento y pena por estas palabras: « Grandemente me aflije la memoria del Padre Viceprovincial y sus compañeros nuestros Hermanos, y el no saver si son vibos o muertos; ofrésceseme sería bien salir desta duda, y que fuesse uno de nosotros a saverlo de cierto, con todo buen recado para lo jornada ». Díxome que ya él lo bía, y no savía qué hazerse, ni qué medio tomarse. Yo le dixe que si a él le

parescía, yo tomaría este travajo de ir a ello, y arriscar mi vida y ponerla
a todo peligro por el vien de nuestros Padres y Hermanos. El Padre lo
estimó en mucho, y me lo agradesció, y hordenó lo tomase a mi cargo; lo
qual yo hize con todas mis fuerças, y en breve tiempo me aparejé de
todas las cossas necesarias de navío, piloto y marineros, mantenimiento y
bestidos y rescates y todo lo necessario cumplidamente; y con este navío
nuestro se aprestaron otros dos con buena y mucha jente, y salimos estos
tres navíos junctos del puerto de la Habana para la Florida, adonde estaba
el Adelantado y su casa y el Padre Antonio Sedeño con el H. Villareal. . . .
[57] . . . Enbarcámonos en aquel navío y en él nabegamos con rezios
temporales y no con menos peligros de la vida; de todas nos libró el
Señor; y nos traxo a Jacán por el mes de agosto de 1572, despeés que el
Adelantado avía dado orden en las cosas que a él tocaban, repartida toda la
jente y soldados en tres navíos; tomamos tierra en la baía de la Madre de
Dios; y en este puerto hallamos una muy hermosa viña, tan concertada y
ordenada como las viñas d'España, puesta en un arenal, cargadas las cepas
de unas muy hermosas uvas blancas y grandes y maduras, que nos tenía
el Señor allí preparadas para nosotros, por lo qual le dimos muchas gracias.
Asimesmo avía dentro de la viña grande suma de árboles de ciruelos y
gindos y míspseros como los d'España, cargados de fruta madura, de la
qual comimos y llevamos para nuestro camino que fue de mucho regalo
y glorificamos al Señor por ello.
[58] [159] Despachó el Adelantado un navío vien armado y con
muchos soldados con el piloto que avía llevado a los nuestros, y savía la
tierra, la baía adentro, y en la tierra del tío de don Luis hizo pressa en
el cacique y otros muchos de los suyos que halló culpados, y los traxo
a la presencia del Adelantado, aviendo muerto el Capitán muchos en su
tierra, y quitado la patena a un indio que la traía al cuello, y otro andaba
con la casulla. Tanbién recojimos al moço compañero de los nuestros, que
el otro cacique tenía en su poder, del qual supimos enteramente las
cossas como pasaron, que es como aquí se an referido.
[59] Puesto el cacique en la presencia del Adelantado, viéndonos a
nosotros vestidos como a los que mataron, que éramos el Padre Rojel y el
Hermano Villarreal y yo, quedó como atónito entendiendo que avíamos
resuscitado. Díxole el Adelantado que le truxese dentro de 3 días allí a don
Luis, si no, que todos avían de ser muertos, y para este efecto inbió un
indio de los prissioneros; y como no viniese al tiempo concertado, los
ahorcó a todas de las entenas del navío, despeés de los aver baptizado
el Padre Juan Rogel al cacique y a los suyos.

[60] Concluído el Adelantado con todo esto, como está dicho, tomó su camino para España en busca de sus armadas, los quales alcançó antes de llegar a España juncto a las islas Terceras. Y nosotros dimos la buelta a la isla de Cuba, a nuestra casa de la Habana.

RELATION OF JUAN DE LA CARRERA [1]

Sent to Bartolomé Pérez, S.J., from Puebla de los Ángeles, March 1, 1600

EXCERPTS

[35] A short time previous to these events, an Indian from Florida arrived in Havana; he called himself Don Luis de Velasco. He was a person of note and had been raised in Mexico by the friars of Saint Dominic and had been baptized there at the instance of the Viceroy Don Luis de Velasco, who was, as I understand it, his godfather and gave him his name. This fellow had been educated at the court of King Philip II and had received many favors from him. Finally the King sent him back to his own country, where he said he was a chief, in the company of some Dominican friars.[2] For some reason or other, he found himself deserted by the friars; so he began to tell his plan to the Admiral, Pedro Menéndez. From what the Indian told him of the grandeurs of his land and the information he already had about the existence of another sea in this region and another navigation route of great importance for the discovery of great kingdoms such as Tartary and others contiguous to it, the Admiral heard the Indian and discussed the matter with Father Baptista [de Segura], who was at that time with the Admiral in Havana, where all this was going on. The two easily came to an agreement, nor was there further discussion. The Father believed that God had granted to him, as to Father Master Francis Xavier, another Paul of Holy Faith and another greater and more important Japan.[3] Longing to spread our holy Catholic Faith, he prepared himself for the trip and had a boat made and equipped with everything necessary for both the sea voyage and that land which was to be stocked with different sorts of animals and birds and many other things. With all this equipment he sailed from Havana in the month of July or August in 1571, by my reckoning.[4] He arrived in good weather at the point of Santa Elena in Florida, where I was staying at the time, and there we all had a meeting.

[36] Since we treated one another with great love and familiarity, he confided to me all the plans and designs and hopes for this journey. These were all clearly praiseworthy, for they came from a holy, sincere Christian heart, and I gave him high praise. But I pointed out the difficulty in the execution of the plan, saying that the Indian did not satisfy me, and judging from what he had told me, I saw that he was a liar. I begged and entreated him to examine the plan more thoroughly, to talk it over with the Fathers present and to decide what was best in conformity with their advice. The idea of a superior wanting to go to such remote and distant lands relying on an Indian, leaving everything behind, without a guard of soldiers or any people other than his own [Jesuits], was in my opinion not as good as that of having another Father go and travel light to look around the country and see what there was in the whole notion and learn if the Indian was lying or telling the truth. That is how it looked to me. All the Fathers assembled there reached the same conclusion except Father Quirós, who was to go along, and he had just come from Spain without any experience. In spite of all this he [Segura] decided to go, according to the arrangements already made, and stay there alone with his companions. This was to prevent anyone from giving a bad example to the Indians. His companions were Father Quirós, Brother Linares, Brother Zavallos, Brother Gabriel Gómez, and three novices, one of whom was named Juan Baptista Méndez, and Gabriel de Solís and Cristóbal Redondo and a boy called Alonso. This mission seemed to him to be more in conformity with the will of Our Lord which he desired to accomplish in everything, and with this resolution he left, firm in his high purpose.

[37] Then his companion, Father Quirós, a man of distinguished learning, came to me with a long list, on which he asked me to give him the best and the larger portion of everything I had in my charge, especially the church goods. When I saw the list I was a little upset and I said to him, "Father, I would gladly give you everything you ask of me, even though I know that it is all going to be lost, were it not for the fact that I know for certain that all this will contribute greatly to the death of everyone going there. Will your Reverence do me the kindness of saying this for me to Father Vice-Provincial [Segura], and after that if he wants me to give you what you ask, well then here it is at your command." He came back with the answer that I should give him everything for which he had asked. I fulfilled his request, but there were also fulfilled the forebodings I expressed. I gave Father Quirós as much as he

wanted, and it was the greater part of the best and richest articles that I had in the way of chalices, monstrances, and vestments and other articles besides church furnishings. With these they completed their equipment for their journey.

[38] The novices that he was taking with him came to say good-bye to me with great tenderness and tears. I was deeply stirred because I loved them kindly as one who had reared them. Now when they told me that they were going to their death, I replied that they should be consoled wherever holy obedience was sending them [5] and that God would be with them and that from Him they would receive the pay and reward of their labors, and that it was a great blessing to die for God and obedience. I felt the same tender sorrow when Father Vice-Provincial and the rest of his companions, whom I was not to see again in this life, departed amidst the tears of all.

[39] They arrived at the country of this Indian Don Luis in August. Its name is Ajacán. They expected through him to do great things in that land, and in all the other lands they hoped to discover, because the Indian was a big chief and a clever talker. Our Fathers and Brothers disembarked in a great and beautiful port, and men who have sailed a great deal and have seen it say it is the best and largest port in the world. [6] So, if I remember rightly, the pilot remarked to me. It is called the Bay of the Mother of God, and in it there are many deep-water ports, each better than the next. I saw this port myself when I went with the Admiral, as I will narrate later. It seemed to me (for as it looked to me and I was given to understand), it was about 3 leagues at the mouth, and in length and breadth it was close to 30. They say that at the end of it the other sea begins. Also there is the very important navigation route, mentioned before, which the Admiral wanted to explore. I understand he would have done this, had he lived long enough. There is a large population on the shores of this port and inland. [7]

[40] After he unloaded all his effects at this beautiful port, [8] Segura decided to remain there without soldiers or guards other than our Fathers and Brothers, and to trust in God's care and protection and the help of His most Holy Mother and of the saints and angels in heaven. He placed himself in the hands of this Indian whom he trusted, for if he was what he ought to be, there would certainly be a rich harvest gathered through him. But it was far to the contrary, for he was very different from what he had seemed to be and what Father Baptista [Segura] had believed about him. The Father bade farewell to all the people in the boat

and remained alone with his own men, who carried all the baggage to the village of a brother of Don Luis. This was very fatiguing labor because of the distance from the port and the poor footpaths and swamps that abounded in the whole region.

[41] Then this wretched native saw himself the master of the Father and his sons and all their supplies. There was no one to fear because he was among his brothers and relatives and friends and many leagues away from the sea. They had no one on land to help them, and aid by water would have been difficult. At the beginning, I understand, he did not show at once his criminal intent, and the Fathers built their poor little hut and chapel and began to treat with him the office of preaching the gospel for which they had come. But this second Judas began to indulge in vices and sins publicly without fear of God or man and then to relinquish their conversation and company. Since he was acting more like a pagan than a Christian in his manners, dress, and habits, he went off and lived with his uncle, a chief, in a country far distant from ours. There he allowed himself free rein in his sins, marrying many women in a pagan way.[10] Neither reasoning nor any other method which Father Baptista tried to release him from his sinful life and draw him back to himself had any effect.

[42] By my reckoning, from the end of August to the Purification of Our Lady these blessed Religious, our Fathers and Brothers, lived in that country in continual fright and alarm, awaiting death each day. It was in the control of this Indian and his kinsmen to take away their lives, when and in what way they wanted without meeting any resistance. Therefore Father Vice-Provincial with several expedients prepared and disposed himself and his companions for a death they held as certain. The first arrangement he made was that all should give themselves to longer and more continual prayer, readying themselves with exhortations and conferences, which he frequently gave them, and with other good spiritual exercises, and he had all of them make a general confession of their past life. Their mortification was great and they must have undergone great austerity even without wanting it, for the supplies they brought ran out, and they were obliged to sustain themselves on the roots and herbs of the countryside, like the Indians who live off the land, for their food usually fails around that time.[11]

[43] The good Father was more despondent over the tiresome work of his sons than his own, because he was naturally compassionate, pious, and meek and very charitable and when he saw them suffering so much his

heart was greatly stirred. It seemed to him that the cure for their misfortunes would be to bring back to friendship that evil and rebellious Indian. So he decided to send Father Quirós and two Brothers to try and succeed. On the way they took some sustenance and some mats which would be some protection against the great cold they endured, because the ground was cold and the house in which they were living was so wretched that its chief covering was palm leaves which served as roof and walls.[12] I know this from experience too, for I have lived many times in similar houses suffering much from the cold, even though the lands were not so cold.

[44] This Father and the Brothers made a cautious trip to the country of Don Luis' uncle, where he was living, as has been narrated. While going along safely with these bundles on their back, lo! the traitor with armed companions suddenly springs out on the path to kill them with bows and arrows. When they saw the sudden attack, Father Quirós turned to Don Luis and asked him what they wanted to do and why they were about to kill them. Then the good Father began to preach to them but the answer was a volley of arrows, and so after wounding them many times they slew Father Quirós and Brother Gabriel de Solís. Brother Baptista Méndez fled to the woods with blood running from his deep wounds. There he hid himself that night and in the morning he was discovered and killed. After that the murderers burned the bodies and stole their clothing and bundles.

[45] Good Father Baptista Segura, who was anxiously awaiting the companions and the successful outcome of their embassy, grieved deeply over their tardiness and feared some mischance and frequently said so to his companions with great sorrow of his heart and soul. Before dawn of the morning of the same day, as I understand, of Our Lady of Candlemas, when he was praying as usual with all his sons, Segura heard someone calling at the door, and all around the house a great noisy crowd of people with their captain and leader, Don Luis. They told the Fathers to give them all the axes and machetes used to cut wood, because they were going into the forests for it. The good Father, oblivious of the evil the Indians were plotting against him, and innocent of their evil intention, said that they would give everything to them, and two of the house would go along to the forest and carry their bundles of wood to warm themselves. The traitor Don Luis, seeing himself in control of the weapons, with which, as he looked at it, they could defend themselves, used the following stratagem.[13]

The Indian archers approached the house from the back, so that if anyone came out he would be killed at once. Don Luis, dressed in the clothing which he had stolen from Father Quirós on the path when he killed him, went inside with some picked followers, keeping the axes and machetes he already had. He assigned his warriors each to a different man, so that all were killed at the same time, without being able to help one another. The wretched and perverse Don Luis attacked Father Baptista first to pay him back for the many kindnesses shown him, and when the Father saw him come in and recognized him he thought he came in for a very different purpose. They say that he spoke joyfully at his sight: "You are very welcome, Don Luis!" Certainly before he got any further the Indian replied with his axe and gave him many blows on the head, the arms, the legs, and his whole body, which lay gravely wounded and maltreated. While the captain was dealing with the Father, the other murderers were occupying themselves similarly with the rest, like wolves among gentle sheep who were doing evil to no one but good to all. They went into the kitchen where they found a Brother named Cristóbal Redondo, who was in soul and body, disposition and speech, more of an angel than a man. When that meek lamb saw himself attacked by those wolves and was wounded by them he raised his voice saying: "Help me, my Fathers, they are going to kill me." But by this time it was useless to look for help, for they were all dead; not one of those who were in the house remained. As to the two who had gone out into the woods, they split the head of one, Brother Zaballos, an old Brother of great virtue, and he lay there dead. They did not touch the boy who had gone with him saying that they did not want to kill him but only the Fathers. When he saw them dead and so badly wounded he asked them in deep sorrow of soul to kill him too. He preferred to die with them rather than live without them among infidels and barbarians. Despite this they spared him. Then he asked the murderers to bury their bodies all naked and cut to pieces by the hands of those enemies of our holy Faith. The Fathers had longed and tried in every way to bring them to the knowledge of their Creator and Lord. As the boy recalls, the wicked Indian who fostered this crime, though evil and hardened in his errors and sins, was so touched at seeing them dead that he wept copiously and called them martyrs. They dug a long ditch and there they buried them each one separately with their crosses in their hands, first Father Baptista and the rest in order.

[46] Then they turned to stealing whatever they found in the house,

leaving nothing that had been brought there except a box in which there was a devotional crucifix surrounded by other pious objects. For when they irreverently opened the box, three Indians fell dead at once; the rest were very frightened and did not dare touch it. They profaned the holy vessels dedicated to the divine service and drank from the chalices and hung the patens [14] around their necks and dressed themselves in the sacred vestments.

[47] It pleased Our Lord that this boy who was called Alonso de Olmos should remain alive in order that from his mouth as from an eye-witness we should learn all these things. Then after all this they wanted to kill him too; so he fled to the territory of a chief who was an enemy of these murderers and defended him with his own hands and kept him in his own custody until we took him from his protection when the Admiral went in person to administer punishment for the massacre and we went with him. Later I will tell how this was.

[49] To resume the thread of our story again, after the departure of the Father and his companions to Ajacán, we remained, as already mentioned, at the port of Santa Elena in Florida, and then all embarked for Havana according to his instructions. There we received letters from the same Father brought back on the boat which had carried them up. A soldier in their service gave them to us. From his report as well as the letters, we saw the great peril in which all our Fathers and Brothers were placed, and so we took steps that a relief ship be dispatched with all speed to bring reinforcements, provisions, and a good stock of supplies. But for all the haste with which we acted, it was God's will that they be already dead.

[50] The Father had given definite signals to the pilot so that when the ship should reach port they would see certain things that the Father wanted, and if they did not find those signals, it was an indication that they were dead. Since the pilot went and did not find the signals, he suspected some foul play, and refused to set foot on land but made for the sea; no matter how many gestures the people on land made calling them in, the pilot, like a prudent man, always refused to land. When they saw this they determined to attack them in numbers with their canoes and capture the ship. These canoes are their ships; [15] and so there was a sharp fight on both sides. The guns that they had on board were not as useful to them as a great pile of rocks which they were carrying for ballast. When they saw so great number of rocks falling on them (a thing they had never seen, for there are no rocks in that region and they

do not know what they are),[16] the natives retired with damage and the loss of two captured Indian chiefs. With these the Spaniards returned, not knowing for certain if the Fathers were dead or alive, nor could they get anything out of the Indians.

[51] This news put us all in a state of great perplexity and anxiety. Now we lived for a long period in deep fear and trembling unable to know anything certain about them. With greater probability we took it as more certain that they had killed our beloved superior and our Fathers and Brothers and in my particular pain and anxiety, I spoke to Father Juan Rogel, who was the superior when Father Sedeño was in Florida with the Admiral Pedro Menéndez. I expressed my sad feelings in these words: "I am deeply afflicted by the memory of Father Vice-Provincial and his companions our brothers, not knowing if they are dead or alive. It occurs to me as a good idea to rid ourselves of this doubt by having some one of us go and find out for certain and bring a good supply of provisions for the journey." He said that he himself saw that already, but did not know what to do or what means to take. I said that if it were agreeable to him I would undertake the task of going up and risking and endangering my life for the welfare of our Fathers and Brothers. This the Father regarded highly and thanking me he ordered me to take charge of the mission. I did this with all possible energy. In a short time I equipped myself with all necessary items: a ship, a pilot and sailors, supplies, clothing and miscellaneous items and everything necessary. Besides this boat of ours, two others were prepared with a large and capable crew, and these three ships sailed together from the port of Havana for Florida, where the Admiral was with his household and Father Antonio Sedeño with Brother Villareal.

[There follows the story of the impounding of this ship by Menéndez and his adventures on the coast of Florida while returning to Havana with Father Sedeño and Brother Carrera. The translation resumes with the history of the second relief ship which left with the Governor's little fleet from Santa Elena.]

[57] We embarked on that ship and sailed amid fierce storms and no less dangers to our lives,[17] but the Lord delivered us from every threat and brought us to Ajacán safely in August, 1572. After the Admiral had given out instructions about his own affairs, he divided all the people and soldiers among the three ships. We made landfall in the Bay of the Mother of God, and in this port we found a very beautiful vineyard, as well laid out and ordered as the vineyards of Spain. It was located on

sandy soil and the vines were laden with fair white grapes, large and ripe.[18] These the Lord had prepared there for us and we gave Him many thanks. Also within the vineyard there was a great number of plum, cherry, and persimmon trees like those in Spain. We ate from the laden branches and took some away for our journey; it was a great windfall and we glorified the Lord for it.

[58] The Admiral sent out a well protected ship, carrying many soldiers and the pilot who had brought Ours there, to reconnoiter the land inside the bay. In the country of Don Luis' uncle he captured the chief and several of his men who were found guilty and brought them before the Admiral. The captain killed many in their country, and took the paten from an Indian who was wearing it around his neck and the chasuble from another who was walking about in it. We also got hold of the boy who was a companion of Ours; he was in the custody of the other chief. We learned from him all about the way things happened, and this has been related here.

[59] When the chief stood in the presence of the Admiral and saw Father Rogel and Brother Villareal and me dressed like those whom they had slain, he was thunderstruck and thought we had risen from the dead.[19] The Admiral told him to bring him Don Luis in three days; if not, they would all be killed. And so he sent back one of the Indian prisoners. Since he did not come back at the appointed time, he hanged them all from the yardarms of the ship. Previously Father Rogel had baptized the chief and his men.

[60] When the Admiral had accomplished this, as has been related, he started on his way for Spain in search of his fleets, which he found before reaching Spain near Islas Terceras.[20] Then we returned to the island of Cuba and our house in Havana.[21]

NOTES

1. The autograph is in the Archives of the Society of Jesus in Rome, *Histor. Soc.* 177 (Vocationes Illustres II) ff. 152-161 (*prius* 1-16, 55-62, 68-69). It is printed in *MAF* 536-570. Father Bartolomé Pérez was assistant to the Father-General, in charge of all the provinces of Spain and its empire. The Relation was sent to him after Father-General Aquaviva had ordered the composition of narratives about the missions in 1598. In the note on the Relation of Juan Rogel more details on this ordinance are given. Much of the early part of the Relation is an eulogistic biography of the martyrs and their Florida labors.

2. For an account of early Dominican activities along the Atlantic Coast, see

V. O'Daniel, *Dominicans in Early Florida* (New York, 1930). This work contains brief bibliographies.

3. Paul of the Holy Faith was the name in Baptism of the first Japanese Christian, named Anjiro. He was an invaluable assistant to Francis Xavier in his work, and the Saint often wrote of him in his letters from Japan.

4. Carrera is approximately right as to the month, but a year off in his date.

5. Actually novices are not bound by any vows to obey the commands of superiors, but they may practice the virtue of obedience.

6. One cannot tell whether the knowledge of the many deep-water ports was already had by the Spanish or whether Brother Carrera is adding information known by the explorations of 1573 and 1588. The mention of 30 leagues' breadth led Father Kenny to suspect that Carrera saw the mouth of the Potomac, but one also gathers an impression of width looking up the James River and back toward the eastern shore from Hampton Roads.

7. The knowledge of a large population on the shores of this port argues a haven of several days around the mouth of the James, where the Kecoughtan on the north and the Nansemond and Chesapeake Indians on the south would have made themselves evident. It took the English some time to discover large numbers of Indians in 1607.

8. "This beautiful port" must be understood as the Chesapeake in general. Carrera evidently did not accompany the pilot on the punitive expedition and thus preserves no sharp recollection of the exact spot where the Segura party finally unloaded its effects.

9. Small tidewater rivulets would present obstacles for land travel in many places between the York and the James. This is the only direct testimony that the Jesuits actually made the removal indicated in Quirós plans.

10. Smith tells us that Powhatan "hath as many women as he will" (1 Arber 80), and Spelman, an unwilling associate of the Virginia Indians for an extended period, says: "The custum of ye cuntry is to haue many wiues and to buye them, so *that* he *which* haue most copper and Beads may haue most wiues. . ." (1 Arber vcii). All in all, the customs and environment of the Virginia Algonkin were such as to constitute grave temptations to the neophyte.

11. In general, Smith gives a picture of improvidence on the part of the Indian. See especially his description of "their planted fruits and how they use them," which has the following: "When all their fruits be gathered, little els they plant, and this is done by their women and children; neither doth this long suffice them: for neere 3 parts of the years, they only obserue times and seasons, and liue of what the country naturally affordeth from hand to mouth. . ." (1 Arber 61 ff.).

12. The cabbage palmetto is not found north of North Carolina. However, Dr. Malcolm Harris of West Point, Va. suggests that the Fathers may have thatched their roof with marsh grass that grows luxuriantly in the river marshes, particularly on the upper York near West Point and along the Poropotank and Chickahominy rivers. That they carried mats with them indicates the necessity of their being gone at least over night. The distance to Don Luis' town is described variously as "far distant," 4 leagues, 10 leagues, and a day and a half journey.

13. Set down thirty years after events, the conversations reported by Carrera are undoubtedly in part imaginative, as also some of the more elaborate details of Don Luis' strategy.

14. A paten is a small flat dish of precious metal that is placed under the Sacred Host during the Mass.

15. Smith describes dugout boats 40 or 50 feet in length capable of bearing as many men (1 Arber 69). Verrazano had reported similar boats along the Atlantic Coast. John White's beautiful reproductions of the boats and boat building of the North Carolina Algonkin may be seen in the Stefan Lorant edition cited in Part I. See also M. V. Brewington, *Chesapeake Bay Log Canoes*, The Mariners' Museum (Newport News, 1937) 17-31.

16. It is true that there are no natural rocks around the mouth of the bay or in the lower James, but Carrera could not have been in a position to say that the Indians did not know what they were.

17. The storms do not seem to have been vivid enough to Rogel to be worthy of mention. See his August Letter above, para. 1, where he mentions a fair voyage.

18. The description of the vineyard, while being a typical pious exaggeration met in this narrative, is nevertheless a clear indication that Carrera is describing Strachey's Kecoughtan: "Yt [Kecoughtan] is an ample and faire countrie indeed, an admirable porcion of land, comparatively high, wholesome, and fruictfull; the seat sometyme of a thousand Indians and three hundred Indian houses, and those Indians, as it may well appeare, better husbands than in any parte ells that we have observed [confirmed by Rogel's August Letter, para. 9], which is the reason that so much ground is there cliered and opened, enough, with little labour, alreddy prepared, to receave corne, or make viniards of twoo or three thousand acres; and where, beside, we find many fruict trees, a kind of goosbery, cherries, and other plombs, the maricock aple, and many prettie copsies or boskes (as it weere) of mulberye trees..." (p. 60). This description reinforces an earlier account of 1610 reprinted in 3 *Force's Tracts* 21, and that of Governor Dale. The only orderly groves spoken of by Smith were the mulberry, but he also speaks of plums, cherries, and grapes as the chief fruits. In one instance he implies that fruit was planted along the Potomac, and he mentions that the Indians have "plentie of fruits, as well planted as naturall...." Verrazano found some indication of vine cultivation about 100 leagues south of the Hudson. Ralph Hamor (*op. cit.* 22) speaks of cherries, persimmons, and grapes, the last-named at least being found near Henrico. One of the native varieties, a large, single grape, was called scuppernong. Bruce (1:98 f.) discusses four native varieties of grapes.

19. Since the chief first saw Carrera in the presence of Menéndez, who remained in port, we have evidence that Carrera remained also.

20. "Islas Terceras" might survive in the present Terceira, in the Azores. These islands were the regular objective of the fleets to and from the Indies. Vásquez de Espinosa describes the route to them as follows: "From Havana the galleons and fleets leave by the Bahama Channel and once out they steer NE up to 32°; thence E ¼ NE to 38° or 39°, on this course they make the Terceras Islands; this is the summer route. On the winter route they steer from the Bahama Channel E. for

the island of Bermuda, which lies at 32° 20′. Passing along its southern coast and following the route, they sail as far as 37° on which lies the island of Santa María; for the island of Tercera they sail to 38°; for San Miguel to 37°; at these they take on necessary fresh provisions" (*Compendium and Description of the Indies*, 102 *SMC*, 2).

21. The return trip, undoubtedly stormy and nearly involving disaster, is told in a vivid and imaginative manner in the conclusion of his Relation.

Vida del Padre Francisco de Borja, Tercer General de la Compañía de Jesús

por Pedro de Ribadeneyra, S.J.

[10] Mas ni a sus compañeros, ni a los otros sus Hermanos, que quedavan en Europa, no los espantó, ni atemorizó esta muerte del Padre Pedro Martínez; antes los animó más, entendiendo que podían más fácilmente alcançar en la Florida lo que deseavan, que era morir por Christo. Y assí el año de mill y 568 embió el P. Francisco, para seguir la empressa començada, onze de la Compañía, de los quales iva por superior el P. Juan Baptista de Segura; y se avían de juntar con el P. Rogel, y el Hermano Francisco de Villarreal, compañeros del Padre P. Martínez, los quales, después de su muerte, se retiraron al pueblo de la Habana, y avían ya buelto a la Florida, para donde partieron de S. Lúcar los onze Padres y Hermanos a los 13 de março deste año de 1568. Iva con ellos un cacique o señor principal de la mesma tierra de la Florida, el qual avía traído della / el adelantado Pero Meléndez de Avilés a España, y aviendo sido enseñado en las cosas de nuestra sancta religión, recibió con grandíssimas muestras de contento el agua del sancto Baptismo y se llamó don Luis. Porque se juzgó que, por ser plático de aquella tierra, y hombre principal, y de muchos deudos, podría ayudar a los nuestros en la conversión de sus vasallos y amigos, como él lo prometía.

[11] Llegados a la Florida, el P. Juan Baptista de Segura y otros siete compañeros (que los demás quedaron en la Habana), se entraron animosamente la tierra adentro, guiados del don Luis, sin consentir que ningún soldado español los acompañasse, aunque muchos se le ofrecieron. Llevaron sus ornamentos, y el recaudo necessario para dezir missa, y algunos libros para su devoción. Passaron grandes desiertos y pantanos de agua, de que ay mucha abundancia en aquella tierra. Faltóles presto el mantenimiento, y huvieron de sustentarse con las yerbas que hallavan por los campos y con el agua que bevían de los charcos. Arribaron a la tierra de don Luis, que estava bien apartada de la mar y de todo humano / abrigo, y habitada de salvajes desnudos. Avisoles don Luis que le aguardasen en un lugar medio despoblado y él se fue a otro donde estava su gente, cinco leguas más adelante. Y como huviessen los B. Padres esperádole seis

días más de lo que estavan concertados, embió el Padre Baptista de Segura un Padre y un Hermano para saber cómo no venía, y si quería que ellos fuessen donde él estava. En llegando (o porque el don Luis avía ya apostatado y buelto a sus idolatrías, y se hallava confuso; o porque ya tenía urdida y tramada la maldad), dio con sus deudos y amigos sobre los dichos Padres y Hermanos y quitáronles las vidas. Y al alva del día siguiente dieron sobre los demás, y sin hablarles palabra, yendo don Luis por capitán y guía, hallándolos a todos seis puestos de rodillas, esperando con devoción y alegría la muerte, se la dieron. Y luego les desnudaron de sus vestiduras, y robaron los ornamentos y adereços del altar, y se los vistieron, y las ropas de los muertos, y bailaron en su borrachera. Tres dellos fueron a abrir una arquilla de los Padres, pensando hallar dentro alguna gran riqueza; y halláranla, si la supieran conozer, porque dentro de la arquilla estava un libro de / la divina Scriptura y misal, y libros devotos, rosarios, imágines, silicios y disciplinas, y un devoto crucifixo, al qual se pusieron a mirar muy attentamente y mirándolo, se cayeron súbitamente muertos. Los compañeros destos tres que estavan a la mira, quedaron tan escandalizados y atónitos de lo que vieron que, sin tocar cosa de las que tenían delante, se fueron cada uno por su parte. [12] Todo esto vio y notó un mancebo español que los Padres llevavan consigo; al qual, por ser muchacho, y por saber que no iva a predicarles y quitarles la adoración de sus ídolos, le dexaron de matar; y estuvo entre ellos captivo algunos años, hasta que el Señor le libró de tan bárbara y fiera nación y contó lo que queda referido. Los que allí murieron por la propagación de nuestra sancta fee fueron el P. Juan Baptista de Segura, natural de Toledo, que por sus grandes virtudes y vida religiosa avía sido en España muy amada del P. Francisco, el P. Luis de Quirós y los Hermanos Gabriel Gómez, Çavallos, Juan Baptista Méndez, Pedro de Linares, Cristóbal Redondo, Gabriel de Solís. He puesto aquí sus nombres para que quede la memoria destos dichosos Religiosos pues por el zelo de las almas derramaron su sangre con tanta / constancia y alegría.

LIFE OF FATHER FRANCIS BORGIA,
THIRD GENERAL OF THE SOCIETY OF JESUS
BOOK III, CHAPTER 6 [1]

by Pedro de Ribadeneyra, S.J.

EXCERPT

[10] This death of Father Pedro Martínez [2] did not frighten or intimidate either his companions or his brothers who remained in Spain, but rather gave them courage with the ideal of being able to attain more easily in Florida their desires to die for Christ. Thus in the year 1568, Father Francis [3] sent eleven of the Company to continue the work begun. Their superior was Father Juan Baptista de Segura and they were to join Father Rogel and Brother Francisco de Villareal, the companions of Father P. Martínez. After his death they had retreated to the town of Havana, but now had returned to Florida, whither the eleven Fathers and Brothers sailed from San Lúcar on the 13th of March of that year of 1568. [4] With them went a *cacique* [5] or important lord from that same land of Florida whom the Governor had brought from there to Spain, because it was thought that an important person, with many relatives, familiar with that land, could help Ours in converting his subjects and friends, as he had promised.

[11] After reaching Florida, while the rest remained in Havana, Father Juan Baptista de Segura and seven [6] other companions boldly went into the interior led by Don Luis. [7] No Spanish soldier was allowed to accompany them, though many volunteered. They took their vestments and the equipment necessary for the altar and some devotional books. They travelled through great deserts and swamps which are very common in that land. Then their supplies failed, and they were forced to sustain themselves by the herbs they found in the fields and they drank water from the pools. They came to the land of Don Luis, which was far distant from the sea and any human protection, and was inhabited by naked savages. Don Luis advised the Fathers to stay in a half-deserted place, and he would go on to another, 5 leagues further, where his tribe was. When the blessed Fathers had waited six days longer than was agreed, Father Baptista de Segura sent one Father and one Brother to find out why he did not come and whether he wished them to go where he was. After their arrival, either because Don Luis had already apostatized and returned

to idolatry and so was embarrassed, or because he had kept secret this wicked plan, he and his relatives and friends fell upon the said Fathers and Brothers and slew them. At dawn of the next day, with Don Luis as captain and guide, they fell upon the rest without speaking a word. They found all six on their knees awaiting death with devout joy. Then they stripped them of their garments, stole the ornaments and vessels of the altar, and danced about in a drunken revel. Three of them went to open a small chest of the Fathers, believing that they had discovered a fine treasure within, and they found one, had they but known. Within the chest was a book of the Holy Scriptures, a missal, devotional books, rosaries, statues, hair shirts and disciplines and a crucifix. When they began to admire it very closely and with interest, they suddenly fell down dead. The companions of those three who were watching were so amazed and astonished at what they saw that, without touching anything they had taken, each one fled to his own place.

[12] All this was seen and described by a Spanish youth [8] whom the Fathers had brought along with them. Because he was a boy and they knew he had not come to preach and take away their idols, they did not kill him. He was a captive among them for some years, until the Lord freed him from such a savage and fierce tribe and he related what has been described. These died for the spreading of our Holy Faith: Father Juan Baptista de Segura from Toledo, who was beloved by Father Francis for his great virtues and holy life while in Spain; Father Luis de Quirós and Brothers Gabriel Gómez, Zavallos, Juan Baptista Méndez, Pedro de Linares, Cristóbal Redondo, and Gabriel de Solís. I set down their names here to perpetuate the memory of these aforementioned Religious, for in zeal for souls they poured out their blood with such joyous courage.

NOTES

1. This account by Pedro de Ribadeneyra, S.J. (1527-1611) was copied out by Bartolomé Martínez with some marginal notes and included in his Relation, which follows. It is taken from the *Vida del Padre Francisco de Borja*, printed at Madrid in 1592 and 1594. It was printed again in 1605 in a collection entitled *Obras del Padre Ribadeneira agora de nuevo revistas y acrecentadas.* A modern edition is available in Pedro de Ribadeneyra, *Historias de la Contrareforma*, [Eusebio Rey, S.I., ed.] (Madrid, 1945) 619-852. The excerpt on Segura printed here from the Martínez MS may be found there on pp. 771 ff.

Ribadeneyra was a prolific writer on historical and theological topics, in addition to his distinguished career as a preacher and administrator in the Society of Jesus. He wrote in a facile, clear, and graceful prose that made his translation of

St. Augustine's *Confessions* and his famous *Flos Sanctorum* very popular. Menéndez y Pelayo comments on his strong influence on Lope de Vega in *Estudios sobre el teatro de Lope de Vega*, 6 vols. (Madrid, 1919-1925), 1: 281, 321; 2: 55. Ribadeneyra's account of the Jesuit martyrdoms influenced Garcilaso de la Vega to add a final chapter to his already complete *La Florida del Ynca* sometime between 1599 and 1605, giving the details of the deaths of Fathers Quirós and Segura (see *The Florida of the Inca* 641 f.). This history has an added interest in that Ribadeneyra wrote the first printed account of the Jesuits in Virginia.

2. Father Pedro Martínez was martyred near the St. John's River on October 5, 1566 (see Pedro Menéndez to Avellaneda, October 15, 1566, *MAF* 95, note 22). For Martínez' life see Zubillaga "P. Pedro Martínez" in 7 *Archivum Historicum Societatis Iesu* (1938) 30-53.

3. I.e., Father Francis Borgia.

4. Segura's party sailed on April 10, 1568 (Sedeño to Borgia, March 17, 1568, *MAF* 349). The Jesuits sailed for Florida at three different times. This was the second expedition in which were Fathers Segura, Sedeño, Álamo, and Brothers D. Agustín Baez and Juan de la Carrera (Avellaneda to Borgia, March 11, 1568, *MAF* 271). Fr. Avellaneda, the provincial of Andalucia, in a letter to Borgia on May 22, 1568, adds that seven catechists sailed with Segura (*MAF* 312).

5. Don Luis was not on this voyage. Rogel Relation (above), para. 8.

6. "Seven other companions," means that Alonso is not being included as a Jesuit. Ribadeneyra knew that he was in the group (para. 12 below).

7. In the margin Martínez wrote: "Los padres del Jacáan no entraron la tierra adentro antes no lejos de la mar hizieron assiento y los martirizaron como lo contó Alonso de Olmos que se libró; y esto que aquí dize succedió al Padre Rogel, Sedeño y Hermanos Francisco y Carrera." ("The Fathers of Ajacán did not travel inland before they settled close to the sea, and they were martyred as Alonso de Olmos, who was freed, recounts; and what he said here he passed on to Fathers Rogel, Sedeño and Brothers Francisco [de Villareal] and Carrera.") A settlement near the sea does not conform to Quirós' or Rogel's accounts. He may have in mind the temporary halt at Newport News, or it is possible that the captain constructed a temporary shelter on College Creek that they could use until they were resettled on the York.

8. In the margin: "Este mancebo se dezia Alonso de Olmos, y no se hallo al martirio, como él contó." ("The youth was named Alonso de Olmos, and he was not present at the martyrdom, as he recounts.") This point is discussed in the Martínez Relation below.

Relación de Bartolomé Martínez

Martirio de los padres y hermanos de la Compañía de Jesús que martirizaron los Indios del Jacán, Tierra de la Florida, de que trata brevemente el Padre Pedro de Ribadeneira, en el libro 3°, capítulo 6 de la vida del B.P. Francisco de Borja

[22] Los terceros Padres y Hermanos de la Compañía de Jesús que entraron en la Florida, fueron los que martirizaron en la provincia del Jacán, y sucedió desta manera. Después que el adelantado Pero Meléndez de Avilés, marqués della, y cavallero del hábito de señor Santiago, ganó al Rey de Francia dos fuerças que tenía en la Florida, y mató dos mill Franceses hereges que tenía en ella, los 600 en el fuerte de S. Matheo, que se nombró assí por ganarse aquel día de los cristianos, y 1200 que se perdieron con tormenta en la punta del Cañaveral, con su capitán y governador, Juan Ribao; yendo la buelta de / España, quiso descubrir la costa de la Florida que corre al norte; y fuesse arrimando a ella más de 450 leguas, hasta que llegó a vista de una tierra, que en lengua de indios se dice el Jacán, que dista del fuerte de Sta. Helena 300 leguas y está de la Habana 150, poco más o menos.

[23] Llegando el adelantado Pero Meléndez, que Dios tiene, al Jacán, descubrió en la costa una gran bahía, entró dentro del puerto y surgió en él. Viendo los indios los navíos, vinieron a bordo en canoas y entraron en la Capitana a donde su Señoría, como tenía de costumbre, que era en esto otro Alexandro, les regaló con comida y vestidos. Entre los indios vino un cacique, que traía un hijo, para indio de muy buen parecer y gracia. Rogóle el Pero Meléndez que se lo diesse para llevallo a que le viesse el Rey de España, su señor, con otros que llevava; que él le dava su palabra y fee de bolvérselo con muchas riquezas y vestidos. Dióselo el cacique, y su Señoría lo llevó a Castilla, a la corte del rey D. Phelippe II, que Dios tiene, y con él y otros indios de la tierra de S. Augustín y Sta. Helena, que llevó el adelantado aquel viaje, se holgó mucho el Rey N. S. y la corte; y su señoría los traxo muy galanes y ricamente vestidos.

[24] El indio del /. Jacán se bolvió cristiano y le pusieron por nombre don Luis y estuvo en Castilla seis o siete años, en una casa de la Compañia,

adonde le instruyeron en las cosas de nuestra sancta fee y religión cristiana, y siendo de lindo ingenio (como lo son los indios de todas aquellas provincias, si tratan desde pequeños con cristianos) vino a ser capaz, que le administraron los sanctíssimos sacramentos del altar y Confirmación. Siendo ya de edad de más de 20 años, dióle desseo de bolver a su tierra, por ventura con designio y voluntad por entonzes, como él dixo, de que sus padres, parientes y naturales della se convirtiessen a la fee de Jesucristo, baptizassen y se bolviessen cristianos como él lo era. Tratólo con los Padres de la Compañía, diziéndoles que se fuessen con él algunos dellos, que él se ofrecía, con el favor de Dios, viéndolos allá, se harían cristianos los indios todos de aquella provincia del Jacán, donde era su padre cacique y señor de lo más della. A los Padres de la Compañía, desseosos del bien de aquellas almas y del augmento y propagación de la religión cristiana, les pareció bien aquel negocio. Dieron quenta dello al Generalíssimo de la Compañía, que entonzes era el Padre Francisco de Borja, y al summo Pontífice Pio V, al rey don Phelippe 2º, que Dios tiene, y con su acuerdo y licencia se hizo el viaje. Supo el negocio el adelantado Pero Meléndez de Avilés, gran marinero y el que sabía la tierra del Jacán /, y avía traído al don Luis. Recibió dello grandíssimo contentamiento, por ser él muy devoto y aficionado a las cosas de la Compañía, el qual se ofreció de poner los Padres, y al don Luis en la tierra de el Jacán con los galeones que guardavan la mar de las Indias, de que era el general: y assí lo hizo.

[25] Su Magestad les mandó dar el avío necessario en la casa de la Contratación de Sevilla, de bastimentos, ornamentos y otras cosas necessarias para el culto divino, y para su viaje. De Roma su Sanctidad y el Generalíssimo les embiaron su bendición con muchas gracias, indulgencias, cuentas benditas, medallas, y Agnus Deyes. Nombraron por superior de los Padres y Hermanos a un venerable Padre que se dezía Juan Baptista de Segura, que avía sido provincial en Castilla, con plena autoridad de su Sanctidad para las cosas tocantes a la conversión de los naturales de aquella tierra del Jacán, y tierra de la Florida.

[26] Embarcáronse en S. Lúcar de Barrameda en los galeones de su Magestad, de que iva por general, como dixe, el adelantado Pero Meléndez, el año de 1568, por principio dél. Tomaron en breve el puerto de la Habana, adonde se quedaron algunos Padres y Hermanos, y de allí prosiguieron los demás su viaje, y lle/-garon al fuerte de Sancta Helena aquel verano, adonde desembarcaron los benditos Padres y estuvieron allí algunos días descansando con los tres Padres y dos Hermanos, que

dixe, estavan allí. El adelantado les prometió como hombre que conocía a los indios, que son traidores, 100 soldados que fuessen en su compañía y los guardassen en el Jacán; y los Padres se lo agradecieron y dixeron que no era menester, que bastava la confiança que ellos tenían en Dios y llevar consigo al don Luis, a quien avían criado en la Compañía, señor y cacique de aquella tierra, que los soldados darían mal exemplo a los indios y los inquietarían con sus cosas. El Adelantado, si no me acuerdo mal, o otro governador de aquellas provincias, solía dezír, y era común plática en ellas: a estos B. Padres paréceles que el ser martirizados y hechos pedazos por estos bárbaros es a sólo lo que su Sanctidad los embía, y la Magestad católica y sus superiores; pues entiendan que, aunque esso es sanctíssimo y don particular del cielo aver mártires en la iglesia sancta de Dios, no los embían a sólo esso, sino a que trabajen muchos años en la conversión destos pobres indios, y en labrar y cultibar esta viña del Señor, y se guarden, y conserven en su gracia muchos años para las ocasiones que adelante se podrán ofrecer de gran servicio de Dios, como lo hicieron algunos sanctos; y a mí me / parece que tenía gran raçón; y la experiencia y el tiempo, que descubre las verdades, lo dio muy bien a entender, y los habitadores de aquellas provincias lo vimos por vista de ojos.

[27] Dióles el Adelantado una fragata muy buena para en que fuessen, y en ella metieron algunas tablas clavazón y otras cosas para el edificio de la casa en que avían de vivir y un carpintero para hazella; y por capitán a un Vicente Gonçález, portugués de nación, famoso soldado y gran marinero, casado en Sevilla, en Triana, que sirvió muchos años de capitán del Buscarruido de los galeones, siendo general della el Pero Meléndez; y la Magestad del rey D. Phelippe 2°, por sus buenos servicios le dio después un hábito y encomienda de Christus.

[28] Partieron para el Jacán del fuerte de S. Helena dos Padres y seis Hermanos, que son los que dize el Padre Pedro de Ribadeneira, y tres mancebos que avían venido con ellos desde Sevilla, de los que se crían en la Compañía, llevando por cabeça al Padre Juan Baptista de Segura; y el otro Padre se dezía Luis de Quirós y los Hermanos, Gabriel Gómez, Çavallos, Juan Baptista Méndez, Pedro de Linares, Cristóbal Redondo, Gabriel de Solís. Uno de los mancebos se dezía Alonso de Olmos, que es el que se escapó del martirio: que de los / dos no se supo su muerte.

[29] Llegaron al Jacán con buen tiempo, desembarcaron en tierra sin que los indios se lo estorbassen; y no lexos de la mar les fabricó el Capitán una casa, la mexor que pudo, y les dexó bastimentos para algunos días,

prometiéndoles sería buen tercero con el Adelantado para que no los olvidasse, y que pues era camino de España, passarían por allí los galeones quando bolviessen a ella; y con mucho gusto y contentamiento de los dichos Padres los dexó, porque el D. Luis los asseguró que no les faltaría lo necessario para la comida, porque la tierra es muy abundante de maíz, pescado y caça; y él y sus padres y parientes los defenderían de los indios; aunque los soldados viejos y baquianos de la tierra siempre pensaron en lo que avían de parar, que era ser mártires de Jesucristo.

[30] Ido el Capitán, vinieron los indios comarcanos, y los que eran subjetos al D. Luis y a su padre, y se alegraron con él, y con los Padres y Hermanos de la Compañía; los quales los acariciaron y regalaron con algunas cosas de las que traían de Castilla. Y començaron a sembrar la sancta semilla del Evangelio en aquellos bárbaros, siendo lengua e intérprete el mesmo don Luis. Y estaban los B. Padres consoladíssimos porque les pareció era buen principio aquel para hazer fructo en aquellos idólatras sus predicaciones.

[31] Es/-tuvo el don Luis con los Padres algunos días, y después que los tuvo assegurados, les pidió licencia, diziendo quería ir en persona a ver su tierra, pueblo, padres y parientes: que con su ida vendrían muchos más indios que hasta allí avían venido. Los bienaventurados Padres, abraçándolo, se la dieron y le dixeron si quería fuesse con él alguno dellos. Respondióles que no era menester compañía, que él solo quería ir, que era la tierra muy montuosa, como era la verdad, y passaría el compañero mucho trabajo aviendo de ir a pie. Fue, que no deviera, porque se bolvió peor que los indios, apostató de la fee católica, bolviéndosse a su idolatría, y se quedó entre los bárbaros.

[32] Viendo los B. Padres que se avían pasado ya muchos días más de los que avía llevado licencia, que se avían retirado los indios, y no venían a la doctrina tantos como antes que el don Luis se fuesse, concibieron mal de su tardança; embiaron a uno de los tres mancebos, que se dezía Alonso de Olmos, por ser grande amigo del don Luis, el qual guiándole Dios, herró el camino, y aportó al pueblo de otro cacique tan poderoso, y más que el don Luis, que le recibió y regaló y persuadió no fuesse en busca del don Luis, / que él le ayudaría de buena gana.

[33] El malaventurado del don Luis convocó sus deudos y parientes y otra mucha gente de guerra para ir a matar aquellos B. Padres y Hermanos, que estavan como ovejas y mansos corderos ofrecidos al holocausto y sacrificio por Jesucristo nuestro Señor. Bien semejante fue esta junta y conciliábulo al que hizieron los pérfidos judíos para crucificar al Salvador

del mundo, por cuyo amor estos benditos Padres y Hermanos murieron
bienaventurada y dichosa muerte, a monos de otra Judas que ellos avían
criado en su collegio y compañía. Llegó este lobo carnizero, aviendo ya
dexado la piel de oveja, y con macanas, dardos y flechas, y con las hachas,
cuchillos y machetes que los benditos Padres avían traído de Castilla para
el servicio de casa, los hizieron pedaços, y mataron, sin dexar a ninguno
con la vida, ni captivalle. ¡Bienaventurados Padres y Hermanos que
padecieron tal muerte, tan cruel y desapiadada por amor de Dios, y des-
dichados los que os la dieron, que padecerán mayores tormentos sin fin en
el fierno! No se escapó persona ninguna que pudiesse dar noticia desta
crueldad y martirio, ni el género de muerte que les dieron a todos ni a
cada uno de por sí.

[34] Llegó la nueva al Alonso d'Olmos que, como dixe, avía salido,
herrando el camino, a otro pueblo de un cacique, el qual, deshaziéndosse
en lágrimas por la muerte de los benditos Padres y Hermanos y por no
aver merecido ser martirizado con ellos, casi perdió la vida de dolor.
El cacique, viéndole tan afligido, le consoló y prometió de defendelle y
liballe de que el don Luis no le matasse, como avía hecho a sus compañeros; que aunque el don Luis se lo pidió muchas vezes para lo
martirizar, no se lo quiso dar el cacique; y el mancebo vivió siempre con
gran rezelo.

[35] Este moço Alonso de Olmos estuvo después en la Habana y de
aí / bolvió a Sancta Helena, donde avía salido; y contaba que le avían
dicho los indios, que al Padre Baptista o a otro Padre le avían martirizado
crudelíssimamente, haziéndole sanctiguar y que, como se iva sanctiguando,
le ivan abriendo con puntas de pedernal, que son tan agudas como navajas;
y a los demás mataron a palos y flechazos y cortaron las cabeças, y de los
cascos hizieron vasos con que se brindavan en sus borracheras, vestidos
con los ornamentos y ropas de los bienaventurados mártires, cantando
sus victorias y hazañas. Y de esto no se admire, ni espante nadie, que
otras mayores crueldades cuenta el Padre Josepho de Acosta de los Indios
de la Nueva España, que son todos unos, porque es su costumbre entre
ellos y tienen por relequia, enseñados del demonio, usar con los cristianos
y con los mesmos indios en sus sacrificios de tales crueldades y sacalles el
coraçón y ofrecelle a sus ídolos y fementidos dioses. . . .

[39] También contava el Alonso de Olmos le avían dicho los indios que,
después de muertos los Padres, avían abierto una caxa y hallando en ella
un Cristo Crucificado y otras reliquias; se pusieron a mirallas, y mano-
seallas, y se cayeron algunos dellos muertos: que parece que el Crucifixo

ofendido de la muerte y crueldades que avían ussado con aquellos Padres bienaventurados, quiso muriesen / súbita y desastradamente. Y visto los muertos, los demás acharon a huir, dexando los cuerpos de los sanctos mártires en el campo: que permitiría la divina Magestad se les diesse sepultura por ministerio de los sanctos ángeles, como lo dezía el mancebo. . . .

[42] . . . partió para Castilla, el verano del dicho año de 1572, yendo costeando la Florida, llevando la mira al norte. Llegaron al Jacán, en busca de los Padres y Hermanos de la Compañía, que ya se tenía alguna nueva que eran / muertos, aunque no cierta. Llegaron sobre tarde a reconocer el puerto; echáronse de mar en trabés a la boca de la barra. El Alonso de Olmos, que dixe se avía escapado del martirio, como tuvo nuevas que avía navíos en la costa, se hurtó del cacique (era su pueblo cerca de la mar), y de noche, marcándola, se fue huyendo a los navíos. Llegó a la playa este día, en frente donde estavan; echósse a nado, y llegando a la Capitana, que estava la primera, se entró dentro. Y como venía desnudo y quemado de sol, nadie le conoció, y entendieron que hera indio. Echó los ojos por el navío y vido a su padre, que se dezía Alonso de Olmos como él, y conociéndole, se echó a sus pies, besándolos y deziendo: este este es padre mío; porque, como avía cinco años que no hablaba nuestra lengua, de repente no acertava a hablar, y por el gran contento que tenía de averse visto en poder de cristianos.

[43] El Adelantado se fue a España, y del Jacán despachó un pataxe a la Habana con el Alonso de Olmos, padre y hijo, y algunos gentiles, que avían traído de la Florida; y de la Habana se bolvieron al fuerte de S. Helena, adonde el Alonso de Olmos tenía también madre, que se dezía Marina de Lara, y dos hermanos Francisco de Olmos y Pedro de Lara, y una hermana y abuela que llamavan María de Lara, que bivían junto a mi casa; y en la suya me guisavan de comer, quando era soltero. Y respecto desto nos comunicábamos; y traté al moço muy familiarmente, y me contó lo referido algunas vezes, y algunas particularidades de la tierra. Al qual le mataron después, en el pueblo de Orista, con 21 soldados, y con ellos al alférez Hernando Moyano (harto infeliz y desastradamente, que le huviera sido mucho mejor aver / muerto mártir glorioso con sus compañeros), yendo a un rescate de perlas, los más bárbaros indios que ay en la Florida, y hizieron dellos las crueldades referidas.

[44] Deste Alonso de Olmos supe ser aquella tierra del Jacán fertilíssima, y aver en ella oro, plata y perlas. Y dixo que, enseñándoles él una crucecita de oro que llevava, la cortaron con los dientes, y le dixeron que en la

sierra, hacia la otra mar, que deve de ser hazia el Nuevo México, avía mucho de aquello. Y los indios de aquella provincia, traían algunas chagualas en la frente y en las muñecas, manillas, y en las orejas, çarcillos de oro. [45] Son los indios desta provincia, según me contava, altos de cuerpo, muy gentiles hombres, más blancos que ningunos otros indios destas partes, grandes nadadores, muy sueltos y ligeros y grandíssimos flecheros. Susténtanse de pescado, maíz y caça, que ay en toda la Florida mucha abundancia destas tres cosas. No tienen rey ni principe poderoso que los govierne y señores; solo este govierno se estiende, quanto dura una lengua, que ay muchas en aquel reino. Los indios de los valles, que están muy estendidos de longitud y latitud, son enemicíssimos de los de la sierra, y se dan los veranos crudelíssima guerra; y de invierno se recoxen a sus pueblos, por ser tierra fría y andar casi desnudos, que no tienen otros vestidos sino pieles de animales, y essas no las alcançan todos. [46] Adoran al sol y a la luna, y al demonio, que se les aparece en varias y diversas figuras, y en pájaros; y entra algunas vezes el enemigo en sus sacerdotes y habla en ellos y los dexa molidos, y medio muertos. Contóme que estando un día en el buhío del cacique, se puso el demonio en un árbol, en figura de un pájaro negro, como cuerbo, y començó a hablar en su lengua. Y / preguntándole al cacique que qué decía aquel pájaro; le respondió, que era Dios, que venía a hablar y le dezía que le matasse. El mancebo le replicó que era el demonio que le traía engañado, y que era enemigo del Dios verdadero de los cristianos; y para que viesse que le dezía verdad, que él lo echaría de allí, en nombre de Jesucristo, Dios de los cristianos, con sola la señal de la Cruz, y saliendo del buhío y haziéndola, se fue, que, nunca más pareció. [47] Esto que dicho tengo, es lo que se platicava en el fuerte de S. Helena, el tiempo que yo estuve en ella (que fueron, como dixe, ocho años), de la muerte de los B. Padres y Hermanos de la Compañía de Ihs., que martirizaron en el Jacán, y lo que contava muchas vezes el dicho Alonso de Olmos, que estuvo quatro años por soldado en S. Helena, después que se libró; y se le dio crédito, por ser virtuoso, hijo de padres honrados y buenos cristianos. Sólo en las crueldades que se an contado, que se entiende fueron mucho mayores que las que se an escrito, podría ser differenciar en algo de lo que succedió; porque verdaderamente, como tengo dicho, no se halló ninguna persona al martirio de los dichos Padres y Hermanos; porque no escapó ningún cristiano que lo viesse; y lo que se a dicho es por avello oído de boca de los indios, que son mentirosos y encubren sus maldades y traiciones.

[48] Las personas que podrán deponer de este succeso y martirio de los dichos Padres son el capitán Vicente González, ya nombrado, commendador del hábito de Christus, casado en Triana, que estuvo dos vezes en el Jacán, la una quando llevó a los Padres, y la otra quando sacó al Alonso d'Olmos, Pero / de Lara, hermano del Alonso de Olmos, que yo dexé soldado en la Florida y deve de estar en ella, y un fulano Yuste, soldado de aquel tiempo que martirizaron los Padres, que yo dexé en Sevilla: que no entiendo ay otros vivos de los antiguos.

Y lo firmé de mi nombre que es fechado en la villa imperial de Potossí a veinte y quatro días del mes de Octubre de mill y seicientos y diez años.

BARTOLOMÉ MARTÍNEZ.

RELATION [1] OF BARTOLOMÉ MARTÍNEZ

The Martyrdom of the Fathers and Brothers of the Company of Jesus whom the Indians of Ajacán, in the Land of Florida, martyred, about which Father Pedro de Ribadeneyra has written briefly in the third book, chapter six, of the Life of the Blessed Father Francis Borgia

From Potosí, October 24, 1610

EXCERPTS

[22] The third band of Fathers and Brothers of the Company of Jesus to reach Florida was of those who were martyred in the province of Ajacán. It happened in this way.[2] The Governor, Pedro Menéndez de Avilés, Marquis of that land and Knight of the robes of Santiago, conquered two strongholds of the King of France in Florida. He slew two thousand French heretics there, 600 in the fortress of San Mateo (so named because the Christians captured it on that day) and 1200 who together with their captain and leader Jean Ribault were lost in a storm off the cape of Cañaveral. Going toward Spain, he sought to explore the coast of Florida that runs northward. He skirted it for more than 450 leagues until he arrived in sight of a land that is called Ajacán, in the language of the Indians. This was 300 leagues away from Santa Elena and 150 [*sic*] from Havana, more or less.

[23] The Governor, Pedro Menéndez, God save him, discovered on the coast a large bay. He entered further into the harbor and sailed up into it. When the Indians saw the boats, they came alongside in canoes and boarded the flagship. There His Excellency, as was his custom, like another Alexander, regaled them with food and clothing. Among these Indians came a chief who brought his son, who for an Indian was of fine presence and bearing. Pedro Menéndez asked the chief for permission to take him along that the King of Spain, his lord, might see him and others whom he had brought along. He gave his pledged word to return him with much wealth and many garments. The chief granted this and His Excellency took him to Castile, to the Court of King Philip II, God save him. The King our lord and his Court were very pleased with him and other Indians from the land of San Agustín and Santa Elena. His Excellency gave them many courtly favors and rich garments.

[24] The Indian from Ajacán became a Christian and they gave him the name Don Luis and he stayed in Castile six or seven years [3] in a house of the Society, where they instructed him in the matter of our Holy Faith and Christian religion. Being intelligent (as the Indians of those provinces are, if they mingle from youth with the Christians) he was made ready and they gave him the holy sacraments of the altar and Confirmation. When he was more than twenty years of age, he wished to return to his native land, with the plan and determination, as he then said, of converting his parents, relatives, and countrymen to the Faith of Jesus Christ, and baptizing them and making them Christians as he was. He discussed the matter with the Fathers of the Society, telling them that, if some of them were with him, he would offer himself, and, with God's favor, they would go there and make Christians of all the Indians of the province of Ajacán, over most of which his father was chief and lord. This proposal seemed good to the Fathers of the Society, seeking as they were the good of those souls and the growth and spread of the Christian religion. They related it to Father Francis Borgia, the General of the Society, and to the Supreme Pontiff, Pius V, and to the King, Philip II, God save him, and with their knowledge and consent, the voyage was made. The Governor Pedro Menéndez de Avilés learned of the proposal. He was a great mariner and he knew the land of Ajacán and had brought Don Luis. He was greatly pleased at the news, for he was very devoted and faithful to the works of the Society. He offered to bring the Fathers and Don Luis to the land of Ajacán in the galleons which protect the sea of the Indies, over which he was commander. And so it was done.

[25] His Majesty ordered the officials in the Casa de Contratación in Seville to give them what was needed in food and clothing and other things necessary for the divine worship and for their journey. From Rome His Holiness and the Father-General sent them their blessings with many favors, indulgences, and Agnus Dei's. They appointed, as superior of the Fathers and Brothers, a venerable Father who was named Juan Baptista Segura, who had been provincial in Castile,[4] with full authority from His Holiness for matters touching on the conversion of the natives of that land of Ajacán and the land of Florida.

[26] In the beginning of the year 1568,[5] they sailed from San Lúcar de Barrameda in the galleons of His Majesty, over which the Governor Pedro Menéndez was commander.[6] In a short time they came to the port of Havana, where some of the Fathers and Brothers stayed behind. From there the rest continued their voyage and reached the fort of Santa Elena that summer; there the blessed Fathers disembarked and stayed for a rest of some days, with the three Fathers and two Brothers who, as I said, had remained there. The Governor, knowing the treachery of the Indians, promised them 100 soldiers who were to be in their company and guard them in Ajacán. The Fathers thanked him and said there was no need of this, for they had confidence in God and were bringing with them Don Luis, whom they had educated in the Society, and who was the lord and chief of that land. Moreover the soldiers would set a bad example for the Indians and disturb them with their activity. The Governor, if I recall correctly, or another official of those provinces, used to say (it was a byword there) that these good Fathers seemed to believe that the sole purpose for which His Holiness and His Majesty and their superiors had sent them was to be martyred and cut to pieces by the savages.[7] They believed that although it is a holy and special gift from above to have martyrs in God's holy Church, the Fathers were not sent for this alone. They were to labor many years for the conversion of these poor Indians, and to plant and cultivate the vineyard of the Lord, to protect themselves and keep themselves in His favor many years for the opportunities in the great service of God that presented themselves. This is what several saints did. This seemed to me to be most reasonable, and experience and time, which reveal the truth, have made it evident, and we inhabitants of those provinces saw it with our own eyes.

[27] The Governor gave them a very good frigate for their journey in which they brought some boards, nails, and other things for the erection of a house, in which they might live, and a carpenter to build it.[8] For

captain there was Vicente Gonzales, a Portuguese, a famous soldier and a fine mariner who was married in Triana in Seville, who spent many years as captain [9] of the small ships with the galleons which were under the command of Pedro Menéndez. His Majesty King Philip II, for his fine services, made him a Knight with the robes and badge of the Order of Christ.

[28] As Father Ribadeneyra reports, two Fathers, six Brothers, and three catechists who had been trained by the Fathers and accompanied them from Seville left the fort at Santa Elena for Ajacán. Father Juan Baptista de Segura was the leader, Luis de Quirós was the name of the other priest, and Gabriel Gómez, Zaballos, Juan Baptista Méndez, Pedro de Linares, Cristóbal Redondo, Gabriel de Solís were the Brothers. One of the boys, Alonso de Olmos, escaped martyrdom; and the death of two was never learned.[10]

[29] They reached Ajacán in good season and landed without any opposition from the Indians. The Captain built them a hut, as best as he could, not far from the sea. He gave them a few days' supplies with a pledge to intercede with the Governor to remember them. The fleets en route to Spain would pass by there on their return; then he left the Fathers contented and happy. Although Don Luis had assured them that food would be available, for the country is rich in corn, fish, and game, and that he and his clan would protect the Fathers from the natives, the soldiers and those who knew the country always believed that the men who stayed there would be martyrs of Jesus Christ.

[30] After the Captain left, the Indians round about, who were subjects of Don Luis and his father, came and were glad at the coming of Don Luis with the Fathers and Brothers of the Society. The Fathers were friendly, gave them some trinkets they had brought from Castile, and then began to sow the holy seed of the gospel among the savages, with Don Luis as interpreter. The Fathers were pleased, for it seemed that their preaching among the pagans was well on its way to bearing fruit.

[31] Don Luis stayed with the Fathers for a few days and won their confidence. Then he asked permission to go in person to see his home country, his village, and his relatives, saying that thus more Indians than before would come. The blessed Fathers, embracing him, agreed and offered to send someone with him. Don Luis replied that he needed no companion and preferred to travel alone, because the terrain was rough, as was true, and a companion would have trouble on foot. He departed, though he should never have done so, for he turned worse than the natives, an

P. Ludovicus Qviros, Gabriel de Solis et Ioannes Mendez S. I. Hispani
in Florida pro Christi fide barbarè enecti. A. 1571. 4. Februarij.
C. Screta del.   Melch. Küsell f.

Plate VI

THE AMBUSH OF FATHER QUIRÓS AND HIS COMPANIONS

An early engraving in the *Societas Iesu Militans . . .*, by Father Mathias
Tanner, S.J., published in Prague in 1675. Melchior Küsell was the
artist. The inscription reads, "F. Luis Quirós, Gabriel de Solís, and Juan
Méndez, Spanish Jesuits, were savagely slain in Florida for the Faith of
Christ, in the year 1571 on the 4th of February."

P. Ioañes Bapt: de Segura, Gabriel Gomez, Petrus de Linarez, Sanctiq Sauelliq,
Christoph. Rotundq Hisp. S.I. in Florida pro Christi fide trucidati A.1571. 8.Febr
C. Screta del.   Melch. Küsell f.

Plate VII

THE KILLING OF FATHER SEGURA AND HIS COMPANIONS

This engraving is from the same source as the preceding illustration.
The Indian costume and weapons reflect the contemporary European
notions. The inscription reads, "F. Juan Bapt: de Segura, Gabriel Gómez,
Pedro Linarez, Sanctus Sauellius (Sancho Zaballos), Christoph. Rotundo
(Cristóbal Redondo), Spanish Jesuits, were murdered in Florida for
the Faith of Christ, in the year 1571 on the 8th of February."

apostate from his Catholic Faith, taking up his idolatry again, and living with the savages.

[32] When the good Fathers saw that more time had elapsed than they had agreed to, and that the Indians had gone and no longer came for the preaching as they did when Don Luis was there, they began to worry over his tardiness. They sent one of the young men called Alonso de Olmos, who was very friendly with Don Luis. Through God's guidance, the boy lost his way [11] and found the village of another chief more powerful than Don Luis, who took him in and warned him not to search for Don Luis, and promised to help gladly.

[33] The renegade Don Luis convened his friends and relatives and many warriors to go and massacre the good Fathers and Brothers who were like sheep and gentle lambs offered as a holocaust and sacrifice to Our Lord Jesus Christ. Such was the council held by the faithless Jews to crucify the Saviour of the world for Whose love these holy Fathers and Brothers died their blessed happy deaths at the hands of another Judas whom they had reared in their own Society's college. This ravening wolf, tossing aside the sheep's clothing, and seizing his swords, darts, and arrows, as well as the hatchets, knives, and axes the Fathers had brought from Castile for their own use, came upon the blessed Fathers and cut them down and slew them. Blessed be the Fathers and Brothers who endured such a cruel and pitiless death for God's love! Hapless murderers who will suffer the eternal pains of Hell! [12] Not a soul escaped to tell about this cruel martyrdom, and whether the manner of death was as a group or singly. [13]

[34] Alonso de Olmos, who, as I mentioned, had lost his way and reached the village of another chief, shed many tears at the news of the death of the blessed Fathers and Brothers. He almost lost his life grieving that he had not deserved to be martyred with them. When the chief saw him so crestfallen, he comforted him and promised to protect him and prevent Don Luis from killing him as he had his companions. Despite the demands of Don Luis that the boy be delivered up to martyrdom, the chief was firm. The boy lived on in fear.

[35] This lad, Alonso de Olmos, later stayed in Havana and then went on to Santa Elena, whence he came. He told what the Indians had said, how they cruelly martyred Father Baptista and another Father, making him bless himself, and as he did so they cut him with points of flint as sharp as a razor. The rest were slain with cudgels and arrows, and then they cut off their heads. Fashioning the skulls into cups, they waved them about in

their drunken feasts, and putting on the sacred vestments and clothes of the saintly martyrs, they sang of their mighty conquests.[14] Let there be no wonder or amazement at this. Father José de Acosta relates greater cruelties about the Indians of New Spain,[15]—they are all the same. For they have a custom and a tradition taught by the devil to torture Christians and even Indians in their sacrifices, cutting out their hearts and offering them to their idols and false divinities.

[39] Alonso de Olmos told something else that the Indians related after the Fathers died. They opened a chest and finding there a crucifix and some relics they tried to see and handle them, but they were struck dead.[16] For it seems that the Crucified One was offended by the cruel death worked on these blessed Fathers and wanted to strike them down suddenly. At the sight of these deaths, the others ran away and left the bodies of the blessed martyrs, for the Divine Majesty willed that they be buried by the angels, as this boy says. . . .

[42] . . . In the Spring of 1572 Menéndez departed for Castile, sailing north along the coast of Florida. They reached Ajacán in search of the Fathers and Brothers, whose deaths were not yet certain. They arrived too late to explore the harbor; so they anchored at its mouth.[17] When Alonso de Olmos, whose escape from martyrdom I have related, heard the report of ships off the coast (the village was close to the sea), he fled at night to the ships. At daybreak he came to the beach off their anchorage, swam out to the flagship, which was nearest, and climbed aboard. Since he arrived naked and tanned by the sun, no one recognized him but thought he was an Indian. Gazing about the ship, he saw and recognized his father, also named Alonso de Olmos, and threw himself at his feet and then he kissed him and cried: "Here! Here is my father!" Because he had not used our language for five years,[18] and was so happy on being in the protection of Christians, he could hardly speak.

[43] The Governor went on to Spain after ordering a ship to Havana with Alonso de Olmos, senior and junior, and some natives he had brought along from Florida. From Havana they returned to the fort at Santa Elena, where, in the house next to mine, there lived Alonso's mother named Marina de Lara, and two brothers, Francisco de Olmos and Pedro de Lara,[19] a sister and a grandmother named María de Lara. When I was a bachelor I used to eat with them. A close friend of the boy told me at different times many of the details of that country that I have set forth. Later, while searching for pearls, he and 21 soldiers under Lieutenant Hernando Moyano were cruelly tortured and slain by the Oristans, the

most savage Indians in Florida.[20] How terribly unfortunate! It would have been much better to have died in the glorious martyrdom of his companions.

[44] From Alonso I learned that Ajacán is a very fertile land, with gold and silver and pearls.[21] He said that when he showed them a small gold cross, they bit it and said it was plentiful in the mountains which reach to the other sea, and this should be as far as New Mexico. The Indians of this province wear some golden circlets on their brows and bracelets on their wrists and ear rings.

[45] According to his report, the Indians of this province are tall, noble, paler than many other Indians in that region, fine swimmers, very swift and nimble and skillful archers.[22] They sustain themselves with fish, corn and game; all three abound in Florida. There is no king or prince who lords it over them, but only that chief is recognized wherever one tongue is spoken, and there are many in that region. The Indians of the long wide valleys are the enemies of those in the mountains and in summer a savage war is waged.[23] In winter they return to their villages because the land is cold and they go about naked. Their only garments are the skins of animals and everyone does not have these.[24]

[46] They adore the sun, the moon, and the devil, who appears in many guises and in the shape of a bird.[25] At times he takes possession of his priests and speaks through them and leaves them bruised and half dead. He said that one day, when he was in the chief's cabin, the devil appeared in the shape of a black bird, like a crow, and, perched on a tree, began to speak in the Indian tongue. When he asked the chief what the bird said, he replied that it was a god who came to tell him to kill the boy. The boy answered that it was the devil trying to deceive, for he was the enemy of the true God of the Christians. In order to show that this was true, he went out of the cabin and in the name of Jesus Christ, the God of the Christians, he drove it away from there with only the sign of the Cross. It went and never appeared again.

[47] What I have told about the death of the blessed Fathers and Brothers of the Company of Jesus, martyred in Ajacán, was on everyone's lips at the time I was in Santa Elena, which was, as I said, for eight years. Alonso de Olmos recounted it to me many times when he was a soldier there four years after his escape. What he says can be believed, for he is a good man from an upright Christian family. There could be a slight difference from later accounts about the tortures which he recounted and which were understood to be much greater than what was recorded. As I said, there

really was no one present at the martyrdom of the Fathers and Brothers. No Christian who saw it escaped; anything said was first heard from the lips of the Indians, who are liars and flaunt their own treacherous crimes. [48] There are people who can give testimony of the martyrdom of the Fathers. They are the aforementioned Vicente Gonzales, a Commander of the Order of Christ, who was married in Triana, and visited Ajacán twice, once when he brought the Fathers and then when he saved Alonso de Olmos. There is a brother of Alonso de Olmos, Pedro de Lara,[26] who was a soldier in Florida when I left and should still be there. There was a person named Yuste, a soldier at the time of the martyrdom of the Fathers, whom I left in Seville. I know of no one else still living. I affix my name to this in the imperial town of Potosí, October 24, 1610.

BARTOLOMÉ MARTÍNEZ

NOTES

1. The text is found in *MAF* 573-604. It is available in a translation done by Father Aloysius J. Owens, S.J., in *Historical Records and Studies of the United States Historical Society*, 25 (New York, 1935) 129-148. The autograph copy, freshened where faint by a more recent hand, is found in the Society's Archivio del Gesù (Fondo Gesuitico), Rome, Vocationes ad Societatem, N. 2. The author was a resident of Santa Elena from 1571 to 1579. Having married a niece of Governor Menéndez' wife, he worked as a minor official under the Governor. As he himself states in para. 47, he heard the story of the death of the Fathers from the residents of Santa Elena and Alonso himself. The Relation is attested by his signature at the request of his confessor, Father Antonio de Vega Loaysa, S.J., Commissary of the Holy Office in Potosí, who was collecting material for a history of the Society. The only other document from his hand that we have found is a letter to the King, February 17, 1577 (in Connor, *Colonial Records of Spanish Florida*, 1: 236-248) reporting on the condition of the province under Hernando de Miranda.

2. It is almost useless to attempt a detailed criticism of Martínez' inaccurate recital. His mind is a jumbled disorder of dates, names, and events. In describing the events at Fort Caroline he more than doubles the number of dead, and falsely credits Menéndez with a voyage to Ajacán. He may have had in mind his victorious penetration of Guale in 1566, but this was six years after Don Luis had been taken (see 2 Lowery 244-263). He likewise greatly exaggerates the distance from Santa Elena to Ajacán.

3. It is quite evident from a study of the Jesuit narratives about Don Luis that he did not stay in Spain as long as this, or in a Jesuit house. Borgia knew of the proposed use of the Indian and perhaps Philip II did, but we have no evidence that Pius V was apprised of the Indian's plan. His letter on the Florida Mission to Menéndez, August 18, 1569 (2 Ruidíaz 299) does not mention Don Luis.

4. Martínez is imaginative and inaccurate in describing the preparations for the

journey. Father Segura had not been provincial, but only a rector of various colleges.

5. The 1570 arrival of the Jesuits is unknown to him, so that he places the Ajacán events two years too early.

6. Segura sailed on April 10; therefore Menéndez could not have captained the fleet, for he writes from Santander on May 12, and was expected at the Azores in June. He apparently visited Havana in April, 1569, and there was opportunity for his stopping there between letters from Spain dated January 4, 1570, and December 3, 1570. After the latter date he remained in Spain until May 17, 1571 (2 Lowery, Appendix CC, 457 ff.).

7. Certainly martyrdom was not the primary purpose of Ajacán, but rather greater conversions than in Florida, which itself afforded abundant chances for martyrdom.

8. There was no carpenter at Ajacán other than the Brothers. Perhaps original plans called for one.

9. Vicente Gonzales is not frequently mentioned in the documents of the period. He evidently was specialized as a pilot of light dispatch ships which visited and mapped the coast and inland waterways. Menéndez Marqués mentions him with high praise to the King (1 Connor 269). He was a pilot to the Chesapeake on four occasions (1570, 1571, 1572, 1588), and his Relation appears below.

10. See Part I, note 61. In the Rogel Letter of December 9, 1570 (*MAF* 478) Alonso is included among the "four catechists." He, in company with his younger brother, may have been one of the three catechists taken by Rogel to Orista to learn the Indian tongue. His ability to survive in Ajacán may have been based on previous experiences in Florida. The other two "boys" spoken of by Martínez either never existed or never disembarked at Ajacán. He wrongly attributes to Ribadeneyra the statement that three catechists went to Ajacán.

11. Alonso may have been lost on an earlier mission, but he found his way back before the murders took place.

12. The Rogel Letter and Relation and the Carrera Relation seem to have been unknown to Martínez, for considerable details of the massacre may be found there. His anger against the murderers would have been mollified had he known they were baptized before death.

13. Martínez rules out Alonso as an eye-witness, as discussed in Part I.

14. The details of this orgy bear signs of invention, but there is no essential exaggeration, as may be gathered from Smith's description of Powhatan's treatment of his enemies and George Cassen in particular (1 Arber 81 ff.).

15. This is the *De Natura Novi Orbis*, Libri duo, Salamanticae, 1589 (1588). It was reprinted at Cologne in 1596; translated into Italian and printed at Venice in 1596; translated into Dutch and published at Enchuysen in 1598; translated into French and published at Paris in 1598. (See Clara L. Penney, *Books Printed Before 1601* in the Library of the Hispanic Society of America.) For an excellent appraisal of Acosta's influence see Leon Lopetegui, S.J., *El Padre José de Acosta, S.J. y las Missiones* (Madrid, 1942).

16. Shea, following earlier histories, says Father Rogel bore away the crucifix

and placed it in the college of Guayala (Shea, "The Log Chapel on the Rappahannock," 22 *Catholic World* [March, 1875] 856). However, from Rogel's Relation, para. 10, it is clear that the crucifix remained in the hands of the Indians.

17. Father Owens' translation states that "they dropped anchor off the bar," but *barra* is often used in old maps and Spanish marine terminology in metonymy for "harbor" or "port." Martínez' description coincides well with the supposed anchorage of Menéndez at Point Comfort.

18. Alonso was among the Indians for only a year and a half. Rogel confirms his loss of the Spanish tongue. See Rogel's August Letter above, para. 9.

19. In Spanish practice, brothers often acquired different family names, one following the father, the other the mother. Ignatius Loyola, for example, took the name López. Pedro de Lara may be identified with Oré's "Juan" de Lara, which name may have been a survival of his catechetical days with Father Rogel, who spoke affectionately of a "Juanico" at Santa Elena (see Rogel to Hinistrosa, December 11, 1569, *MAF* 402). Father Sedeño also speaks of two "Juanicos" in his letter to Rogel of Dec. 19, 1568, from Tegesta to Havana (*MAF* 373), which implies the use of a nickname for young catechists or assistants. As late as Virginia days, the early colonists and missionaries relied on young boys who could quickly pick up the Indian language from contact and then act as interpreters.

20. Oré says the Spanish went to Escamacu to recover stolen clothing, but official reports indicate that 21 soldiers under Moyano were attacked at Orista when they seized food there (1 Connor 192-203).

21. If Alonso is correct about the pearls, the country he describes must be inland from the bay. Drs. Harald A. Rehder and Joseph P. E. Morrison, of the Division of Mollusks, Smithsonian Institution, inform us that "the Chesapeake oyster, like all true oysters, never produces pearls of value." Pearls in the Virginia area came from the Naiades, or Pearly Freshwater Mussels, which do not invade even brackish water and are found a considerable distance west of Jamestown Island and also on the Pamunkey and Mattaponi rivers. Significantly, Weanoc was said to be a land "full of pearl muskles" (1 Arber xli), and the Pamunkey is elsewhere described as a "land rich in copper and pearl."

Smith and others seem to have the Indians of the lower James collecting pearl oysters, but they may have made an improper inference from seeing them in possession of pearls, and collecting oysters. All commentators on Lane's narrative (6 Hakluyt (EL) 143) interpret the Chowan king's remarks to refer to pearl fishing around Craney Island, but there was neither "deep water" there nor pearl mussels. The remark, if it has any foundation at all, might better be applied to Eppes Island or Turkey Island in Weanoc territory. "If the Indians actually found the pearls (rather than possessed them) near the mouth of the James River, they must have gathered them from the smaller tributaries running down from the upland, in this Tidewater area" concludes Dr. Rehder. It might be added that reports of a king on a pearl island had already been circulated in the West, and Lane may have been reading this into his conversation with the chief.

22. The large stature of the Virginia Indians is confirmed by T. Dale Stewart, "The Finding of an Indian Ossuary on the York River in Virginia," *Journal of*

the Washington Academy of Science, Washington, D.C., 22 (1940) 356-364. Many of the bones were found at the very edge of the stream. They indicate a race six feet tall. Alonso de Olmos had described them to Martínez as tall and of considerable physical ability. There is no doubt of their ability as swimmers and archers. Percy tells how in 1607 the Indians that met them at Point Comfort swam across the river or inlet to Kecoughtan with their bows and arrows in their mouths (1 Arber lxiii). Smith is in accord with Alonso in describing the Indians as tall, "of a colour browne when they are of any age, but they are bourne white," "very strong, of an able body and full of agilitie," "forty yards will they shoot levell, or very neare the mark" (1 Arber 69 ff.). The prevalence in the diet of "fish, corn and game" is too well known to need comment.

23. The description of tongues and rule is similar to that given by Hariot for North Carolina. There was little difference in language among the various Algonkin tribes; so Alonso, as is evident from the mention of wars between the Tidewater and Piedmont Indians, knew at least about the Sioux and perhaps the Iroquoian tribes to the south and north of the Algonkin. He indicates that the Powhatan empire had not yet been forged, though he attributes a headship to Don Luis' father.

24. Here there is an echo of Smith, who says: "For their apparell, they are some time couered with the skinnes of wilde beasts; But the common sort haue scarce to cover their nakednesse but with grasse, the leaues of trees, or such like" (1 Arber 66).

25. The account of the religion has an authentic ring. Among the traits listed by Regina Flannery as characteristic of coastal Algonquian culture are the regarding of the sun and moon as deities. Perhaps the story of the crow explains the taboo on killing the crow (heretofore not recorded for Virginia or Maryland). The taming of hawks was known to the coastal Algonkin. In summary, the following traits are verified in the documents that we have here presented:

Agriculture–maize (Quirós).
Stalking in disguise–(Virginia only) illustrated by Don Luis' approach in the stolen garments, though it applies chiefly to animal stalking.
Corncribs–the *garita* of Oré.
Tamed pets–Alonso's crow?
Copper ornaments–trade mentioned by Rogel.
Dugout canoes–their use is described by Rogel and Carrera.
Falchions and clubs set with stones–the clubs mentioned by Rogel as used by assassins: *macanas, botadores.*
Smoke signaling–the Ecija relation (heretofore doubtful for Virginia).
Polygamy–Don Luis' wives.
Adopt prisoners–attitude of Don Luis' brother and the friendly chief who protected Alonso.

See Regina Flannery, "An Analysis of Coastal Algonquian Culture," *Catholic University of America Anthropological Series,* No. 7 (1939), 167-176.

26. Here is another indication that Pedro de Lara, a survivor in Florida, is the Juan de Lara known to Oré.

CARTA DE PEDRO MENÉNDEZ MARQUÉS

Junio 22, 1587

A dos de mayo passado reçebi un pliego de su magestad en la florida, por el qual me manda, sepa y entienda q ay algun cosario poplado en la costa y si ay un estrecho que dizen passa a la otra mar, dentro de çinco dias como lo reçebi, me parti de sant agustin con la misma fragata que llebo el despacho, y dos barcas a saber lo que su magestad me mando, dexando primero en santa elena muniçiones y mas xente de la que tenia. fui corriendo la costa asta altura de treinta y siete grados, muy cerca del Jacan, ques la baya de Santa Maria. asta llegar alli ay tres bajos muy ruines que salen mucho a la mar. en lo demas la costa es mucho mejor ansi en el fondo como en la tierra, que no de santa elena para el cabo de cañabaral, por que tiene muy buenos puertos y dentro de aquello que andube, no ay memoria de cosario ninguno y no passe adelante, porque el dia que abia de entrar en el Jacan me dio tan grandisima tormenta que me desgarro de la costa y un palmo de bela, y me echo en los Lucayas y desta isla, y de dos barcas que llebaba perdi la una con todo su aparexo y fue bentura poder tomar la xente. bine a esta billa a tres dias y saldre de aqui dentro de quatro. Para el año que biene lo tomare mas de proposito y saldre un poco mas tarde porque en el mes de mayo es berde en aquella costa. yo doy cuenta de todo esto a su magestad y tambien le suplicome de lizencia para correr toda la costa asta la isla de San Juan, para que de una bez sepamos el secreto de esta costa y que de alli yo propio baya a dar cuenta de lo que ay y su magestad mande lo q fuere servido. pues ay tiempo para ello que no saldre de sant agustin asta fin de mayo, y realmente ay nezesidad de saver toda la costa, por que lo que yo andube esta muy diferente de lo que la carta tiene pintada, y en esto podra Vuestra Señoria saber mesmo de adbertir a su magestad lo que mas conbenga. *(alia manu)* y con tant. dios guarde a Vuestra Señoria Sn lazar [?] a 22 de Junio 1587 de Jc.

PEDRO MENÉNDEZ MARQUÉS

166

LETTER [1] OF PEDRO MENÉNDEZ MARQUÉS
June 22, 1587

On the second of last May I received a document in Florida from His Majesty, whereby he orders me to take cognizance of the fact that there is a pirate settlement [2] on the coast and ascertain if there be a strait which they say passes to the other sea. Within five days of receiving the document I set out on the same frigate that brought the despatch, with two small boats [3] to find out what His Majesty ordered me. Leaving first supplies at Santa Elena and more men than they had, I proceeded along the coast to the latitude of 37°, very close to Jacán, [4] which is the bay of Santa María. On approaching it, there are three very dangerous shoals [5] that stretch out far into the sea. For the rest, the coast both as to the depth of the sea, and the land, is much better than the part from Santa Elena to the cape of Cañaveral, for it has many fine ports. In the parts I travelled there is no record of pirates. I did not go farther, because on the day I was to enter Jacán, I was met with a very fierce storm which tore me from the coast and ripped a stretch of sail. I was driven into the Lucayas and away from this island. [6] Of the two small boats, one was lost with all its rigging; by good fortune we were able to save the crew. I arrived at this village three days ago and I shall leave within four. Next year [7] I shall undertake the enterprise with more caution and I shall set out later because in the month of May that coast line is green. I shall report all of this to His Majesty and I shall also ask for permission to follow the whole coast as far as the island of San Juan, [8] so that once and for all we may know the secret of this coast. I myself am going to make my report and His Majesty can then command his will. There is, indeed, time for all of this because I shall not set out from San Agustín until the end of May, and really it is necessary to know the coast, for the parts that I visited are different from what is drawn on the map, [9] and likewise Your Excellency can also advise His Majesty what is most expedient.

[In another hand] And so God protect Your Excellency. From San Lazar [?],

June 22, 1587 of Jesus Christ.

PEDRO MENÉNDEZ MARQUÉS

NOTES

1. The original is in AGI, Casa de Contratación, 42-1-8/3. There is a photostat in the Connor Papers, Library of Congress, which our text follows. From the cryptic style of this letter, it is possible to reconstruct only partially this voyage to Ajacán. Oré (41) makes a brief reference to this voyage. On May 7, 1587, the Governor, on receipt of an order to hunt for pirates and find out more about the passage to the "other sea," sailed north from San Agustín. On the way he reinforced Santa Elena and then observed the coast line up to 37°. He was not able to enter the bay, but was driven down to the Bahamas by a fierce storm in which he lost one of his three ships. He wrote this report during a stay of a week on one of the islands which seems to be named San Lazar (The place is the only illegible word on the manuscript). This letter gives no open reference to the recipient's name or office. Obviously he was someone intimate with the King and more likely a member of the Casa de Contratación since the letter is found in that collection. There are two suggested persons. The first is the Marqués de Santa Cruz, who was finishing plans for the Armada against England at this time and desired the Indies clear of pirates before the Spaniards drew off strength for the attack. The other is the Duke of Medina Sidonia, who wrote to Pedro Menéndez Marqués in the winter of 1587-88 to be ready to sail to the island of San Juan by May of 1588. See Letter of Pedro Menéndez Marqués, July 17, 1588 (3 *Historical Magazine* 275).

2. This was the Raleigh colony of North Carolina. Had the Governor waited for about two months before sailing, he would have encountered John White's ships, which reached the colony in July. The small colony which had been left at Roanoke was attacked by the Indians and all had been killed or taken prisoner by the time Pedro Menéndez Marqués arrived. See also Appendix E.

3. There is frequent reference in the remaining documents to "two ships" accompanying the expeditions. In his *Ordenanzas de Poblaciones* of 1563 (see *Recopilación de las Leyes de Indias*, II, 5, 6) Philip II ordered every explorer to take at least two vessels of not over 60 tons each in order to enter inlets and cross the bars and shoals along the coast. The larger ships remained in a safe harbor until another was reached by these pinnaces.

4. The latitude given indicates that Marqués believed the Chesapeake to be above 37°. Thus he is consistent with his 1573 estimate of 37 1/2° and with the 1588 estimate of 37 "and some" degrees at the first port west of the mouth. Perhaps overestimates were due to failure to correct properly for refraction.

5. The changes in the coast line do not permit accurate identification of these shoals. He may refer to Wimble Shoals and Platt Shoals south of Oregon Inlet, though they were not dangerous for small sailing vessels, or he may refer to the shoal in front of Oregon Inlet which would have been extremely dangerous. Farther south he would have encountered dangerous shoals off Cape Lookout (the *Promotorium Tremendum* of White's map) and Cape Hatteras.

6. These are today the Bahamas, although the 1529 map by Ribero places them east of the "isla de Bahama." The phrase "away from this island" is obscure, but it

would appear that he was driven past this *villa*, where he knew he could make repairs. Oré (41) makes this island Cuba, but it is difficult to reconcile this with the Spanish text.

7. This most successful voyage of 1588 is described in the documents that follow.

8. On the Wytfliet map "Norvmbega et Virginia, 1597," the "isla de S. Juan" is placed at 44°. However he might be referring to the Cabo de San Juan or the Río de San Juan, which on the earlier Spanish maps is shown at about 39°.

9. Although voyages north of Santa Elena to Ajacán had been made by the Spanish in 1570, 1571, 1572, and 1573, the information from these trips seems to have been lost in transmission to the cartographers of the *Padrón General* map at the Casa de Contratación. There was no cartographer on the 1573 voyage or, probably, on the others. A more widespread education in map construction would have accelerated geographical knowledge. An essay on the history of the cartography of the Chesapeake is found in Part III below.

Relación de Luis Gerónimo de Oré

Relación de los mártires que ha habido en las provincias de la Florida; doce religiosos de la Compañía de Jesús, que padecieron en el Jacán, y cinco de la orden de nuestro Seráfico P. S. Francisco, en la provincia de Guale. Pónese asimismo la descripción de Jacán, donde se han fortificado los Ingleses, y de otras cosas tocantes a la conversión de los Indios

Hecha por el P. Luis Gerónimo de Oré. Lector de Teología y Comisario de la Provincia de Santa Elena de la Florida e Isla de Cuba.

Del descubrimiento del Jacán y martirio de doce religiosos de la Compañía de Jesús.

Cerca del año de mil y quinientos y setenta, gobernando el Adelantado Pedro Menéndez los presidios de la Florida, se desgaritó de el puerto de Santa Helena un navío la vuelta del Norte, en altura de treinta y siete grados y medio, y se metió en una gran bahía que llamaron de la Madre de Dios, y de algunos indios que vinieron a bordo, cogieron un mancebo cacique y le llevaron a España, y después de catequizado le bautizaron y pusieron por nombre don Luis, a quien Su Majestad mandó dar el sustento necesario, todo el tiempo que estuvo en España, y lo pusieron al estudio con los Padres de la Compañía de Jesús.

Y por el año de 77 trajo el Adelantado cincuenta pobladores, y los repartió en dos fuertes de Santa Helena y de San Agustín; y el año siguiente de 78, fueron ocho religiosos de la Compañía a la conversión de los naturales de la Florida, y estos religiosos asistían en la ciudad de Santa Helena, y dos dellos fueron a la provincia de Guale, catorce leguas de allí, entre San Agustín y Santa Helena, para dotrinar los naturales, y el uno fué a la banda del Norte, a una provincia que llaman Escamacu, y llevó en su compañía un muchacho de diez años, llamado Juan de Lara, hijo de un poblador, para deprender la lengua, el cual vive hoy en San Agustín. Asistiendo, pues, año y medio con los naturales, considerando el poco fruto que hacía, se volvió a Santa Helena, donde estaban los demás religiosos.

El Padre Álamo (que así se llamaba uno de los religiosos de aquella Congregación) vino a España a dar cuenta a los superiores de las condiciones y calidades de los naturales, y de la tierra, y del poco provecho que se hacía entre ellos, pues, por su resistencia y dureza, les pareció a los Padres no convenir bautizar a alguno, en todo este tiempo. Estaba entonces en la casa de Sevilla el cacique don Luis, aprovechado en la lengua española, en leer y escribir, y otros estudios que le enseñaron, el cual, viendo que habían pasado a la conversión de la Florida religiosos, dijo a el / fol. 4 v. / Padre Rector y a otros, que él se atrevía a llevar a su tierra algunos sacerdotes, y que con el ayuda de Dios y su buena diligencia se convertirían a la fe los indios della. Estas palabras causaron en los religiosos gran deseo y zelo de la salvación de las almas, y con esta determinación se ofrecieron a Su Majestad, y pidieron licencia y el avío necesario para ir a aquellas partes, y llevar consigo al cacique don Luis.

Concedida la licencia y lo que pedían por Su Majestad, salieron de España, y llegaron en salvamento a Santa Helena, y de allí el Adelantado les dió un navío y sustento para un año, y que los llevase un capitán llamado Vicente Gonzáles. Fueron, por todos, doce sacerdotes religiosos y un muchacho llamado Alonso de Lara, hermano mayor del otro que se hizo mención, hijos del poblador de Santa Helena. Llegados a la bahía de la Madre de Dios o al Jacán, subieron el río arriba doce leguas, en cuya ribera tenía el cacique don Luis sus pueblos y dos hermanos caciques, los cuales y los demás indios los recibieron y los hicieron alojar, con demostracion de mucho contento.

Viendo la buena disposición de la tierra, desembarcaron la ropa y alojaron en una casa que luego hicieron de palma, con un apartado pequeño a una banda para decir Misa, hasta que se hiciese iglesia más cómoda. De allí se vino el navío a Santa Helena a dar cuenta al Adelantado dónde dejaba a los religiosos. Y como el enemigo del género humano procura estorbar siempre semejantes obras, enderezadas a la salvación de la almas, instigó al cacique don Luis, puesto ya en la ocasión de estar entre los suyos, a darse al vicio deshonesto, tan desenfrenadamente que el P. Juan Bautista, superior de aquellos religiosos, le reprendió severamente, y después con palabras caritativas y religiosas lo amonestó y exhortó y rogó diciéndole que mirase que habían venido movidos por sus promesas hechas in España, y debajo de su amparo; y que si él daba tan mal ejemplo, no podrían plantar el Evangelio, en cuyos ministros e intérpretes es importantísima la limpieza de la vida. Con estas y otras palabras blandas que él y los demás religiosos le dijeron, no le pudieron mover a blandura, antes fueron ocasión para endurecerse, y que el demonio reinase en su corazón, como en el de Judas, donde forjó la traición en su pecho, y queriéndose quitar de los ojos de quien lo reprendía, dijo que iba a buscar / fol. 5 r. / castañas y nueces a un pueblo suyo, que estaba cuatro leguas de allí, y que vendería muy presto dentro de tantos días. Los Padres le dejaron ir, y viendo que no volvió al día y tiempo señalado, le escribieron una carta, rogándole que por amor de Dios viniese y / mirase que estaban sin intérprete, y que del pendía aquella conversión, después de Dios.

No hubo remedio con el cacique apóstata ni para venir ni querer responder, con la cual se vieron aquellos siervos de Dios en grande confusión, por la cual determinaron de enviar adonde él estaba un Padre de respeto, que era predicador, y otro compañero con él, para que le amonestasen se viniese con ellos, presumiendo que no se le perderían, viéndolos ir personalmente; pero como el demonio estaba ya apoderado de su alma, luego que llegaron los dos embajadores sacerdotes, los mató, y se partió para acabar los demás, víspera de la Purificación de Nuestra Señora, día del ínclito mártir San Ignacio, en cuyo corazón se halló escrito el nombre de Jesús, y en tal día derramaron su sangre estos dos bienaventurados mátires de la Compañía de Jesús.

Llegado al lugar adonde los demás estaban, dijo el cacique don Luis que los Padres quedaban atrás con los indios que traían las castañas y nueces para su regalo; que llegarían por la mañana, y que pues el día siguiente era fiesta tan solemne de nuestra Señora de la Candelaria, quería ir con todos los indios a cortar madera para hacer una iglesia a la Virgen; y que dijese la misa de mañana, y le diese los machetes, hachas y otras herramientas para repartirlas entre los indios. Con estas razones se apercibieron los Padres para dar principio al edificio de la iglesia, y al amanecer se dijo la Misa. El mancebo Alonso de Lara estaba en casa de un cacique hermano de don Luis, conjurado con él para la muerte de los religiosos, y teniendo lástima del, por no matarlo a vuelta de los demás, lo llevó a su casa para darle de almorzar.

Estando, pues, el sacerdote en el altar celebrando la Misa, y los demás oyéndola y oficiándola, llegó don Luís y le dió en la cabeza un grande golpe con el machete, y luego hirió y mato a los demás compañeros, que como corderos estaban entra aquellos lobos carniceros. Saliendo el mozo Alonso de Lara al ruido, le cogió del brazo el cacique que lo había llevado a su casa, y lo detuvo no fuese allá. Y da después de muertos todos, salió el muchacho y vió al sacerdote / fol. 5 v/ que celebraba tendido en el suelo, boqueando. Dijo a don Luis que ayudase a enterrar los cuerpos, y en medio del temor que concebiría de ver este hecho, tuvo ánimo para pedir con lágrimas la piedad de la sepultura para aquellos sacerdotes, sus compañeros y buenos maestros. Abriendo las sepulturas, los enterraron como pudieron. Y estos fueron los árboles que cortaron, y quedarán en perpetua memoria por doce columnas de la iglesia que en el Jacán se erigiere, cuando Dios fuere servido de que vuelva aquella tierra regada con sangre de mártires a retoñar plantas para el cielo.

Dice el santo Job, cap. 14: *Lignum habens spem, si precisum fuerit, rursum virescit et rami eius pullulant.* Bien hay que interpretar en estas palabras, las cuales quise de paso aplicar a la muerte y sepultura destos inocentes mártires que el apóstata sacrílego los entretuvo aquella noche con pláticas de cortar madera para edificar la iglesia, las cuales pronosticaron su preciosa muerte en el acatamiento del Señor, cuyos nombres están escritos en los cielos, que en la diligente pesquisa que he hecho, no los he podido descubrir, sino sólo el del P. Juan Bautista, su prelado y superior.

Un caso milagroso sucedió: que andando los indios ocupados en los despojos de la ropa, cálices, patenas y ornamentos sacerdotales que repartieron entre sí, profanando los vasos y cosas sagradas en abominables usos, hallaron una caja donde estaban Reliquias y un crucifijo que para su devoción y consuelo habían llevado los mártires. Quiso un indio dar un golpe con una hacha en la caja, y levantando los brazos y cogiendo aire para hacer el golpe, se cayó muerto, con lo cual temieron todos los otros y no osaron llegar más a ellas. Alonso de Lara dijo a don Luis que aquella caja de Reliquias sería bien ponerla en una garita, que las hay en toda la tierra de la Florida para guardar el maíz de su sustento, y son unas despensas armadas sobre cuatro palos altos y gruesos, leventadas de la tierra, y las llaman garitas, y a una de aquéllas subieron la caja de Reliquias y el crucifijo Alonso de Lara y don Luis, el cual no es posible menos sino que de tan nefasto hecho y traición como puso por obra, tenía el alma confusa y los pensamientos en el castigo del cielo y horror de su condenación.

Este fué el martirio destos siervos de Dios. Y como los indios fueron señores de la tierra y desta abominable traición, lo fueron / también del secreto pa- / fol. 6 r. / ra que no lo supiesen los españoles, y así no se descubrió ni divulgó hasta el año siguiente; y pasó desta manera:

De cómo se descubrió la traición de los indios y muerte de los religiosos.

Pasado un año, fué el mismo capitán Vicente González [Gonzales] a

llevar bastimento a los religiosos, y llegando a vista del pueblo, vió en la
playa gente vestida con los sotanos y ropas de los religiosos, pareciéndole
que eran ellos. Estuvo aguardando a que alguno llegase a bordo, y acercándose una canoa en que venían indios, por señas preguntó que¿ cómo no
venían los Padres a bordo? Escribió dándoles aviso que era Vicente
González, y no volviendo la respuesta de la carta, se tuvo mala sospecha,
y de los indios que volvieron al navío prendió dos, y los demás se echaron
al agua, y de ahí a poco espacio vió que venían muchas canoas llenas de
indios, y haciéndose a la vela, vino a Santa Elena, tomaron su confesión
a los indios; dijeron como todos los religiosos fueron muertos, y cómo
había quedado un muchacho llamado Alonso de Lara.

En este tiempo envió Su Majestad a llamar al Adelantado, y antes de
ir a España, se le ofreció venir de Santa Elena a San Agustín, adonde tenía
dos fragatas nuevas que aún estaban por acabar, que por ser por el mes de
julio, saliendo del puerto para la vuelta de España, se acabaron en el
Jacán, y a importunación de los religiosos que quedaron en Santa Elena,
hubo de ir a sacar a Alonso de Lara, llevando de los dos presidios ciento
y cincuenta soldados, y entre ellos, a Juan de Lara, hermano menór del
cautivo. Todos los cuales fueron en cuatro navíos. Llegados a la bahía,
hallaron dos indios del cacique con quien se había amparado Alonso de
Lara de la furia de don Luis, sacándole una sobrina del mismo cacique de
noche, porque no lo matase su tío.

Dieron fondo los navíos, y acercándose los dos indios, preguntó Juan de
Lara por su hermano Alonso. Respondieron que estaba en poder de su
cacique, una jornada de un día hasta allá donde estaba. El Adelantado les
mandó decir era su hijo, y que dijesen a su cacique se lo enviase, enviándole
juntamente algunas dádivas. El día siguiente envió al capitán Vicente
González con un patage y treinta soldados al pueblo de don Luis, por si
acaso le pu / fol. 6 v. / diesen coger y prender. Llegados a la ribera
del pueblo, mandó el capitán se escondiesen los soldados debajo de
cubierta, y como los indios no vieron más que seis hombres, vinieron a
bordo en canoas sesenta personas, los cuales traían las patenas de los
cálices por chagualas, que es un ornato de que usan a la garganta, y
estando desnudos (como es el uso de los indios de toda aquella tierra)
se cubrían con los corporales las partes pudendas. Convidólos el capitán
a comer melado y biscocho que llevaban, y estando al mejor gusto, salieron
debajo de cubierta los soldados, y prendieron trece indios de los más
principales, y mataron más de veinte; con la cual presa volvieron a la
bahía, adonde quedó el Adelantado, y de ahí a dos días llegaron doscientos

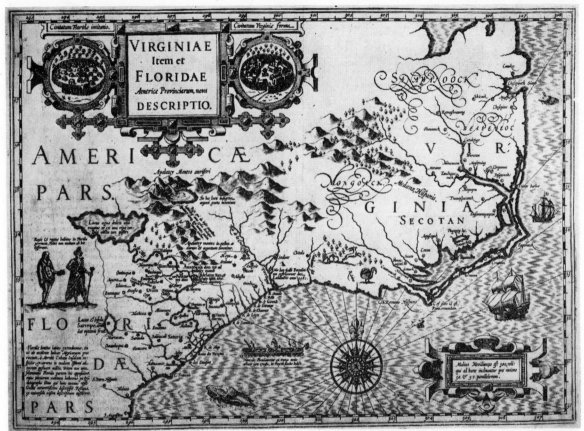

LEGENDS OF APPALACHIAN WEALTH PERPETUATED BY
MERCATOR, 1630

Of particular interest are the auriferous lake at the left center
of the map, just as it was described to Juan Menéndez
Marqués and Gonzales in Maryland, and in the foreground
an Indian dugout canoe with the note, "They have the same
in Virginia."

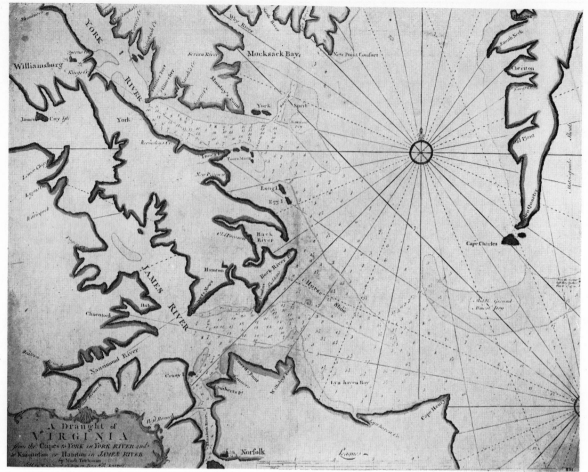

Plate X   *The Mariners' Museum*

CHART FROM "THE ENGLISH PILOT," 1737

Probably drawn as early as 1706, this chart gives a good idea of the ports
that seemed most accessible to the early navigators. The fathom figures
given here seem to support our analysis of the 1588 expedition of
Gonzales, in which he lists ports or anchorages in the Elizabeth River,
Newport News, behind Point Comfort (here shown incorrectly without its Mill Creek), and opposite Gloucester Point.

indios, los cuales trajeron y entregaron a Alonso de Lara desnudo, en traje de indio, el cual dió larga y verdadera relación del martirio de los Padres, de la manera que se ha referido.

El Adelantado envió cien soldados y a don Diego de Velasco, su yerno, y que llevase a Alonso de Lara y a su hermano con ellos a ver la disposición de la tierra y a hablar con el cacique que defendió y tuvo en su poder a Alonso de Lara, que por lo que el informaba parecía ser tierra rica. Volvieron con poca o ninguna relación de lo que deseaban saber, porque los indios andaban remontados y huídos. Y a los trece prisioneros que el capitán Vicente González trajo, hizo el Adelantado muchas preguntas, y les propuso si alguno dellos se atrevía a traer vivo o muerto a don Luis; y ofreciéndose uno a ello, le dijo pidiese término, porque si al plazo no viniese con la empresa, los había de ahorcar a todos. Ellos pidieron diez días de plazo, y enviaron al que salió a hacer lo que el Adelantado les dijo. Fué y nunca volvió, aunque pasaron algunos más días del término señalado. El Adelantado les mandó decir que habían de morir todos, y les propuso si querían ser cristianos, los cuales lo aceptaron y pidieron el bautismo de buena gana; y catequizándolos un religioso, y exhortándolos a lo que convenía, los ahorcaron de los peñoles. Lo cual hecho, el Adelantado se fué a España en 24 de agosto de 1572, enviando en un patage al religioso y a Alonso de Lara a la Habana. . . .

* * *

El año siguiente de 1588, por fin del mes de mayo, partió del puerto y presidio de San Agustín el capitán Vicente González, y en su compañía el sargento mayor, Juan Menéndez Marqués, con treinta soldados y marineros, en un barco luengo de San Lúcar, que había venido de aviso a la Habana el año antes, y se compró para efecto deste viaje, con orden que fuese corriendo la costa, hasta la bahía de la Madre de Dios del Jacán, y procurasen tomar lengua y reconocer la población y fortificación del inglés. Y habiendo hecho su viaje de luengo de costa, llegaron a Santa Elena, y hallaron los indios de paz, y lo mismo en el puerto de Cayagua, el cual juzgaron por buen puerto; y siguiendo la costa, habiendo pasado el cabo de San Román, hablaron con indios, cuya len- / fol. 10 v. / gua no entendieron los intérpretes que llevaban, y prosiguiendo el viaje, pasaron el cabo de Trafalgar y el de San Juan y otros dos puertos, después de los cuales llegaron a la bahía de la Madre de Dios del Jacán, por el mes de junio del año de 88, la cual tiene cerca de tres leguas de boca, sin bajos ni arrecifes, y más de ocho brazas de fondo en su entrada, que corre

Norueste Sueste. Hace un grande golfo en rendondo, y desde la boca hasta llegar a la tierra firme, yendo la vuelta del Oeste y Norueste habrá como tres leguas, y Este Oeste con la boca está en la tierra firme un buen puerto que en su entrada tiene tres brazas de fondo. Y cosa poco menos de dos leguas está otro puerto, la vuelta del Norueste, adonde dijo el capitán Vicente González que había saltado en tierra cuando llevó los religiosos de la Compañía que martirizaron don Luis y los que fueron con él, como ya queda referido; y dijo que en un llano que está sobre una barranca, donde había unos pinos juntos, se había hecho un altar donde se dijo misa, y que de allí volvió a salir en la vuelta del Leste, adonde en la tierra firme de aquella banda y dentro de la bahía, cerca de unas isletas y de una encenada, estuvo el Adelantado, y acabó las obras muertas de dos fragatas, en que salió de allí para Castilla.

Partieron de el dicho puerto, y costeando la bahía por la banda de la tierra firme en la vuelta del Norte, se descubrió otro puerto, al parecer bueno y mucho fondo, y en su ribera mucha piedra grande, y en la punta de la banda del Norte un morro alto. Están estos tres puertos a una vista de la boca de la bahía, y deste postrero casi no se ve. Prosiguiendo, pues, la vuelta del Norte, fué pareciendo la tierra del Leste por dentro de la bahía, y prosiguiendo, fué ensangostando, de manera que en lo más angosto de toda ella, desde la costa y ribera de la parte del Oeste, por donde se iba hasta la costa y ribera de la parte y banda del Leste, habrá dos leguas. Y prosiguiendo y descubriendo caletas, encenadas y ríos por aquesta banda del Oeste, llegaron a un grande río de agua dulce, que en la boca donde entraba y se encorporaba en la bahía, tenía más de seis brazas de fondo, y de la banda del Norte, tierra muy alta, abarrancada, sin arboleda, raso y como campo verde y apacible a las vista. De la banda del Sur deste río tiene la playa y ribera muy apacible de guijas menudas, y por el mis- / fol. 11 recto / mo río arriba, en banda del Sur, parecía valle de arboleda claro y tierra agradable, y al parecer fértil para crianza y labranza. Estaba este río en altura de treinta y ocho grados. Pásose nombre San Pedro. Prosiguiendo la vuelta del Norte, por la banda del Oeste, llegaron a hacer noche en una caletilla, al abrigo de una tierra alta y bien asombrada. Otro día vinieron a la playa muchos indios, y el que dellos parecía de más respeto tenía una sarta de chagualas al cuello, que parecían ser de oro fino. Aquí prendieron un indio mozo de hasta quince anos.

Prosiguiendo adelante, descubrieron otros muchos puertos y ríos caudalosos que por aquella banda del Oeste venían a entrar en la bahía, hasta que en altura de treinta y cinco grados se comenzaron a descubrir sierras muy altas que venían echadas al Sudeste en la vuelta del Nordeste, y se descubrieron mas ríos. Y luego pareció en medio de la bahía una isleta, y por la banda del Oeste comenzó a disminuir el fondo, y fué de manera que no se pudo pasar adelante, y fué forzoso ir arribando en la vuelta del Leste, que en el paraje y frente de la islata hacía tierra alta abarrancada y poblada de arboleda. Cerca de la isla, por la banda del Leste, hace bancos de más y menos fondo; y más arrimado a la tierra firme de la banda del Leste se halló canal de mucho fondo. Y prosiguiendo la vuelta del Norte, fueron las sierras haciendo cerco en redondo a una vista, y en diferentes partes bocas de ríos y abras. Y este redondo adonde fenece la bahía, será tan ancho como la bahía de Cádiz. Y más de dos o tres leguas antes de llegar al remate, se halló ser el agua dulce, y aquella tarde se llegó a entrar por un río en la vuelta del Oeste-Norueste entre unas grandes sierras y peñascos. Tenía en la boca de pleamar más de tres brazas, y a cosa de un cuarto de legua, por ser ya noche, se dió fondo, y al amanecer era baja mar, y casi milagrosamente quedó el barco entre unos peñascos de que se vió el río cercado de una parte a otra, y con harto riesgo, bota aqui, guarda de allí, se fué saliendo hasta la boca del río que estaba limpio, donde vieron un sábalo pequeño sobreaguado muerto, que no fué de provecho, y en un arroyo que bajaba por entre unos peñascos abajo se vieron truchas pequeñas, como las de las montañas. Este día fué víspera de señor San Juan Bautista, y a su devoción se puso nombre al río San Juan de las Peñas.

Subieron arriba a la sierra en lo llano; vióse / fol. 11 v. / de la otra banda otro río, y a una vista todo sierras y montañas grandes y dobladas, y abajo en la falda desta sierra hacía un valle de arboleda muy clara, y tierra fértil y agradable. Desde altura de treinta y ocho grados hasta el remate hay mucha cantidad de castaños y nogales grandes, muchas parras silvestres y la uva gruesa. El mismo día partieron del mismo río, y de luengo de costa y de la ribera fueron buen rato en la vuelta del Leste, y se descubrió una muy agradable ensenada poblada de arboleda, donde parecían muchos venados. Entraron por ella en la vuelta del Norte, hasta el remate de todo. Saltaron en tierra en una playa agradable debajo de unas barrancas pequeñas, y en aquel remate había un apacible y ameno valle de arboleda clara sin arcabuco, en el cual había muchos venados, y se mató uno, con que hicieron fiesta el día del glorioso San Juan Bautista. Pesaron el sol el capitán Vicente González y el piloto Ginés Pinzón, y se hallaron en altura de cuarenta grados largos, y asimismo la tomaron en el primer puerto, después de haber entrado en la bahía en la tierra firme della, y hallaron por su cuenta estaban en treinta y siete grados y tantos minutos.

El mismo día de San Juan partieron de aquel remate de la bahía en la vuelta del Sur, y por toda la banda del Oeste no parecieron indios, respecto de la presa del referido atrás, hasta que el día de los Apóstoles San Pedro y San Pablo por la mañana atravesaron a la banda del Leste, y llegaron a las isletas que están a vista de la boca de la bahía, y saltaron en tierra, y de allí a un poco más adelante a vista de la encenada adonde estuvo el Adelantado, llegaron a tierra y por hacer aplacelado de poco fondo, no pudo llegar el barco a tierra. Vinieron muchos indios y indias a la playa, y como llegaban algunos al barco, el agua a la rodilla, prendieron uno, y luego se hicieron a la vela, y aquella tarde salieron fuera de la bahía, y toda aquella noche se navegó la vuelta del Sur con viento Oeste recio, y otro día hasta el poner del sol, y por ir cargando el viento, desarbolaron, y con fuerza de remos llegaron a la costa, y entraron en una barra de muy poco fondo, y dentro hacía grande encenada, que de baja mar por la banda del Sur quedaba casi en seco. A una vista y por la del Norte quedaba gran pedazo de bahía, y mostraba un grande brazo en la vuelta del Norueste de luengo, de arboleda muy espesa. Y en la costa, por la banda del Nor- / folio 12 r. / te, hacía otra boca, al parecer mejor que la por donde entraron. Y el pedazo de costa, cosa de una legua, entre una barra y otra es baja y pelada de arena, y por la parte de dentro adonde llegaron, había veradero señalado de chalupas y en tierra cantidad de pozos hechos de pipas inglesas y otras señales de despojos, como de haber estado allí golpe de gente.

Relation [1] of Luis Gerónimo de Oré

An account of the Martyrs of the Provinces of Florida: twelve Religious of the Society of Jesus, who suffered in Jacán, and five of the Order of Our Seraphic Father Saint Francis, in the Province of Guale. Offered also is a description of Jacán where the English have fortified themselves; and of other matters relating to the conversion of the Indians.

Written by Father Luis Gerónimo de Oré, Lector of Theology and Commissary of the Province of Santa Elena of Florida and the Island of Cuba. (Translated by Maynard Geiger, O.F.M.)

EXCERPTS

The Discovery of Jacán, and the Martyrdom of Twelve Religious of the Society of Jesus.

About the year 1570,[2] while the *Adelantado*, Pedro Menéndez, was governing the *presidios* of Florida, a ship from the port of Santa Elena lost its course towards the north, at a latitude [3] of 37½° and put into a large bay which the sailors called the Bahía de Madre de Dios. From among some Indians who came aboard they retained a young *cacique*, whom they took along with them to Spain, where after instructing him in the Faith, they baptized him and gave him the name Luis. The King ordered that the necessary sustenance be given him all the time he remained in Spain. They placed him with the Fathers of the Society of Jesus to be educated.

In the year 1577 the *Adelantado* brought fifty settlers to Florida and divided them between the two forts of Santa Elena and San Agustín. In the following year, 1578, eight Religious of the Society came for the purpose of converting the natives of Florida. When they arrived they exercised their ministry in Santa Elena, while two of them went to the province of Guale,[4] 14 leagues from there, between San Agustín and Santa Elena, in order to instruct the natives. One went to the northern district to a province called Escamacu, taking in his company a boy of ten years of age, named Juan de Lara,[5] a son of a settler, in order to learn the language. Today Juan de Lara lives at San Agustín. After serving the natives for a year and a half, considering the little progress that he made, the Father returned to Santa Elena, where the other Religious were.

Father Álamo [6] (this was the name of one of the Religious of that Congregation) went to Spain to give an account to his superiors of the condition and character of the natives of that land, and of the meager progress he made among them. For, owing to their resistance and obduracy, the Fathers did not deem it fitting to baptize [7] any during this entire period. At that time the *cacique* Don Luis was living in the [Jesuit] house at Seville, advancing in the Spanish language, both in reading and writing, together with other branches of knowledge which they taught him.

When he learned that Religious had gone for the conversion of the natives of Florida, he told the Father Rector and others that he would venture to take some priests to his country and that with the help of God and his own industry, the Indians of that land would be converted to the Faith. These words aroused in the hearts of the Religious an intense desire and zeal for the salvation of souls. Moved to resolution, they offered themselves to the King, and asked for his permission as well as for the necessary provisions to go to those parts, and to take with them the *cacique* Don Luis.

When His Majesty had granted permission and the supplies they had asked for, they set out from Spain and arrived at Santa Elena [8] in safety. From here the *Adelantado* gave them a ship and provisions for a year,[9] and ordered that a captain, Vicente Gonzales by name, should take them thither. There were altogether 12 Religious priests [10] and a boy, Alonso de Lara, the elder brother of the other mentioned before, sons of a settler of Santa Elena. Having arrived at the Bahía de Madre de Dios at Jacán, they ascended the river for a distance of twelve leagues. On the banks of this river, the *cacique* Don Luis had his towns. Two brother *caciques* [11] of Don Luis together with other Indians received them and gave them lodgings amid demonstrations of great joy.

Seeing the good condition of the land [12] they unloaded their provisions and found lodging in a house which they soon constructed, made of palms. This had a small apartment to one side where the Fathers were to say Mass, until they could build a more commodious church. From here Vicente Gonzales returned to Santa Elena to give an account to the *Adelantado* as to where he had left the Religious. And as the enemy of the human race always tries to impede works of this sort, dedicated to the salvation of souls, he instigated the *cacique* Don Luis (now placed in the position of being in the midst of his own people) to give himself over to immorality in so shameful a manner that the superior of those

Religious, Father Juan Baptista, reprimanded him severely. Afterwards, in words couched in the spirit of religion and charity, he admonished and begged him, telling him that he should remember that they had come, moved by the promises he had made in Spain, and under his protection. Moreover, if he gave such a bad example, they would not be able to implant the Gospel, in whose ministers and interpreters, cleanness of life is so very important. Despite these and other gentle words which he and the other Religious spoke to him, they could not soften him, but rather they were the occasion of spiritual hardening of the heart, for the devil reigned in his heart as he did in the heart of Judas. He forged the treachery in his breast. Wishing to withdraw from the sight of him who had reprimanded him, Don Luis said he was going to look for chestnuts and nuts of other varieties, in one of his towns, which was 4 leagues from there, and he would return very soon, within a definite number of days. The Fathers let him go, but seeing that he did not return on the day and at the time specified, they wrote him a letter, asking him for the love of God to come, and to remember that they were without an interpreter and that, after God, the conversion of the natives depended on him.

But it had no influence on the apostate *cacique*, either to induce him to come or to answer the letter. On this account those servants of God were in great confusion. Wherefore, they determined to send a Father whom he respected, and who was a preacher,[13] together with a companion, to the place where Don Luis was. These were to admonish him to come along with them. They presumed they would not be killed when he saw them coming personally. But as the devil had the upper hand in his heart already, he killed the two priest ambassadors as soon as they came; then he set out to kill the others, on the vespers of the Purification of Our Lady, on the day of the renowned martyr, St. Ignatius, in whose heart was written the name of Jesus. On such a day these two blessed martyrs of the Company of Jesus shed their blood.

Having arrived at the place where the others were, the *cacique* Don Luis said that the Fathers remained behind with the Indians who were bringing the chestnuts and other varieties of nuts [14] for his repast; that they would arrive in the morning, and that the next day being the solemn feast of Candlemas, he wished to go with all the Indians to cut wood in order to construct a church for the Virgin; and that a Father should say Mass in the morning. Therefore he asked for hatchets and other tools in order to distribute them among the Indians. On hearing this the Fathers perceived that a church could be constructed. In the morning [one of the priests] said Mass. The youth Alonso de Lara was in the house of a *cacique*, a brother of Don Luis, who also was a conspirator with his brother for the death of the Religious. He had pity on Alonso for he did not kill him after the others, but took him to his house to give him some breakfast.

When the priest was celebrating Mass at the altar, and the others were assisting and officiating at it, Don Luis came and gave him a heavy blow on the head with a cutlass, and then wounded and killed the other companions, who were like sheep among those wolves and butchers. At the sound of the noise, Alonso de Lara came forth, but the *cacique* who had taken him to his house caught him by the arm and detained him from going to the scene. When all were dead the boy went out and saw the priest who had been celebrating Mass stretched on the ground and breathing his last. The boy told Don Luis to help him bury the bodies, and in the midst of the fear which he felt on seeing this deed, he took courage to ask with tears that respect be shown to those priests, his companions and good masters, that they should receive burial. Digging the graves, they buried them all as well as they could. These were the trees they cut down, which will remain in perpetual memory as twelve columns of the Church which was erected in Jacán, when God was willing that the land be watered with the blood of martyrs so that new plants should sprout for heaven.

Holy Job says: "A tree hath hope: if it be cut, it groweth green again, and the boughs thereof sprout." [15] Well may we apply these words, at the same time, to the death and burial of those innocent martyrs whom the sacrilegious apostate deceived that night when he said he was going to cut wood to build a church. These words foretold their precious death in the sight of the Lord and their names are written in heaven. These names I have not been able to find out in the diligent inquiry I have made, [16] except that of Father Juan Baptista, their prelate and superior.

A miraculous thing happened: while the Indians were going about busily in despoiling the clothing, chalices, patens, and sacerdotal vestments which they divided among themselves, profaning the vases and sacred objects in an abominable manner, they found a chest which contained relics and a crucifix which the martyrs had brought along for their devotion and consolation. An Indian wanted to give the chest a blow with a hatchet, but on raising his arm and on swinging to strike it, he fell dead. At this, fear fell upon the others with the result that they did not dare to approach it any more. Alonso de Lara told Don Luis that the relics should be placed in a *garita*. These are found all over Florida and in them the Indians place the maize they keep for their sustenance; it is a type of barn supported by four posts, high and bulky, raised from the earth. These they call *garitas*.[17] Up into one of these, Alonso de Lara and Don Luis together raised the box of relics and the crucifix. It is hardly possible but that the soul of Don Luis was confounded and that his thoughts turned on the punishment of heaven and the horrors of condemnation over such a nefarious act and treasonable deed which he committed.

Such was the martyrdom of these servants of God. And as the Indians were the lords of the land and the authors of this abominable act of treachery, they held it a secret lest the Spaniards find it out. Thus it was not discovered, nor divulged until the following year. It happened in this way:

The Discovery of the Treachery of the Indians and of the Death of the Religious.

After a year had passed, the same captain Vicente Gonzales set out to carry provisions to the Religious. When he arrived within sight of the town,[18] he saw, along the beach, people vested in cassocks and religious robes, and it seemed to him that these were the Religious. He was waiting until someone should come on board. Then a canoe came containing Indians. He asked them by signs why the Fathers did not come on board. He wrote giving them notice that he was Vicente Gonzales, and when no answer was forthcoming, suspicion of evil arose. Of the Indians who returned to the ship, he seized two while the others jumped into the water. From yonder in a short time he saw that many Indians were coming in canoes. Then he took to sail and came to Santa Elena, where he took the confession of the Indians. They said that the Religious were dead[19] and that there remained there a boy called Alonso de Lara.

At this time the King called the *Adelantado* to Spain, but before going thither, it happened that he went from Santa Elena to San Agustín, where he had two new frigates which were just being completed. Since it was the month of July, he sailed from that port to Spain. At the importunity of the Religious who remained at Santa Elena, they stopped at Jacán, to go and hunt for Alonso de Lara. He took with him a hundred and fifty soldiers of the *presidio* and among them Juan de Lara, the younger brother of the captive. All these sailed in four ships. Arriving at the bay, they found two Indians who belonged to the *cacique* by whom Alonso de

Lara had been protected from the fury of Don Luis. The *cacique* had disguised him during the night to make him look like Don Luis' niece, for he knew Alonso's "uncle" would not kill him.[20]

They anchored the ships. Approaching the Indians, Juan de Lara asked for his brother Alonso. The Indians answered that he was in the power of their *cacique*, a day's journey from there. The *Adelantado* told them to say that Alonso was his son and that they should tell their *cacique* to send him to him. At the same time he sent some gifts. The following day he sent Captain Vicente Gonzales with a tender and thirty soldiers to Don Luis' town so that he could perchance catch and apprehend him. Arriving at the edge of the town, the captain commanded the soldiers to hide below the decks. Since the Indians saw no more than six men, sixty Indians in canoes came on board, wearing the patens belonging to the chalices as ornaments about their necks. Since they were naked (which is the custom of the Indians of the whole land) they covered their private parts with the corporals. The captain invited them to eat honey-cakes and biscuits which he brought. Then while they were in the midst of their meal, the soldiers sallied forth from below the decks, seized hold of thirteen of the more important Indians, and killed more than twenty. With this booty of prisoners they returned to the bay, where the *Adelantado* had remained. At that place there arrived within two days, two hundred Indians who brought with them Alonso de Lara, whom they handed over. He was naked, in Indian fashion. It was he who gave a true and lengthy story of the martyrdom of the Fathers in the manner in which it has been related.

The *Adelantado* then sent Don Diego de Velasco, his son-in-law, with a hundred soldiers, as well as the two Lara brothers, to look over the condition of the land and to speak to the *cacique* who had defended and taken under his protection Alonso de Lara. From the information obtained regarding the territory, it appeared that the land was rich. They returned, however, with little or no news concerning the things they desired to know, for the frightened Indians had fled. The *Adelantado* put many questions to the thirteen prisoners whom Captain Gonzales brought with him. He made a proposal to them saying: would anyone venture to bring Don Luis to him dead or alive? One offered to do this. He gave him a definite time to return and said that if at the time determined he would not come through with his undertaking, he would have to hang them all. They asked for a period of ten days [21] in which to carry out their enterprise. They sent him out to accomplish that which the *Adelantado* had told them to do. He never returned though more days passed beyond the time stipulated. The *Adelantado* then gave orders that the captured Indians be put to death. He asked them if they wished to die as Christians, and this they accepted. Willingly they asked for baptism. A Religious instructed them and exhorted them as was fitting. Then they were hanged from the yardarms. When this was accomplished, the *Adelantado* went to Spain [22] on August 24, 1572, sending a Religious and Alonso de Lara in a tender to Havana. . . .

[A Later Exploration of Jacán]

In the following year, 1588, at the end of the month of May, Captain Vicente Gonzales left from the port and *presidio* of San Agustín. With Gonzales went the sergeant-major, Juan Menéndez Marqués, and thirty soldiers and sailors in a long bark which had come from San Lúcar to Havana the year before as a dispatch boat. This boat was bought for the expedition to Jacán.[23] The purpose of this expedition was to run along the coast up to the Bahía de Madre de Dios, in order to obtain knowledge of and to reconnoiter the English settlement and fortification. After they made the journey along the coast, the party came to Santa Elena and found the Indians at peace; the same was true at the harbor of Cayagua, which they judged to be a good port. Then they followed the coast, having passed the Cape of San Román. They spoke with the Indians, but the interpreters whom they had brought along did not understand their language. They continued their journey, passing the Cape of Trafalgar and that of San Juan; likewise two other ports. Whereupon they arrived at the Bahía de Madre de Dios de Jacán, in the month of June, in the year 1588.

The mouth of the bay is about 3 leagues wide, without shoals or reefs, and is more than 8 fathoms deep. It runs northwest-southeast and forms a large round gulf. Between the entrance and the place where one reaches the mainland, it extends toward the west and the northwest for about 3 leagues. In the east-west direction with the mouth,[24] on the mainland, there is a good port which at its entrance has a depth of 3 fathoms. A little less than 2 leagues from there, there is another port toward the northwest, where Captain Vicente Gonzales said he had landed when he brought the Religious of the Society, whom Don Luis and his accomplices put to death, as has already been told.

He [Captain Gonzales] said that on a plain which is beyond a bluff [25] and where there was a group of pine trees, an altar had been erected and Mass had been said and that from there he returned toward the east,[26] where on the mainland on that side,[27] and within the bay and near some small islands and an inlet, the *Adelantado* had been. It was there that the *Adelantado* finished the gunwales of two frigates in which he sailed for Castile from that place.

Thereupon they departed from the said harbor,[28] and coasting along the shore of the mainland toward the north, they discovered another port which appeared to be a good one and of great depth. On the shore there was an abundance of large stone, while the cape of the land to the north formed a high headland. These three ports can be seen at one glance from the mouth of the bay: the last however, only faintly.

As they continued to sail north, the land from the east jutted into the bay. It became narrower in such a manner that at its narrowest place, from the western shore whence it stretched toward the eastern part, it was 2 leagues.[29] After that they discovered inlets and coves as well as rivers along the western shore. Then they came upon a large fresh-water river, which, where it entered the bay, was more than 6 fathoms deep.[30] To the north there was very high land, with ravines, but without trees, delightful and free, which had the aspect of a green field and was pleasant to behold. On the south shore of this river the beach is very calm and is lined with small pebbles. Farther up on the south bank of the same river there appeared a delightful valley, wooded, and pleasant land which seemed to be fertile and adaptable to stock-raising and farming. This river was located in a latitude of 38°. They named it San Pedro.

They continued to sail north along the western shore and passed the night in a small inlet under the protection of high and well-shaded land. The next day many Indians came to the beach, and the one among them who appeared to have the greater dignity, wore a necklace, which seemed to be of fine gold. There they seized an Indian youth of about fifteen years of age.

Advancing farther, they discovered many other ports and important rivers which entered the bay from the western shore until they came to latitude 35° where they discovered mountain ridges which were very high and which ran in the direction of southwest-northeast. Still more rivers were discovered. Soon in the middle of the bay there appeared a small island [31] while along the western shore the depth began to diminish to such an extent that they could go no farther. They found it necessary to turn eastward. In front of the island, the land was high and broken and well wooded. Near the island on the eastern shore there were shoals of greater or lesser depth. Sailing closer toward the eastern shore, they found a channel of great depth. Continuing still farther north, they found that the hills began to encircle the view.

In different parts they found mouths of rivers and coves. Where this semi-circular [32] bay ends, it is about as wide as the harbor of Cádiz. More than 2 or 3 leagues before they reached the terminus of the bay, they found that the water was fresh. That evening they were on the point of entering a river toward the north-northwest [33] between some high hills and rocks. At high tide the mouth was more than 3 fathoms deep. Because it was already night, at about a quarter of a league from there, they cast anchor. At dawn, there was low tide. It was almost a miracle that the bark remained between the rocks by which the river was enclosed from one side to the other. At great risk, and amid shouts and orders, it sailed forth as far as the mouth of the river which was clear. There they saw a small shad,[34] dead and floating on the water, which was of no use. In a brook which came down between the rocks, some small trout were seen like those of the mountains. This was the eve of the feast of St. John the Baptist, and out of devotion they called the river San Juan de las Peñas.

They went up to the sierra, on the level place, and beheld on the other side another river,[35] and together with it ranges of hills and rolling land. Below in the fold of this range there was a fair valley with trees, with fertile and pleasing land. From the latitude of 38° up to the end, there is found a great quantity of chestnuts and large walnuts as well as wild vines with bulky grapes. The same day they departed from that river and went along the coast toward the east at a good rate, where they discovered a very agreeable inlet, thick with trees, where many deer appeared. They entered it toward the north, and sailed as far as its extremity. Then they landed on a pleasant beach, below some small ravines. At that termination there was a quiet and pleasant valley, containing trees, without any craggy place. In it they found many deer. They killed one of these and made a feast of it on the day of the glorious Saint John the Baptist.[36]

Captain Vicente Gonzales and the pilot Ginés Pinzón took the latitude [37] which they found to be a good 40°. They had taken it also at the first port after they had entered the bay and there they found it to be 37° and some minutes. On that same day, the feast of Saint John, they left that end of the bay and sailed south along the western shore. In view of the fact that one of the Indians had been captured there (as mentioned before) no Indian appeared along the western shore [38] until the feast of Sts. Peter and Paul. In the morning they crossed to the eastern shore and came to some small islands [39] which are within view of the mouth of the bay. There they landed.

From that place to a spot farther on, and in view of the cove where the *Adelantado* had been, they steered for land, but because the water had little depth, they could not reach it. Many Indians, both men and women, came to the beach. When some came to the bark, after wading in water up to their knees, the Spaniards seized one of them and sailed away. When they departed from the bay it was evening. All that night they navigated toward the south with the help of a strong west wind. The same was true all the next day till sunset. The wind, however, became too strong, and they were forced to unmast the ship. By rowing they came to the shore and interned at a bar of very shallow depth.[40] Within the bar there was a large bay to the south, which at low tide remained almost dry. The view toward the north showed a great portion of the bay as well as a large arm to the northwest, while the land was thickly wooded. Also, along the coast, to the north, there appeared another mouth which seemed to be better than the one they had entered. That portion of the coast, for about a league, between one bar and another, is low and broken by sand. In the interior of the region where they were, there was a ship-yard, indicated by the presence of sloops, while on the land there were some remains of English barrels. Besides, there were other signs of debris, indicating that people had been there.

NOTES

1. The text of the translation by Father Geiger is taken from "The Martyrs of Florida," *Franciscan Studies*, No. 18 (New York, 1936) 20-25, 28-30, 44-48. The original Spanish book is extremely rare, but fortunately Fray Atanasio López, O.F.M., edited a republication of the *Relación* under the title *Relación histórica de la Florida escrita en el siglo XVII*, vol. 1 (Madrid, 1931). The Spanish text here reproduced is from this edition, pp. 63-70, 78-81. From internal evidence the Relation can be dated between 1617 and 1620 (see "The Martyrs of Florida" xiii). Fray Oré (1554-1629) was a zealous and learned missionary who in addition to this Relation composed catechisms and books of devotions. The material for this history was gathered during his official visits to Florida, Georgia, and Cuba in 1614 and 1616. In Florida he acquired knowledge of "Juan," Brother of Alonso de Olmos, the sole survivor of the Segura Mission. Possibly, too, he met Vicente Gonzales who, Martínez indicates, was still living in 1610 (see Martínez' Relation above, para. 47). Oré gives such a careful summary of the Juan Menéndez Marqués expedition of 1588, which bears clues about the Segura site, that he must have read

the report made of it. It hardly seems necessary to remark on the evident mistake concerning "twelve priests" in the title. There is an undated letter by Fray Oré summarized in the Lowery Papers, vol. 6 (Library of Congress), which asks for more Religious for the Florida Mission and describes his two visits to Florida (AGI, "Memorial de Fray Luis Gerónimo, sin fecha" 54-5-20).

2. Oré is consistently ten years off in his dating of the finding of Don Luis and the activities of the Jesuits in Florida and Virginia.

3. Significantly, Oré is constant in the latitude he assigns to the mouth of the Chesapeake. Later he gives 37° and some minutes as the latitude of the first port, east-west from the mouth after entering the bay, another proof that the first port in the series cannot be north of the James.

4. Father Sedeño and Brother Báez worked in Guale, and Father Rogel went to Escamacu and Orista near Port Royal.

5. If Juan de Lara was ten years old in 1568, his older brother Alonso was thirteen years old or more when the Jesuits set out in 1570.

6. He was unsuitable for the Florida Mission and returned to Europe in 1569. The state of the mission had been reported by Segura and Sedeño. See also Sacchini Excerpt below, note 3.

7. Actually, according to Rogel's letter of Dec. 9, 1570 (*MAF* 477), seven had been baptized, of whom four were infants and all in danger of death. The Jesuits feared to confer the sacrament in cases of doubtful dispositions. See also letters of Sedeño, March 6, 1570 (*MAF* 423) and Villareal, March 5, 1570 (*MAF* 419), and the Carrera Relation, paras. 22 f., *MAF* 546 f.

8. As we have seen, neither Segura nor Don Luis went from Spain to Santa Elena, directly, but were for some time in Havana.

9. In the Quirós-Segura letter it is stated that the meager provisions were partially consumed by the ship's crew.

10. All agree on the youth of Alonso, but there were only two priests present, Segura and Quirós.

11. Three and possibly four brothers of Don Luis are mentioned in the sources. All, except a three-year-old boy, are called *caciques*. The uncle of Don Luis appears to be the most important *cacique* (See Rogel, August Letter above, para. 2). Sacchini mentions the death of an older brother and the survival of a younger ruling brother (Book VI, no. 270). One brother seems to have lived near the stream where the capture was effected in 1572, another near the settlement of the Jesuits, since he was on hand to protect Alonso.

12. This contradicts the first report of the Quirós letter, unless Oré intends a good location and potentialities.

13. Perhaps we have here a parallel to the high evaluation Sedeño evidently placed on the spoken word in criticizing Segura to Borgia as poor in the art of preaching. See above, Part I, note 58. Elsewhere Oré cites preaching ability as a requisite for mission work (Geiger edition 120).

14. Smith mentions chestnuts, walnuts, chinquapins, and acorns in the diet of the Indians. Acorns were treated before eating (1 Arber 352-354).

15. Book of Job, 14:7.

16. This is an indication that he did not talk to Gonzales, who possibly would have remembered more of the names of the Jesuits. But see note 26 below.

17. The description given by Oré agrees perfectly with a drawing by John White of the granary in which the North Carolina Algonkin kept "their rype corne." It does not so much resemble the Florida granary drawn by Le Moyne and cited by Father Geiger from Bushnell, 69 *BAE,B* Plate 16. The White drawing is shown in Plate 5.

18. The impression could be that Gonzales went directly to the final settlement, because "he arrived within sight of the town." However, the same town is mentioned later in connection with the 1572 events, and we are quite sure they occurred at the point of debarkation in 1570, where there was no town. Gonzales probably did not see the final settlement, since the way was uncharted and he received no directions. Had he known the way to the town, he would have gone there directly again in 1572, instead of to the point of first landing. There may have been, and indeed from the Quirós Letter and the Rogel Relation there must have been, an Indian settlement within an hour's walk from the narrow stream originally entered.

19. From the Rogel August Letter it seems that they were convinced that the Religious were dead, but we do not know definitely that the Indians gave them this information except by suspicious silence.

20. This account sounds fanciful. Rogel, Carrera, and Martínez plausibly attribute Alonso's safety to the power of the friendly chief, who neither needed this ruse nor could sustain it for a year and a half.

21. Rogel, who was there, says five days were allowed the *cacique* to deliver the murderers (August Letter above, para. 8).

22. The date of the Rogel Letter is August 28, a few days before the expiration of time granted the prisoners. Therefore his departure could not have been before August 29. Menéndez remained in Spain and was appointed Captain-General of a large armada at Santander of at least 150 ships. He died at that port on Sept. 17, 1574 of an attack of indigestion. His body was not taken to Avilés until 1591, when it was placed in a vault on the gospel side of the altar in the Church of San Nicolás. The epitaph mentions among other things the Order of Santiago and the title of *Adelantado*. The only ornament on his tomb was his coat of arms (2 Lowery 383 ff.). His son-in-law, Don Diego de Velasco, succeeded him as governor from 1574 to 1577.

23. Pedro Menéndez Marqués says of this boat and the expedition: "After the completion of [San Agustín], I sent Captain Vicente Gonzales and a nephew of mine in a vessel very fast of sail and oar, to go running the coast as high as the thirty-ninth degree of latitude, which is above the Bay of Santa Maria. He took thirty skillful men with him, that should the English have settled in that direction, he might make discovery of whatever existed. He set out at a good time, in the beginning of June" ("Relación dando cuenta S.M. del estado de equella provincia," from Havana, July 17, 1588, AGI 54-5-9, in Lowery Papers, vol. 6, Library of Congress. Also translated by Buckingham Smith, *Historical Magazine* (1859) 275 f.).

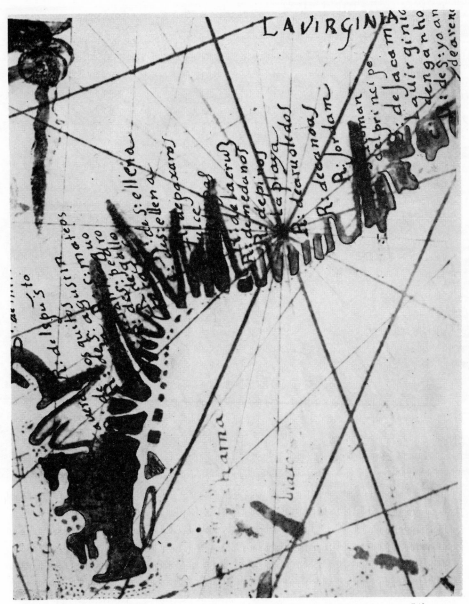

SÁNCHEZ MAP OF 1618 SHOWING "JACAM"

"Jacam" is the Portuguese spelling for "Jacan," which rarely appears on extant maps. (Place names have been darkened in this reproduction.)

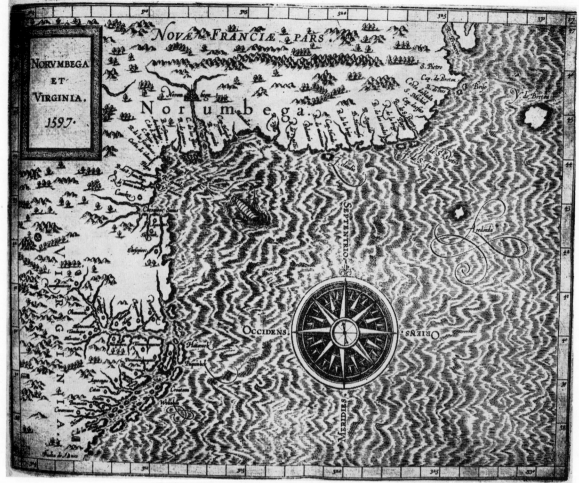

Plate XII

WYTFLIET MAP OF 1597, A JUMBLE OF SPANISH
AND ENGLISH CARTOGRAPHY

Here is a good example of what can happen when entirely new cartographical knowledge is incorporated into a section of a coast line.
Wytfliet decided to introduce the whole of Virginia north of the "C. de
las arenas," thereby elevating the "Chesipooc Sinus" to nearly 43°,
bringing it next to the "R. de Buena Madre (compare with this river on
the *padrón* maps, Plates I and XIV). Some of the difficulties in the *padrón*
maps may have come in the same way, the map-maker not knowing
where to place the new discoveries, which were often accompanied by
erroneous reports of latitude.

24. Father Geiger translates this as "at the mouth," but from the geography of the place, "with relation to" is clearer and more faithful to *con la boca*.

25. The word *barranca* may mean a "bluff," although Father Geiger translates it "ravine." We prefer "bluff" because it is a more noticeable landmark and conformable to the terrain. There may be reference here, however, to a ravine on the site of the present yacht basin at Newport News.

26. We have slightly amended Father Geiger's translation here; in the Spanish the indirect discourse continues. Gonzales is made to testify that from where Mass was said he returned to the east, so that the immediate inference is of the 1570 trip, but the context suggests that Oré is returning here to the 1588 excursion, for the next move is north. Moreover, observing the sequence of tenses, Gonzales could not have returned in 1570 to where Menéndez "had been" in 1572. It should be noted that unless Oré is carelessly letting the second *que* slip in here, he must also have had either the written or spoken testimony of Vicente Gonzales in composing his account of the 1588 trip. In his Relation given below, Gonzales implies that he gave information to the Franciscan provincial of Florida, from whom, in turn, Oré could have derived it.

27. Father Geiger has "on the mainland of that area." By our more literal translation of the word *banda*, it can be seen that the first mainland referred to was on the south bank of the James.

28. The word "harbor" is used instead of Father Geiger's "port" because Oré has not called Menéndez' anchorage a port. He would have regarded Norfolk, Newport News, and Point Comfort as being in one "harbor."

29. It is about 14 miles from New Point Comfort to Savage Neck on the eastern shore, much farther than is here estimated. The Menéndez Marqués letter of November 1605, whose text is given further on, also says "2 good leagues in width" for the narrowest part. But the Vicente Gonzales report of 1588 states correctly that "it is 4 at the narrowest part of the bay." See his Relation below.

30. It is difficult to say whether the Rappahannock or the Potomac is meant. The latitude is right for the latter, but Gonzales' latitudes are consistently too high. The depth and description of the southern bank applies to both rivers. The valley could be either Urbanna Creek or Yeocomico River. The land on the north bank of the Rappahannock rises to 80 feet, that on the Potomac to 100 feet. Father White, S.J., in his *Relatio Itineris*, described the banks of the Potomac as free enough of trees to permit the passage of a carriage anywhere, but not as unwooded as Oré's account indicates. Perhaps the strongest argument for the Potomac is the fact that he speaks of the good condition of the land from the 38th degree north, a natural division to make of the western coast line if the Potomac is taken as the starting point.

31. Latitude 35 is a mechanical error, possibly for 39. The island in the middle of the bay would have been Spesutie, or perhaps Poole's but not Kent, for they could not have sailed along the east shore there.

32. A good summary description of the entire upper part of the Chesapeake.

33. The river entered toward the north-northwest is the Susquehanna. Here John Smith met the Susquehannock and Iroquois Indians. Menéndez Marqués and

Vicente Gonzales say nothing about it but their tarrying here may have been the origin of a coin of 1558 commemorating Ferdinand I of the Holy Roman Empire. It was found near Athens, Pa., on the east side of the Susquehanna, 8 feet below ground (L. W. Murray, *Old Tioga Point and Early Athens, Pa.* [Athens, 1908] 67).

34. Shad migrate to fresh water and were taken in great numbers here by the early colonists.

35. This may have been the Octoraro Creek.

36. From the liturgical calender these dates can be known: the Nativity of St. John the Baptist is June 24, the feast of St. Peter and St. Paul on the 29th.

37. It is not clear where the latitude was taken, at the beach or in the valley, but presumably the former, in which case there is an error of at least 25′, for the true latitude is 39° 35′ at the extremity of the Northeast River, in which they probably were. Herrman's map shows enough depth for them to have entered Elk River also.

38. On the western shore at the mouth of the Rappahannock there were several Indian villages.

39. The islands on the eastern shore may have been the Cherrystone Islands. The 1852 Coast and Geodetic Survey reveals that Cherrystone Island itself was much larger than today. Four hundred years ago the shore here may have been considerably different from its present state. It is intimated that the mouth of the bay could be seen from here, and that where they next touched shore, the Menéndez *ensenada* was in view. Just below the ferry landing at Butler's Bluff the channel comes close to the land. From here one can look across to Buckroe Beach and into the mouth of the James. George F. Carter discusses changing shores of the Chesapeake in "The Sea and the Land," *Research Reviews* (November, 1952), Office of Naval Research, Department of the U.S. Navy. Erosion in the upper Chesapeake is treated in detail in "Shore Erosion in Tidewater Maryland," Bulletin 6 (1949), Dept. of Geology, Mines and Water Resources, State of Maryland, Baltimore, Md.

40. It is difficult to identify the inlet entered because of the changes in the shore line. Even White's three maps do not agree. We would select the inlet south of Pea Island at 35° 35′, but the English would not have had shallops in there. More probably they entered the Oregon Inlet (Hatarask Inlet on White's De Bry map) and thought the other inlet, shown there above Oregon, was a better one. From there they could have seen Roanoke Sound and the beginning of Croatan Sound. White indicates a cove south of Oregon Inlet that is less pronounced today on the maps, but Oré may mean by *ensenada* the whole sound to the south.

Relación de Vicente Gonzales

Relación que dió el Capitán Vicente Gonzales de lo que observo en el viage que por mandado de Pero Meléndez Marqués Gobernador de las probincias de la Florida hizo con 50 soldados y dos lanchas al reconocimiento del fuerte que se entendío havia hecho Franceses en la costa de Santa Elena, con un discurso mui suscinto al fin sobre la fortificación de la misma costa y fuertes que en ella tenia su Magestad, etc.

El Capitan Vicente Gonzales dice: que Pero Meléndez Marqués, governador de las Probincias de la Florida tuvo nueva por via de los Indios de la Costa de Santa Elena que havia un Fuerte de Franceses, donde le mando fuese con cincuenta soldados y dos Lanchas con todo el recato ser pudiese, porque no cayese en las manos del enemigo, y assi lo hizo costeando la costa ácia los Bacallaös, entrando en todos los Puertos que hallava, por que muchos donde fue á dar en un puerto que tiene dos leguas de boca, y va treinta leguas a la tierra adentro, y tiene de ancho cinco ó seis, y lo mas angosto quatro hasta llegar al pie de le sierra donde está un cazique muy principal con mucha gente que sujeta á todos los Caziques de aquella comarca, y halló un Cacique que andava con quatro ó cinco chagualas de oro en las orejas, y en la cabeza de un palmo y medio de largo, y seis dedos de ancho, y los demas Indios trahian de la propia manera de cobre, y al Cazique le preguntó que a donde havia aquello que trahia? el qual le respondió que del piel [pie] de aquella sierra á donde havia tres jornadas de un Indio cargado que podrian ser veinte y cinco ó treinta leguas, la qual era una sierra que no tenia otra cosa: dixole que si havia mucha cantidad de aquello por que en su tierra tambien havia mucho, y que no valia nada, y asi dixo él lo propio, que allá tampoco lo estimavan, y lo que trahian los Indios, que era el cobre que aquello estimavan en mucho, y lo mismo le respondió el dicho Capitan Vicente Gonzales que acá nosotros lo estimavamos, por que entendiese, que no ybamos á saber áquello, por que si él lo quisiera traher pudiera, y no le pareció conbenia por no alterarlos, por que muchas personas que con él fueron vieron lo mismo que él vió.

Hay muchas perlas, y grandes, eceto que son moradas; detras de esta

sierra está el nuevo Mexico, que dicen, que será entre todo desde el pie
de la sierra hasta allá cinco jornadas: Aqui hay casas grandes de quatro
ó cinco sobrados, y embarradas por de fuera: hay muchas Vacas pequeñas,
y mucha plata, por que los propios Indios se lo dixeron: de esta tierra que
dice ázia el Sur hay muchas minas de plata, y hay minas de cristal. Hay
otra sierra pequeña de diamantes que en la Florida los han tenido los
soldados, y los han vendido en España no saviendo su estima, uno en
quinientos Ducados, y otro en cien Doblones, que por no saver lo que
valian perdieron mucho en ellos, y en la Florida hay soldados que han estado
en las minas de plata que dice, y en la serrezuela de los diamantes con
gran deseo de yr á allá: puede informar cerca desto, un Frayle Francisco
Probincial de la Florida, que tambien está informado de lo dicho, y otro
soldado que está en esta corte. En esta tierra hay mucha comida de Mayz,
Fresol, que es su comida dellos: hay muchas guindas, ciruela, vba, castaña
apilada, que la tienen todo el año: hay manzanas, nisperos, nuez, mucha
caza de todas las suertes naturalmente como en España: el temple de la
tierra es como el de esta.

El Ingles conforme los Indios han dicho está poblado desde este Pueblo
ázia el Norte en un rio donde tiene por cierto el dicho Capitan Vicente
Gonzales que pasa la Mar del Sur, por que tratando con los Indios si
havia algun rio que pasava á la otra Mar, le respondieron, que adelante
donde ellos estavan havia uno que pasava á la otra Mar, y assi tiene por sin
duda, que estan alli los Ingleses: para yr á este Puerto no tiene necesidad
de yr á parte ninguna de la Indias, sino su viaje derecho, por que no tiene
que embocar canal, ni desembocar la canal de Baama, y asi mismo en la
buelta se puede venir dentro de un mes, y quando mucho mes y medio, que
es á lo mas que se puede tardar. Es de parecer el dicho Capitan Vicente
Gonzales, que se mande juntar el Fuerte de Santa Elena con el de San
Agustín, y con parte de aquella gente y la que de acá se podria yr, y hazer
esta jornada, y descubrimiento sin recivir ningun daño por estar los
soldados que hay en la Florida con gran voluntad de yr allá por la noticia
que tienen de su riqueza por lo haver visto algunos por vista de ojos.
—VICENTE GONZALES.

RELATION [1] OF VICENTE GONZALES

Relation given by Captain Vicente Gonzales of his observations made, by command of Pedro Menéndez Marqués, Governor of the Provinces of Florida, with 50 soldiers and 2 boats to reconnoiter the fort which it is understood the French have made on the coast of Santa Elena, with a very brief discourse at the end on the fortification of the same coast and forts that His Majesty possesses there, etc.

Sometime after 1588

The Captain Vicente Gonzales says: that Pedro Menéndez Marqués, Governor of the provinces of Florida, had news through the Indians of the coast of Santa Elena that there was a fort of the French, where he ordered him to go with fifty soldiers and two boats with all caution possible since he should not fall into the hands of the enemy.[2] This he did, sailing along the coast toward Los Bacallaos and entering into all the ports he discovered, for there were many. In one of them he found himself in a harbor [3] which was 2 leagues at mouth and 30 leagues inside in length, and had a width of 5 or 6, and 4 at the narrowest until the foot of the mountains is reached, where there is a very important chief [4] with a large tribe who rules all the chiefs of that region. He discovered a certain chief who went about with four or five gold rings in his ears, and on his head there was a band of a span and a half's length and six fingers wide.[5] The rest of the Indians wear copper in a similar fashion. They asked the chief where he got what he wore. He replied that at the foot of these mountains, which are reached in three days by an Indian carrying a pack (this would be 25 or 30 leagues), there is a mountain that has nothing else in it. He said they have a great amount of gold, because there is a lot in his land, and that it is worth nothing. In this he spoke the truth—that they think little of it. The Indians have a high opinion of the copper they were wearing. The aforesaid Captain Vicente Gonzales replied, in a similar fashion, that we had the same opinion here, so that he would think that we did not go to find out about gold. For if he wished he would be able to bring some.[6] It did not seem wise to disturb them, for many persons who came with him saw the same as he did.

There are many large pearls, except that they are purple.[7] Beyond that mountain range [8] there is New Mexico, which they say would be, all in all, five days' journey away from the foot of the mountains. Here there are large huts of four or five sections, daubed with mud on the outside.[9] There are a lot of small cattle and a great amount of silver, for the Indians themselves are reported to say that in the land that is said to be southward there are many silver mines and crystal mines. There is another small mountain of diamonds out of which the soldiers in Florida took and sold in Spain, without realizing their value, one for 500 ducats and another for 100 dubloons. Since they did not understand the value, they lost a great amount by this. In Florida there are soldiers who have been at the silver mines and at a small mountain of diamonds. He [the Captain] says the soldiers have a great desire to go there. Able to give information about this [10] is a Franciscan friar, the provincial of Florida, who is also informed about what has been said, likewise another soldier who is in this court. In that land there is a great amount of provisions: maize and berries, which are their fare; there are wild cherries, plums, grapes, dried chestnuts which they keep the year round;[11] there are apples, persimmons, walnuts, and a lot of game of the types common in Spain; the climate of the land is similar, too.

Moreover the Indians said that the English have settled away from these people toward the north, on a river, which, Captain Vicente Gonzales believes for certain, goes into the South Sea. For he asked the Indians whether there was a river which goes into the other sea and they replied that farther on from them there was one which went into another sea.[12] Thus he has no doubt that the English are there. In order to go to this port, there is no need to go to any part of the Indies, but only of a direct voyage without having to enter a channel or go out through the Bahama Channel. Likewise one can come up here in a month or at the most a month and a half, which is the latest that one can be. That is the opinion of Captain Vicente Gonzales, who was ordered to visit both the fort at Santa Elena and the one at San Agustín, and with some of those men and some from here, he could go and make that journey of exploration without any unpleasantness. For the soldiers in Florida are most eager to go there because of the reports they have of its riches which some have seen with their own eyes.

—VICENTE GONZALES

NOTES

1. The Connor Papers in the Library of Congress include a photostat of the original from AGI, Audiencia de México, 92-2-1. This text is from a copy in the Museo Naval, Madrid, in Navarrete, *Colección*, vol. 14, Doc. 54. A typed transcript is in the Lowery Papers, "MSS Florida 1608-1620," in the Library of Congress. There is a notation at the end of the document saying the original is in the Archivo General de Indias, among papers brought from Simancas "in a folder with the notation: various undated papers."

There are three other documents from Vicente Gonzales available, none of which mentions the Chesapeake expedition. The first deals with his expedition to Guale on Oct. 4, 1580: "De lo que hiço el Capitan Vicente Gos. sobre la Rebelion de los Yndios de Guale a 4 de Ote 1580 y como los Yndios Tractaron y contractaron con los franceses." AGI 2-4-4, Doc. 46-D. Mary Ross has described this rebellion in "French Intrusions and Indian Uprisings in Georgia and South Carolina, 1577-1580," 7 GHQ 251-281. There are also two letters of Vicente Gonzales to the King. One dated Dec. 18, 1595, AGI 54-5-16, Doc. 77, is in the Connor Papers in photostat; the other is dated Oct. 26, 1596, AGI 54-5-16, Doc. 77.

The title is misleading, for it emphasizes what is apparently a search for French traders along the coast, whereas Gonzales devotes most of his attention to that which interests us more, his view of the Chesapeake and the Indians of Maryland, as observed by him in 1588.

The exaggerated description which he gives of the riches of the interior reveals an uncritical mind prone to peddling the stories of fabulous wealth that were current in his day.

2. Gonzales seems to be reporting the same events given in Juan Menéndez Marqués' letter. As Oré explains, the purpose of the 1588 expedition was to reconnoiter the English settlements, but Pedro Menéndez Marqués in his letter of 1588 mentions only one boat and says nothing at all about the French incident, but he may not yet have had news of the capture. From Oré we know that the Gonzales party stopped at Santa Elena and Cayagua on their way north.

3. He is undoubtedly describing the Chesapeake. It is interesting that he gives the same length as Carrera and, later, Molina, 30 leagues, a gross underestimate unless he pictures the bay as ending at the Potomac. His widths, on the other hand, are more nearly true than Juan Menéndez Marqués' 2 leagues.

4. The "important chief" must have been the ruler of the Patuxent Indians, numbering about six hundred, or some Susquehannock chieftain whose village was located but a few miles above the bay. Between the Patuxent and the Susquehanna Smith's map shows no villages, a result of the Iroquoian and Susquehannock attacks on the Algonkin tribes of Maryland. One is inclined to believe that Gonzales is here talking about Algonkin Indians, since the conversation swings to the old familiar strain of precious metals to be found in the mountains. The interpreters mentioned by Oré could not understand the southern languages. They seemed to have no trouble in the Chesapeake. Perhaps Alonso's friend, taken by Avilés in 1572, was an interpreter in 1588.

5. Gonzales' remarks on the Indians' gold ornaments support Menéndez Marqués' observations. As to the method of wearing copper, Father White in his *Relatio Itineris* 38 notes that "Some of them wear on their foreheads the figure of a fish, made of copper." The *Declaratio* attributed to Cecil Calvert and depreciated perhaps more than it deserves, has the remark, "There is hope of finding gold, for the neighboring people wear bracelets of gold, which indeed is as yet unwrought, and long strings of pearls." Gonzales, much better than Menéndez Marqués, gives the source of the gold as three days' journey away, rather than a half day.

6. The point of Gonzales' remarks here, almost unintelligible in the Spanish, seems to be that he gave the Indians the impression that the Spaniards were not interested in gold, hoping thereby not to frighten the Indians into thinking the Spaniards would be back to start a gold rush. For the same reason he did not try to acquire samples of it; moreover, it was not a question of one man's word as to its existence, since many of his companions were ready to bear the same witness.

7. The purple color of the pearls came from their being heated when the mussels were cooked.

8. "That mountain range" refers to the Appalachians, where the gold is to be found. Now Gonzales is reporting information that he picked up from the southern Indians, in 1588 and at other times, and reports of soldiers who enlarged on their observations while on expeditions with Pardo and Moyano into the southern Appalachian regions (2 Lowery 275-298). Pardo's own letters reveal that these stories were greatly exaggerated. In their most extreme form they appear in the relation of Pedro Morales to Hakluyt, 1586, and Nicholas Burgoignon to Hakluyt and Heriot (9 Hakluyt (ES) 112 f). Burgoignon was captured by Drake at San Agustín in 1586. Both he and Morales speak of gold, rubies, and diamonds up the River Santa Elena at a place they call "La Grand Copal," the mythical *Ursprung* of the Aztecs, a rich "new" Mexico concocted by Ybarra in 1563. The diamonds were so brilliant the explorers were warned to shield their eyes as they advanced. Beginning in 1598, Governor Canzo encouraged the spread of these legends to attract colonists (Quinn 1 *TRHS* 21). Espinosa, in his *Compendium* 109, speaks of crystals and diamonds in the Sierra de Tama, a province north of Guale and 40 leagues south of "Xacal, an English settlement."

The distance that Vicente Gonzales gives to New Mexico reflects contemporary geography. Pardo on his journey seems to have believed that the silver mines of Mexico were not far beyond the Appalachian. Ribault was persuaded that he could reach Cibola in 20 days by boat from Port Royal.

9. Lederer in 1670 reported that the Oenock and mountain Indians "build not their houses of bark, but of watling and plaister." This is probably what the Indians meant, but Gonzales had in mind the pueblo dwellings of the West.

10. Since the "Province of Florida" was not created for the Franciscan administrative system until 1612, this Friar may have been a provincial on visitation from Spain or Cuba. See M. Geiger, *Biographical Dictionary of the Franciscans in Spanish Florida and Cuba, 1528-1841* 8.

11. Oré (47) seems to be echoing this description of trees and fruits when he states their abundance from 38° northward, anticipating a similar account by Father White in 1634.

12. Gonzales indicates that he knows it is easy to enter the river that goes to the South Sea. Doubtless he was thinking of the James and the story he picked up from the Indians in 1570. We need not suppose that the English here in question are the 1607 colony, for the idea that Raleigh's colony remained in North Carolina persisted, at least until 1602. It may be objected, and rightly, that the course of his 1588 expedition indicates the Susquehanna rather than the James as the hoped-for passage to the Western Ocean. But Gonzales probably visualized more than one possibility, for according to the Irishman Francis "Maguel" (deposition of July 1, 1610, Brown, 1 *Genesis*, 397), the Indians spoke of three routes: the James, the Roanoke (?) and the Susquehanna (?). The plans for going to that river reveal two things: that he is thinking of a ship sailing from Spain or Santo Domingo, not from Havana, and that he was still vigorous enough to be entrusted with a command. Evidently he was not writing in 1609, when Andrés Gonzales, probably a relative, took over. Lowery may have been influenced to date this Relation between 1608 and 1620 because of a reference to a Florida provincial and to an English colony that could have been that at Jamestown. We would prefer to connect this Relation with the letter and Relation of Juan Menéndez Marqués. It is difficult to date the original composition of any of them, since they seem to have been recopied and retransmitted at various times.

Carta de Juan Menéndez Marqués

Noviembre 21, 1605

Aqui sse tubo nueua de vn nauio de enemigos que estaba cargando de
ssasafraz en esta costa en la prouinçia de guale çerca de ssanta Elena en la
baya de los bajos despacho el Señor Governador vna Armadilla en su
busca y fue Dios seruido de darles tan buena suerte que con solo perdida
de la muerte de dos honbres lo rrindieron y trugeron a este pressidio trayan
papeles ynstruçiones y Patentes del Rey de françia tocantes a contrataçion
comerçio y descubrimiento de minas en esta costa y Poblaçion que a
muchos dias se tiene notiçia avia de ynglesses—de todo esto creo avissa
a su magestad el señor governador y que a de caussar algun cuydado—Este
Vuestra Paternidad a la mira y adbertido que desde Altura de 33 grados
asta la de 40 en esta costa en la buelta del norte ninguno tiene Platica y
esperiençia por vista de ojos que ssea español sino solo el capitan Viçente
gonzáles y gines pinçon Piloto que en compañia del dicho capitan y mia
siendo yo aqui sargento mayor fue por orden del general queste en el
çielo a que supiessemos y tomasemos lengua desta poblaçion—y confiriendo
los yndiçios y Rastro que allamos con la Relaçion que daban Pero diaz
pimienta piloto vzo de gerachico y dauid glauid yrlandes que estubieron
en la mesma poblaçion—allabamos ser en vn puerto que esta en Altura
de treinta y çinco grados escassos y ti(e)ne por sseñas en la playa tres
medanos grandes de Arena tiene dos bocas la de la banda del norte es la
buena y por donde podian entrar nauios pequeños dentro açe gran baya y
en la buelta del ceste suoeste es norueste açe demostraçion de tierra
montuossa y grande arboleda diçen ser ysla y que alli estaba la poblacion
que tenia el ingles.

la baya de la madre de dios del jacan esta en Altura de 37 grados entrasse
de norueste sueste o por mejor deçir de ssueste norueste porque su
trabessia es sueste tiene çerca de tres leguas de boca sin genero de bajo
ni Arreçife en la boca y del medio della para la banda del sur tiene siete
o ocho braças de fondo cossa de tres leguas en la buelta del norueste
y todo en rredondo açe gran baya que cassi pierde la tierra de vista y
luego costeandola en la buelta del norte se uen por la costa de la banda
del oeste muchos y muy buenos Puertos y Rios caudales de agua dulçe y

en lo mas angosto tiene buenas dos leguas de ancho asta que en Altura de quarenta grados largos remata açiendo un grande golfho de agua dulçe rodeado de sierras de que bajan Rios caudales con balles y tierra bien asonbrada y al pareçer fertil para criança y labrança—y dentro de la misma baya en Altura de 38 grados vimos chagalas de oro a los yndios que las trayan al cuello esta baya sospecho a de ser donde los ynglesses y françesses llaman el gran rrio de la gama / y si pareçiere a Vuestra Paternidad conbendra auissar desto a los susodichos del quomo * lo podra açer con ssatisfaçion de que esta Relaçion es çierta y bernadera y ruego a Dios confunda los malos yntentos de los enemigos de nuestra sancta fee catolica y de ssiempre Victoria a su magestad contra ellos Amen.

del ssubçesso del Viaje que digo y descubrimiento del dicho Puerto a baya di vna Relaçion muy amplia por scripto en el consejo a muchas dias (Rubricado) /

Relaçion de la costa de Jacan a donde diçen esta poblado un fuerte de enemigos yngleses

En 21 de nouiembre 1605

Vista y que se junte con los demas papeles que tratan de la florida (Rubricado)

LETTER [1] OF JUAN MENÉNDEZ MARQUÉS TO A RELIGIOUS
[From San Agustín ?] November 21, 1605

An enemy ship was reported here to be loading sassafras [2] on this coast in the province of Guale near Santa Elena in the Bay of the Shoals. The Lord Governor sent a small fleet in search and God was served by granting a successful outcome, for with the loss of only two killed they took the ship [3] and brought it to this fort. They captured written instructions and patents from the King of France dealing with the trade, business, and discovery of mines on this coast and also touching on the English settlement [4] which they had observed for many days. I believe the Lord Governor has advised His Majesty about all this and it caused him some worry. Let it be known to Your Paternity's watchful care that no Spaniard has reports or experience concerning this coast in a northern direction from the latitude of 33° up to 40° except Captain Vicente

* This seems an apt transliteration for the abbreviation: ss del q°.

Gonzales and Ginés Pinzón, a pilot, who accompanied the said Captain and myself, the sergeant-major, under orders from the General,[5] God rest him, to go to where we understood the settlement was from the reports received.

Comparing the signs and the evidence we discovered with the report which was given by Pedro Díaz Pimienta,[6] a pilot of the "Gerachico," and David Glavid,[7] Irishman, who lived in that same settlement, we found the settlement was in a port which was at about 35°. For signs, there are on the beach three large mounds of sand that make two entrances. The one on the northern shore is the better and small ships can enter therein.[8] There is a large bay in the direction of the west-southwest. To the northwest, there are indications of hilly country and thick forests. They say that it is an island where the English made their settlement.

The Bay of the Mother of God of Jacán is at a latitude of 37°. One enters northwest-southeast, or to put it more nicely, southeast-northwest, because it stretches to the southeast. It has a mouth 3 leagues wide, without any type of shoal or bar in the mouth and center. Along the southern shore there is a depth of 7 or 8 fathoms[9] for about 3 leagues in a northwest direction. All around there is a great bay where the land almost disappears from view. Then sailing in a northern direction one may see on the coast of the western shore many fine harbors and plentiful rivers of fresh water and in the most narrow part it is 2 good leagues in width up to a latitude of more than 40° where it ends in a large gulf of fresh water. This is surrounded by mountain ranges down which plenteous streams flow amid valleys and a land of pleasing aspect that appears fertile and fit for grazing and cultivation. Within the same bay we saw Indians with rings of gold which they wear about the neck. This bay I suspect must be the one which the English and French call the great River of the Deer.[10] If it should seem fitting to Your Paternity to inform the aforementioned persons as to the question, Your Paternity can do so with the assurance that this relation is certain and true. I ask God to confound the enemies of our holy Catholic Faith and to always grant victory to His Majesty against them, Amen.

I have been giving a fuller relation in writing in the council for many days about the outcome of the voyage of discovery which I mentioned, from the said port to the bay. (Rubric)

A relation of the coast of Jacán where it is said there is a fort[11] inhabited by the English, our enemies.

On the 21st of November, 1605.

Approved. It is joined with the following papers which deal with Florida.

(Rubric)

NOTES

1. The original is in the AGI 54-5-9. This text is from a transcript in the Connor Papers, Library of Congress. Mrs. Connor has a notation on the transcript, "Is this from Ecija?" but the author is unquestionably Juan Menéndez Marqués, since he describes himself here as the sergeant-major on the 1588 expedition. The letter is written to a Religious, who is addressed in the text as "Your Paternity." We believe this person may have been Fray Miguel de Avengozar, to whom Juan Menéndez addressed his long Relation (see text below) seven months later. Fray Miguel held the very important post of Commissary-General of the Franciscan Order in the Spanish Empire. (For a description of this post created in 1572, see L. de Aspurz, O.F.M., *La Aportación Extranjera a las Misiónes Españoles del Patranato Regio* [Madrid, 1946] 119 ff.). Juan Menéndez treats this Religious as a man of considerable influence who would be duly alarmed at the Spanish ignorance of the northern coast line of Florida and at the English settlements there.

The depths of water given enable us to plot the course of the 1588 vessel from the cape to the mouth of the James. The reference to the Río de Gamas reveals that the Spanish still had a confused knowledge of cartography, one of whose results was to compress the distance between Santa Elena and Los Bacallaos, or Newfoundland.

From Menéndez Marqués' letter it appears that he was at the time compiling a more detailed relation, *en el consejo*, as he says, possibly referring to the *curia* of Governor Canzo, at San Agustín. It would also appear that this letter was approved by the Governor and joined to other reports on Florida, possibly including Menéndez Marqués' final draught, all then being sent to "the Religious." It is certain that Oré later acquired more information from Menéndez Marqués than is to be found in either of the reports we reproduce. Perhaps it is to the longer account Menéndez Marqués was preparing *en el consejo* that Oré refers (48) when he says: "This trip of exploration and discovery, from start to finish, they made in a month and a half, according to this report, so exact and prolix, which was made by the said sergeant-major Juan Menéndez, who at present is the royal treasurer in the city of St. Augustine." In his 1606 relation, Marqués reveals that he and his first cousin Pedro presented themselves to the King and Council toward the end of July 1589 and gave a full report of the 1588 journey, addressing themselves particularly to Don Juan de Diaguez and Juan de Ibarra, but we have found no record of what they told the Council at that time. The King desired the fortification of the Chesapeake, but the course of history prevented this. Being a Franciscan, Oré could naturally avail himself of any records kept by his order.

2. The habit of drinking sassafras tea was sweeping Europe. Strachey tells us

that "of sassafras there is plenty enough, the rootes whereof, not monie yeares since, were sold for twenty shillings per lb. and better . . ." (*Historie* 129). Barcia (145, 160 f.) relates stories showing the ridiculously exaggerated prestige of this root among the Spanish.

3. A ship which had been outfitted in Plymouth in January, 1604, was captured by Ecija in 1605. The letters patent on board were dated 1600 and 1604 and were to be used when setting up French claim plates along the coast. A full report on the events is in the document "Carta de Pedro Ybara a S.M. de fecha de Mayo 1605," AGI 54-5-9. The story of the capture is told vividly by Mary Ross in "The French on the Savannah, 1605," in 8 *GHQ* (1924) 167-194. The events bear much resemblance to those reported by Juan Menéndez Marqués here, but we think he is reporting a similar incident of 1588.

4. The English population mentioned here is evidently the Raleigh colony.

5. Juan Menéndez Marqués' first cousin, Pedro Menéndez Marqués.

6. In Havana in March, 1589, Pedro Díaz, a captive of the English from 1585 to 1588, composed a report on the English activities at Roanoke and northward. The text is in Connor Papers, Library of Congress, AGI 54-1-34. There is a brief summary in Quinn, "Some Spanish Reactions to Elizabethan Enter-prizes," *TRHS* (5) 18 f.

7. For Glavin's Relation, see the discussion in Part I. Glavin, too, had been captured by Grenville and was twice taken to Ajacán, but on the second trip he escaped while the English were stopping at Puerto Rico.

8. Menéndez Marqués is describing Roanoke Island and Pamlico Sound as it would be seen from Oregon Inlet. Notice that Menéndez Marqués gives 35° while Oré, aiming for greater accuracy, gives 35½°, just as later Menéndez Marqués gives 37° for the Bay of Jacán where Oré gives 37½°, evidently basing upon a more accurate and detailed report of Menéndez Marqués.

9. The depths given for the journey along the southern shore, if at all ac-curate, indicate that the party sailed in through the Thimble Shoal channel, the deepest course leading toward the James River.

10. The River of the Deer, or Río de Gamas, was farther north. On Wytfliet's map of 1597 it is shown in the position of the modern Hackensack River, in New Jersey. From Oré's Relation we know that they found many deer near the mouth of the Susquehanna, which undoubtedly caused Menéndez Marqués to associate the upper part of the bay with the Río Grande (Hudson) or the Río de Gamas, which flows into Newark Bay. See the essay on cartography, Part III below, for other interpretations of the Río de Gamas.

11. The belief in the English fort probably stems from the Glavin and Diaz relations of experiences in 1586. There is, however, a remote possibility that reports of Raleigh survivors may have trickled in from the Indians farther south, who always maintained communication of a kind with the north.

Relación de Juan Menéndez Marqués

*Relación escrita en el Fuerte de San Agustín por el Tesorero
Juan Menéndez Marqués, sobrino de Pero Menéndez, al
P. Comisario General de Indias Fr. Miguel Avengoçar, en la que
describe las provincias de la Florida, distancias, etc.*

... desde la dicha baya de Santa Elena hasta la baya de la Madre de
Dios de Jacan, que está su entrada en altura de treinta y siete grados, yo
me ofrezco á mostrar puertos, siendo necessario, capaces para entrar y
poder surgir y repararse en ella navios, aunque sean de porte de quinientas
toneladas, en particular en el dicho puerto y baya de la Madre de Dios,
que su entrada está de Norueste Sueste, sin género de baxio ni arrecife
en toda la boca, ni fuera della, la buelta la mar á una bista tiniendo fondo
de suyo á ocho braças para arriba, y de ancho en la boca mas de dos
leguas, a mi parecer, y entrando para dentro hace tanto golfo que casi se
pierde la tierra de bista de una parte á otra, y aviendo entrado cosa de
tres leguas en la buelta del Norueste, se llega á la costa de la Tierra
Firme, y ay otro puerto grande que en la boca tiene de tres braças de
fondo para arriba, y luego costeando la baya por la banda de la Tierra
Firme en la buelta del Norte, ay maravillosos puertos y rios dulces caudales,
y balles bien asembrados, y al parecer tierra fertil, en particular desde
altura de treinta y ocho grados para arriba hasta altura de cuarenta grados,
donde remata la baya y puertos en sierras altas, y faldas y balles en ellas
al parecer fértiles y de linda disposicion para criança y labrança; y es
tanta la fuerça de los rios caudales que baxan de las sierras, que hacen en
el dicho remate de la baya un golfo grande de agua dulce, y en lo más
angosto de la baya ay desde la entrada al remate me paresce que ay de
travessia por lo menos dos leguas.

Y en altura de treinta y ocho grados yo bí por mis ojos traer á un
yndio chagualas de oro al cuello, y aviendo traydo de aquella parte á
este pressidio un yndio, mostrándole yo una cadena de oro dijo que en
su tierra avia mucho, y que se llamava *Tapisco;* y mostrándole un can-
delero de açofar, dijo que tambien mucho, y que se llamava *guapaçina;* y
mostrándole cobre, dijo que tambien mucho, y que no balia nada, que
los yndios no hacian caso dél, y que se llamava *ococo,* y preguntado que

donde lo avia y como sacava, dijo que saliendo de su lugar por la mañana al salir del sol á medio dia se llegava al pie de una sierra grande, y que de allá caya un gran golpe de agua, que en lo llano hacia una gran repressa y remanso de agua que rompia en un rio grande, y que çambullendo los yndios en aquel remanso, al salir sacavan los manos llenas de guijas y arena, y á las bueltas señalava que sacavan granos como garbanças y otros mayores y menores de los dichos tres géneros; y preguntado de qué manera desacian aquellos granos y hacian las chagualas dellos, dijo que echándoles en la candela y dándoles golpes.

Y de la bondad de la tierra y su fertilidad decia maravillas; y aviendo bisto en la Yaguana bacas, dijo que en su tierra avia muchas, pero que eran mas pequeñas y mas ariscas. Y aviendo llevado este yndio a España el biaje de las galiçabras á Cartajena, de buelto de biaje con ellas cargadas de plata y oro, murió en Biana del Camino, y por ser ya christiano lo enterramos en el Conbento de Santo Domingo; . . .

RELATION OF JUAN MENÉNDEZ MARQUÉS [1]

Relation composed at Fort San Agustín by the treasurer Juan Menéndez Marqués, nephew of Pedro Menéndez, for the Reverend Commissary-General Fray Miguel Avengozar, wherein there is a description of the Province of Florida, the distances, etc.

From San Agustín, June 7, 1606

EXCERPT

. . . from the Bay of Santa Elena to the Bay of the Mother of God of Ajacán, which is at 37° latitude, if necessary I offer to point out ports of suitable entrance where even vessels of fifty tons can be anchored and repaired, especially in the said port and bay of the Mother of God, whose entrance lies northwest-southeast without any kind of sand bar or reef inside or outside the entire mouth. Here in the sea's direction, at one observation, there was a depth of 7 or 8 fathoms or more, and the width of the mouth was more than 2 leagues in my opinion. After entering inside, there is such a gulf that the land almost disappears from one side to the other, and when one has entered about 3 leagues in a northwest direction, the shore of the mainland ["west," in 1602 version] is reached

Plate XIII   *Photostat of original in the John Carter Brown Library*

MADRE DE DIOS ON A DUTCH MAP, ABOUT 1655

This is a section of a map of the Atlantic entitled "Mar de Nort" as found in
Jansson's *Novus Atlas*, Volume V. Mr. Lawrence C. Wroth states that this copy
has an *Au Lecteur* dated in 1650, so that the map itself may be of that date. This
is the earliest reference we have found in Dutch cartography to the Chesapeake
as the Barra (or Bahía) de Madre de Dios. We have been unable to locate any of
the Spanish maps which must have antedated the Dutch use of Spanish nomenclature for the region between Albemarle Sound and the Chesapeake. The earliest
reference to the Chesapeake as the Bahía de Madre de Dios is the heading of Father
Rogel's letter of August, 1572.

and there is another large harbor[2] with a depth of 3 fathoms or more at its mouth. Then in the bay, while sailing along the shore of the mainland in a northern direction, there are splendid ports and abundant freshwater streams, fine arable valleys and apparently fertile lands. Especially from 38° or more to 40° latitude, where the bay and the harbor ends at high ranges, there are slopes and valleys there which seem to be fertile and of beautiful contour, fit for grazing and cultivation. Such is the force of these abundant streams which descend from the mountain heights, that they make at the edge of the bay a huge gulf of fresh water. In the narrow part of the bay, from the entrance to the edge there is a distance of at least 2 leagues.

At 38° latitude, I beheld an Indian with a necklace of gold about his neck; I captured him and took him from there over to where I was. I showed him a chain of gold and he said they had plenty of it and called it *tapisco;* then I showed him a candlestick made of brass and the Indian said they had plenty of this and called it *guapaçina;* then I showed him copper and he said they also had plenty of this and that it cost nothing and that the Indians made nothing of it and that it was called *ococo*.[3] To questions about the source and the method of obtaining it, he replied that if they left their place in the morning at dawn, at noon they arrived at the foot of the mountain range and that from this range there descended a torrent of water which formed in the flatland a huge basin of water, which in turn flowed down into a large river.[4] He said that the Indians used to dive into this basin and on coming up they had their hands filled with pebbles and sand. He made signs that sometimes they took grains of the three kinds mentioned above, as big as Spanish beans and others bigger and smaller. When asked how they crushed those grains and made necklaces out of them, the Indian said that they threw them into the fire and then pounded them. . . .

He spoke wonders of the bounty and fertility of the land; and when he saw the cattle at Yaguana, he said that there were many such in his land, but that they were small and very timid. The voyage of the sloops to Cartajena took this Indian to Spain when they returned loaded with silver and gold. He died in Biana del Camino, and since he was a Christian, we buried him in the Convent of Santo Domingo. . . .

NOTES

1. The autograph is in the AGI 1-1-1/19. This text was edited by Ruidíaz y Caravia in *La Florida* 495-509. The portion translated here is practically identical with a letter of Juan Menéndez Marqués to the King from San Agustín, Sept. 20, 1602, AGI 54-5-14, in Lowery Papers, "Florida," vol. 4. Juan Menéndez Marqués describes the purpose of his voyage in an earlier part of the relation: "y aviendo por el año de 88 ydo al descubrimiento de la baya de la Madre de Dios de Jacán y tomar lengua de la población del ynglés juntamente con le Capitan Vicente Gonzales, por orden del dicho General..." (*La Florida* 498). This section of the report deals with his explorations in the Chesapeake with the same pilot who made the 1570-1572 voyages (see Rogel Relation above, para. 9). His description of the bay is the best that is available for this early date. In connection with his office as treasurer, Juan Menéndez Marqués was later suspended by one of the frequent arbitrary actions of the Council of the Indies, which found him "chiefly concerned in certain unregistered sales of merchandise in fraud of royal rights". (AGI, Saec. Aud. de S. Dom.: 54-5-10; Lowery Papers, "Florida," vol. 6, Library of Congress).

2. This "harbor" suggests entry of the mouth of the James at Hampton Roads.

3. The mention of these three metals at this early date by an Indian of the Rappahannock or Potomac region poses an interesting problem for the anthropologist: Is it possible that behind this and numerous similar stories there is more than native cooperation with European wishful thinking? The report of Juan Menéndez Marqués strengthens the report of Alonso to Martínez (see the Martínez Relation above, para. 44), where Ajacán is described as rich in gold, silver, and pearls. An Indian reported there was much gold in the mountains that reach to the other sea. No doubt this is an exaggeration, but it is remarkable how consistently such reports appear in the early relations of the Virginia region. See Appendix E, "Early Reports of Metals in Virginia."

4. In the map by Mercator, "Virginia item et Floridae" (1630 edition), there is an illustration showing a large torrent of water gushing from the "*Apalatcy montes*" to form a pool like that in the Indians' story quoted by Menéndez Marqués. This merely continues the same description as found in Le Moyne's map of Florida (Lorant, 34 f.), drawn in 1564 or 1565. Francis Lister Hawks, in his *History of North Carolina* (1857) 1: 123, thinks the copper and gold stories of the Indians may have had a true foundation. For further instances of gold among the natives, see the notes following the Vicente Gonzales Relation, in this part.

Relación de Francisco de Ecija
y
Relación de Andrés Gonzales
1609
[I]

Y savado *25* del dicho mes de Gullio al amanescer se puso un marinero
sobre el tope y descubrio el dicho navio estar como estava el dia antes
y aque se acavo de echar de ver ser enemigo que [e]stava de guardia
y centinela que aviendo tenido el viento terral, y luna, y marea, no avia
salido ni venido en nuestra busca, y ansi nos pusimos del todo a la orden
y no nos levamos por vaciar el agua y no aver viento hasta las *9* que
començo a crecer la marea y vino entrado la viraçon por el nordeste y a
esta punta nos hicimos a la vela estando de contino la posta en el tope la
qual descubrio que el dicho navio hacia tambien la vela la vuelta de
nosotros, procurando nosotros siempre ganalle el varlovento siendo
nosotros (14) aventajado en ello por havernos hecho a la vela desde
fuera y correr el agua acia dentro que lo grigava a el como nosotros
y ansí no nos pudo ganar el barlovento y fuimos en su demanda llegandonos a el tiempo que el dicho navio se hiço a la vela que fue quando
nosotros, alçaron una gran humada en la tierra de la vanda del norte, y
luego respondió otra a uesnorueste que's donde esta un rrio muy caudaloso
segun dijo el alferez Juan de Santiago y otros que en dias pasados avian
ydo con el Capitan Vicente Gonçalez, y de aqui se ynfirio y conocio ser
centinela el dicho navio con las causas que atras quedan dichas, pues en
haciendose a la vela alçaron el humo y luego respondieron donde tienen el
presidio segun lo declarado por los yndios y que los humos ni mas ni
menos que nos hacian por la costa eran asimismo señas.

Pues yendo prosiguiendo nuestro camino reconocimos era navio sin
comparacion de mas porte que nosotros porque vimos trayados velas de
gavia y una gran bandera de tope y ser el dicho navio largo y raso y
llegandonos mas viniendo el dicho navio de nuestra vuelta cada uno por
ganar el barlovento y conociendo el dicho Capitan y todas los demas y
que a este tiempo era el viento poco y escaso y llevarnos ensenando y el

dicho enemigo por entretenernos con las velas de gavia sobre la borda
para que nos enseñase la corriente donde el quisiese.

[II]

Señas de la Vaia del Xacan

De la varra de santiago a la vaia de la madre de dios ques la del xacan
es costa de norte sur y es costa toda poblada de monte alto y el mas del
es parexo y quando quieras ver que esta çerca de la vaia veras que la tierra
de la vaia haçe de la vanda del sur de la voca una punta taxada a la mar
y luego te pareçe que se acava la tierra manda ir un hombre arriba en
estando çerca de la propia punta y veras que de la otra parte del norte
cosa de quatro leguas echa una tierra la vuelta del esnordeste no tienes
sino costear la costa de la vanda del sul y yras para adentro luego veras
en estando dentro que haçe una vaia muy grande que la vuelta del
noroeste se pierdre la tierra de vista y la tierra que haçe camino del oeste
esta de la punta que haçe la vaia de la vanda del sul mas de dos leguas
buenas y de la punta de la vaia de la vanda del sul a la tierra de la otra
vanda de la voca ay como dijo arriba cosa de quatro leguas toda es tierra
parexa y toda esta costa es muy hondable porque cosa de un tiro de
mosquete de tierra ay diez o doçe vraças de agua y en yendo avriendo
mas la vaia hallareis catorçe y deçiseis vraças esta esta vaia en altura de
treinta y siete grados largos que yo tomé el sol en ella a la entrada en la
punta de la vanda del sul y ay de la varra de santiago a ella cosa de siete o
ocho leguas.—andres gonsales— (con su rubrica)

The Ecija Reports

[The two documents that follow supplement each other. They are
from the Spanish expedition that scouted the English settlements in the
summer of 1609 and they offer valuable geographical notes. On June 19,
1609, Governor Pedro de Ybarra issued instructions to Ecija: "to go to
the latitude of 37 1/2° where it is rumored the first English settlements are
in a place which they call Virginia or Cortuan [*sic*] and in our language

is called the Bay of Jacán, where one sails into a mouth 6 leagues wide; and to try to scout the heads of the rivers, on one of which is the settlement, and other islands which are in the middle of the bay . . ." (AGI 2-5-3/16, Lowery Papers, "Florida," vol. 6, Library of Congress).

[On July 23 the expedition was off the North Carolina coast and reported signal fires. The next day they reached Ajacán. The Commander's report for the 25th shows the short distance this expedition went into the Bay of the Mother of God. But an important sentence refers to a smoke signal near a "rrio caudaloso," which river some of the crew recalled from the earlier expedition on which Vicente Gonzales was pilot (see the Juan Menéndez Marqués reports above). Therefore Gonzales and Marqués knew the James and could not have overlooked its ports in an official report. Thus Ecija's account helps to interpret Oré's description of the same expedition, which is discussed at length in Part I. The second document gives the pilot's report for navigation in the bay.]

EXCERPTS

I. THE REPORT OF THE COMMANDER [1]

At dawn on Saturday the 25th of the said month of July, a sailor climbed to the top of the mast and saw that the said ship [2] was the same as the day before. Hence it was easy to see that it was an enemy on watch, for even with the off-shore breeze, moon, and tide it had not sailed out and come to look for us. So we made everything ready but did not raise anchor because we had to pump water and there was no wind. Then at nine the tide began to come in and the wind shifted to the northeast. At this point, keeping the lookout on watch all the time, we set sail and discovered the ship was making sail in our direction. We kept trying to keep to the windward, for we had the advantage in that we sailed from outside and the current ran inwards, which bothered them as much as us. And so the other ship could not get to our windward and, at the time that the said ship put on sail just as we did, we sailed straight taking the vantage point. They started a great smoke cloud on the northern shore, and then one replied from the west-northwest,[3] where there is a river that carries much water according to Lieutenant Juan de Santiago and others who previously had gone with Captain Vicente Gonzales.[4] From this they reasoned and understood, from the reasons mentioned above, that the ship was on watch, because as soon as we set sail, they started smoke clouds and there was a reply from where they kept their garrison, according to the reports of the Indians. The smoke clouds made on the shore were nothing more nor less than signals.

Then proceeding on our course we saw that it was a ship larger than ours beyond comparison and we looked at its topsails and the large banner on the top of the mast, and the ship was big but still indistinct.[5] As we were getting near, the ship came towards us trying to get to the windward. The captain and all the rest knew about this advantage, namely, that when the wind was slight and faint and taking us into the bay, the enemy, by enticing us with the topsails across the gunwale,[6] would thus let the current lead us where he wanted us.[7]

II. The Report of the Pilot [8]

Description of the Bay of Ajacán

From the Bar of Santiago [9] toward the Bay of the Mother of God, or Ajacán, the coast lies north-south, the entire shore has high shrubbery, the greater part is fairly level. When you wish to recognize the approach to the bay, you will see that the land at the southern edge of the mouth of the bay forms a steep point into the sea.[10] Then as soon as it seems to you that the land ends, send a man up [11] as you near the point itself. There you will see that at the northern shore, some 4 leagues away, the land makes a turn toward east-northeast. You have only to sail up the coast of the southern shore and you will go into the interior. Then you will see, once inside, that there is a bay so large that towards the northwest the land disappears.[12] The land which goes to the west is more than 2 good leagues from the point which the bay makes at the south. From the point of the bay at the southern shore to the land of the other shore at the mouth there are, as I said above, some 4 leagues. All this is fairly level land and all the coast line is navigable since at about a musket shot away from land there are 10 or 12 fathoms of water. And as the mouth of the bay opens up you will find 14 and 16 fathoms.[13] This bay is at a latitude of 37°, for I shot the sun at the bay's entrance on the point of the southern shore.[14] The Bar of Santiago is some 7 or 8 leagues away.

Andrés Gonzales. (Rubric)

NOTES

1. The autograph is in the AGI 2-5-3/16. A transcript, from which our text is taken, is in the Lowery Papers, "Florida" 1608-1620, vol. 6, Library of Congress.

2. When they arrived they saw a ship anchored near the shore, but they were not certain that it was English. They had then decided to wait the night and see what the ship would do.

3. Probably between the Kecoughtan and their Algonkin brethren on the eastern shore. Strachey (50) informs us that Powhatan had sentinels posted to relay all information concerning ship movements.

4. From the rest of the report this conference was attended by Juan Rodríguez de Cartaya and Juan de Santiago, lieutenants; Andrés Gonzales, the pilot; and Juan Rodrigo, the master-gunner.

5. Irene A. Wright, "Spanish Policy to Virginia, 1606-1612," 25 *AHR* (1920) 464, gives the following paraphrase of the Ecija Report in a *consulta* of the Council for War in the Indies, dated March 5, 1611 (AGI 147-5-17): "On the 25th having come to the Bay of Jacán (which by another name they call Virginia) he perceived a ship anchored in it and since it was of much greater tonnage than that in which they were, for it carried two topsails and a great banner at its masthead, and since he perceived that it desired to entrap them in the bay where it could be master, because it withdrew before them, they did not venture to follow it." The Spanish ship was also bothered by leaks.

6. A vague expression, but the idea seems to be to keep the sails slack and apparently out of use. Sailors of wind-driven vessels will be able to interpret the factors entering the promised engagement of the two ships. A breeze off the southern shore, striking the English sail at a slight angle, added to the tidal current, would have given the English ship a smart speed essential for maneuvering. Then the wind and tide shifted in favor of the Spanish ship *Asunción de Cristo*, but since the wind was so slight there was danger of the current's bringing the *Asunción* within range of the English ship, which meantime was trying to trap the Spanish by getting to their windward side.

7. Had Ecija known the true state of affairs in the Virginia colony, he might have made bold to attack the English ship. So far as we can discover, except for barges there were only two ships in Virginia waters at this time. A pinnace had been left behind when Newport sailed to England in November, 1608. In this, Phettiplace, under Smith's command, had sailed up the York to trade with Powhatan (1 Arber 131). The famed Captain Argall, with Robert Tindall as master, brought a ship into the James about July 16, 1609, to fish for sturgeon, according to a letter of Captain Gabriel Archer dated August 31, 1609 (1 Arber xciv). This ship was found at Jamestown when a battered English fleet arrived on August 11, more than three weeks (the Julian calendar of the English was 10 days behind) after Ecija's departure. Thus it was either Argall's craft or possibly the pinnace which, in compliance with long-standing orders of the Virginia Company, was standing in the mouth of the James.

If there was any garrison at all at Point Comfort, it consisted in a score of men under Lieutenant Percy, sent there during the spring or summer by Captain John Smith to fish "but in 6 weekes, they would not agree once to cast their net" (1 Arber 155). Some dissenters in the colony were conspiring with Powhatan and secretly hoping for a Spanish invasion. Smith himself was prepared for it, alerted no doubt by Ecija's appearance, and the first hazy reports of the sighting of the August English fleet led him to expect and prepare for battle with the Spaniards. Ratcliffe, newly arrived captain of the *Diamond*, second flagship, reported on October 4, 1609: "I am raysing a fortification vpon point Comfort" (1 Arber xcix). He was joined there by the crew of Captain Davis, who arrived in October with 16 men in a small pinnace (1 Arber 170). This enterprise was doubtless motivated by Ecija's scouting, but it was abandoned temporarily when Ratcliffe and some of his party were killed on a visit to Powhatan.

8. The autograph is in the AGI 1-1-1/19. A transcript is in the Lowery Papers previously cited.

9. This "bar" would have been a sand bar or inlet of Back Bay or Currituck Sound. The famous Blaeu atlas thus shows a "Barra de S. Iago oft van Cheseapeac" and a "B. de la Madalena" opposite Albemarle Sound, earlier mentioned by Vicente Gonzales and possibly identified with White's "Trinety Harbor." Most Dutch maps place S. Iago off Currituck Sound.

10. The elevation at Cape Henry near the shore is 80 feet. These directions show good judgment. In an 18th-century MS "Directions for Virginia," attributed to a Captain Bowater, there is this warning about the Cape: ". . . in coming from the southward with the Cape you will make a point, which may be mistaken for the Cape, and is called the false Cape between which and the real Cape is a bay. You must therefore be cautious of hauling around until you make the real Cape" (from the Library of the Virginia Historical Society).

11. Here "as a lookout" should be understood. From his post of observation, the eastern shore was plainly seen.

12. To make the statement about the direction of the northern coast, he must have been able to see at least 15 miles. He must likewise have seen the Point Comfort area, since he reckons it at only half the distance that he assigns for the northern coast. It is more than 15 miles from Point Comfort, a fact of importance in our analysis of the Oré report of the 1588 voyage.

13. The depths given are true only within a mile or two of Cape Henry, an indication that Ecija did not go far in. The maximum depth on modern charts is 16 fathoms.

14. Irene A. Wright, *art. cit.*, 465, note 63, states that all of Ecija's latitudes exceed the actual by about the same amount. He is more than 40' too high for Cayagua, but this pilot was only 4' too high at Cape Henry.

Historiae Societatis Iesu Pars Tertia, siue Borgia

Auctore R. P. Francisco Sacchino Societatis eiusdem Sacerdote

LIBER VI

Iam in Florida quoque paulo mox imponendae Sociorum per eam euangelizantium ceruicibus Cruces adornabantur. Tres ad numerum ceterorum circa medium ver accessere, Ludouicus Quirius, Gabriel Gomius, & Sanctius Sauallius: Consaluus vero Alamus, cum Petro Menende Praefecto, quod plus molestiae Socijs quadam ingenij pertinacia, quam auxilij rerum scientia afferret, in Hispaniam reuocatu Praepositi Generalis reuectus est. Ceterum Rogerius, & Ioannes Carrera in Prouincia Sanctae Helenae: Sedennius, & Franciscus Villaregius in Quala, prope sine fructu cum annum egissent, deplorata iam Floridanorum salus videbatur. Ad res diuinas silice duriores, frustra blandis sermonibus, frustra captui ipsorum accommodata catechesi tundebantur. Quamdiu de bonitate diuina, quamque summus ille rerum omnium auctor amaret bonos, eisque benefaceret, loquerere; aures praebebant non illibenter: ad supplicia noxiorum, post secretum a corpore animum, ad animi immortalitatem plane erant surdi. Quin etiam, siue prae hebetudine insigni, non intelligentes vim nominis, siue, prae improbitatis pertinacia, cum Satanam detestari iubebantur, negabant id se facturos: iuuenum esse illum Deum affirmantes, multumque se illi debere. Super haec tentata inter indigenas commoratio, difficultates, quae ab Europaeis militibus accidebant, nequaquam pro spe sustulerat, sed contra opinionem duplicarat. Quippe, cum vna ex parte milites necessaria destituti annona, per longinquas etiam in mediterranea excursiones vndecunque quaeritarent: ex altera indigenae, quos eaedem premebant angustiae, nil sibi relinqui perdolerent, & tutelam Patrum requirerent; famuli Dei in medio constituti, quia nec satis tueri poterant innocentes, nec militum egestati prospicere, odio erant vtrisque. Igitur quoniam his difficultatibus Prouinciae, quae non magno interuallo ab Hispanis castellis distabant, obsidebantur; Segura in omnes partes sagacitatem caritatis intendens, ac versans, ad nouam expeditionem animum adiecit. Est Axaca Floridae Prouincia perampla, ab aequatore in Boream erecta triginta septem gradibus, ab Sancta Helena leucis centum septuaginta disiuncta. Caciquae Reguli eius regionis frater, vndecim ante annis,

266
Res difficiles in Florida.

267
Segura cum Socijs in Axacam proficisci meditatur.

nauigantibus prope Axacam Hispanis, tradiderat sese nemine suorum conscio. Is in Hispaniam vectus, perque honeste, & humane habitus, & sacro fonte ablutus, ab Ludouico Velasco, qui pro Rege Mexico praefuit, Ludouicus Velascus nomen accepit. Postea Philippus Rex, vbi tempestiuum est visum, in Prouinciam suam duci hominem iusserat, cum aliquot e Dominicana familia Religiosis. Sed aliquot annis frustra in varijs Insulis praestolatus, Habenae agebat hoc tempore. Homo erat quinquagenarius, Patrique Segurae magna viri boni argumenta praebuit, eamque spem (quid enim caritas non credit, speratque) vt ad explorandam Axacanam Prouinciam, de qua vulgo egregia praedicabantur, non dubitaret se se ei duci committere. Verumtamen, vt in grauissima re, exquirendas ante per literas Sociorum sententias existimauit. Illi fere omnes dissuaserunt. Quae Ludouicus Neophytus de Axaca sua praedicaret, nequaquam omnia ab ijs, qui regionem vidissent, affirmari: sed item poene, vt ceteram Floridam, solo arenoso, infelici, paludibus, & stagnis obruto esse: hominum vero ingenia plane esse eadem, mutabilia, nullius fidei, in vitijs, & superstitionibus obfirmata. Neque credendum Barbaro. Satis superque inter armatorum praesidia militum, qui possint terrore, quo & belluae coercentur, in officio continere, perspectum, nullam esse Floridanis nec humanae, nec diuinae fidei verecundiam. Quid porro ausuros vbi nullum praesidium, nulla arma, nulla formido, sed summa impunitas sit? Haec, aliaque in eandem sententiam, cum singuli e stationibus suis Habanam Socij scripsissent, nauigio, quo vehebantur literae, ex tempestate diu aberrante, Segura eas tempori non accepit. Quippe Petrus Menendes, qui initio non probabat modo profectionem (tametsi post euentum aliter cupiebat videri) sed etiam vrgebat; jussit nauigium, quo illuc Ludouicus, cum Socijs deueheretur, egregie adornari. Itaque Segura, re Deo plurimum precibus, & sacrificijs commendata, antequam commoda tempestas efflueret, conscendit : iussisque ex itinere socijs a Prouincia Qualae, & Sanctae Helenae, in quibus frustra laborabant, collectis quotquot possent Caciquarum pueris, Habanam redire; ipse cum Patre Ludouico Quirio, Gabriele Gomio, Sanctio Sauellio, & Petro Linare Socijs veteranis: itemque Christophoro Rotundo, Ioanne Baptista Mendio, & Gabriele de Solis Tyronibus, alioque adolescente, cui nomen erat Alfonsus, tertio Idus Septembris in Axacam prospero cursu peruenit. Indigenas reperere fame, morbisque toto septennio misere conflictatos. Excesserat e vita Ludouici frater natu maior: minor imperitabat: cui Ludouicus imperium offerenti magno animo remisit : subijciens non se terrenarum rerum cupidine in patriam redijsse, sed vt eos Christi Domini religione imbutos viam caeli doceret. Quae visi

268
Ab itinere dissuadetur per literas Sociorum.

269
Non acceptis literis proficiscitur.

270
Axacae calamitates.

sunt audire non iniucunde. Procul a portu in mediterraneis, inter quaedam gentis tuguria domunculam Segura suam constituit, nauigio statim, & humano omni munimento Habanam remissis. Haec via si minus procederet, nulla videbatur mortalis industria superesse earum terrarum mortalibus edocendis. Sed quemadmodum processerit, non longe post exponetur.

271
Ludouici
Vilasci
Neophyti
integritas.

LIBER VII

Prouincia Florida suo ingenio gloriosas, et steriles non modo aerumnas, verum etiam neces peperit. Omnibus frustra tentatis, cum illud Ioanni Baptistae Segurae, quanquam periculo intelligebat, & praedicabant omnes plenissimum, tentandum visum esset, vt in regiones non dum Christianorum odio ex militum iniurijs imbutas penetraret, Ludouico neophyto duce (quemadmodum superiore anno memoratum est) in Axacam prouinciam, se cum comitibus octo contulerat, omnia Neophyto pollicente : qui summo Dei beneficio particeps baptismi factus, omnique humanitatis genere in Hispania a Rege, atque Dynastis, & nuper Habanae, atque in itinere a Segura habitus; maluit Iudae proditoris imitari perfidiam, quam hominibus se, Deoque fidelem, & gratum praebere. Paucis apud Patres exactis diebus (vt feris hominum industria mansuefactis vsu venit, si forte patria lustra nancisci contingat) natali solo, vnde barbariem hauserat, pristinos suggerente spiritus, popularium inuitante licentia, ad haec impunitate proposita, sensim redire ad ingenium coepit : donec impatiens christianae disciplinae, ab vsu famulorum Dei in totum abstulit se, atque ad populum inde sesquidiei itinere disiunctum contulit. Non redeuntem, semel, atque iterum, misso vno fratrum, Segura reuocauit. Quippe non ad alia modo, sed ad interpretis quoque vsum prorsus necessarium hominis auxilium erat, quod lingua propria vterentur indigenae nulli dum Sociorum cognita. Nullis delinimentis verborum, nullis promissis cum pellici potuisset, nullis precibus flecti; iam haud dubiam pusillus ille Domini grex, tanquam in luporum faucibus constitutus, expectabat in dies necem. Nam ad effugium nulla patebat via. Hinc mare, inde vastissima barbaries obsidebat : & ad facinus, praeter cetera, etiam spes praedae rapacissimam gentem, atque egentissimam inuitabat : cui exigua illa supellex ad sacrum maxime apparatum ex alio allata mundo pro diuitijs, ac miraculo erat. Quo rerum in statu Segura tum pro Ludouico frequentes indicebat preces, tum domesticos omnes adhortabatur, vt corpora sua, & animas in holocaustum continuum offerentes, expediti dies, ac noctes ad effundendum sanguinem

203
Interfecti in
odium fidei in
Florida.

204
Ludouici
Neophyti
perfidia.

205
Sociorum
patientia.

essent. Itaque totum in precibus, sanctisque collocutionibus, & religiosis functionibus, & meditatione beatae vitae ponebant tempus. Iamque non solitudo, non solicitudo, imminensque in momenta singula mors ita perturbabat, vt cibariorum macerabat penuria, & fames : quicquid commeatus Habana secum detulerant dudum absumpto. Amplius quatuor mensibus in his angustijs, inque praeparando ad mortem animo, ac Deo precibus, vt Ludouicum respiceret, fatigando transactis; statuit Segura tertio barbari animum pertentare. Tres e Socijs ad eum legat : dato simul negotio, vt diligenter conquirerent si quid vsquam ad famis remedium offerretur. Pater Ludouicus Quiros, duoque non Sacerdotes Gabriel de Solis, & Ioannes Baptista Mendes vna profecti. Quos Ludouicus Neophytus, postquam inani reditus spe alacriores dimiserat, conuerso itinere, quibusdam onustos sarcinulis redeuntes, cum globo barbarorum, nec opinantes aggressus, Quirio cor ipse sagitta transfixit, duos eius Socios ceteri peremerunt, Dominico die, qui proxime Purificationis solemnia exceperat. Segura spem inter, ac metum rogando Deo, vt legationem secundaret, anxius insistebat auide Sociorum reditum expectans : qui vbi longiorem, quam pro itinere, moram faciunt; iam scelus Apostatae haud dubium habens, eo intentius cum suorum reliquis omne studium ad geminandas preces, & exposcendam ab Deo pacem contulit. Ecce autem quinto post trium caedem die, cum stolida dissimulatione proditor multis popularium stipantibus, duobusque germanis simulant lignatum se pergere; rogant, quae ad id, vt in desertam regionem secum Patres detulerant, ferramenta commodent : ea fortasse causa, ne Dei famuli, quibus nulla praeterea erant arma, ijs propulsare vim latronum vellent. Sed frustra adhibebatur artificium paratioribus illis ad ferendam, quam barbaris ad inferendam necem. Nec poterat obscurari sermone fraus, quam res loquebatur : cum detractis Patri Quirio exuuijs, religiosum in morem proditor ipse vestitus incederet, vt nihil ambigeres deuoratae ouis pelle indutum lupum. Igitur, quod rogarant, cum accepissent; contra inermes, atque mitissimos homines, de seque tam benemeritos, tanquam rabidi lupi contra agnos, furore conuerso omnes concidere securibus, praeter vnum adolescentulum Alfonsum nomine, qui e Societate non erat. Hunc alter apostatae fratrum initio seruauit, moxque Ludouici omnia extinguere indicia enitentis furori subductum, finitimo Caciquae tradidit, per eum Deo gloriosum finem suorum manifestum Ecclesiae suae facere destinante. Barbari ab dira caede ad direptionem pauperis tugurij, quod ipsimet sibi Patres suo labore concinnauerant, versi, neque sacrae, neque profanae rei parcunt, profano vsu sacra temerantes : eo dementius,

206
*Tres primo
occiduntur.*

207
*Deinde occi-
duntur reliqui.*

quod sacri, profanique discrimen plumbea corda ignorabant. Sacrificalem patinam argenteam vnus Caciquarum sibi ab ceruice suspendit, & quasi pretiosum monile, & bullam nobilem gloriosus gestabat : alius sacerdotali casula pulcher incedebat : iam sacer calix pro magnifico erat poculo. Ad clausam multi arcam cum accessissent, tanquam thesaurum ibi inuenturi; plane inuenere, si aestimare nouissent. In eam quaedam religiosa, & Crucifixi mediocre signum Patres condiderant. Quod signum dum curiosius, & contemptius sacrilegi spectant; narrauit Alfonsus (cui quidem fidem abrogare non ausim, cum alij rem absque dubitatione ante me vulgauerint) tres eorum continuo mortuos concidisse, ceterosque conterritos in diuersa dilapsos. Idem referebat, post editum dirum nefas monitu suo, antequam sibi quoque exitium moliretur, mortuorum corpora Ludouicum proditorem, sua cuique in manu Cruce posita, tegenda humo curasse. Ignorabant haec Patres, qui in Cuba insula manserant Rogerius, & Sedennius, tamen assidua animi solicitudine dirum aliquid praesagiebant. Itaque vnum e suis Salsedum nomine ad rerum statum cognoscendum, & commeatum deuehendum in Axacam mittunt. De cetero ipsi ad iuuandos Habanae conuenas, & inquilinos serio conuertuntur.

... Inter haec nauigium in Axacam missum ad commeatum Segurae, Sociosque deportandum, resque eorum cognoscendas : neque ijs, neque Ludouico Neophyto repertis, Habanam redijt. Sed Nauclerus pariter, ac Salcedus, referebant multis argumentis constare Patres ab indigenis interfectos. Signa quae Segura dixerat ad cognoscenda loca fixurum, nulla vspiam extitisse. Axacanos multa ex rebus quae Segura detulerat, conspectos habere. Postremo duo indigenae a militibus, qui in nauigio ibant, excepti, aperte affirmabant vniuersos extinctos. Quae Rogerius vbi cognouit, minime cunctandum ratus, vt certa explorarentur, & auxilium, si posset, afferretur in tempore, nauigium de integro adornandum curat. Ioannes Carrera magno animo subiturum se discrimen Sociorum causa professus, conscenso nauigio, ad Sancti Augustini praesidium idem sub tempus, quo & Menendes cum Sedennio, venit. Hic milites necessarias vitae copias, haud minus miserabili casu, quam praesidiarij Sanctae Helenae, amiserant. Ita praeter modum intumuerat, se seque effuderat mare, vt refluens & horreum secum, & prope omnia ad remedium necessitatis recondita abstulisset. Itaque herbis, erutisque radicibus mors arcebatur. Quae videns Menendes, missum a Deo Carreram existimans, cum hyems iam inhorresceret, tempestatem minus commodam ratus Axacanae nauigationi, pollicitusque, vbi tractabilius foret mare, ipsum se cum classe iturum;

208
Barbarorum stolida impietas.

209
Crucis contemptores diuinitus puniti.

211
In Florida res aduersae.

commeatu, quem ille aduxerat, vtriusque praesidij Sancti Augustini, & Sanctae Helenae fami subuenit. Eodemque conscenso nauigio, cum Sedennio, & Carrera Habanam versus cursum intendit.

LIBER VIII

Rogerius interim, Carrera, et Villaregius in Axacam delati, cum Menende Praefecto de Segurae, atque Sociorum nece Alfonso potiti, captisque a Menende sceleris adiutoribus, ea, quae superiore libro posuimus, cognouerunt. Proditor Ludouicus euasit longe in mediterranea. Fuere qui dicerent, poenitentia eum facti perculsum, per montes, ac loca deserta in assiduo luctu, ad expiandum nefas, vagari. Menendes, quos comprehendit,

supremo affecit supplicio : sed ante quam morerentur, fortasse eorum precibus, quos enecarant, placato Numine, petierunt, et impetrauerunt baptismum, inenarrabili Dei prouisu, per oblatam innocentibus mortem immortalitatis occasionem adepti.

BORGIA, THE THIRD PART OF THE HISTORY OF THE SOCIETY OF JESUS [1]

By Francisco Sacchini, S.J.

EXCERPTS

BOOK VI

In Florida there were being prepared the crosses that would soon be placed on the shoulders of the brethren preaching the gospel throughout that land. Luis Quirós, Gabriel Gómez and Sancho Zaballos [2] were three, among others, who fell toward the middle of spring. Meanwhile Gonsalvo de Álamos was brought back [to Spain] by Pedro Menéndez at the summons of the General, because he brought more trouble to his companions by his stubborn ideas than help with his knowledge of affairs. [3] After Rogel and Juan Carrera in the province of Santa Elena, and Sedeño and Francisco de Villareal in Guale had spent the year with small reward, the salvation of the natives of Florida seemed in jeopardy. They were stolid and obdurate toward spiritual things; soft words were useless, the catechism adapted to their understanding was wasted. As long as the Fathers spoke of the divine goodness or how the most high Creator of all things loves and rewards the good, the Indians listened willingly. Yet they were deaf to the teaching about the pains of the damned after the soul leaves the body, or the soul's immortality. Whether with unusual sloth they failed to see the meaning of the word or because of deep-rooted malice, they refused to deny Satan when ordered to do so and asserted that he was the god of their youth to whom they owed so much. In addition to these efforts just mentioned, the European soldiers made other difficulties that did nothing to nourish hope but rather the opposite. Thus, when the soldiers ran short of supplies and foraged everywhere, even into the forests, they attacked the natives who were also starving. Should the Indians ask the protection of the Fathers, the ministers of God were caught in the middle and hateful to both groups, for they could neither protect the innocent nor provide for the needs of the soldiers.

And so since these trials from proximity to the Spanish garrisons beset the province, Segura, in his quest for charity's wisdom in all things, decided on a new expedition. Ajacán [4] is a large province in Florida, 37° north of the Equator and 170 leagues distant from Santa Elena. Some eleven years earlier, the brother of a principal chief of that region gave himself up to some Spaniards sailing near Ajacán. None of his family knew of this. After he was brought to Spain and treated honorably and kindly, he was baptized by Luis de Velasco, Viceroy of Mexico, whose name he received. When King Philip thought it fitting, he later ordered the man to be returned to his province in company with some Religious of the Dominican order. After spending some years fruitlessly on various islands, he was living at this time in Havana. A man of fifty years, [5] he afforded Father Segura very convincing proofs that he was a good man, and he expressed the hope (for does not charity believe and hope?) that in exploring Ajacán, about which marvelous tales were abroad, Segura would not hesitate to use him as a guide. Nevertheless, as in any important matter, Segura first sought the opinions of his brethren by letter. Practically everyone was against it.

*267
Segura plans
to go to Ajacán
with companions.*

They said that the stories of Luis the neophyte about his land of Ajacán were in no way confirmed by those who had seen the region, but rather like the rest of Florida it was only sandy, inhospitable, and filled with marshes and swamps. They said the character of the people was patently the same, changeable, untrustworthy, confirmed in vices and superstitions. Never believe a native! It was more than evident among the garrisons of armed soldiers, who restrained the natives as wild beasts are checked, that for the Floridans there was no decency in human and divine faith. What

*268
Letters of
the brethren
reject the
journey.*

would happen when terror from soldiers under arms was gone and freedom from reprisal remained instead? These and other remarks in a similar
vein, which each of the Brethren had sent to Havana from his post, were
never heard by Segura, for the ship bearing the reports was long delayed
in a storm.[6]

Pedro Menéndez had both approved and encouraged the departure,
although after the event he wanted to appear otherwise. He ordered that
the ship, in which Luis and the Fathers would sail, be well supplied.
Then, after commending the enterprise to God in prayers and Masses,
Segura departed before the good weather would end. He had ordered the
Fathers to leave the provinces of Guale and Santa Elena, where they
labored in vain, and return to Havana with as many of the sons of the
caciques as they could. Segura, with Father Luis Quirós, Gabriel Gómez,
Sancho Zaballos, and Pedro Linares, all professed Brothers, and Cristóbal
Redondo, Juan Baptista Méndez and Gabriel de Solís, novices,[7] and a boy
named Alonso, after a fair voyage [8] arrived at Ajacán on the third day
before the Ides of September.[9]

They found the natives afflicted with famine and disease for the past
seven years. An older brother of Luis had died, a younger one was ruling.
Luis generously returned the rule [10] to him when offered, asserting that he
had not returned to his fatherland out of a desire of earthly things but
to teach them the way to heaven which lay in instruction in the religion of
Christ Our Lord. The natives heard this with little pleasure.

Some distance [11] from the port, among some native huts in the forest,
Segura built his small house. The ship and any human protection were sent
back to Havana immediately. This procedure would be of little avail
though no human effort was spared in instructing the people of this region.
The outcome will be shortly described.

BOOK VII

Characteristically the province of Florida produced honorable but
useless sufferings and death. When all ventures had failed, despite the
knowledge of the dangers which everyone fully predicted, Juan Baptista
Segura decided to try this plan. Under the guidance of Luis the neophyte,
he and eight companions were to journey to parts of the province of
Ajacán not yet infected with hatred of the Christians because of the out-
rages of soldiers. Everything had been sworn to by the neophyte, who in
God's great generosity, had partaken in Baptism and had been treated with

every human kindness by the King and the royal officials in Spain and later in Havana, and on the journey by Segura himself. Yet he was to prefer to imitate the treachery of Judas the betrayer, rather than show himself faithful to God and grateful to men.

As sometimes happens to wild beasts gentled by the efforts of men, if by chance they return to their original haunts, after a few days with the Fathers the native soil whence he took his savage nature excited in Luis his early character. The vice of the natives was alluring, the sanction for it was absent. Slowly he began to revert to type until, chafing under Christian discipline, he left the company of the servants of God completely and went off to his people, a journey of a day and a half away. More than once Segura sent one of the brethren to call him back but he would not come. Among other benefits, he was a valuable assistant especially in interpreting, for the natives spoke a tongue as yet unknown to the Fathers. Since Luis could not be coaxed by any kind words or promises, or moved by any prayers, the little flock of the Lord, as if left to the hunger of wolves, now awaited death from day to day. There was no way of escape. On the one side the ocean, on the other the numberless savages blocked them off; besides other mischief, the hope of spoils was an attraction to the greedy and destitute natives for whom the smallest sacred vestment appeared to be a miracle, brought from another world for the rich.

204
The treachery of Luis, the neophyte.

In this situation Segura ordered constant prayers for Luis and urged all his subjects to prepare their bodies and souls as a constant holocaust, ready to shed their blood any day or night. Thus they passed the time in prayers, pious conversations, religious duties, and meditation on the blessed life. Still no solitude or anxiety or imminent death so disturbed them as starvation and want of food which kept weakening them after the provisions from Havana had been consumed. Four months more passed amid these trials in preparing their souls for death and praying to God that He might protect Luis and make him weary of his past. Then Segura decided to try a third time to move the mind of the savage. He called three of the brethren to him and entrusted them with the task of learning if there was any way at all of relieving their hunger. Father Luis Quirós and two nonpriests Gabriel de Solís and Juan Baptista Méndez set out together.

205
The patience of the brethren.

Luis the neophyte sent them hurrying back with foolish hopes, a little grain and no suspicion of an ambush. Then at the head of a pack of warriors, Luis pierced the heart of Quirós with an arrow and the others killed his two companions. It was the Sunday after the feast of the Purification.

206
First three are killed.

In fear and hope, Segura kept praying to God to bless the embassy and eagerly awaiting the return of the brethren who were tarrying longer than the journey required. Then with little doubt about the treachery of the apostate, he made devoted efforts with all the rest of the Fathers to re-double their prayers and to beg peace from God. Five days after the murder of the three, under a dull-witted pretext, the traitor arrived at the head of a milling crowd of his people. He pretended that he and his two brothers [12] had come to cut wood; they asked for a loan of tools for this and that the Fathers accompany them to a deserted spot. This was the plan: these servants of God who had no weapons might find them helpful in resisting the attacks of robbers. But the snare was wasted on men more prepared to endure death than the savages were to inflict it. Deceit could not be masked in speech when the evidence spoke; the traitor himself, clothed in the garments stripped from Father Quirós, walked about like a Religious. One has no doubts about a wolf clothed in the fleece of the murdered sheep.

207
Then the rest.

When their request was fulfilled, like hungry wolves on lambs they set upon the Fathers furiously with the axes and murdered such defenseless, gentle and deserving men. Only a boy named Alonso escaped and he was not of the company. One of the apostate's brothers saved this young man in the beginning, and after hiding him from the frenzied Luis, who strove to remove all evidence against himself, he handed him over to a neighboring chieftain. God had destined the boy to make known to His Church the glorious end of His own. After the terrible murders, the savages turned to the destruction of the wretched hut which the Fathers had laboriously built. Nothing sacred or profane was spared, and their flagrant abuse of the sacred things was all the more inane because their leaden hearts knew no difference.

208
The hardened impiety of the savages.

One *cacique* hung the Mass paten around his neck, and proudly strutted as if it were a precious necklace or a fine medallion; another walked about resplendent in a priest's chasuble; soon the sacred chalice was only a pretty cup. Later some savages came upon the locked chest in the hopes of discovering spoils. Had they known its worth, they really had a treasure! The Fathers had placed in it some religious articles and an ordinary crucifix.

209
The profaners of the Cross are punished from above.

While the profaners examined the crucifix with curious contempt, Alonso relates that three of them immediately fell over dead and the rest fled elsewhere in terror. (I would not try to disbelieve the boy, for others told me the incident without hesitation.) Alonso also relates that, after the terrible deed was done, he warned Luis the traitor, even before he should kill the boy, to see that the bodies of the dead, each with crucifix in hand, were buried in the ground. Fathers Rogel and Sedeño, who stayed on the island of Cuba, knew nothing of these events; yet in the deep anxiety of their minds they had some dread forebodings. So they sent up to Ajacán one of their men named Salcedo to find out the situation and bring along supplies, while they continued their ministry to the poor and the outcasts of Havana.

Meanwhile the ship sent to Ajacán to bring supplies to Segura and his companions and get news about them returned to Havana without finding the Fathers or Luis the neophyte. Salcedo and the pilot agreed that there were many indications proving that the Fathers were slain by the Indians. The signals which Segura had said he would place for recognizing his location were never set up.[13] The Indians of Ajacán had been seen with many of the belongings of Segura, and finally two natives captured by the soldiers on the ship had openly stated that all had perished. Rogel hearing the news and convinced that there must be no delay, saw to it that the ship was refitted at once in order to get at the truth and bring help if it were still needed. Juan Carrera generously promised to go and learn the fate of the Fathers and, setting out in the ship, reached San Agustín at the same time that Menéndez arrived with Sedeño. Here the soldiers were without the necessities of life and in as miserable condition as the garrison at Santa Elena. The ocean was so unusually rough and raised such waves that after flooding the granary it washed away almost all the stores of food. When Menéndez saw this, he thought Carrera had been sent by God. With the terrors of winter beginning he considered the weather unsuitable for a voyage to Ajacán, but he promised that when the seas would be more favorable, he would sail up with his fleet. He then helped the starving garrisons at San Agustín and Santa Elena with the supplies Carrera brought. Then setting sail in that same ship with Carrera and Sedeño, the Governor tried to get back to Havana.

211
Difficulties in Florida.

BOOK VIII

Meanwhile Rogel, Carrera, and Villareal arrived at Ajacán with Governor Menéndez. There they rescued Alonso. They captured those who took part in the crime and learned of the death of Segura and his companions, events which I related in a previous book. The traitor Luis went away into the deep forests. There are some who relate that, stricken with

295
Affairs in Florida.

sorrow for his action, he wandered through the wilderness weeping in atonement for his crime. Menéndez punished his captives with death. Before their execution (perhaps the Divine Majesty was moved by the prayers of the very men they murdered) the Indians begged for Baptism.

In the inexplicable Providence of God, by the deaths inflicted on the innocent, they received a chance for immortality.

*296
Divine
Providence.*

NOTES

1. The title page reads: *Historiae Societatis Iesu, Pars Tertia siue Borgia,* auctore R.P. Francisco Sacchino, Societatis eiusdem Sacerdote, Romae Typis Manelfi Manelfii, Anno MCIL. The following sections are used: Book VI, nos. 266-270, pp. 323-324; Book VII, nos. 203-209, 211, pp. 374-375; Book VIII, nos. 295, 296, p. 426. This history is the most important secondary source available on the Segura mission. In the preface, it is evident that Father Sacchini (1570-1625) composed the work in 1622. Thus he wrote only three years after Juan Rogel's death; in fact he intimates that he checked part of his account with those acquainted with the events (See Book VII, No. 209). Certainly he made careful use of many of the letters and relations we present. On him several other Jesuit historians depend, especially Alegambe and Tanner and to a lesser degree, Alegre. Sacchini composed his narrative chronologically, so that his story of the Society's activities under Father-General Borgia covers every phase under that year. The entire history is pieced together here. Since a literal version of the complex, rhetorical Latin would be awkward in English, we give here a free translation that is faithful to the thought but not always to the grammar.

2. These names are picked at random; they did not die on the same day. For Quirós' companions see Rogel's August Letter above, para. 6.

3. Gonsalvo de Álamos was born in Córdoba in 1540. He entered the Andalusian province of the Society of Jesus in June, 1559. After his novitiate in Granada, he studied theology in Seville. He was sent to the Florida Mission with Father Segura, but because of disobedience, he had to be recalled. The complaints of Segura against him may be found in *MAF* 392 in a letter to Borgia dated July 5, 1569. For his subsequent career in the college at Seville, see *ibid.* 344, note 1.

4. The modern spelling is substituted because while *Axaca* is convenient for Latin declensions, it should keep the final "n" to be close to the original name.

5. For Don Luis' age see Part I above.

6. While the Ajacán mission was discussed at Santa Elena (see Carrera Relation above, para. 36) there is no record of any canvass of the other Jesuits' opinions beyond that.

7. Actually when these three men departed they were catechists. Sacchini seems to believe or to have actually heard that they were admitted into the Society at Ajacán (see also the Introduction to Part II.)

8. Quirós indicates a difficult voyage, marked by the "discomforts of the weather" (see Quirós-Segura Letter above, para. 1).

9. September 10. The Quirós-Segura Letter says the 11th.

10. From what we know of Virginia customs, the rule was passed down from brother to brother as in Powhatan's case, but the female line was the controlling factor.

11. All accounts agree significantly in placing the settlement inland from the coast.

12. Sacchini is either inconsistent or the third brother mentioned earlier in the narrative was not present. Since these Algonkin were probably following the classificatory kinship system in which brother could mean "relative," we need not suppose that all the brothers mentioned in the various accounts were sons of the same father or mother.

13. For this plan of signals, see Quirós-Segura Letter above, para. 7.

PART THREE

AJACÁN AND THE
CHESAPEAKE

Navigable Waters and Indian Settlements
of Ajacán in 1570

THIS is an attempt to recreate the natural and ethnological background against which Gonzales and the Jesuits staged the events of
1570-1572 and 1588.

The principal sources for this reconstruction are the writings of
several members of the Raleigh and Virginia colonies, found chiefly in
Hakluyt's Voyages, the Arber-Bradley edition of Smith's works, *Force's
Tracts*, and the histories of Virginia by Strachey (1616) and Beverley
(1705). This we have complemented with an examination of three maps
by John White, governor of the Raleigh colony, two by John Smith or
Nathaniel Powell, and one by Robert Tindall. We have also consulted
later Virginia maps in the Mariner's Museum at Newport News, the
Library of Congress, the U.S. National Archives, the Maryland Room
of the Enoch A. Pratt Library, Baltimore, and the Peabody Institute
Library of the same city. The United States Coast and Geodetic Survey has also kindly permitted us to examine topographic and hydrographic surveys dating from 1852 to 1875, before the days of large-scale
harbor improvements and installations. From these varied collections the
following maps have been of particular value: Augustine Herrman's
1670 (1673) map of Virginia; Walter Hoxton's "Mapp of the Bay of
Chesepeack," published in London in 1735 or later and showing depths;
a chart from the *English Pilot* drawn in 1706, also giving depths as far
as Newport News and Yorktown; Anthony De Mayne, "A Survey of

the Chesapeake," 1814; "Reconnoitering of Chesapeake Bay, 1818," by U.S. topographical engineers; and "Map of the State of Virginia," 1826, engraved by H. S. Tanner and drawn by Herman Böÿe, giving depths of water.

Details concerning the salinity of the bay in different areas and the location of oyster beds were supplied by Dr. Donald T. Pritchard, director of the Chesapeake Bay Institute.

An opportunity to check on many points of this analysis by actual observation was afforded the writers in company with nine members of the Virginia Historical Society during a cruise in the state patrol boat *Chesapeake* on October 31, 1951. With documents and navigational charts in hand, the party cruised the lower part of the Chesapeake from Point Comfort north to the Back River, then south to a point within sight of the lighthouses and towers of Cape Henry, then back toward the James, following the Thimble Shoal channel. The boat kept to the southern edge of the channel, swinging in past Sewalls Point, then up the river past Newport News to Mulberry Island, and from there back to Point Comfort. Not all the conditions of 1570 were of course present. There were no pine and poplar trees towering over a hundred feet to form a uniformly dark skyline. There was no rigging into which one could climb to a height of forty feet, thus vastly enlarging one's horizon. An autumn sky, somewhat darkened by smoke from ships and factories, was not so clear as a July or September sky of 1570. Such clarity is confirmed by the documents themselves, which reflect no difficulty in seeing from Cape Henry to Cape Charles or from either of the capes to Point Comfort. Mathematically, it would have been quite possible. It is nearly 20 miles from Cape Charles to Old Point, and 16 from Cape Henry to Old Point. From the rigging of the ship, a sailor on a clear day could have made out the tops of trees on Point Comfort. On a clear June day the writers were able to test this on the balcony of the Chamberlain Hotel at Point Comfort at an altitude of about 90 feet above sea level. From there the eastern shore was clearly seen almost as far as Old Plantation Creek, or about 22 miles. To sailors coming in from the capes, Newport News would have been visible shortly after Old Point, for loblolly pines as high as 120 feet standing at a 30-foot elevation would have been detected from a 40-foot ship elevation for a distance of nearly 25 miles. In a communication to the writers Admiral Robert W. Knox, Acting Director of the Coast and Geodetic Survey, says concerning this possibility: "As to your specific case, it would be possible for an observer whose eyes are 38 to 40 feet above the water to see in clear weather the tops of pine trees, about 150 feet above the water, at a distance of 25 statute miles." Captain Bowater, in a set of eighteenth-century directions, to which reference is made in the notes to Andrés Gonzales (Part II above), announced that in approaching Cape Henry "in clear weather you will see the Land at the distance of about 5 leagues" (over 17 miles).

We need not suppose that the Spanish made all their observations from their ships, for where possible the pilots put ashore to take latitudes and on occasion climbed to elevated spots to scan the horizon. Atop Cape Henry's pine trees they would have had the advantage of a height of 125 feet above sea level, giving them a range exceeding 30 miles. The far vision of a trained lookout was almost incredible, especially before the use of the telescope.

SOUTH SHORE OF THE JAMES

We shall start at Cape Henry and proceed as if we were navigating the coast of Virginia with Gonzales, observing points of interest as we go in relation to the documents we have cited. Juan Menéndez Marqués, who was with Gonzales in 1588, speaks of there being "7 or 8 fathoms of depth" for 3 leagues along the southern shore. This indicates that they came toward Point Comfort in the Thimble Shoal channel, which has a depth of about 36 to 40 feet, exactly what Menéndez Marqués says, a fathom for the Spanish consisting in about 5 feet. The first shelter for boats is Lynnhaven Roads, used by the early tobacco fleets, but the entrance to Lynnhaven Bay is no more than 3 feet deep, too shallow for ocean-going vessels. Most of the maps, however, show Lynnhaven Creek as a watering place. The experience of the English in 1607 as reported by Percy and the evidence of all the maps demonstrate the fact that the Spanish would have found no port worth mentioning until after they entered the James River. Little Creek was unnavigable until dredged in modern times.

Shoals off Willoughby Point would have forced them into the channel of the James River, bringing them toward Point Comfort on their way in, though evidently not in the deepest part of the channel.

The relations of the 1588 expedition lead us to believe that the ship traced the coast line of the Chesapeake, especially on the west side, going into each of the large rivers only far enough to find suitable ports. To have traversed each river would have required an enormous amount of time. As a ship approached Point Comfort it would have seen what appeared to be two islands, for as Walter Hoxton said (c. 1735), "Point Comfort is chiefly covered with woods, but there are two places on it where no trees grow, which makes it appear like two islands." The lack of trees was probably due to low spots which have been filled in during the construction of modern roads. When Oré speaks of an English sentinel ship in the mouth of a large river "in the region of the islands" he can mean only Point Comfort as it appeared to the distant Ecija ship in 1609. He uses the Spanish *cayos*, or "keys." That Point Comfort was an island is indicated by the first land patents of the English who speak of it as "Point Comfort Island" and refer to the creek that separated it from "the maine land."

When Gonzales entered with the Jesuits in 1570 he would not have been tempted to throw out anchor at the low-lying points encircling the mouth of the river, but would have headed for the long-visible higher land in the background and its promise of fresh water not too far from the anchorage. John Smith's party, it will be recalled, could find scarcely any drinking water while navigating the bay shore. Actually, as Bruce (102) says, quoting Devries' *Voyages from Holland to America* (49, 53), there was a fine spring at Newport News, where all outgoing ships took on water, and of this spring Don Luis was probably aware. Everything in the Quirós Letter and common sense tell us that the Jesuits had some general preconceived notions of where their mission was to be, as recommended by Don Luis, and ruled by the necessity of going far enough inland to escape annoyance by pirates. A difficulty arises in trying to understand why Don Luis or the Indians they met in this vicinity did not give them information on how to reach this goal by an all-water route by the York, since Father Quirós states that a water route was possible. No doubt the Indians knew all about the York River and approximately where to enter it, but as dugout canoe sailors they would have known little about shoals, and what they did know would have been translated with great difficulty into terms Gonzales could understand and apply. No doubt he foresaw a much longer trip by way of the York, with the necessity of proceeding cautiously and taking soundings frequently as he went. Father Segura, anxious to reduce the time and conserve supplies for the sailors, might well have urged the shorter route up the James, although it involved a portage of 3 or 4 miles, which they undoubtedly foresaw before putting into College Creek.

·When Gonzales was mapping ports in 1588 his thorough methods would have led him south after entering the mouth of the James. In Willoughby Bay he would have found 9 or 10 feet, but its unsheltered condition would have caused him to pass it by, just as the English did. Below Sewalls Point he would have found 12 feet of water within perhaps a hundred feet of shore. A deep but narrow channel led up the Elizabeth River. Somewhere in this general vicinity, either on the east or west side of the river, must have been the first port mentioned by Oré on main land west of Cape Henry. The growth of the entire Norfolk harbor area testifies to the naturalness of such a designation. Since the entry to this port was only 3 fathoms, or about 15 feet, we may assume he was not speaking of Hampton Roads itself, too exposed for small ships, but an area to the south of the deep channel of the James.

On the right bank of the Elizabeth River, according to Smith's map, the Chesapeake Indians had a village. When the original party of English landed inside Cape Henry and built a shallop, they had an encounter with these Indians and found their fires but no dwellings in the cape area, nor does Smith's map show any other dwellings of this tribe except their main village. The Elizabeth River is easily recognized because it flows into the bay west of Willoughby Point and opposite Point Comfort, a relationship perfectly familiar to Smith and visible to anyone sailing up the James. From Bagnall's relation (2 Arber 430 ff.), we have a detailed description of the first exploration up the Elizabeth River, and following that the Nansemond. Indians were found fishing with weirs at the mouth of the Nansemond, and farther up this river a skirmish was had with the combined forces of the Chesapeake and Nansemond, which seem also to have fought together against the English at Cape Henry. In two of White's maps (Lorant 186 f.), he shows the Chesapeake village between what resemble the Elizabeth and Nansemond rivers. In the map published by De Bry he shows but one of the rivers, this resembling the Nansemond, and places the Chesepiooc on the left bank. On a peninsula at the head of this river he shows a village named Apasus, possibly the dwelling of a tribe which Lane calls Opossians (6 Hakluyt (EL) 142).

The next inlet of importance is the Pagan River, with a bay in its mouth, where the Warraskoyack (in Tindall, Ooriskeyek) tribe lived. Smith visited this river in a barge and obtained corn from them. It is hard to overlook the resemblance between this river and its tribe's name to the Skicoak (Scicóac) that appears on all White's maps. Gerard, finding the word "swamp" in both words, unconsciously relates the two. It also suggests the name Chiskiac. There are two arguments in favor of the latter identification, neither of them at all conclusive. One is that Barlowe refers to the village as "their greatest citie, called Skicoak, which this people affirm to be very great: but the Savages were never at it, only they speake of it by the report of their fathers and other men, whom they have heard affirme it to bee above one houres journey about" (6 Hakluyt (EL) 129). Warraskoyack, it would seem, should have been more familiar to the North Carolinians. The second indication in favor of Chiskiac is the supposition that White did not know about the James River and that the branched stream that he shows is the York, with the tributary Pamunkey and Mattaponi. In this event Chiskiac is correctly placed in relation to present-day West Point.

Perhaps the reader might be tempted to choose one of the southern tributaries of the James, some of which are wide at the mouth, as the port at which the Jesuits disembarked. From several of these streams they could have gone 2 leagues to the headwaters of the Chowan. From there they could have drifted down to the villages in the Chawanook area. If this was Don Luis' territory, it would explain easily how Villafañe might have picked him up. We reject this possibility on the basis of the distances given by Father Quirós, which at the most could not have taken him more than 15 miles from the point where they landed. Strachey (28) said he believed the upper branches of the Chowan unnavigable. Lane, however, visualized a three-day trip by canoe in the less-navigable portion of the Chowan, added to a four-day march by land before he could reach the lower James. He exaggerated the difficulty, but the undertaking still was one certainly beyond the scope of our narrative of 1570 (6 Hakluyt (EL) 143). Grays Creek opposite Jamestown is a stream capable of being entered but one would probably have to travel many miles down the nearby Blackwater River before reaching Indian habitations.

NORTH SHORE OF THE JAMES

Crossing over the James to the north side we find the Chickahominy River, navigated by Smith in a barge almost to the present Providence Forge. It is a wide stream for nearly 10 miles. On its banks lived the compactly settled Chickahominy Indians, ruled by priests and elders rather than werowances, which does not exactly fit the picture given us by the documents. It is a bit too far from Menéndez' port to afford a proper harmonization of events. It is wide for a distance of some miles and not merely at the mouth. It could have been the stream to which Don Luis retired when frightened by Menéndez. Another objection to this stream is the fact that the Jesuits would scarcely have found it deserted. The population was large, the corn crop the best to be found, wildfowl plentiful in September. If they entered a small stream trending toward the York from the Chickahominy, it would have had to be Gordon's Creek or Yarmouth Creek, on the banks of which Smith indicates population. It would be rather pointless to characterize these meandering streams as "wide at the mouth." The only other possibility on the Chickahominy is Diascund Creek, going past Lanexa in the direction of the Pamunkey, doubtfully navigable by a sloop and heavily populated at its mouth, near the Indian village of Ozenies. Here we are indeed a long way from the mouth of the James.

The Thorofare back of the Jamestown Island was navigable for three miles and wide of mouth, but Powhatan Creek which once flowed into it, as maps of the Smith period show, does not trend toward the York. Furthermore, a portage from there to the Chickahominy would scarcely have been made when the ship could have quickly reached the Chickahominy from that point by returning to the James. The area between Jamestown and the Chickahominy, according to surface indications, was heavily populated by Indians. It was evidently under control of the Paspaheghs at the founding of Jamestown, for they sold this land to the settlers and were frequent visitors and even attackers of the fort. They apparently controlled both sides of the mouth of the Chickahominy at least as far as Gordon's Creek and perhaps farther. Their political relations were under the veto of Powhatan, but Smith does not list them as part of Powhatan's inheritance, which includes the Powhatan, Appamatuck, and Arrahotack of the upper James, the Youghtanund and Pamunkey of the Pamunkey, the Mattapanient of the Mattaponi, and the Chiskiac. It is interesting that Smith does not list the Mattapanient on the Mattaponi, but shows a small settlement of this name on a branch of the Chickahominy River just a few miles above Jamestown. Though this name, like many others, is often repeated in other geographical contexts, it suggests that the larger part of the group may have withdrawn from here to the Mattaponi after contact either with the Spanish or the English. At any rate, it helps to strengthen the possibility of family relationships between the Chiskiac and the Indians of Paspahegh territory and explains how Don Luis might have had a brother among the Chiskiac and a brother and an uncle somewhere around the mouth of the Chickahominy. The relations between the Chiskiac and Paspahegh seem to have been good, from the fact that they hunted together. Obviously the Paspaheghs or the Quiyoughcohannocks (across the river from the Paspaheghs) were the owners of the canoes which surrounded the Spanish ship in 1571 and 1572. The injury inflicted on them on these occasions may explain their great fear of the English ships years later (1 Arber lxxvi).

About five miles from Jamestown we have the mouth of College Creek, first known as Archer's Hape (Hope) Creek and navigable for five miles to a point one mile from Williamsburg (16 *WMQ* (1) 11). A check through the historical magazines of Virginia reveals that a wharf was built on the creek near Williamsburg and named Princess Anne Port. A canal was also once planned between the streams. A paper mill was erected on a branch of Archer's Hope Creek. Today the mouth of this creek contains an island and is confronted by a sand bar which even at low tide is partially covered with water. A portion of the bar was probably built up after cultivation of the land. Allen Sinnott, district geologist of the U.S. Geological Survey, believes the bar was built up by the James. Despite the obstacles, the mouth is well characterized as "very wide," for just before emptying into the James it forms a bay nearly a mile wide and a quarter of a mile long. Smith's map shows the stream, but the scale is too small to indicate the nature of the entrance. The 1854-55 survey (H-529) reveals 3 or 4 feet of water at low tide at the entrance, 6 feet below the entrance near the James shore. In the river before the entrance, in 6 feet of water, there was the remains of an old wharf. In this area the shore line has greatly receded and grown shallower; so we may conclude changes around the mouth of College Creek. Smith and Newport were able to tie their ship to trees at Jamestown, impossible today. A brief history of Queens Creek and College Creek with their ports written by Lloyd Williams appears in the *Newport News Daily Press* under date of August 17, 1947. Something of the character of James River at College Creek can be learned from Mr. John Clayton's letter to the Royal Society, May 12, 1688 (*Force's Tracts* 3:24). He was arguing for a change of location of the Jamestown fort to Archer's Hope Point, where "The Channel . . . lies close by the Shoar . . . and generally when they about the ship as they call it, they are so near the Shoar, that a Man may almost fling a Finger-stone on Board." Percy realized the importance of Archer's Hope on their very first voyage to Jamestown: "The twelfth day [of May], we went backe to our ships; and discouered a point of Land, called *Archers Hope*, which was sufficient with a little labour to defend our selues against any Enemy. The soile was good and fruitfull, with excellent good Timber... We found store of Turkie nests and many Egges. If it had not been disliked because the ship could not ride neere the shoare, we had settled there to all the Collonies contentment" (1 Arber lxvi).

This account gives meaning to Quirós' description of the site as *desierto*, a spot where, as Percy has it, birds of all colors sang, turkeys laid eggs undisturbed, with no human habitation about.

Herrman's map of 1670 and the Desandroüins and other maps of the Revolutionary Period give prominence to Archer's Hope Creek. The Hydrographic Survey of 1854-1855 indicates that Skiffe's Creek, the next below College Creek, was deep inside, but with only 1 or 2 feet at the entrance. It too is large at the mouth and trends in the direction of Felgate Creek. Although nearer to the Chiskiac Indians, it is not as satisfactory as College Creek because the channel of the James there is far from the shore, the entrance is too near Menéndez' port, and it is so far from known Indian settlements that we cannot explain their quick appearance when the Spanish arrived. Warwick Creek, though still nearer Point Comfort, is wide at the mouth, navigable for several miles, and a hundred years ago showed 6 feet in the entrance and a greater depth in the stream itself. However, if this were the port of disembarkation, Father Rogel would hardly be surprised that those at Point Comfort should soon hear of the capture of the Indians.

A point of small weight favoring Skiffe's Creek and Warwick Creek is the presence of oyster beds off Mulberry Island. However, we know that the Paspaheghs had at least dried oysters and must have had access to the same beds, which do not extend beyond Deep Water Shoals. These they could have offered in trade to the Spanish, or oysters may have been clams like those that are now found across from Jamestown Island.

From Deep Creek to the point of the cape at Newport News the northern shore of the James is characterized by a precipitous bank ranging from about 20 feet to 35 in height. The channel swings toward the northern bank, but does not actually touch it until near the point itself. The 1863 survey by Blunt and Farley shows 5 fathoms at this point. The 1706 *English Pilot* map reveals 7, both short of the 68 feet in this port today, a depth which may be partly due to dredging.

KECOUGHTAN

The curving shore line from there to Hampton Creek is now, and was then, navigable only for small boats. The Newport News and Hampton bars separate this area from the channel itself. In the 1854 survey Hampton Creek is given 6 feet, with a minimum of 6 feet from there over to Point Comfort. A dredged channel today gives access to Hampton Creek for tugs having a draught of more than 10 feet. On the left shore of Point Comfort the 1854 map shows 8-10-12 feet, where the 1706 map gives 2 or 3 fathoms. Point Comfort itself had 22 to 39 feet close to shore. In his Madrid deposition, February 18, 1613 (Wright, 25 *AHR* 478) John Clark, English pilot, made the following statement:

"Being asked what roadsteads and of what quality and what forts and of what sort there are from the bay up to the said city of Jacobus, he said that the bay is seven or eight leagues wide and with good soundings, although ships have not security or shelter in it, and so go in until they shelter themselves behind Point Comfort, as he did, where there is room for thirty ships up to 800 tons to anchor, for although when the wind is north some sea is felt there, it is not a matter of much importance; and on that same point there is a fort beside the shore where seven pieces of artillery are mounted, each of about thirty hundred-weight, placed alongside the water in such a way that, since the entrance is narrow and the channel not more than a musket-shot broad, ships cannot enter or anchor without the artillery doing them damage. . . ."

Percy says they met five Indians on Point Comfort, who swam across (Mill Creek?) to the mainland, carrying their bows and arrows in their mouths. They then directed the English to their village, which from this account and those of Smith must have been about where Smith's map indicates, between Phoebus and Hampton Creeks, their orchards and cornfields occupying the little peninsulas and bays in that area (1 Arber 9 ff.). Smith speaks of Kecoughtan (Tindall, Chechotanke) as a "convenient harbour for fisher boats or smal boats" (ibid., 50) and Strachey (35) includes smacks and frigates. Elsewhere we have related Strachey's description of Kecoughtan to the orchard of Brother Carrera. Dale to Salisbury, August 17, 1611 (Brown, 1 *Genesis* 504) speaks of "2. or 3.000 acors" of cleared land there and an abundance of natural vines.

THE YORK

Oré mentions "leaving the harbor" after discussing Menéndez' anchorage, from which we might infer that he anchored somewhere inside rather than outside the Point. The next port toward the north is that of Back River, possibly the Gosnold's Bay of Smith's map, in which he once sought shelter in a storm. Dotted lines on both the 1646 (Dudley) and 1706 maps seem to discourage use of either Back Bay or Poquoson Bay farther on, but a map of the state of Virginia in 1826 by Herman Böÿe shows 21 feet of water in Back River. A survey of the old maps reveals considerable change in the coast line between the James and the York. Just north of Back River there were several islands known as "Plumbtree," now numbering but one and commemorated only by Plumtree Point. Near the entrance to Poquoson Bay were a series of spits known as the "Egg Islands," including one called Long Island, all now under water. Tindall's map, like Smith's, makes this whole coast consist of islands, overemphasizing their importance. We do not know to what degree they might have interfered with navigation. Strachey, who had an eye for geology, noted that the coast was undergoing constant change (*op. cit.* 32).

The entrance to the York River was difficult because of the narrow though deep channel. Once inside, navigation was good for many miles beyond the forks at West Point. The 1857 Hydrographic Survey gives a depth of 15 feet near the mouth of Kings Creek and Felgate's Creek and 6 feet inside the creeks. Queens Creek has 6 feet near the mouth but only 4 feet some distance inside. It was once navigable to the bridge on Route 168 near Williamsburg. An oyster bank in early days partially obscured the entrance to Kings Creek, as it does today, and small boats trying to enter sometimes got caught fast on the bar. The settlement of Chiskiac is almost unanimously ascribed to the level area known as Indian Fields, between Indian Fields Creek and Felgate's Creek, at an elevation of from 20 to 40 feet just inside the Colonial Parkway. So far, however, very few surface indications of occupation here have been discovered. The villages themselves probably were located on various elevations back from the river but commanding a view of it. Land grants mention an Indian path that led from Chiskiac toward the James, at the point once occupied by Camp Wallace.

The Chiskiac Indians are described by Smith as the nearest to the mouth of the York. They were usually hostile to him, whereas the

Kecoughtan were uniformly tolerant, which might be expected in the light of the events of 1572, if indeed many were still living after the wars and famines that intervened. Tindall shows the Chiskiac on his map as being located near the York at the right bank of the tributary that may well be Felgate's Creek. He spells the word Cheskoyek. One also finds Chescaik, Chiskiack, Chisquack, Chesiack, Kiskyack, Kiskiack, Kiskirk and even, in more modern times, Cheesecake. The Powell [?] 1608 map implies settlement around the mouth of Queens Creek. After their re-settlement north of the York, they gave their name to the Cheesecake Path leading east from West Point. Smith estimates their warriors at about 40 or 50, which would mean a population of not more than two hundred. He and Strachey describe them as part of Powhatan's "inheritance and chief alliance." Strachey (62) says their "werowance" was named Ottahotin. He was probably the Chiskiac chief who traded peacefully with Jamestown (Brown, 2 *Genesis* 585) and led Smith to Powhatan.

Across the river and 10 or 12 miles farther up was Werowocomoco, Powhatan's capital in 1608. Smaller settlements were scattered above and below this center. Just above Purtans (Powhatan's) Bay is the Poropotank River, navigable by barges for some distance in the direction of the Piankatank River, which in its turn was navigable by small boats for a short distance up Dragon Run. Two settlements south of Werowocomoco and opposite Queens Creek were called on Smith's map Cantaunkack and Capahowasick, respectively, but the 1608 map shows them in reverse order. There is a possibility that the Jesuits might have settled there, though that would presume a greater population in that area than the 1612 map indicates. Strachey, however, assigns 100 warriors to Cantaun-kack, which we believe was located near the oyster shell deposits at the mouth of Carter Creek. Capahowasick was probably where the 1608 map and modern maps indicate. It may be Strachey's Kaposecocke (400 warriors) or Cassapecock (100 warriors). Jefferson and Fry in 1775 assign Capahosack to the south side of the York.

Powhatan himself may have inherited as his kingdom the tribes neighboring Powhatan settlements. Powhatan's remarks on the "death of his people thrice" may well indicate considerable decimation of population between 1570 and 1607.

Beverley, in *The History and Present State of Virginia*, in 1705 lists as rivers capable of receiving the biggest merchant vessels: Elizabeth, Nansemond, Chickahominy, Poquoson, Pamunkey, and Mattaponi, in the area in which we are interested. The smaller streams, he said, made the river water fresh sometimes within 30 or 40 miles of the bay.

Smith and Clark both indicate that the James was quite free for ships up to Jamestown, the least water in the channel being 3½ fathoms. From there barges could go "30 leagues" farther up the river.

To sum up this reconstruction, not complete but intended only to supplement notes throughout the study, it seems to us that the number of deductions we can make of the Tidewater area and its people in 1570 is sufficient to fit the events of 1570-88 into a pattern in which many of their locations emerge as logical conclusions from the data.

THE MEANING OF AJACÁN

Its Orthography

FUNDAMENTAL to a knowledge of the meaning of Ajacán is its spelling by the Spanish. We immediately run into variants, but these are not as significant as they might seem at first glance. In his section of the Quirós letter Segura spells the word *Axacam*, according to the Buckingham Smith transcript. The second time the word was written, apparently, was in the December 9, 1570, Letter of Juan Rogel: a virtual proof that it was Don Luis who had taught them the name, since Rogel had not yet met the ship that returned from the Chesapeake. Rogel in his letters of March 10 and June 27, 1572, always spells the word *Ajacán*. In his two letters of February 8, 1572, Father Sedeño spells it *Jacán* and *Jacám*, but it is an occasional Spanish practice to drop the initial *a* of such words. Nadal, replying to a lost letter of Sedeño, June 20, 1572, has *Ajachán*. Brother Carrera's relation gives *Jacán*, as does Oré. Later spellings of *Xacán*, *Axacán*, and *Xacál* do not represent any real departure, for *x* and *j* are interchangeable, and occasionally *n* and *l* replace each other. The *Axaca* in Sacchini is merely an adaptation to the Latin tongue. Lowery gives sources for many of these spellings in 2: 458 ff., but he had almost none of the letters of the early Jesuits in which the common early spelling of *Ajacán* occurs.

ITS USE BY THE SPANISH

Regardless of the meaning or locality designated by the word as used by the Indians, the Spaniards applied it to the Chesapeake Bay and to the whole coast of North Carolina and Virginia. This is first evident when they speak of Ajacán as a "province." The English pilot Clark, captured by the Spanish on the James River, said he was the "pilot for the coast of Xacan," which "is the name for Virginia" (Brown, 1 *Genesis* 517).

The Irishman David Glavin (Glavid, Glauin), who was captured by Richard Grenville and taken to North Carolina in 1584, speaks of the English settlement in 35½° to 37° as being at Jacán, or at least his report was so interpreted by those taking the deposition. But in the letter of 1587, which we have reproduced in Part II, Pedro Menéndez Marqués speaks of Jacán as being identical with the Bahía de Santa María, and he places it just beyond 37°. His cousin Juan Menéndez Marqués, who shared the distinction of having explored the Chesapeake, speaks of it as the Bay of the Mother of God of Jacán, and he locates it at 37°. Oré writes of the "Bahía de Madre de Dios in Jacán, where the English have now fortified themselves and peopled it in latitude of 36°," but earlier he had described the 1570-1572 events in the same bay as taking place in 37½°; so for him Madre de Dios and Jacán are probably not coextensive.

A study of the relations of Juan Menéndez Marquéz and Andrés Gonzales makes it clear that one does not reach the Bay of Jacán until one comes to Cape Henry. However, the expression "coast of Jacán" was universally used to include North Carolina. The Spaniards probably took the name of a specific Indian location and expanded it to cover a whole province, as they did in many other instances in the South.

An Attempt to Find Later Equivalents

From the expansive application of the term by the Spaniards we get little help in finding the Jesuit mission site, but if we knew the meaning of the word and its local application by the Indians we would have an important clue.

Lured by this promise, Shea, Kenny, and many following them were led into choosing as the mission site places near Occoquan [Ocoan, Ocoghuan, Ohoquin, Ochaquim, Aquacond, Accaquon, etc.] Creek, a tributary of the Potomac south of Washington, D.C. Brown (1 *Genesis* 488) went so far as to concede that the Xatauahane appearing in the margin of the Spelman Relation and applying to Nacottawtanke, a village on the Rappahannock or Potomac, might be the equivalent of Occoquan, or Xacan.

Greenhow, on the other hand, observed that "the Spanish sound of this

name is scarcely distinguishable from Wocokon, the name of the place
according to its English pronunciation, at which colonists of the latter
nation landed in 1685 [1585]." Thus he concludes that "This province
of Axacan comprised the lower part of the present state of North Carolina..." (*Memoir* 487). Despite Shea's objections, Charles Campbell followed Greenhow in his history of Virginia, 1860. Wokokon is the name
given on White's map, published in 1590, to either the island today known
as Ocracoke, or, more probably, Portsmouth Island, which is identical in
shape to White's Wokokon. In William Hack's map of Carolina, 1684,
in the Crown Collection, Wokokon is spelled Okok. The Smith map of
1608 and the stolen map of 1610 both have a Wococon, which in 2
Hodge 392 is interpreted as "curve" or "bend." The neighboring
Ocracoke Inlet has an early variant spelling *Ocacock*. Amadas and Barlowe in 1584 speak of "the great river called Occam by the inhabitants
on which standeth a towne called Pomeiock" (6 Hakluyt [EL] 129), and
it "runneth towarde the Citie of Skicoak..." (*ibid.* 127). Occam is
probably Albemarle Sound. Perhaps this is the river indicated in Fran-
quelin's map of 1703 in which he places a R. Otocan just north of
C. Transfalgar.

The identification of the above variants with Ajacán rests upon the
assumption that the Spanish Jesuits pronounced Ajacán in the modern
Spanish way, making the *j* equivalent to the German *ch*, which the
English would render by the hard sound *k*. Working upon this assumption, which we have not admitted, Ajacán might mean "copper-land
people" or "beaten copper." The Algonkin natives of both North Carolina and Virginia set a high value on copper. The Roanoke River was an
avenue along which copper was carried from the mines of Virgilina and
possibly from as far away as Lake Superior, according to Mooney and
Swanton. The Pamunkey Indians were noted for their use of copper.
Somewhere near the Patuxent or Potomac in 1588, Juan Menéndez
Marqués was told that the word for copper was *ococo*. *Ococ*-ham
resembles Quirós' Axacam. The ending *ham* signifies "beaten" or
"pounded," according to Gérard. Early Virginia literature, on the other
hand, gives *caquassan* and *matassun* as words for copper.

A very serious difficulty with the above equivalents is the belief of
philologists that the Spanish of the sixteenth century pronounced *j* and *x*
like *sh*. Dr. Margaret Bates, assistant professor of Romance Languages,
The Catholic University of America, gives as examples English *sherry*,
older *sherris*, from Spanish *Jérez*, and the French *Quichotte* from Spanish

Quixote. Mooney, in "Siouan Tribes of the East" (22 *BAE,B* 57), and Swanton, in 137 *BAE,B* 167, also make *sh* equal to *j* or *x*. Dr. James A. Geary, instructor in the Algonquian language at The Catholic University of America, in reply to a query, gives his opinion that the word is Algonquian, spelled and accented *Áshacàn*. He has kindly supplied the following references to equivalents which we take from William M. Beauchamp. The first is found in his *Aboriginal Place Names of New York* (New York State Museum Bull. 108, Archaeology 12) 236: "Sho-kán was sometimes written Ashokan, and is now a village in Olive. It was called Shokaken in the Marbletown records of 1677, and was often mentioned. It may be derived from chogan, *a blackbird*, or sokan, *to cross the creek*, the last being preferable."

Olive is in Ulster County, N.Y., and there is a reservoir at the same place called Ashókan.

The second reference from Beauchamp is from *Indian Names in New York, with a Selection from Other States* (Fayetteville, N.Y., 1893) 96: "Ashaagoona, *Big knife*, or *Sword*, is now their Iroquois name for Pennsylvania and the states farther south. It was formerly given to Virginia, and is thus described in the conference of 1721: 'Assarigoe, the name of the Governors of Virginia, which signifys a Simeter or Cutlas, which was given to Lord Howard, anno 1684, from the Dutch word Hower, a Cutlas.' The name, however, is purely Iroquois, but thence came the term of 'Long Knives,' rather than from Gen. Wayne's campaign. The Iroquois were fond of playing upon words."

In the days of the Raleigh colony and later Virginia colony there were Iroquois (Meherrin, Mangoags, and possibly Weanoc) living south of the James and somewhat inland from the coast. Perhaps they gave the name Ashaagoona to the Algonkin tribes because of their wooden "swords" or *macanas* that characterized them and are mentioned in Spanish, Raleigh, and Jamestown colony accounts. The only difficulty is that we do not believe Don Luis was an Iroquois or that an Algonkin would call his own people by an Iroquois name. The Algonquian word for Virginia was Tsenahcommocah (Strachey 195), while the Roanoke Indians called residents of the whole coast Renapoaks.

We have found several other terms, any one of which, considering the errors inevitable in transmission, may stand for the original Ajacán. From Smith's Indian vocabulary (1 Arber 44) we have *shacquohocan*, "a stone," which Strachey (194) spells *Shacahocan*. The word might apply quite well to the region occupied by the Chiskiac. The only visible stone of any size crops out on the York River just below Yorktown and again at King's Mill Wharf a mile below the mouth of College Creek. A word equally applicable is Strachey's *ahshaham*, "lobster" (190) missing the Axacam of Quirós by only one letter. From Smith's map we might add Cekakawwon (Chicacoan, Chickacoon, Sekacawone, or Coan), near the mouth of the Potomac. Better still is his small settlement Chesakawan at the mouth of the Rappahannock. Of similar flavor are Herrman's Cicocoan and Achquank on the Nantikoke River. Shackaconia might have significance were it not so far in Sioux territory on the upper Rappahannock. To this name might be related the Shaccoe Valley of Richmond. To complete the list of resemblances we have the Shakori (137 *BAE,B* 187), thought to be the tribe of Ayllón's Chicora, which Swanton believes may have migrated to the "Schockoores old fields" between the Meherrin and Nottoway after 1566. If our word were Siouan we would separate it into Ash-acan; -acan or -occan, according to Speck, is a Siouan terminal modifier meaning "people" (of the land). ("Siouan Tribes of the Carolinas," 37*AA* (L935) 201-225, 213). MacLeod, incidentally, thinks the Siouan tongue was a sort of *lingua franca* among the Virginia Algonkin.

Here we should like to interpose a question concerning the general rule that *x* and *j* are to be rendered *sh*. It seems probable that the rule must be modified not only to fit provincial differences in pronunciation but also different vowel and consonant combinations. In going through the vast index to Espinosa's *Compendium and Description of the Indies*, we found that *x* and *j* were perfectly interchangeable, and in many instances were the equivalent of soft *s* or *z*. But, more important, initial *x* was often the equivalent of initial *s*, and especially before the vowel *a*. Examples: *Xacxaguana—sacsahuaman, saguan—xaguan, sapallanga—xapallanga*. *S*, on the other hand, was interchangeable with *c* and *z* but not with *ch*, which had no alternatives. Examples: *Sianca—Ciancas, Sicaya—Cicaya, Sicicaya—Zizicaya*. From this, one would conclude that Ajacán or Axacám was probably pronounced *Azacan* or *Azhacam*.

The nearest name to the former pronunciation, *Azacan*, that we have found is that of the Roanoke Island friend of Chief Wingina—an enemy of the Raleigh colony called Osacan or Osocan.

We do not know to what extent the variety of forms found in English and Spanish sources for any Indian word is reflected among the Indians themselves. Lederer, for instance, in his map of 1672 lists a Shikcham between the Pamunkey and Mattaponi, which from his journal we know he intends for the Chickahominy. Did the Chickahominy refer to themselves also in this abbreviated form? If so, Shikcham is not far from Shakam. Also, did the Indians, like the Spanish, occasionally drop the initial *a?* Beauchamp, in giving Shokan and Ashokan, implies that they did. Lowery discusses the Spanish practice in 2:App. X 444 f, regarding it as common, but we have been unable to find many examples of it.

Perhaps the Spaniards carelessly fell into the use of Jacán or Xacal because of the Mexican Jacal, three of which are mentioned in the American Geographical Society's *Index to Mexico.* These variations recall Chickhan, or Chuckahann, Creek in old Northumberland County, cited by Nugent (252). Allowing for the even greater differences in Spanish and English renditions, one would not wish to exclude the possibility that Ajacán and Chickahominy are identical.

Those interested in a further study of the Old Spanish use of these letters are referred to J. D. M. Ford, *Old Spanish Readings* (New York, 1911) xl, and to Rufino J. Cuervo: *Obras Inéditas* (Bogota, 1944), "Disquisiciones sobre antigua ortographía y pronunciación castellana" 353-493. In looking for survivals of the word Ajacán we have consulted modern maps and postal guides of Virginia and North Carolina, the early relations of both colonies, many old maps of both regions, and in particular E. G. Swem, *Virginia Historical Index,* and Nell M. Nugent, *Cavaliers and Pioneers: Abstracts of Land Patents and Grants, 1623-1666.*

In summary, it should be said that, in view of the widely different interpretations of Virginia place names, illustrated by the discussions of Tooker and Gerard in a previous generation, it does not seem wise to expect to derive location from an analysis of the meaning of Ajacán.

CARTOGRAPHY OF THE CHESAPEAKE

With Annotated List of Maps

W E HAVE undertaken a study of the early maps of the Chesapeake only to establish beyond all doubt the fact that the Spanish knew of its existence long before the mission of 1570, that it was this body of water that they first called the Bahía de Santa María, and that it was somewhere inland from this same body of water that the Jesuits with Don Luis had planned to establish their mission.

From the maps we also learn something of the geography as pictured by the sixteenth-century mind, in accordance with which the distance from the Atlantic to the Pacific was shortened and waterways connecting the two were imagined. It becomes evident, too, that the early name for the James was El Río del Espíritu Santo (River of the Holy Spirit), while the upper part of the bay was thought of as a river and called the Río Salado (Salt River). We have found confirmation in the maps for the Spanish name Ajacán as applied to the Chesapeake area. The Spanish also called the bay Bahía del Jacán and Bahía de Madre de Dios (Bay of the Mother of God). Without completely supplanting the name Santa María, this terminology was in vogue from about 1570 to 1620 in Spanish circles. The name Bahía de Madre de Dios appears on the Dutch maps up to the seventeenth century.

In appraising and classifying these maps we have relied chiefly on Father Delanglez' essay on the cartography of the Gulf Coast and adjacent territory during the sixteenth and seventeenth centuries, published under the title *El Río del Espíritu Santo*, supplemented by Walter Thiele, *Official Map Publications*, various essays on cartography in Winsor's *Narra-*

tive and Critical History of America, and Woodbury Lowery, *A Descriptive List of Maps of the Spanish Possessions within the Present Limits of the United States, 1502-1820.* For later English maps our chief reliance has been on E. G. Swem, "Maps Relating to Virginia in the Virginia State Library and other Departments of the Commonwealth, with the 17th and 18th Century Atlas Maps in the Library of Congress," *Virginia State Library Bulletin* (April, July, 1914), Richmond, Virginia, and P. L. Phillips, "Virginia Cartography," 37 *SMC* (1896).

We have studied English maps to learn the locations of ports and Indian tribes and to see if there have been any survivals of the word Ajacán. It is an interesting sidelight that, with few exceptions, the English maps depicting the middle coast of the present eastern United States after the time of the Raleigh settlement abandon Spanish nomenclature and cartographical influences, in some instances dropping the Chesapeake entirely and substituting for it the sounds of North Carolina.

Cartography as an exact science was slow in developing. Exactness was sacrificed to a desire to profit by the sale of maps labeled "new," although the printers kept turning out virtually the same product for fifty years at a time. This was true of the maps of Agnese, Homem, and Mercator for the Spanish period, while the maps of White, Smith, and Herrman were models repeatedly copied by English map-makers for more than a century.

By far the greater part of Europe's knowledge of the Atlantic Coast originated in Spain in the sixteenth century, but unfortunately most of the Spanish maps have been lost. Their character must be deduced from French, Portuguese, and Dutch imitations.

The task of determining, by a comparison of coast line and nomenclature, the interrelations of all the available maps that show the Chesapeake has never been completely achieved, but we leave this interesting undertaking to historians of geography. In the lists that follow we shall note only the more obvious and important interconnections among the maps.

To facilitate reference to these maps we have employed the following abbreviations: LC— In the Library of Congress collection; if a number is added, it is that given in Lowery's *Descriptive List;* WL—Woodbury Lowery Collection, the number being that given in the *Descriptive List;* S—page number in the Swem list; P—page number in the Phillips article; KC—the Karpinski Collection. We viewed duplicates of this collection in the Enoch A. Pratt Free Library, Baltimore, based on the photostat file possessed by the William L. Clements Library, Ann Arbor, Michigan.

ANNOTATED LIST OF THE PRINCIPAL MAPS USED
IN THIS MONOGRAPH

THE SPANISH PERIOD

1525?—Salviati. Europe, Asia, eastern coast line of the Americas. LC 24. Unsigned, undated, untitled. Delanglez (16 f.) thinks it based on a prototype earlier than the *padrón* (pattern) map of 1527-29, but it gives more detail for the Atlantic Coast than the *padrón* map of 1527. There are two indentations in the *costa baxa* that may correspond to the Delaware and the Chesapeake, though it is better to suppose from their formalized shape that they are only conjectures of the cartographer. The map is supposed to represent exploration done between 1520-1525, presumably by Quexos, Gordillo, and Gómez. It derives its name from the Salviati family's coat of arms, one of the family being papal nuncio to Spain from 1525 to 1530. As a possible line of future research we suggest the possibility of identifying the "baya de S. Antonio" with the Chesapeake because of its shape, rivers, and nearness to "R. de las Canoas," a southern stream. Perhaps differing and independent descriptions of the Chesapeake brought back by explorers led the cartographer to incorporate both into the 1529 map under the impression that they were reports of two distinct bays. Certainly this might explain the southeasterly trending bay above "C. de Arenas," a monstrosity in the *padrón* that has given interpreters a headache ever since Ribero's time.

1527—Viconte di Maiollo. Map of the world. WL 25. A beautifully colored manuscript planisphere preserved at Milan. Believed to reflect the voyage of Verrazano in 1524, it is similar to Hieronimus de Verrazano's map in picturing an isthmus between the Pacific and the Atlantic in the vicinity of Cape Hatteras. The latitudes of the Atlantic Coast are about 5° too low, whereas Verrazano's were much too high. Of the two, Maiollo is far more detailed on this coast. The map is worth restudying in the light of modern findings on the true course of Verrazano's voyage, though any possible indication of the Chesapeake in this Italian map could not be a reflection of Verrazano's knowledge, unless he were deliberately concealing its discovery on his brother's map.

1527—Ribero?. The Weimar map, *Carta Universal*. WL 26, 27. Delanglez and Thiele believe this map to be the work of Ribero; Kohl in *Die beiden ältesten*...cites Ferdinand Columbus (Hernando Colon) as the author; others say Nuño García de Toreno. This is an example of the *Padrón* ("pattern") *General*, the official Spanish map of the world, drawn according to the direction of the geographical department of the Casa de Contratación, which controlled the affairs of the New World. In 1526 it succeeded the *Padrón Real*. All Spanish navigators were required to submit corrections

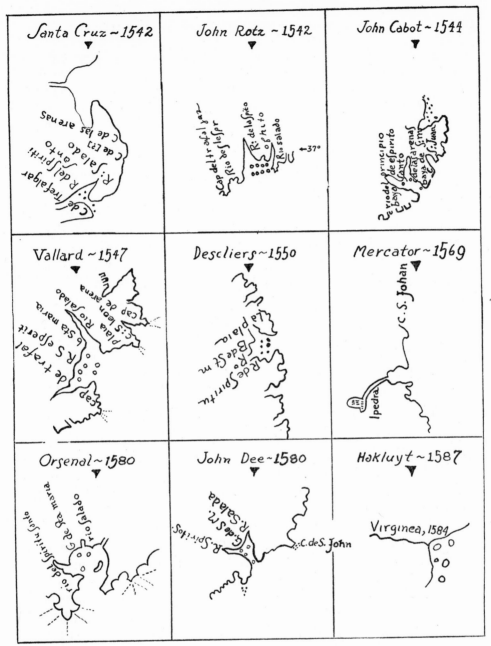

Plate XIV

EARLY CONCEPTIONS OF THE CHESAPEAKE

These are free-hand drawings. The shape of the Chesapeake as given here should be compared with the Ribero prototype of 1529, in Plate II. All the cartographers are evidently trying to depict a really existing Bahía de Santa María, with the possible exception of Mercator. That he too is trying to show the Chesapeake will be seen by comparing his map with Vallard's, in which the next major indentation below "C: S Ieon" (C. S. Johan) is the "b Sta maria." The Orsenal map shows the tendency to "pretty up" the coast line.

to this map suggested by their explorations. This *carta universal* is thought by some to give us the first representation of the Chesapeake, immediately below the inscription *tierra del licencia de Ayllón,* but the shape and location correspond better to the Río Jordan into which Ayllón's 1526 expedition first entered. Kohl believes that a Meruelo and Jordan exploration of 1520 may have furnished data for the South Carolina coast.

1529—Hieronimus de Verrazano (Gerolamo da Verrazzano). Map of the world. LC 30. Propaganda Museum, Rome. For a discussion of the voyage and the map, see Part I.

1529—Ribero-Weimar. Map of the world. LC 31. Kohl has a large-scale color reproduction of this and the 1527 map in *Die beiden ältesten...* We have discussed this map in Part I, explaining the wide mouth and the islands of the "B. de S. Ma." as an impression an explorer would get in sailing along the Delmarvian peninsula. This wide-open mouth was infrequently copied in later maps; one of the notable imitators was John Rotz, 1542. From "Cabo de arenas" north, this Ribero map is almost identical with that of 1527. From Florida to the Chesapeake, however, we have an entirely new survey. Harrisse thinks Quexos and Gordillo discovered up to 37° in 1521, and Quexos to 39° in 1526-27. The data of this 1529 map therefore came from the second expedition of Quexos under Ayllón's direction. Kohl believes that the paper detailing the discovery did not reach Spain before the making of the 1527 map.

1529—Ribero, 2nd Borgian. Map of the world. LC. Vatican. Description, Lowery list, p. 41. Substantially the same as the Weimar 1529, but the coast line is drawn a bit more skilfully. Thiele (73) mentions a 1525 member of the Ribero group known as the "Castiglioni" or Mantua map which we have not seen.

1530—Battista Agnese. Map of the world. WL 32. This is the earliest of the prolific output of the Genoese map-maker, whose work has more artistic than cartographic merit. Among several sources on which Agnese draws are the Spanish *padrones.* In listing a "C. d. S. María," he seems to follow Maiollo, but since he puts it north of "C. d. san Juan" we cannot conclude that a Chesapeake cape is intended. The remainder of the coast is almost identical to that of the Weimar 1527 map. The Agnese portolan map we reproduce is dated 1580 from the Karpinski Collection S-15-5, but it is scarcely unchanged from the Atlantic Coast shown in the Agnese atlas of 1530-40 in the J. P. Morgan Library (M-460 in LC). A 1540 edition in the LC collection is somewhat superior; it may attempt to show the Chesapeake. In all his reproductions the shape of the North American continent reflects Verrazano's notion of an isthmus-like east coast.

1540—Diogo Homem (Diego Homen). Map of the Atlantic and eastern coast of the United States. LC. The date given on this copy in the Library of

Plate XV

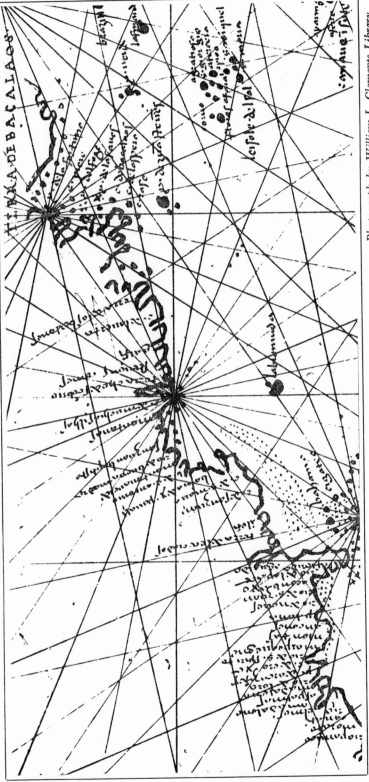

Photograph by William L. Clements Library

THE CHESAPEAKE AREA AS IT APPEARS IN THE AGNESE ATLAS, 1530-1580

This map is from the 1580 atlas but differs little from the version that appeared as early as 1530. The nomenclature is much like that of the 1527 *padrón*, but there is added a "c. de s. maria" north of the "c. de San Juan," thus carelessly changing the "R: de s Juhan" of the 1527 map to a cape, and the "b: de S. Ma" of the 1529 map also to a cape, while transposing their respective locations.

Congress is probably too early. The "G. de S. Ma." and "R. Salado" are much as they are on the map we reproduce from the KC S-207-5, dated 1585 [?]. A 1568 version remains virtually unchanged. About the year 1536, under Chaves, the *Padrón General* underwent some improvements. One of these is the shape of the Chesapeake Bay. The mouth was narrowed and the Río Salado was given a more proper northern trend. The more realistic Spanish maps reduced the number of islands to four, but copiers outside Spain tend to herd all Ribero's seven together inside the bay, so that in some of the more formalistic maps they are arranged as neatly as bowling pins. Chaves' own map has been lost, although its nomenclature survives in his writings.

1541—Nicolas Desliens. Map of the world. LC 37. The first known map of the Dieppe school of cartographers. Father Delanglez utilizes it to prove that the cartographers of the *padrón* were free to use some originality, since Desliens, who obviously copies from them, has some features and nomenclature which do not appear on the earlier *padrón* but are in the *padrón* subsequent to Desliens, and of course not copied from him, therefore Spanish reinterpretations of earlier data, the later interpretation having been followed by Desliens.

1542—Alonso de Santa Cruz. Map of the world. LC 39. All agree that Santa Cruz, an official Spanish cosmographer, modeled after the lost Chaves map. The Chesapeake mouth is narrowed down and only five small islands are shown. The bay is not named, but the terms Río del Spiriti Santo [sic] and Río Salado are retained. The only reproduction is in E. W. Dahlgreen, *Map of the World by Alonso de Santa Cruz, 1542* (Stockholm, 1892). Internal evidence indicates that the map was originally constructed in 1539.

1542—John Rotz. LC. A very elaborate map dedicated to Henry VIII. It is done in the Dieppe tradition by a man whose real name was Jean Roze, son of a Scot emigré, Ross. His nomenclature for the Chesapeake area is strangely corrupted, but there is no doubt that he retains Río de la Spirito Sancto for the James and Río Salado for the Chesapeake proper. The islands and rivers show that he went back to the Ribero 1529 map for his model. He is clumsy in handling the cryptic Spanish abbreviations.

1542?—Harleian Mappemonde. LC. Commonly classified as c. 1536, this fine Dieppe creation gives evidence of composition after 1542. Delanglez (32 f.) believes that it is based on a Portuguese copy of the *padrón*. It is shown in Biggar opp. 128. The "B. de Se Marie" is shown at 36½°; the Salado is translated "R: de Sal."

1544—Sebastian Cabot. Map of the World. WL 44. Harrisse reproduces it in his French book on the Cabots. Our copy is after Kretschmer, 14 *BAE,R* 352. The authorship is not entirely certain. Delanglez (28) believes this map to correspond closely to Chaves. We are interested in the shape the cartog-

Plate XVI   *William L. Clements Library*

ATLANTIC COAST AND "GOLFO DE SANTA MARÍA"
IN HOMEM'S MAP, 1585 (?)

This is substantially the same as Homem's 1558 map and illustrates the
prominence given the Chesapeake on the Atlantic Coast. The bay
with the wide single opening could not be thought to resemble
Pamlico Sound. The sand bar below the bay may represent shoals
near Cape Hatteras. (The top two names have been retouched.)

rapher gives the Chesapeake, narrowing the entrance, but limiting the islands to three small dots which in reality could correspond to Fisherman Island, Point Comfort, and Cherrystone, which a hundred years ago was a mile long. The shape is an improvement over Santa Cruz, the bay being deeper; the James trends in the right direction and makes a point where it flows into the bay. It seems that no one except Cabot would have been in a position to improve on Ribero's work of 1529. Cabot had been in Spanish employ since 1512; he was a prominent member of the geographical department of the Casa. He was on a voyage when Ribero drew his 1527 and 1529 maps, which may explain why he did not suggest a more correct way of showing the Chesapeake at that time. The reason why he did not bring about its inclusion in earlier Spanish maps may have been his own desire to use secret information as a bargaining point in selling his services to various countries, or it may have been Spanish reluctance thus publicly to recognize Cabot's English-sponsored prior discoveries. Whatever the case, it is plain that someone who had actually *seen* Chesapeake Bay submitted the information that improved over Ribero and the data supplied by the Ayllón expedition. Cabot has distinctive terminology, as will be seen from our sketch. Probably he means to call the Chesapeake "baya de espírito Santo," reserving the title "baya de S:m" for an indentation farther north. He also shows an indentation that may correspond to Delaware Bay.

In this same year Medina also shows the Bahia de Santa Maria.

1546—Freire. 4 Winsor 86. Freire is a Portuguese map-maker employing French and Spanish sources. His Chesapeake resembles that of Rotz.

1546—Descliers Mappemonde. Biggar 192. The latitudes follow Ribero rather closely. The "B de Se Marie" is at 35°, "c de arenas" at 40°. The corrugated coast line is unrealistic and the Chesapeake is represented as a small round gulf with two rivers emptying into it, and containing five small islands.

1547—Vallard. Map of New Spain, in Nicolas Vallard's atlas. LC 44. Biggar 160, but more correctly in M. B. Davidson, *Life in America,* 2 vols. (Cambridge, 1951) 1: 26 f. Original in Huntington Library, San Marino, California. In the Dieppe style, but an improvement over his contemporaries. The "b. Ste. Marie" is shown at 37°. The shape is a compromise between Ribero and Cabot. R. de S. Esprit and Río Salado provide a blend of French and Spanish. Much like Vallard's Chesapeake is that of the *Planche de l'Atlas de Le Testu* (No. 28 in Gabriel Marcel). It probably dates from about the same period. This map shows the Río Salado as the R. de L'esprit.

1550—Diego Gutiérrez. The Western Hemisphere. KC 5-38-5. Gabriel Marcel, No. 31. This map by the Casa cosmographer shows a Bahía de Santa María much like Vallard's and the Río del Espíritu Santo in the position of the James. Cf. Delanglez (42) on his maps.

1550—Descliers Planisphere. Biggar 224. Same bay as in 1546 edition, but adds "R. de Spiritu Sto" title to the lower river entering the bay.

1563—Lazaro Luis. World. LC. MS atlas in the *Académie des Sciences*, Lisbon. The "b de Sa Ma" resembles that in Rotz. "R Salado" shown. Some earlier writers supposed that this map dealt with Portuguese explorations dating back to 1521.

1564—Jacques Le Moyne. Map of Florida. Lorant 34 f. First published by De Bry, 1594. Tying in with the remarks of Gonzales, Morales, and Burgoignon, we find the "Montes Apalatci, in quibus aurum argentum & as inuenttur." (The Appalachian Mountains, in which gold, silver, and brass are found.) From one of the mountains spurts a stream into a lake which bears the following inscription: "In hoc lacu Indigenae argenti grana inveniunt." (In this lake the natives find grains of silver.) These inscriptions are also found in the 1630 Mercator map which we reproduce.

1566—Nicolas Desliens. Map of the world. KC S-15-1. The North American continent retains something of the narrow shape with which Verrazano and Agnese endowed it. The Chesapeake is not named, but shown.

1569—Mercator. Planisphere of the world. LC 55. The first example of his famous projection, but of far less value than the *padrón* maps. The Chesapeake, identifiable because placed between "C. S. Johan" and the "R. del Principe," has a round shape resembling the 1546 Descliers map, with one curving southern tributary ending up in a castle-like rock named *Ipedra*. We have not found the origin of this word, evidently Spanish and apparently garbled from reports of the De Soto expedition. Mercator copied from a variety of sources, including Jerome Cock, and felt free to extend rivers into the interior to suit his fancy. Ortelius in his atlas of 1570 copies the Mercator map. In general, the Ortelius, Mercator, Plancius, and Hondius maps are of little value for our subject. Ortelius is said to have had 99 families of maps at hand in constructing his 1570 opus, and not one of them of direct Spanish origin.

1570?—Jean Cossin. Carte geographique ou universelle description du monde. KC S-15-2. Included not only because he shows a Cabot-like Chesapeake Bay, but because he presents a northwest passage to Japan and the Moluccas and a waterway from the Atlantic to the northwest passage, the sort of bizarre cartography that misled Menéndez de Avilés.

1573 c.—Juan López de Velasco. Geografía y Descripción Universal de las Indias. LC 58. First published in Madrid, 1894. Velasco was made chief cosmographer of Spain in 1572. Lowery 2:381 believes that he must have published his geography before Pedro Menéndez Marqués' exploration of the Chesapeake in 1573, since he makes no mention of it. On 172 Velasco says the Río Salado is east of the Cabo de Trafalgar and that the Cabo de

San Juan, 65 leagues from Trafalgar, is at 36°, thus preserving something of Ribero's early mistake in latitude.

1573—Teixeira?. MS in French A.S.H. Ea 11. KC S-15-1. Shows the "R del Spo Santo" and the "B de Santa María."

1576—Ignazio Dante. Mappamonde. Terra Logia (Vatican). LC. Clear representation of the Chesapeake.

1580—Orsenal-Paris. KC S-38-3. Highly formalized drawing, with frequent *fleur-de-lis* patterns; shows the Chesapeake at 36½° having three tributaries, the southern still being called the River of the Holy Spirit, the western tributary the Salado, and the northern one unnamed. The bay is called the "G d Sta María."

1580—John Dee. Spherical projection of a part of the northern hemisphere including all America north of the Equator, and the western part of Europe and Africa (8 Hakluyt (ES) end of volume). In general, Dee employs Spanish nomenclature. His Chesapeake, labeled "G. de S.M.," with its four small islands resembles Cabot, though he fails to indicate a sharp point at the mouth of the James, which he calls the "R. Spirito S." The northern branch is labeled "R. Salada." Since he was frequently consulted by Queen Elizabeth, it cannot be said that the English court was ignorant of Spanish pretensions along the Atlantic Coast.

THE ENGLISH PERIOD

1585 c.—John White. I Chart of the East Coast or Chart of Virginia. WL 71. Lorant 186 f.; 8 Hakluyt (ES) 320. Reproduced in color in Lorant, but names more distinct in Hakluyt. John White, or With, whose identity we shall not discuss here, made three maps while in North Carolina. For a century they influenced the cartography of this section of the coast. The Spanish *padrón* with its terminology was dropped by all except the Spanish and Portuguese, and to some extent the Dutch. Considering the limited opportunity for observation, White's cartographic accomplishments are as notable as Smith's and are of inestimable value to the anthropologist. This sketch is the most generalized and probably the least accurate of his three maps. Phillips discusses White's maps in 37 *SMC* 4-18.

———, II. The Coast from Chesapeake Bay to Cape Lookout. Lorant 186; 8 Hakluyt (ES) 400. This map shows two openings in the coast south of Hatteras, as the reports of Gonzales and Menéndez Marqués would indicate. More Indian village sites around the Chesapeake are marked here than in the other two maps; on this one alone is Mashawatee shown, on the eastern shore of Virginia.

———, III. *Americae pars, Nunc Virginia dicta*. Published by De Bry, 1590. S 41. The lengthened streams, ending in snake tongues, are partly ascribable to the demands of "art." Two inlets are indicated at Hatorask and three entering Currituck Sound. The latter could explain the existence of such bars as Madalena and Santiago in the reports of Ecija and Andrés Gonzales. The islands shown near Apasus [Kecoughtan?] may refer to the Indians' report of a pearl-vending chief on an island, though as we have noted elsewhere any such island, if it existed, must have been in the fresh-water area. The implications of this map for Virginia ethnology are briefly discussed in the essay on the Indian settlements of Ajacán, in this Part.

1587—Dedicated to Richard Hakluyt. 8 Hakluyt (ES) 272. "Virginea" is shown above an open bay filled with islands. The bay has only one tributary. It is difficult to say just what the cartographer had in mind.

1589—Wright-Molyneux. Globe. LC. An interesting interpretation of White's maps, showing the Albemarle Sound and Chesapeake Bay.

1590?—Juan Martines. Map of eastern part of United States area. KC S-38-3. A portolan chart from the *Bib. Nac.*, Madrid, revealing a coast line composed of artistic patterns like the Orsenal map discussed above. Tributary to the "b de sta. María" are the Río de Spirito Santo and the R: Salado.

1592—Thomas Hood. Eastern coast of North America, from *Atlas zur Entdeckungsgeschichte Amerikas*, by Kunstmann and others, Munich, 1859, Plate xiii. 3 Winsor 197. It shows no English influence. The nomenclature is Spanish and Portuguese. The Chesapeake is shown on the Chaves model, with branching Río de S. Spo. and Río Salado.

1597—Cornelius Wytfliet. Norumbega et Virginia. LC 84; S 41; P 18. Published first in his *Descriptionis Ptolemaicae Augmentum...*" in 1597. The map we show is from the French edition of 1607. The second map of Virginia, it combines the maps of White with those of Spanish origin. Evidently he had not seen White's map of Florida and Virginia or any of those showing the proper latitudes, for he supposes that Virginia is north of the "C. de las arenas," and thus he pushes the "Chesipooc" up to 43°. Much of the nomenclature north of the Chesapeake is to be found as early as 1529 in Ribero's map. Hudson must have thought that the "R. grande" of this map was the river to which the Dutch gave his name, for he calls it "the Great river." On many Spanish and Portuguese maps it is called the Río de Gamas, but some writers think it is meant to represent other streams, perhaps as far east as the Penobscot. It is true that if we equate the Río de Gamas with the Hudson, there is little we can do with the numerous other bays that intervene between there and the Chesapeake. If this criticism is correct, it only serves to emphasize what a limited knowledge of geography still prevailed in Florida when Gonzales and Menéndez Marqués imagined they were exploring the Río de Gamas in 1588 when they came to the Susquehanna.

This is one of the first maps to ascribe a longitude (31°) to the Chesapeake.

An interesting feature is a compass showing the declination of the magnetic needle from the true north, and in the correct direction. This may be the map referred to by Shakespeare in *Twelfth Night* (3 Winsor 217).

1599—Jean Dirckx. West Indies and Caribbean Coast. KC S-201-5. Same nomenclature as in Martines 1590, but adds Cape Trafalgar and shows a slightly different coast line.

1600—Florimini. [No title.] LC. A hodge-podge eclectic map showing a R de Santa María instead of a bay. Several maps refer to the Chesapeake as a river rather than a bay.

1600?—Torre de Tombo. Caribbean and north part of S. America. Lisbon, in a Vaz Dourado atlas. KC S-601-5. At 37° is shown the "b (or c?) de S. m." with a square bay and rivers off the now familiar points. Vaz Dourado technique subordinated accuracy to artistry.

1600—Emeric Molineaux. World. LC. Based on the globe which he started in 1589. 1 Hakluyt (ES) 356. Edward Wright may be the real author. In addition to the features we have already mentioned in the 1589 map, we call attention to the elaborate inland sea and waterways leading to it which resemble the cartographical dreams of Menéndez.

1608?—John Smith. A description of the land of Virginia. Actually, it is Smith's map of North Carolina. Public Record Office, London, M.P.G. 584. Copied in Brown, 2 *Genesis* 596f. The map was sent to Lord Bacon in 1618. For discussion, see note 17, Part I.

16—?—Antonius Millo. World. British Museum add MS 27,470. Chesapeake shown with three branches. The James is called the R. S. María. The streams are elongated in imaginative fashion. A good example of the slow progress of cartography.

1608—Nathaniel Powell? Chart of Virginia. S 42; P 24. Brown (1: 184) thinks this chart was sent to England by Captain Francis Nelson, who left Virginia June 2, 1608. It was intended to illustrate Smith's *True Relation*, which was published in August of that year, but apparently the chart was never engraved. Brown also thinks this is the chart Hudson received from Smith. Brown translates the almost illegible legends for us in 1: 184-189. This map has the appearance of being a rather careless free-hand copy of a more accurate map. Its geography is certainly far less correct than Smith's 1612 publication. The ethnology of the two maps is so consistent, however, as to point to a common source or experience. The 1608 map is more detailed for the James-York area, much less attention being given to the Rappahannock and Potomac. The rendition of some areas, particularly Poquoson, is suggestive of Tyndall. As Brown says (1: 461), Tyndall, Isaac Madison, and Nathaniel Powell were employed by the Virginia Company as cartographers from the beginning. Perhaps it will never be possible to determine just how interdependent are the various maps they and Smith have drawn.

Powell may have drawn this, though only Smith could have indicated the route he followed as a prisoner of the Indians. Powell was with Smith on most of his explorations in the colony of Virginia.

1608—Robert Tindall. Draughte of Virginia. S 42; P 25. For a discussion, see note 68, Part I above. It is reproduced in color, one-half the size of the original in the British Museum, in 58 *PMHS* 224-227. A copy which varies slightly is given in Brown, *Genesis,* with a discussion on 1: 151. He shows Chechotanke [Kecoughtan], Cape Comfortt, Nassamonge, Ooriskeyek, Jamestowne, Poetan, Cheskoyek, and Pamaunkee in the area in which we are interested.

1610—King's Surveyor. Map of America. Brown, 1 *Genesis* 456. Contour resembles Smith, but fewer islands are shown.

1612—John Smith. Map of Virginia. S 44; P 19-24. Clayton Torrence, in *A Trial Bibliography of Colonial Virginia* (Richmond, 1908) 32 f., discusses the various reproductions of this map. Those that we have seen in the Library of Congress differ from one another very little. There are clear prints in 2 Arber and in L. G. Tyler, ed., *Narratives of Early Virginia* (New York, 1930) 77. Until Augustine Herrman's map in 1670, Smith's map remained the model for all who depicted the Chesapeake. His map of New England has a similar importance. Phillips (19-24) gives 1608 as the date of composition. Obviously the final drawing is by a professional artist, not Smith.

1618—Sánchez. Map of the Atlantic Coast. KC S-202-5, north sheet. From MS in Bibl. Nat., Paris, GE AA568. This Lisbon map is the only one on which we have found the Spanish name for Virginia. Here it is spelled "B? de Jacam," it being Portuguese orthography to substitute *m* for *n*, as will be noted in "R. Jordam" farther down the coast. Jacam is so juxtaposed with La Virginia as to leave no doubt that the term applies specifically to the Chesapeake. Its appearance on a Portuguese map argues for its use on lost Spanish charts. The coast line is drawn more with an eye to artistic convention than to navigation. Unusually complete nomenclature, though at times misplaced, enhances the value of the map. In our reproduction we have taken the liberty to retrace most of the titles, which otherwise would have been unreadable. We are not sure of the titles immediately north of R. de Gallo and R. dulce. Perhaps they are Tocabago, which would be misplaced, and R. de Uxpal, which we cannot identify.

16—?—Portuguese. World. LC. Photostat British Museum add MS 27,303. Based on an early *padrón.* The Chesapeake is shown without islands, the James is the "R: de Spirito," the Chesapeake "b: de S: Ma," its upper part Río Salado.

1630—Mercator. Virginiae item et Floridae Americae provinciarum, nova descriptio. From his atlas. S 45. LC. We reproduce it to show how the

French and Spanish legends concerning wealth in the Appalachians were perpetuated. The Chesapeake is that which White drew for De Bry; Smith has not been used. Villages and dugout canoes on the Virginia plan are shown.

1646—Robert Dudley. From his *Arcano del Mare.* LC 133; P 27. This map is titled *Carta seconda Generale del' America,* and was drawn possibly by the Italian artist Lucini. Dudley, an expatriated Englishman who had been interested in maps as early as 1590, published his atlas in Florence. Although he relies almost exclusively on White, Smith, and the Dutch sources, his resultant product is strikingly modern. His shoal markings exclude any ports from Cape Henry to Willoughby Bay. Phillips (27) lists a map of this title drawn by Lucini in 1634 [?].

MADRE DE DIOS ON THE DUTCH MAPS

1655 c.—Jansson. Mar de Nort (Atlantic). From *Novus Atlas,* vol. 5. Contains an "Au lecteur" dated 1650. The John Carter Brown Library. This is the oldest map we have been able to locate applying the name Madre de Dios to the Chesapeake. The bay is shown here without the word Chesapeake, simply as Barra de Madre de Dios. *Barra* literally means a shoal or sand bar, but the early Spanish used it loosely enough to include navigable entrances, even applying it to the Barra de San Lúcar. It is interesting that the Dutch maps from this date on often give Madre de Dios as at least an alternate name for the Chesapeake. Barra de la Madalena for an entrance to Albemarle Sound, and Barra de Santiago for an entrance to Currituck Sound had appeared in Blaeu and other atlases before this time. It must be acknowledged that the Dutch had read documents or seen Spanish maps in which the name Madre de Dios was thus used. During the period in which they were furiously publishing sea charts, the Dutch had reason to favor the Spanish claim. The original Dutch claims based on the 1609 "discoveries" of Henry Hudson while "searching for a passage to the west" fared poorly against England's counterclaims; so the Dutch pushed their case back almost another century, to the early Spanish explorations, claiming to have inherited their effects while The Netherlands was a part of the Spanish kingdom, an inheritance specifically made over by Spain in the Treaty of Münster, 1648. Augustine Herrman, while still a citizen of New Amsterdam, urged this type of argument successfully while acting as a member of a boundary dispute commission attempting a settlement between New Amsterdam and Maryland in 1659. Mr. Lawrence Wroth, to whom we are indebted for most of our information about the Dutch maps, states that the so-called Witsen map of 1616, one of the earliest Dutch maps of Virginia, does not contain Madre de Dios. The same may be said for Anthony

Jacobsz, 1621 (*Pennsylvania Archives* 5 : 2), an indication that it did not come to Dutch knowledge until a later date. The Jacobsz map places the "c. de las Arenas" at about 39½°, even with the head of the Chesapeake, probably intending Cape Henlopen.

1666—Peter Goos. Pas caerte van Nieu Nederlandt en de Engelesche Virginies van Cabo Cod tot Cabo Canrick. From *De zee-atlas oft Waterweereld.* LC. S 50. In this map and in a more general map of the entire Atlantic Coast we have "Barra de Madre de Dios oft Chesepeac." In 3 Winsor 333, note 1, it is stated that the 1666 Goos maps appeared at Middleburgh and The Hague in a tract in which the Dutch States-General defended the Netherlands claims against Sir George Downing of England. However, the maps which Winsor reproduces in 4: 440 and 3: 333 are not from Goos but from a later atlas of Van Keulen. A 1675 edition of Goos in The John Carter Brown Library keeps the name Madre de Dios for the Chesapeake. Mr. Wroth thinks that this atlas and a 1676 edition of Roggeveen show, in their place names, a decided influence of the Visscher *Novi Belgii* of c. 1651 or of a common prototype, but the Visscher does not have Madre de Dios, nor does the Doncker of 1660. The Roggeveen atlas of 1676 employs Spanish texts, and in a text descriptive of the "Pascaerte vande Virginies" a paragraph begins, "El Rio Chesapeack, o Madre de Dios segun el appelido de los Espanoles...." The same maps found in the 1666 Goos, are contained in the Johannes Van Loon atlas of 1666 and 1667: *Klar-lichtende Noort-star ofte Zee-atlas,* also in LC and the Hispanic Society of America. Of Roggeveen's 1680 atlas, Barcia (160) says that he reveals less knowledge of the coast than Menéndez Marqués' report of 1573 "and did not venture to explain what little he drew on the maps."

1670—Augustine Herrman. Virginia and Maryland. S 52. Herrman (Herman, Heermans, Harman, etc.) a tobacco merchant of Bohemian descent in New Amsterdam, became a citizen of Maryland in 1661 under romantic circumstances and because of his promise to draw up an accurate map of Virginia and Maryland. The map he claims to have finished in 1670 and which was engraved by W. Faithorne in London in 1673, in substance had been drawn at least by 1660, for Lord Baltimore mentioned it in the past tense in conferring citizenship on Herrman (C. C. Hall, *Narratives of Early Maryland,* New York, 1925, 313, note 2). It was not in existence in 1659, the year in which Hermann wrote to Stuyvesant detailing the need for a better map of the area for the clarification of Dutch claims. There are some who believe that Herrman helped in the construction of Visscher maps, but as Wroth says, Herrman's map of Virginia and Maryland stands quite apart from those of his predecessors, though he doubtless utilized some of them. Herrman certainly claims originality for his map when he inscribes on it: "Virginia and Maryland as it is planted and inhabited this present year 1670 surveyed and exactly drawne by the only labour and endeavour of Augustine Herrman, Bohemiensis." He slips now and then in the spelling of English names, finding it necessary to insert an H after he has finished Dorcester and giving us Nantemond for Nansemond. There is a Dutch flavor in his title: "The Great Bay of the Cheseapeake," a translation of "De Groote Bay van Cheseapeake." He pretends to show the upper courses of the streams, but in most cases these sinewy branches have only decorative value. In his journal of 1659 Herrman avers that prior rights of Spanish discovery of Maryland "could be proved from Spanish journals and chronicles" (Hall 324).

F. S. McGrath discusses Herrman at length as a map-maker in *Pillars of Maryland* (Richmond, 1950), *passim,* and reproduces his map of Virginia and Maryland (224). P. L. Phillips has a fine reproduction in his monograph *The Rare Map of Virginia and Maryland by Augustine Herrman* (Washington, 1911). Mathews, *op. cit.,* has a more extended analysis of the accuracy of Herrman's map. It still remains something of a mystery how or when he could have taken the soundings and made the inland surveys that enabled him to show harbor depths in detail and indicate locations of all white and Indian dwellings.

1681—Johannis van Keulen. Pas kaart van de zee kusten van Virginia tusschen C. Henry 'en t Hooge Land van Renselaars Hoek. Door Vooght geometra. t' Amsterdam. From the atlas *De lichtende zeefakkel,* vol. 2, Amsterdam, 1681-96. S 52. LC. One of the charts in this atlas shows the lower half of Virginia and gives "de Bay van Cheseapeke off Bahia de Madre de Dios."

1695?—Johannis van Keulen. Same title as the map immediately above. From *De Groote Nieuwe Vermeerderde Zee-Atlas ofte Water-Werelt . . . t' Amsterdam.* S 54 f. The Spanish nomenclature still clings: De Groote Bay van Chesapeake off Bahía de Madre de Dios. Maryland and Virginia are both shown on the same map, which is in almost every detail a copy of Herrman, except that streams have not been extended beyond their navigable portions, and fewer place names are given. The style of lettering is the same as on the 1681 map. The names of Van Keulen and Herrman are brought into interesting juxtaposition in the *Journal of Jasper Daenckaerts,* October 10, 1680. Daenckaerts, leader of a sect which had converted Herrman's son, was in Amsterdam. "I went to Joannis van Ceulen, mathematician, who has made a new sea-atlas, a copy of which he had sent to the king of England, and also to the king of France. It is a beautiful work; but he was surprised, after having corrected it so much as he had, that I should point out several errors. I endeavored to obtain a chart of Maryland, from Augustine Herman's draught, but could not find it here; nor could I in England." This journal is edited by James and Jameson as one of the *Original Narratives of Early American History* (New York, 1913). Evidently Van Keulen acted on the tip given by Daenckaerts and built his later atlases on the Herrman plan. Of Herrman, Wroth says, "His map influenced an amazing number of later productions. If *he* had said *Madre de Dios,* the name would probably have been fixed on the bay. The fact that he, working upon the spot, does not use it is pretty good evidence that locally its use had not taken hold, and that its appearance upon the Dutch maps of later date was simply the transmission of an historical memory."

In concluding this section on Dutch maps, which was intended only to follow up the use of "Madre de Dios," we shall briefly consider the origin of this name. The earliest use we have found is in Rogel's letter of 1572. Oré intimates that it was thus known to the sailors who picked up Don Luis a dozen years earlier. There was no universal feast of the Church under that title in the sixteenth century; so it is not likely that the name stems from a date of discovery. Many Dominicans took the name Madre de Dios; in fact, there was a Brother Madre de Dios who stayed behind to nurse the sick in Florida while his confrères went on with Villafañe up the Atlantic Coast in the 1561 exploration that may have reached the Chesapeake. It is entirely possible that the Dominicans may have added this title to "Santa María."

LATER CARTOGRAPHY

1735 c.—Walter Hoxton. Mapp of the Bay of Chesepeack. London. LC. Probably the best mariner's map of the Chesapeake up to that time, showing depths of water in considerable detail. Describes Point Comfort as having the appearance of two islands.

1737—A Draught of Virginia. *Mark Tiddeman.* From *The English Pilot,* 4th book. S 59 f. Dr. Swem traces the map's origin as far back as John Thornton in the 1706 edition of *The English Pilot.* From Cape Henry to Mocksack Bay the only navigable ports shown are those we believe Oré indicates: (1) the waters from "Sowalls Point" to Norfolk; (2) Newport News; (3) the waters inside Point Comfort; and (4) Yorktown.

1765—Fernando Martínez. La Florida en el ano 1765. WL 497. 1 Ruidíaz, post xliii. A quite inaccurate map interesting only because the Chesapeake is shown as the B. de Santa María and its discovery is attributed to Pedro Menéndez Marqués in 1573, false if first discovery is intended. Description, Lowery list, p. 342. Cape Henry is referred to as Cabo de Santa María. Whenever this designation is found, we believe it to be a confusion with a cape of that name farther up the coast on early maps.

Without comparing, we believe this is identical with a map attributed to Fernando Murnoz, 1765, entitled *Descripcion geografica de la parte que los Españoles poseon actualmente en el Continente de la Florida* (Crown Coll., vol. 5, no. 36).

1780—Joseph Frederick Wallet Des Barres, Esq. A Chart of the Coast of New York, New Jersey, Pensilvania, Maryland, Virginia, North Carolina &c. composed from the deposit of surveys of the Right Honourable Lords of Trade with Soundings and Nautical Remarks. U.S. National Archives. This map is one sheet of a large atlas prepared for the British armed forces and embodying almost all of the cartography of that period, with reference to Eastern United States. Its treatment of the North Carolina Coast in general substantiates the work of White and the reports of Spanish navigators beginning with Pedro Menéndez Marqués in 1573. Wimble Shoals near Hatteras and the Three Sand Hills off Currituck Sound are clearly the same features noted in the 1573 account conserved by Barcia. Chickinoke Inlet and Grant Inlet correspond to the two openings south of Roanoke reported by Juan Menéndez Marqués in 1588.

1781—Desandroüins. Map of the British and American battle lines north of Jamestown Island. LC. Of interest because it shows the course of Powhatan Creek and indicates that it was possibly navigable at an earlier day as far as Poheran (Powhatan) Mill north of the road to Williamsburg. This presents the possibility of the Jesuit Fathers' having ascended this stream in 1570, from which they could have crossed over to one of the villages of the Paspaheghs or Chickahominy on the Chickahominy River or its vicinity. The ferry indicated north of Jamestown crosses an area once land-locked, as indicated on the Smith and Powell maps. Thus the mouth of Powhatan Creek in 1570 was doubtless the Thorofare, certainly wide at its mouth.

1781?—Desandroüins. Map of College Creek and Williamsburg. LC. This map is useful for indicating the navigability of the creek at least as far as College Landing, about a mile from Williamsburg. In the hypothesis that the Jesuits ascended this stream in 1570, it is probable that they would have portaged from College Landing to Queen's Creek, a distance of less than three miles. Extensive cultivation is indicated on the war maps. This may account for the building up of the low sand bar, covered at high tide, shown at the mouth of College Creek.

1781—Chantayoine ? Carte de la Virginie. KC S-461-12. We select this map as one of many Revolutionary War maps emphasizing the importance of College Creek and showing the Egg Islands around Poquoson and Back Bay that have now disappeared.

17—?—"W.P.M." A Sketch of the East End of the Peninsula Whereon is Hampton. Clinton Map No. 263, Clements Library. Dr. Swem believes that this very detailed map dates from the Revolutionary War period, chiefly because of the emphasis on roads and windmills, a source of food for foraging soldiers. This map was probably prepared for the British Army. It provides a fairly accurate view of the streams and roads of Hampton and vicinity. Assuming that Point Comfort is drawn with equal accuracy, it is evident that Mill(s) Creek was once a stream rather than a bay, and that the shallow water that today reaches nearly a mile from the Phoebus shore was then part of the mainland. It does not seem likely that Percy's Indians, bows and arrows in mouth, would have swum a stretch of water as wide as Mill Creek is today.

1814—Anthony De Mayne. A Survey of the Chesapeake. Maryland Room, Pratt Library. Shows 9 or 10 fathoms of water off Old Point Comfort, about 7 fathoms just north of the point at Newport News.

1818—Major Roberdeau, U.S.T. Engineers. Reconnoitering of Chesapeake Bay. U.S. National Archives. Map drawn by topographical engineers under the direction of General John G. Swift and J. D. Elliott. Lynnhaven Bay and Creek are shown, but not Little Creek. Navigable channels leading to Hampton Creek and Mill Creek are shown. By the time of this survey the mouths of Warwick Creek and Skiffe's Creek were considerably shoaled.

1826—H. S. Tanner, engraver, Herman Boye, draughtsman. Map of the State of Virginia. Acc. no. 203 ns., Coast and Geodetic Survey. P 69. "Archer's Hape Creek" given importance. Plumbtree Islands and remains of Egg Islands shown. Cf. S 109, where a Tanner map is listed under date 1827.

United States Coast and Geodetic Survey. Use has been made of all the modern charts for the Chesapeake and the James and of old topographic and hydrographic surveys for various years from 1852 to 1875. To list them all here is needless.

United States Geological Survey. The following modern survey quadrangles were examined: Cape Henry, Newport News, Hampton, Yorktown, Williamsburg, Toano.

Recapitulating, we find that Spanish cartography dominated representations of the Atlantic Coast until White's maps were published. In practically all Spanish-published or Spanish-influenced maps, a bay resembling the Chesapeake is called Bahía de Santa María, and a river corresponding to the James is named the Río del Espíritu Santo. The northern part of the Chesapeake, which has a slight current, was called the Río Salado. These maps were known in part in England, but after the maps of White and Smith appeared, their nomenclature and coast lines no longer influenced English cartography. Only the Dutch, relying on Spanish explorations to support their claims to New Netherlands, and the Portuguese, who had divided the world with the Spanish, continued to make free use of Spanish sources. The names Jacán and Madre de Dios for the Chesapeake were current in Spanish usage for a little more than a half century, beginning with the taking of Don Luis from Ajacán. We have found but few cartographical survivals of these names, none of them on Spanish maps. Time, inexorable as the ocean tide, has all but washed out the memory of them and the events they commemorated.

APPENDICES
BIBLIOGRAPHY
INDEX

APPENDICES

APPENDIX A

Cartographical Knowledge of Smith and Hakluyt

AN immense amount of research would be required to establish the extent of Smith's cartographical knowledge and especially how much might have been available to him through the indefatigable Hakluyt. Smith himself raises the question of how "those spatious Tracts of Land ... can be thus long vnknowne, or not possessed by the *Spaniards*." In his answer he tells us of great efforts he went to in securing several practically worthless maps of the Atlantic Coast, he hints that some discoveries may have died with their authors, and he calls attention to the vastness of the territory and the difficulty in getting a good description of even a small portion of it. By 1614 he had abandoned the idea of a near-by western ocean, for he speaks of "those large Dominions which doe stretch themselues into the maine, God doth know how many thousand miles ..." (Arber 2: 702 ff.). Smith frequently quotes John Dee on matters such as trade and the British Navy, and we may suppose that he had seen John Dee's map of 1580 in which he clearly shows the Bahía de Santa María after the shape of Cabot's map of 1544.

It seems reasonable to suppose that Hakluyt, in urging the Raleigh colony to transfer to the Chesapeake, was relying on a cartographical hunch even more heavily than on the vague information picked up from the Indians by Lane. A fair idea of the extent of Hakluyt's own knowledge can be gained from a list of geographical works published in England during his time (G. B. Parks, *Richard Hakluyt and the English Voyages*, Appendix IV, 269-277). The long enumeration includes the Spanish histories by Peter Martyr and López de Gómara, the works of Dee and Ribault, and the Agnese portolan atlas dedicated to Henry VIII.

APPENDIX B

The Aboriginal Population

Judging from figures given by Swanton, based on a posthumously published manuscript of Mooney, "The Aboriginal Population of America North of Mexico," 80 *SMC* 1-40, there were more Indians in Florida, North Carolina, or South Carolina than in Virginia. However, as Mook demonstrates in his article in *AA* already cited, the Powhatan Indians had a greater density of population than their immediate neighbors. Father Rogel's estimate should not be taken lightly, for he had worked in east and west Florida, Georgia, and South Carolina. Carrera too had been impressed with the number of Indians; "On the bank of this port there is a large population, and also inland" (para. 39). A contrary testimony, less valuable because more remote from the scene, is that of Father Sedeño, writing to Borgia from Guale May 14, 1570, and trying to throw cold water on the projected Ajacán venture: "Another enterprise is now presenting itself, as I believe Father Vice-provincial will write Y[our] P[aternity]; it appears to me it will be like what we've had so far, for after all, it is in Florida, and the population is so dispersed and even more than this; for an Indian, already a Christian, who comes from there, says that in an area 500 leagues long by 250 wide, there are probably not thirty thousand souls in all, etc. Your Paternity can see how we'll have to go about preaching to them. Father will write at length about all this to Your Paternity, that you may be better informed" (*MAF* 430).

APPENDIX C

Rumors of the Lost Colony

Opechancanough, Powhatan, and other Indians independently affirmed to Smith the report of "men clothed like us" at Ocanohowan (1 Arber 17, 20). The "Spaniards" seen there may have been four Englishmen "lost by Sr Walter Rawley, which escaped from the slaughter of Powhatan of Roanoke upon the first arivall of our Colony..." (Bushnell, "Virginia from Early Records," 9 *AA* 34, quoting instructions of the government to Sir Thomas Gates, "knight governour of Virginia"). Bushnell discusses the import of references linking Powhatan and his father with the early Spanish and English settlements in "Virginia Before Jamestown" (100 *SMC* 130 ff.). These four Englishmen had been protected by Sepanocon, a rival of Powhatan. Bushnell thinks that inasmuch as Powhatan is a generic name, the Virginia Powhatan was perhaps not the chief implicated in the Roanoke slaughter. But Strachey, who apparently derives his information from Machumps, brother-in-law to Powhatan, clearly puts the blame on Virginia's chief. He states that the Raleigh colony of men, women, and children lived for twenty-odd years inter-mixed with the Indians. Then Powhatan, incited by his sorcerers, slaughtered the colony. Of this number, seven (four men, two boys, and a young maid) escaped and fled up the "river of Chanoke" where they were protected by a chief named Eyanoco [Sepanocon?], who employed them to beat out his cop-per at a mine at Ritanoe. Machumps reported Indians with walled houses of stone at "Peccarecamek and Ochanahoen," the English having taught them that type of construction (see Strachey 26, 86). Strachey expresses anger over the failure of White in 1590 and Mace in 1602 to search diligently for the survivors.

It is a strange fact that the Spanish, who picked up their information from the southern Indians, in all their relations assume the continuous existence of the Raleigh colony from 1585 to at least 1602. They sent ships to investigate in 1585, 1587, and 1588, but without result. Neither of the last two expedi-tions got inside the sounds.

Opinion divides concerning the location of Ritanoe and Ocanohowan. Mooney in Hodge, *Handbook* 103, suggests an identification of Ocanohowan with Occaneechi, on the Roanoke River in Mecklenburg County, Virginia. It is true that in Brown's *Genesis* (discussion 1: 185-188) a 1608 map of Vir-ginia shows Ocanohowan as a river that might be identified with the Roanoke, but we might also link the name with the town of Ohaunoock on John White's map of 1590, obviously on the Chowan River, probably the same as Strachey's "Chanoke." Lane (1 Arber 312) speaks of Ohanock, a town subject to Chawa-nock. It is significant that when the Virginia colonists set out to find the lost Raleigh men they went to Chawanook to find them, but concluded that they were dead (1 Arber 158). Perhaps they did not go far enough south. One of these parties was guided by the Quiyoughcohannock Indians from near the Falls of the James, probably because they lived near the headwaters of the Chowan. The first attempt to find clothed men ended when the Paspahegh king refused to go beyond Warraskoyack while conducting "two of our men to a place called Panawicke beyond Roonok" (1 Arber 23). Here we have some basis for interpreting Ritanoe as Roanoke. Instructions issued by the government to Gates speak of the copper mines of Ritanoe and the possibility of finding the four Englishmen at Peccarecamicke. One gets the impression that they regard the copper mines as on one branch of the river and the Englishmen on another. White's map is no help in identifying Peccaracamicke. On his map of the East Coast, however, he lists what seems to be a Ritahokene or Ricahokene which could easily have been misread Ritanokene and then shortened to Ritanoe. This village was located near the mouth of the Chowan; the prefix Rica- signifies a dividing point. There are no copper mines there, but if one followed the Roanoke River which flows in there he would eventually come to copper mines. We know of no evidence that the Roanoke River itself acquired that name in very early times. It was known to Lane and White as the Moratoc. Lederer in 1670 spoke of the "Shawan, alias Rorenock-river." In puzzling fashion he speaks of Rickahokans as seated far to the west on a "land of great waves."

The 1608 map by Powell[?] gives the most coherent explanation of the place names mentioned in Arber's documents. Pananiock can be identified with White's Pomeiock (modern Engelhard, N.C.). "Here the King of Paspaheghe reported our men to be and wants to go." The Packrackwick River of this map can be identified with Peccarecamek, probably the Neuse, and "Here remaineth 4 men clothed that came from Ronock to Ocanahawan," as the 1608 map proclaims.

To reconstruct the picture as well as possible from the jumble of information, it seems logical that the English should remove to Ohaunoock on the Chowan (perhaps after a brief interlude on Croatoan) for Lane had planned his first fort there in the move toward the Chesapeake, it having the added feature of being close to the Roanoke River and the road to the copper mines. It is also logical that Powhatan, like Hamor, should have imagined that these clothed people were Spanish, and his enmity toward them would be explained in terms of the punishment of 1572. Opechancanough's tyranny in this region makes it easy to concede a similar treatment by Powhatan. That a few of the young should be spared is consistent with Indian habits. That the old survivors should be put to work beating out copper is a parallel to Powhatan's avid employment of English laborers in building houses and in constructing implements of iron. The fact that the few survivors were never found is explained by the fact that it was long before the Virginia English penetrated the Virgilina region where copper was found or to the Neuse where the captives ultimately were reported. If Strachey can be trusted, the English evidently placed the blame for the murders on Powhatan, for they meted out punishment to his priestly advisers who agitated the project.

That part of the Roanoke party may have attempted to reach the Chesapeake is implied in the relation of Alonso Ruiz, who was captured by William Irishe and taken to the Bahía de Santa María. Somewhere along the coast they saw traces of cattle and a stray dark-brown mule (1 *TRHS* (5) 18). This was in the year 1588. There is evidence from the relation of Pedro Díaz, March 21, 1589, that the Roanoke colony possessed such animals. Díaz was captured by Grenville in 1585, and escaped on May 1, 1588. His account adds interesting details to the Roanoke story. He gives the location as 36¼° and indicates gold, silver, and a route to the South Sea as part of the colony's objectives. In an ungrammatical sentence he seems to place the population "beyond" the Bahía de Santa María, but if correctly interpreted, he probably follows this order: Roanoke, Cabo de San Juan 12 leagues north, Bahía de Santa María 30 leagues north. Juan Menéndez Marqués also gives a Cabo de San Juan south of the Chesapeake. Díaz' relation is in A.G.I. 54-1-34.

Brown (1 *Genesis* 189 f.) relates a tradition of the Croatan tribe as late as 1864 of their intermarriage with the English. John Lawson in 1709 had reported that the Hatteras Indians frequenting Roanoke Island showed traces of white blood (137 *BAE,R* 137). Wirt (3 Winsor 115 f.) follows Strachey's account and links the survivors with the Hatteras Indians.

APPENDIX D

Methods of Estimating Distance

In a communication to the writers, the late Jean Delanglez, S.J., whose work on the discovery of the Mississippi is cited elsewhere, thus summarizes his own research: "We aren't at all certain of the value of the land league in Spain during the 16th Century. The league spoken of by Lowery (see preface to *Spanish Settlements*) is the so-called judicial league. All assume this is the standard league used on land. No one has given any reason for such an assumption. As for the sea league used by Spanish explorers in the sixteenth and seventeenth centuries, we know beyond doubt that there were 17½ leagues to the degree of latitude (value 68.704 miles at the equator, 69.407 miles at the poles) average 69 miles divided by 17½, gives 3.943 miles for one league." In the *Final Report of the U.S. De Soto Expedition Commission*, 76th Congress, 1st Session, Document No. 71, Vol. 9, p. 104, the judicial league is given a value of 2.634 statute miles. De Soto is reported to have marched 5 or 6 leagues a day, actually between 13 and 15.6 miles, giving his league a value of between 2 and 3 miles. In Appendix C, p. 303 of the *Report* there is a list of the distances given by the chronicler of "The Gentleman of Elvas," illustrating how inaccurate were his guesses. S. E. Morison in his *Admiral of the Ocean Sea* (New York, 1942) 262, note 28, cites Pigafetta of Magellan's expedition as saying that he was using 2.2 nautical miles (6080 feet each) for the land league. Columbus' alongshore league was about 1.5 nautical miles (*ibid.* 248). Father Sedeño, an associate of Father Quirós, estimated the distance from Havana to Santiago in Cuba at 225 leagues by land. Actually the distance is close to 500 miles, giving a value for the league of 2.2 miles. He estimated the distance from Cape Cañaveral to San Agustín in a straight line at 30 leagues, giving a value of 3.60 miles per league, but he probably was applying the common estimate of distance by sea, commonly held to be 30 leagues. In eleven instances, exclusive of the deliberate underestimates of Menéndez, the value of the land league or alongshore league of Father Quirós' contemporaries in the Florida Mission ranges in application from 2.2 miles to 3.63 miles, with

2.75 as the most frequently recurring figure. Thus we can say that Quirós' 2 leagues must have been between 4 and 7 miles, if he made a good estimate.

APPENDIX E

Early Reports of Metals in Virginia

It is remarkable how consistently appear reports of such metals as gold and copper in the Rappahannock or Potomac region. The Spanish captive Molina, in a letter smuggled to Velasco, May 28, 1613, from Virginia, reports that "they say that at the headwaters of the rivers, after they have come forth from the mountains, there is a great quantity of grains of gold and silver, but as they do not attach any value to them, but only to copper which they esteem very highly, they do not collect them" (Brown, 2 *Genesis* 647). Glavin in his deposition said that he saw Ricard de Campoverde [Grenville] bargain for more than one *arroba* of gold. The chiefs wore nose rings of gold. They procured the metal from gold mines 40 leagues up a river, at the foot of a range at the source of a river (8 *GHQ* 227).

An Apalache Indian boy named Pedro, supposed by De Soto's party to have been possessed by the devil, assured the Spanish they would find quantities of gold, silver, and precious pearls at Cofachiqui, and he gave an elaborate description of how gold was mined, melted, and refined (see *The Florida of the Inca* 280; Swanton, 137 *BAE,B* 42). Menéndez in a letter to Borgia January 18, 1568 (*MAF* 230), says that the Indians "sent gold and silver from their mines" to his soldiers who had penetrated 300 leagues inland. Hariot gives a description of the taking and refining of a metal called *wassador* (a generic metal term, but probably copper) as related by the North Carolina Algonkin Indians, and this account is almost identical with the one given to Menéndez Marqués here. In his analysis of this story Swanton (137 *BAE,B* 490-498) comes to the conclusion that a copper ore containing silver was obtained by trade from the Lake Superior region, the Mangoags, Iroquois ancestors of the Nottoway, acting as the middlemen along a route they had kept open after migrating from the West toward the Atlantic Coast. He admits the possibility of limited mining of copper on the Roanoke, near Virgilina, Va., and the gathering of gold nuggets after rain is suggested by George F. Becker in "Reconnaisance of the Gold Fields of the Southern Appalachians" in the 16th Annual Report, U.S. Geological Survey 9.

Lorant, *The New World* 117, reproduces a picture from the early French colony of South Carolina showing natives collecting gold in the streams. It is possible that the gold ornaments reported by Alonso, Menéndez Marqués, Gonzales, and Glavin were highly burnished copper or may have been gold trade items picked up from Indians who gathered them from wrecks along the

Carolina coasts. John Smith and other early Virginia writers speak of gold and silver only in a vague way and give little evidence of actual observation of its use by the Virginia Indians. Smith speaks of brass but twice, Powhatan having told him of a country called "*Anone*, where they haue abundance of brass, and houses walled as ours" (1 *Arber* 20).

Two considerations seem to make worth while a more serious examination of the evidence for a knowledge of gold, silver, copper, and brass smelting on the part of the Indians of this region. The first is the widespread idea of the Indians that they actually had such resources. The second is that, in the analysis of the mineral deposits of the East, silver is associated with copper in the ores of Virgilina and elsewhere in the Appalachian region, gold is found with copper, and even tin is reported for Virginia. Gold placer deposits have been worked in Goochland, Louisa, Spotsylvania, and Stafford counties, to name but a few. Bruce, *Economic History of Virginia* 1: 82, describes the beginnings of these workings. Gold is found in a greater number of places and in larger quantities in Georgia and North Carolina. Many higher producing sites were near the Indian Trail in North Carolina. See Sanford and Stone, *Useful Minerals of the United States*, Bulletin 585, U.S. Geological Survey (1914) for the mineral resources of this region.

BIBLIOGRAPHY

MANUSCRIPT COLLECTIONS

Buckingham Smith Papers: New York Historical Society.
Several volumes of transcripts from Spanish Archives collected in the middle of the last century. Smith wrote on a wide range of problems, but his collection is hardly complete. A transcript of the Quirós-Segura letter is here.

John Gilmary Shea Papers: Georgetown University.
As far as the Segura mission is concerned, Shea collected excerpts from secondary sources and transcripts of some of the letters of the Jesuits reproduced in Part II. In the Archives of William and Mary College there are the letters of Charles Campbell and Shea on this question. Campbell refers to them in vol. I of his *History of the Colony and Ancient Dominion of Virginia*. In the Archives of Woodstock College there are two letters to Father John Morgan, S.J., pertaining to Shea's article in the *Catholic World* for 1875. Since all previous studies on this topic can be traced to Shea, the following summary of his sources is informative: "I wrote my paper with Menéndez correspondence, reports of official pilots, letters of Fathers Segura and Quirós, as well as Tanner and extracts from the Chrono-Historia de la Provincia de Toledo" (Shea to Morgan, Sept. 20, 1884).

Lowery Papers: Library of Congress.
Nine volumes of hand-copied transcripts from Simancas and Seville. These cover the entire period of Spanish occupancy in Florida. We have examined every document that referred to Ajacán and the Chesapeake from 1570 to 1610. The collection has all the principal relations and letters of this era, but there are large omissions in the minor documents.

Connor Papers: Library of Congress.
Several thousand pages of photostats and typed transcriptions from Euro-

pean Archives pertaining to the history of Florida. This excellent collection far surpasses Lowery in comprehensiveness. All the relevant Florida documents have been examined.

PUBLISHED DOCUMENTS

SPANISH FLORIDA AND THE JESUIT MISSION
(See also the General List following this.)

Monumenta Historica Societatis Iesu. A collection, at present numbering over seventy volumes, that offers excerpts from the various archives of the Society of Jesus. The original Latin or vernacular is given in a critical edition with a Latin commentary. We have used the following:

Monumenta Antiquae Floridae. Rome, 1946.

Sanctus Franciscus Borgia, quartus Gandiae Dux et Societatis Iesu Praepositus Generalis tertius. 5 vols. Madrid, 1894-1911.

Lainii Monumenta. Epistolae et Acta Patris Jacobi Lainii . . . 8 vols. Madrid, 1912-1917.

Polanci Complimenta. Epistolae et commentaria P. Ioannis Alphonsi de Polanco . . . 2 vols. Madrid, 1916-1917.

Barcia, Andrés. [Gabriel Cárdenas y Cano] *Ensayo cronológico para la historia general de Florida.* Madrid, 1723. Translated with introduction by Anthony Kerrigan as *Barcia's Chronological History of the Continent of Florida.* Gainesville, 1951. (References in the text are to the English translation.)

Connor, Jeannette T. *Colonial Records of Spanish Florida.* 2 vols. Deland, 1925. (Original Spanish with English translations.)

Devitt, E. I. "Axacam: The Martyrs of the Rappahannock," *Records of the American Catholic Historical Society,* 19 (1908), 1-17. (English translations.)

Geiger, Maynard. *The Martyrs of Florida 1513-1616, by Luis Gerónimo de Oré.* New York, 1939. *Franciscan Studies,* 18. (English translation.)

López, Atanasio. *Relación historica de la Florida escrita en el siglo XVII.* vol. 1. Madrid, 1931. (Modern transliteration of Spanish of Oré.)

Loomie, Albert J. "The Jesuit Mission in Ajacán, 1570: A Documentary History," *The Woodstock Letters,* 80 (1951), 351-386. (English translations.)

Marcel, Gabriel. *Reproductions de cartes et de globes relatifs à la découverte de l'Amérique du XVIe au XVIIe siecle.* Paris, 1892.

Navarrete, M. Fernández. "Viajes Apócrifos," vol. 15 (1848) in *Colección de Documentos Inéditos para la Historia de España.* 75 vols. Madrid, 1842-1880.

Priestley, Herbert I. *The Luna Papers.* 2 vols. Deland, 1929. (Original Spanish with English translations.)

Ruidíaz y Caravia, Eugenio. *La Florida, Su Conquista y Colonización por Pedro Menéndez de Avilés.* 2 vols. Madrid, 1893. (Spanish texts in second volume.)

Vargas Ugarte, Rubén. "The First Jesuit Mission in Florida," *Historical Records and Studies, The United States Catholic Historical Society*, 25 (1935), 59-148. (English translations.)

Varner, J. G. and J. J., ed. *Garcilaso da Vega, The Florida of the Inca.* Austin, 1951. (English translation.)

Ware, Henry. "Siete Cartas escritas al Rey, años de 1565 y 1566," *Proceedings, Massachusetts Historical Society*, 2nd Series. 8, 416-468. (English translations.)

GENERAL LIST

(This list includes both general reference works and documentary collections on problems not directly concerned with the Spanish in the Chesapeake. Full bibliographical references to other works of less importance in this study are given in the notes to the text.)

Alcázar, Bartolomé. *Chrono-Historia de la Compañía de Jesús en la provincia de Toledo.* 2 vols. Madrid, 1710.

Alegambe, Phillipus. *Mortes illustres et gesta eorum de Societate Iesu qui... confecti sunt.* Romae, 1657.

Alegre, Francisco Jávier. *Historia de la Compañía de Jesús en Nueva España.* 3 vols. Mexico, 1841-1842.

Arber, Edward, and A. G. Bradley, eds. *Travels and Works of Captain John Smith.* 2 vols. Edinburgh, 1910.

Astraín, Antonio. *Historia de la Compañía de Jesús en la Asistencia de España.* 7 vols. Madrid, 1902-1925.

Beverley, Robert. *The History and Present State of Virginia.* Chapel Hill, 1947. Edited by Louis B. Wright.

Blair, Emma H. and James A. Robertson. *The Philippine Islands, 1493-1898.* 55 vols. Cleveland, 1903-1909.

Bolton, Herbert E. *The Spanish Borderlands.* New Haven, 1921.

Brown, Alexander. *The Genesis of the United States.* 2 vols. New York, 1890.
———. *The First Republic in America.* Boston, 1890.

Brown, Lloyd A. *The Story of Maps.* Boston, 1949.

Bruce, Philip A. *Economic History of Virginia in the Seventeenth Century.* 2 vols. New York, 1896.

Campbell, Charles. *The History of the Colony and Ancient Dominion of Virginia.* Philadelphia, 1860.

Cascón, Miguel. *Los Jesuitas en Menéndez Pelayo*. Valladolid, 1940.

Clark, Charles Upson, ed. *Antonio Vásquez de Espinosa, Compendio y Descripción de las Indias Occidentales*. Washington, 1948. And *Antonio Vásquez de Espinosa, Compendium and Description of the West Indies*. Washington, 1942. *Smithsonian Miscellaneous Collections*, 102, 108.

Chatelaine, Verne. *The Defenses of Spanish Florida, 1563-1573*. Washington, 1941.

Craven, Wesley Frank. *The Southern Colonies in the Seventeenth Century*. Baton Rouge, 1949.

Delanglez, Jean. *El Río del Espíritu Santo*. New York, 1945.

Fernández Duro, Cesáreo. *Disquisiciones Náuticas*. 6 vols. Madrid, 1876-1881.

García, Genaro. *Dos antiquas relaciónes de la Florida*. Mexico, 1902.

Geiger, Maynard. *The Franciscan Conquest of Florida, 1573-1618*. Washington, 1938.

―――. *Biographical Dictionary of the Franciscans in Spanish Florida and Cuba, 1528-1841*. Paterson, 1940. *Franciscan Studies*, 21.

Granero, Jesús María. *La acción misionera y los métodos misionales de San Ignacio de Loyola*. Burgos, 1931.

Hakluyt, Richard. *Hakluyt's Voyages*. Everyman's Library, London, 1926, and *The Extra Series*, Glasgow, 1904.

Hall, C. C., ed. *Narratives of Early Maryland*. New York, 1925.

Hamor, Raphe. *A True discourse of the Present Estate of Virginia* ... London, 1615. Reprinted Albany, 1860.

Hanke, Lewis. *The Spanish Struggle for Justice in the Conquest of America*. Philadelphia, 1950.

Haring, C. H. *Trade and Navigation between Spain and the Indies in the Time of the Hapsburgs*. Cambridge, Mass., 1918.

Harrisse, Henry. *The Discovery of North America*. London and Paris, 1892.

―――. *John Cabot, The Discoverer of North America and Sebastian, His Son*. London, 1896.

Hodge, Frederick W. *Handbook of American Indians North of Mexico*. 2 vols. Washington, 1907-1910.

Hulbert, Archer. *Crown Collection of Photographs of American Maps*. 5 vols. Cleveland, 1904-1908.

Kenny, Michael. *The Romance of the Floridas*. Milwaukee, 1943.

Lanning, John Tate. *The Spanish Missions of Georgia*. Chapel Hill, 1935.

López de Velasco, Juan. *Geografía y Descripción Universal de las Indias* [1573 ?] Madrid, 1894.

Lorant, Stephan. *The New World*. New York, 1946.

Lowery, Woodbury. *The Spanish Settlements in the United States*. 2 vols. New York, 1911.

Mathews, E. B. *The Maps and Map-Makers of Maryland*. Baltimore, 1898.

Nugent, Nell M. *Cavaliers and Pioneers, Abstracts of Land Patents and Grants, 1623-1666*. Richmond, 1934.

O'Daniel, V. F. *The Dominicans in Early Florida*. New York, 1930.

Parks, G. B. *Richard Hakluyt and the English Voyages*. New York, 1928.

Parry, J. H. *The Spanish Theory of Empire in the Sixteenth Century*. Cambridge, 1940.

Pérez de Ribas, Andrés. *Historia de los triunfos de nuestra santa fe entre gentes las más bárbaras y fieras del nuevo Orbe* ... Madrid, 1645.

Robinson, Conway. *An Account of Discoveries in the West until 1519, and of Voyages to and along the Atlantic Coast of North America from 1520 to 1573*. Richmond, 1848.

Robertson, James A. *List of Documents in the Spanish Archives, relating to the History of the United States*. Washington, 1910.

Sacchini, Francisco. *Historiae Societatis Iesu, pars Tertia, sive Borgia*. Rome, 1649.

Salley, Alexander. *Narratives of Early Carolina*. New York, 1911.

Sánchez Alonso, Bernardino. *Fuentes de la historia española e hispano-americana*. 2 vols. Madrid, 1927 and 1946.

Smith, John. *The Generall Historie of Virginia*. 2 vols. Glasgow, 1907.

Strachey, William. *Historie of Travaille into Virginia*. [c. 1616]. London, 1849.

Swem, E. G, *Virginia Historical Index*. 2 vols. Roanoke, 1934-1936.

Tanner, Mathias. *Societas Iesu usque ad sanguinis et profusionem vitae militans* ... Prague, 1675.

Thiele, Walter. *Official Map Publications*. Chicago, 1938.

Tyler, L. G. *Narratives of Early Virginia*. New York, 1917.

Wertenbaker, Thomas J. *Virginia under the Stuarts*. Princeton, 1914.

White, Andrew. *Relatio Itineris in Marylandiam*. [1634] Baltimore, 1874.

Winsor, Justin. *Narrative and Critical History of America*. 8 vols. Boston and New York, 1884-1889.

Wright, Irene A. *Early History of Cuba, 1492-1586*. New York, 1916.

———. *Documents concerning English Voyages to the Spanish Main, 1569-1580*. London, 1932.

Zubillaga, Felix. *La Florida. La Misión Jesuítica y la colonización española*. Rome, 1940.

ARTICLES IN PERIODICALS

Bushnell, David I., Jr. "Virginia—From Early Sources," *American Anthropologist*, 9 (1907), 45-56.

———. "Virginia Before Jamestown," *Smithsonian Miscellaneous Collections*, 100 (1940), 125-158.

————. "Indian Sites Below the Falls of the Rappahannock," *Smithsonian Miscellaneous Collections*, 96 (1937), 1-65.

"The Discoveries of John Lederer . . . together with a General Map of the Whole Territory He Traversed," reprinted in *Quarterly Bulletin, Archeological Society of Virginia*, 5 (1950).

Griffin, Rosemary. "Rogel, Padre of the Ports," *Mid-America*, 30 (1948), 3-43.

Mook, Maurice. "The Aboriginal Population of Tidewater Virginia," *American Anthropologist*, 40 (1944), 193-208.

————. "The Anthropological Position of the Indian Tribes of Tidewater Virginia," *William and Mary College Quarterly*, 2nd Series, 23 (1943), 27-40.

————. "The Ethnological Significance of Tindall's Map of Virginia, 1608," *William and Mary College Quarterly*, 2nd Series, 27 (1947), 371-408.

Mooney, James. "Siouan Tribes of the East," *Bureau of American Ethnology*, Bulletin 22 (1895).

————. "The Powhatan Confederacy, Past and Present," *American Anthropologist*, 9 (1907), 127-152.

Quinn, D. B. "Some Spanish Reactions to Elizabethan Colonial Enterprizes," *Transactions of the Royal Historical Society*, 5th series, 1 (1950), 1-23.

Reding, Katherine. "Letter of Gonzalo M. de Canzo, June 28, 1600," *Georgia Historical Quarterly*, 8 (1924), 214-228.

Ross, Mary. "French Intrusions and Indian Uprisings in Georgia and South Carolina, 1577-1580," *Georgia Historical Quarterly*, 7 (1923), 251-281.

————. "The French on the Savannah, 1605," *ibid.* 8 (1924), 167-194.

Scisco, Louis Dow. "Discovery of the Chesapeake, 1525-1573," *Maryland Historical Magazine*, 40 (1945), 275-286.

————. "The Voyage of Vicente Gonzales, 1588," *Maryland Historical Magazine*, 42 (1947), 95-110.

Shea, John Gilmary. "Log Chapel on the Rappahannock," *Catholic World*, 22 (1875), 847-856. Also in *The Indian Miscellany*, edited by W. W. Beach, Albany, 1877, 333-343.

Speck, Frank G. "Chapters on the Ethnology of the Powhatan Tribes of Virginia," Heye Foundation, *Indian Notes and Monographs*, 1 (1919), 223-455.

————. "The Ethnic Position of the Southeastern Algonkin," *American Anthropologist*, 26 (1924), 184-200.

————. "Siouan Tribes of the Carolinas," *American Anthropologist*, 37 (1935), 201-225.

Stewart, T. D. "The Finding of an Indian Ossuary on the York River in Virginia," *Journal of the Washington Academy of Science*, 30 (1940), 356-364.

Swanton, John R. "The Indians of the Southeastern United States," *Bureau of American Ethnology*, Bulletin 137 (1946).

———. *Early History of the Creek Indians, Bureau of American Ethnology*, Bulletin 73 (1922).

———. "The Aboriginal Population of America North of Mexico," *Smithsonian Miscellaneous Collections*, 80 (1927), 1-40.

———. "Aboriginal Culture of the Southeast," *Bureau of American Ethnology*, Bulletin 42 (1928).

Wright, Irene A. "Spanish Policy toward Virginia, 1606-1612," *American Historical Review*, 25 (1920), 448-479.

Zubillaga Félix. "Padre Pedro Martínez (1533-1566). La primera sangre jesuítica en las misiones norteamericanos," *Archivum Historicum Societatis Iesu*, 7 (1938), 30-53.

———. "Métodos misionales de la primera instrucción de San Francisco de Borja para la América española," *Archivum Historicum Societatis Iesu*, 12 (1943), 56-88.

INDEX

Acosta, José de, writes of New Spain, 160, 163*n*15

Acuña, Juan de, 24

Adelantado, title explained, 77, 77*n*. *See also* Menéndez de Avilés, Pedro

Agua dulce, where found in Chesapeake, 37*n*

Ajacán (Axacám, Jacán, Jacám, Xacál, etc.), reached by Jesuits and described by Carrera, 28 f; as a pirates' nest, 30*n*; location of discussed, 36-43; route to, 42 f; mentioned in 1636 as strait to Orient, 57; mentioned by Governor Canzo, 62*n*; navigable waters and Indian settlements of, 231-43; orthography and meaning of name of, 244-49

Álamos, Gonsalvo de, life of, 226*n*3; mentioned, 215, 220

Albemarle Sound, 29

Alegre, Francisco, reproduced Rogel Relation, 121*n*1

Algonkin, stability of settlements of, 30; culture of, 165*n*25; Algonquian name for Virginia, 247

Alonso, boy on expedition. *See* Olmos, Alonso de

Anian, Strait of, rumors concerning, 18*n*

Aquaviva, Claudio, 121*n*1

Archer's Hape (Hope) Creek, 38. *See also* College Creek

Arredondo, Antonio, on Spanish claims, 4

Ashaagoona, compared with Ajacán, 247

Ashókan, compared with Ajacán, 247

Astraín, Antonio, on rescue of Jesuits, 45

Asunción de Cristo, Ecija's ship, 213*n*6

Avilés. *See* Menéndez Avilés

Ayllón, Lucas Vásquez de, 7, 12

Báez, Domingo Agustín, 25

Bahama Channel, 50

Bahamas, the, and wreck of Pedro Menéndez Marqués, 167, 168*n*6

Barcia, Andrés, history of Florida by, 70 f

Bay, Spanish equivalents of word explained, 80

Borgia, Francis, Saint, General of Society of Jesus, mission policy of, 21*n*, 76*n*; Segura reports to, 25; advice of to Segura, 27; life of, 74*n*

Bowater, Captain, early directions of for entering the Chesapeake, 214*n*10

Burial (Indian), manner of, 48, 113*n*15; ossuary on York River, 164*n*22, 242